IMAGINING
TORONTO

Amy Lavender Harris

Mansfield Press

IMAGINING TORONTO

Amy Lavender Harris

Mansfield Press

Library and Archives Canada Cataloguing in Publication

Harris, Amy Lavender, 1972-
     Imagining Toronto / Amy Lavender Harris.

Includes bibliographical references and index.
ISBN 978-1-894469-39-5

     1. Toronto (Ont.)--In literature. 2. Imagination in literature. 3. Cultural
pluralism in literature. 4. Canadian literature (English)--Ontario--Toronto--
History and criticism. 5. Canadian literature (English)--20th century--History
and criticism. 6. Canadian literature (English)--21st century--History and
criticism. I. Title.

PS8101.T67H37 2010   C810.9'9713541   C2010-901312-3

Editor for the Press: Denis De Klerck
Copyeditor: Stuart Ross
Typesetting & Design: Denis De Klerck
Cover Photo: Gother Mann, Plan of Torento (sic) Harbour,
courtesy of University of Toronto Map & Data Library.
Author Photo: Peter Fruchter

The publication of *Imagining Toronto* has been generously supported by
the Canada Council for the Arts and
the Ontario Arts Council.

Canada Council
for the Arts
Conseil des Arts
du Canada

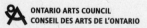
ONTARIO ARTS COUNCIL
CONSEIL DES ARTS DE L'ONTARIO

Mansfield Press Inc.
25 Mansfield Avenue, Toronto, Ontario, Canada M6J 2A9
Publisher: Denis De Klerck
www.mansfieldpress.net

to Peter
urban explorer

and

Katherine Aurora
city child

CONTENTS

"The city, however, does not tell its past, but contains it like the lines of a hand, written in the corners of the streets, the gratings of the windows, the banisters of the steps, the antennae of the lightning rods, the poles of the flags, every segment marked in turn with scratches, indentations, scrolls. [...] At times all I need is a brief glimpse, an opening in the midst of an incongruous landscape, a glint of light in the fog, the dialogue of two passersby meeting in the crowd, and I think that, setting out from there, I will put together, piece by piece, the perfect city, made of fragments mixed with the rest, of instants separated by intervals, of signals one sends out, not knowing who receives them."

Italo Calvino, *Invisible Cities*

"The city scrolled away from us like a vast and intricate diagram, as indecipherable as the language of the Hittites. Lights dim as stars cut into the vast blackness of Lake Ontario, all quivering in the rising remains of the heat of the day. Here was a religion, I thought. My religion. My secret book, my Talmud."

Robert Charles Wilson, "The Inner Inner City"

– 1 –

THE IMAGINED CITY

THE CITY WITHIN THE CITY

In the iconic Toronto novel *In the Skin of a Lion*, Michael Ondaatje writes, "Before the real city could be seen it had to be imagined, the way rumours and tall tales were a kind of charting." With vivid language Ondaatje shows us how the city is conjured into being by acts of imagination that flesh out and give form to its physical and cultural terrain. As we navigate the city in restless pursuit of accommodation, commerce and community, we give the city meaning through narrative, through stories that help us chart a course between the concrete, lived city and the city as we understand, fear, remember and dream it. Ondaatje's observation echoes the words of essayist Jonathan Raban, who wrote in *Soft City* that "[t]he city as we imagine it, the soft city of illusion, myth, aspiration, nightmare, is as real, maybe more real, than the hard city one can locate on maps, in statistics, in monographs on urban sociology and demography and architecture." Ondaatje and Raban remind us that the cities we live in are made not merely of brick and mortar, or bureaucracy and money, but are equally the invention of our memories and imaginations. We realize that our cities unfold not only in the building but in the telling of them.

Toronto is a city of stories that accumulate in fragments between the aggressive thrust of its downtown towers and the primordial dream of its ravines. In these fragments we find narratives of unfinished journeys and incomplete arrivals, chronicles of all the violence, poverty, ambition and hope that give shape to this city and those who live in it. In *Thirsty*, Toronto poet Dionne Brand calls these narratives "the biographies of streets," and adds, "at these crossroads, transient selves flare / in the individual drama, in the faith of translation." It is here at these interstices that the city's stories gain their deepest resonance, in the liminal spaces between the pavements and the shadows of the passersby who leave their imprint upon them.

In his story "The Inner Inner City," science-fiction writer Robert Charles Wilson describes a "paracartographic map" of Toronto in which the visible city is only a mirror of the imagined city, an unchartable labyrinth of hidden avenues laid deep within its core. "There's a city inside the city," he writes, "the city at the center of the map." This book, too, is a pilgrimage into the city within the city. Beginning with the familiar terrain—the ravines, downtown towers, neighbourhoods and inhabitants who give shape to Toronto—it ventures deep into the imagined city, dowsing for meaning in literary representations of Toronto as its inhabitants experience and narrate it. It explores how we arrive and who we become in this city; how we live, love and make the city home, and how the city changes us even as we shape its contours. In doing so, the book seeks to craft a literary genealogy of Toronto, tracing for the first time the long and interwoven heritage of writers and works engaging imaginatively with this city. At the same time, it seeks to do more than simply inventory Toronto's literary history: it is also motivated by a conviction that literature, given its unique capacity to confront the most pressing contemporary urban concerns—bigotry, poverty and violence, as well as tolerance, asylum, desire and ambition—can help Torontonians transcend difference in this most culturally diverse of cities. This book is predicated on a belief that rather than comparing Toronto to the world's other great literary cities and finding it wanting, we should instead realize that Toronto's literature reflects an entirely new kind of city, a city where identity emerges not from shared tradition or a long history but rather is forged out of a commitment to the virtues of diversity, tolerance and cultural understanding.

A CURE FOR CULTURAL AMNESIA

Imagining Toronto is the first full study of this city's literature to appear in print. Although a number of other Canadian cities—among them Montreal, Saskatoon, Winnipeg and Vancouver—have inspired book-length explorations of their literature,[1] and while burgeoning interest in the shape of the city has stimulated investigations into Toronto's history, architecture, photography, public art, urban form, ecology, politics and cultural demographics,[2] curiously this interest has extended to Toronto literature only peripherally. John Robert Colombo's *Canadian Literary Landmarks* references Toronto at length, but focuses mainly on literary personalities and the establishments they founded or frequented. Similarly, Greg Gatenby's *Toronto: A Literary Guide* offers an encyclopaedic collection of literary walking tours identifying where (and sometimes with whom) notable writers have slept while living in Toronto, but mentions works actually set in Toronto only in passing. William Keith dedicates three chapters to Toronto's literary history in *Literary Images of Ontario* and Noah Richler discusses fictional representations of post-colonial Toronto in *This Is My Country, What's Yours? A Literary Atlas of Canada*, but both authors tailor their observations of Toronto literature to suit their focus on regional or national themes. Biographers and

1   See, for example, Elaine Decoursey, Donn Kerr, Dan Ring and Matthew Teitelbaum's *Saskatoon Imagined* (1989), Bryan Demchinsky and Elaine Kalman Naves' *Storied Streets: Montreal in the Literary Imagination* (2000) and David Arnason and Mhari Mackintosh's *The Imagined City: A Literary History of Winnipeg* (2005).

2   See, for example, Eric Arthur's *No Mean City* (3rd edition, 2003), Michael McClelland and Graeme Stewart's *Concrete Toronto* (2007), Mark Osbaldeston's *Unbuilt Toronto* (2008), Sally Gibson's *Inside Toronto: Urban Interiors, 1880-1920* (2006), Edith Firth's *Toronto in Art* (1983), John Warkentin's *Creating Memory: A Guide to Outdoor Sculpture in Toronto* (2010), John Sewell's *The Shape of the City* (1993), Wayne Grady's *Toronto the Wild* (1995), Julie-Anne Boudreau, Roger Keil and Douglas Young's *Changing Toronto: Governing Urban Neoliberalism* (2009), Paul Anisef and Michael Lanphier's *The World in a City* (2003) and Coach House Books' five-volume *uTOpia* book series.

literary scholars who have examined individual Toronto writers,[3] specific local settings[4] and particular urban experiences[5] have done so without fully extending their analyses to the deeper urban themes that underlie and connect them. A special two-volume series of articles on Toronto literature appearing in *Open Letter* in 1994 did call for synthesis between the "social real" and the "literary symbolic" in readings of Toronto literature, but limited its analyses primarily to small press and "ethnic" writing of the 1980s.[6]

Perhaps so little attention has been paid to Toronto literature because of a curious belief that it does not actually exist. In 1961 Canadian chronicler Pierre Berton lamented that "Toronto has not provided the background for much great literature."[7] In *City Hall & Mrs God*, a critical examination of civil society published in 1990, Cary Fagan suggested that people feel no loyalty to Toronto "because this city, unlike New York or Montreal, has created no myth of itself to hold them," pointing out that "without memory there is no past, and without past no identity." In a 2005 essay called "Making a Toronto of the Imagination," journalist Bert Archer asserted that Toronto is "a city that exists in no one's imagination, neither in Toronto, nor in the rest of the world," adding, "Toronto is a place people live, not a place where things happen, or, at least, not where the sorts of things happen that forge a place for the city in the imagination." Similarly, author Andrew Pyper has claimed that "there's a reluctance in our fiction to engage Toronto directly as a place,"[8] a sentiment

---

3   Notable literary biographies of Toronto writers include Rosemary Sullivan's *Shadow Maker: The Life of Gwendolyn MacEwen* (1995), Nathalie Cooke's *Margaret Atwood: A Biography* (1998) and Matt Cohen's memoir, *Typing: A Life in 26 Keys* (2000).

4   See, for example, Justin D. Edwards' "*Strange Fugitive*, Strange City: Reading Urban Space in Morley Callaghan's Toronto," published in *Studies in Canadian Literature* (1998) and Stephen Cain's essay "Mapping Raymond Souster's Toronto," in *The Canadian Modernists Meet* (2005).

5   See, for example, Batia Boe Stolar's "Building and Living the Immigrant City: Michael Ondaatje's and Austin Clarke's Toronto," published in *Downtown Canada: Writing Canadian Cities* (2005), and Emily Johansen's essay "Streets are the dwelling place of the collective": Public Space and Cosmopolitan Citizenship in Dionne Brand's *What We All Long For*, in *Canadian Literature* (2008).

6   "Toronto Since Then," Parts 1 and 2, *Open Letter* (Nos. 8 and 9; Winter 1994 and Summer 1994). The considerable cultural and literary significance of small and micropress publishing and writing in Toronto has not yet received much critical attention, and a considered analysis is beyond the scope of this book. Interested readers are directed to this two volume series of *Open Letter* as well as to two monographs that helped prompt them, Clint Burnham's *Allegories of Publishing: The Toronto Small Press Scene* (Streetcar Editions, 1991) and Beverley Daurio's *Internal Document: A Response to Clint Burnham's Allegories of Publishing* (1992). A special issue of *Open Letter*, "Canadian Small Presses and Micropresses" (12(4)), published in 2004, brings a national perspective to small press writing and publishing. Stuart Ross's *Confessions of a Small Press Racketeer* (2005) and "In the small press village: New trends in adequate stapling" (in Wilcox, Palassio and Dovercourt, 2006) add much to this subject, but a full history of small press publishing in Toronto has not yet been written.

7   Berton, 1961. Oddly, Berton makes this claim in an essay referencing Toronto novelists Morley Callaghan, Phyllis Brett Young and Hugh Garner, all internationally regarded authors at the time.

8   Quoted in Pupo, 2006. Pyper's 2008 novel, *The Killing Circle*, is set mainly in Toronto, as are

echoed by literary critic Philip Marchand, who wrote flatly of the "bland and featureless reputation" of Toronto's literary landscape and insisted that "our city awaits its great novelist."[9]

Where commentators do acknowledge the accumulation of literary works engaging with Toronto, they tend to do so grudgingly, managing to imply at the same time that even if Toronto *does* have a literature, it cannot possibly be any good. This propensity seems to originate in a curiously bifurcated resentment of Toronto, a city an unhappy Ottawa-based reviewer of Michael Ondaatje's *In the Skin of a Lion* described as "a catastrophe," adding, "ugly, formless, without character, it sits upon the banks of Lake Ontario like some diseased organ in the body, spreading pollution about it."[10] Stephen Henighan, a respected novelist and academic, is nonetheless best known for asserting, in a 2006 essay published in *Geist* magazine, that the Scotiabank Giller Prize is controlled by a Toronto-centred conspiracy of behemoth publishers, corporate booksellers and literary kingmakers.[11] The most damning evidence of this conspiracy, Henighan insisted, was that nearly every winner in the history of the Giller "lived within a two-hour drive of the corner of Yonge and Bloor," the symbolic epicentre of the conspiracy. Henighan's opinions on the merits of Toronto literature may be traced to "Vulgarity on Bloor," an essay appearing in his 2002 book *When Words Deny the World*, in which Henighan claimed that Canadian literature had been replaced by TorLit, a "slick, image-obsessed, Toronto-centric" literary culture where "one becomes a writer by being seen at certain parties" and where "publication is less important, literary accomplishment barely relevant." Henighan's views are echoed by author Stephen Marche, who has compared Toronto to an "old folks' home" and described the city's literature as "something your smartest aunt does once she's cozied up in her favourite sweater," adding, "innovation, whether in language or form, is a dirty word."[12]

Other commentators dismiss Toronto in slightly kinder tones, suggesting the city's literature might be taken more seriously if only its writers would learn to emulate their betters in Paris or London. Among them is Philip Marchand, who in a 2002 *Toronto Star* column lamented the failure of Toronto's writers

---

several stories in his debut collection, *Kiss Me* (1996).

9   See Marchand, Philip, 5 November 2006. "What's Toronto's story." *Toronto Star.* Incidentally, Marchand is the author of *Deadly Spirits* (1994), a crime thriller set in 1980s Toronto.

10   See Hyde, Anthony, 1 August 1987. "Turning Toronto the Terrible into Myth." *Ottawa Citizen.*

11   The Scotiabank Giller Prize is a juried prize awarded annually for excellence in Canadian fiction. Currently Canada's most lucrative literary prize—shortlisted finalists receive $5,000 each while the Giller winner receives $50,000—each year the prize is the subject of intense public speculation, media scrutiny and criticism within literary spheres.

12   See Marche's essay, "Raging against the tyranny of CanLit." *Toronto Star*, 20 October 2007. Despite his low opinion of the city's literature, Marche is himself the author of a Toronto novel, *Raymond and Hannah*, that was shortlisted for the 2006 Toronto Book Award.

to harness the city's "extraordinary sophistication and energy" and its "culturally charged atmosphere," and added, "what a gift to Toronto if some latter-day Balzac or Dickens were to recreate this new urban milieu in fiction."[13] Pointing out that none of the Giller Prize–winning works had, at that point, ever been *set* in Toronto,[14] Marchand suggested, in contrast to Henighan, that a conspiracy *against* Toronto was afoot, claiming, "Everybody hates Toronto. Even people who live in Toronto hate Toronto, and if they're writers they would rather write about Uganda or Bolivia or Manitoba than the city they inhabit." Examining Marchand's claim might help explain why the city's literature has remained so strangely underappreciated.

Harbouring enmity toward Toronto is a long-standing Canadian tradition, a phenomenon Scott Gardiner sums up in his 2007 novel *King John of Canada*:

> It's an ancient joke among Canadians that the only thing they could all agree about was how much they hated Toronto. Torontonians themselves would typically chuckle at this, and dip their heads politely and say ha ha very funny, and try their best to treat the whole thing as if it really were an exercise in good-natured familial bantering. But it wasn't. People from outside the city honestly and unreservedly loathed the place.

More surprising—and telling—is the revelation that hating Toronto is a recognizable trope in the city's own literature. In Francis Pollock's 1936 novel *Jupiter Eight*, the protagonist, an aspiring stock-market mogul, muses of Toronto,

> He had been accustomed to abuse his city, as all his friends did. All the sporting set, all the arty crowd vilified it as one of their staples of conversation. The sportsmen despised it because it did not sufficiently resemble Chicago and Havana; the artists because it did not sufficiently resemble Paris and Munich. They called it a slow place, a dull place, where English snobbery met American vulgarity and each thrived on the other; where the police would not let you drink standing up, and where there was no subsidized theatre. They called it a half-grown city, a nest of Methodists and Orangemen, of Puritans and Pharisees, who had not yet learned that Queen Victoria was dead. They called it a rube town, a hick town, an overgrown tank-town, with half a million people who confused Dada with Santa Claus.

---

13 See Marchand, Philip, 23 November 2002. "Literati Leave Big Smoke Out in the Cold: Book Prize Judges, and Our Authors, Snub Toronto." *Toronto Star*.
14 Two Scotiabank Giller Prize–winning works have subsequently been set in Toronto. The first, Vincent Lam's *Bloodletting & Miraculous Cures*, won the prize in 2006. The 2008 winner, Joseph Boyden's *Through Black Spruce*, is set partly in Toronto.

In *Self Condemned*, a scathing indictment of a renamed but otherwise thinly fictionalized version of wartime Toronto first published in 1954, Wyndham Lewis writes,

> Momaco was so ugly, and so devoid of all character as of any trace of charm, that it was disagreeable to walk in. It was as if the elegance and charm of Montreal had been attributed to the seductions of the Fiend by the puritan founders of Momaco: as if they had said to themselves that at least in Momaco the god-fearing citizen, going about his lawful occasions, should do so without the danger of being seduced by way of his senses.

In *City Boys*, a collection of stories about ambitious young men chafing against the confines of early-1960s Toronto, David Lewis Stein's narrator intones simply,

> How could one be sensitive, important, alive, in Toronto? The city was the original backwater of western civilization. Toronto was where they would put the pipe if they wanted to give the world an enema.

Raymond Souster, Toronto's most persistent chronicler and usually generous in his judgements, lambasted the city in "Sleep Toronto," writing

> Sleep on, knowing full well you're both spendthrift and miser,
> bigoted, hypocrite, little wise, much foolish,
> sleep with the dreams of profits, mergers, margins,
> sleep with the dreams of garbage-dump and dole.
> Sleep city sleep
> your Yonge Street narrow as the hearts that own you.[15]

The protagonist of Margaret Atwood's 1988 novel *Cat's Eye* offers a similarly scathing sentiment, evaluating how much—and how little—the city has changed during her absence:

> Once it was fashionable to say how dull it was. First prize a week in Toronto, second prize two weeks in Toronto, Toronto the Good, Toronto the Blue, where you couldn't get wine on Sundays. Everyone who lived here said those things: provincial, self-satisfied, boring. If you said that, it showed you recognized these qualities but did not partake of them yourself. [...] Now you're supposed to say how much

---

15   Raymond Souster, the author of hundreds of poems engaging with Toronto, won the Governor General's Award for Poetry for *The Colour of the Times* (1964). "Sleep Toronto" was originally published in *Shake Hands with the Hangman* (1953).

it's changed. *World-class city* is a phrase they use in magazines these days, a great deal too much. All those ethnic restaurants, and the theatre and the boutiques, New York without the garbage and muggings, it's supposed to be.[16]

In his novel *Your Secrets Sleep with Me*, Darren O'Donnell draws these sentiments toward their logical conclusion, describing Toronto simply as a city whose greatest desire is to be any place other than itself:

It wishes it were other cities: Chicago, New Delhi, Istanbul, Mexico City, Montreal, San Jose, Algiers, Moscow, London, Karachi, Caracas, Tokyo, Kathmandu, Barcelona, Bogota, Cairo, Perth, Berlin, Kinshasa, Manila, Singapore, Shanghai, San Francisco, Brussels, Paris, Seoul, São Paulo, Stockholm, Rome, Marrakech, Sarajevo, Cape Town, Lahore, Taipei, Athens, Prague, New York City, Casablanca, Kiev, Madrid, Nairobi, Dublin, Tijuana, Lisbon, Hanoi, Calcutta, Baghdad, Tel Aviv, Hong Kong, Santiago, Bombay, Copenhagen, Addis Ababa, Los Angeles, Helsinki, Kuala Lampur, Las Vegas [...], Colombo, Havana, New Orleans, Mecca, Beijing, Managua, Jakarta, Oslo.

Taken together, these observations suggest that the real trouble with Toronto has less to do with any obvious cultural deficiency than with a striking and persistent self-loathing.

In an 1899 essay, "Literature in Canada," published in *The Canadian Magazine*, novelist and critic Robert Barr lamented Torontonians' prejudice against their own writers, commenting,

The bald truth is that Canada has the money, but would rather spend it on whiskey than on books. [...] What chance has Canada, then, of raising a Sir Walter Scott? I maintain that she has but very little chance, because she won't pay the money, and money is the root of all literature. The new Sir Walter is probably tramping the streets of Toronto to-day, looking vainly for something to do. But Toronto will recognize him when he comes back from New York or London, and will give him a dinner when he doesn't need it.[17]

Margaret Atwood—whose works include seven novels, numerous short stories and a wide variety of poems engaging with Toronto[18]—acknowledges having

16 The "Toronto prize" is an old urban joke; it also appears a generation earlier in Phyllis Brett Young's novel *The Torontonians* (1960). In the introduction to the 1991 edition of *Fodor's Toronto*, Allan Gould reports that a similar rejoinder was popular in Quebec during the 1920s and 1930s.
17 Barr [1899] 1973. "Literature in Canada, Part One." Originally published in *The Canadian Magazine*, XIV(1); reprinted in *The Measure of the Rule*. Toronto: University of Toronto Press.
18 In "The Allure of Atwood's Toronto," (*Americas*, November/December 2005), Guylaine Spencer describes dozens of recognizable Toronto settings that have figured prominently in Atwood's novels;

set her first published novel, *The Edible Woman*, in Toronto with considerable trepidation, commenting, "[I] was so embarrassed by the location that I never actually named the city and disguised the street names as best I could. Everyone knew that real novels were not set in Toronto."[19] Finally, novelist Russell Smith, a sometimes beleaguered advocate of urban fiction, has struggled to explain the truculence of local authors who would rather mythologize rural landscapes than write about events actually happening in Toronto, musing, "This lag, this disconnect, between the real and the fictitious, baffles me. I can't explain it—except perhaps by accusing Canadian writers of being so lofty-minded that they are unwilling to sully their hands with contact with the corrupt and superficial city."[20]

In the 2007 documentary film *Let's All Hate Toronto*—an homage, in many ways, to Jack McLaren's illustrated 1956 satire of the same title[21] and Listair Sinclair's 1948 radio play, "We All Hate Toronto"[22]—filmmakers Albert Nerenberg and Rob Spence travel across Canada hoping to discover why hating Toronto is such a rewarding national pastime. Posing as "Mr. Toronto" and hosting "Toronto Appreciation Day" events in such Toronto-hating cities as Halifax, Calgary and Vancouver, Spence compiles (and then attempts to rebut) a list of the top ten reasons Canadians hate Toronto. Among the predictable—and predictably valid—reasons Toronto deserves to be loathed, two are startlingly prescient: first, that nobody hates Toronto more than Torontonians ourselves; and second, that Toronto is a city that doesn't know itself.

In "Mapping Wonderland," a 2005 essay discussing Toronto's quixotic relationship with its own literary heritage, literary scholar Germaine Warkentin suggests that one reason the city does not know itself is because it suffers from cultural amnesia. Warkentin writes,

> A key difficulty in constructing the city's metaphors is the handling of meaning from one generation to the next, or across barriers of birth, class and circumstance. For a large part of its history, Toronto has been in a state of near-amnesia, seeking desperately for its own memory.

Atwood's Toronto novels are also popular subjects for geographers and literary scholars writing about literature and place.

19 See Atwood's essay, "The City Rediscovered," in the *New York Times*, 8 August 1982.

20 Russell Smith, 11 December 2002. "Dear [non-] reader, it might not be your fault." *Globe & Mail*.

21 See McLaren's book, *Let's All Hate Toronto* (1956). Other Toronto-bashing books include Rick Trask's *Tronna Roast #1: Toronto Jokes* (1989), in which Toronto is made the brunt of jokes more commonly told against Newfoundlanders, and Michael B. Davie's *Why Everybody Hates Toronto* (2004), a self-published compilation of criticisms of the city.

22 Lister Sinclair's radio play, "We All Hate Toronto," appears in *A Play on Words & Other Radio Plays* (1948).

Warkentin connects Toronto's amnesia to a city-building compulsion that has "destroyed and rebuilt, destroyed and rebuilt" the city's monuments as well as its memory in competition for colonial, corporate and cultural attention. Her thesis is compelling because it identifies not only a plausible cause of Toronto's literary forgetting (strikingly reminiscent of Toronto's well-known propensity for destroying its own heritage buildings) but accounts for many of its symptoms as well. As Anne Denoon writes in the Toronto novel *Back Flip*, "It seemed that progress, not content with destroying the material evidence of the past, had to demolish memory itself."

In light of the above, a diagnosis of cultural amnesia would seem to explain why—in a city where nearly everybody seems to be a writer or aspires to be one, where books have their own festivals and television shows, where celebrity authors are jostled and fawned over in the street—books, no matter how enthusiastically they may be read, reviewed and rewarded when they are first published, soon slide irretrievably into oblivion like flotsam beneath a somnolent sea.

Toronto's undeservedly neglected "mythopoeic" poet Gwendolyn MacEwen[23] engages directly with the problem of cultural forgetting in her story collections *Noman* and *Noman's Land*.[24] MacEwen's eponymous protagonist is an amnesiac who emerges lost and naked from the Ontario wilderness and hitchhikes to Toronto to search for his identity. Shortly after his arrival, Noman realizes that Toronto's amnesia mirrors his own and observes,

> Sometimes he couldn't even remember how long he'd had the amnesia. But one of the nice things about not remembering anything was that the world was almost unbearably beautiful; everything was fresh and new. The city was full of surprises.

To MacEwen, Toronto's amnesia seemed rooted in the absence of a shared cultural mythology, and so she sought to remedy this deficiency by revisiting familiar Toronto locations and events. Her recurring protagonist Noman, for example, views the city from inside the famous bronze Henry Moore sculpture anchoring Nathan Phillips Square, rescues a weary Sun King from colliding with a popcorn cart at the Caribana parade and jostles among the crowds rummaging for bargains at Honest Ed's. Later, Noman re-enacts Marilyn Bell's legendary 1954 swim across Lake Ontario, and while doing so realizes that

---

23 MacEwen published nearly two dozen collections of poems and stories and was a two-time winner of the Governor General's Award for Poetry before her death at forty-six. Rosemary Sullivan's beautifully written biography, *Shadow Maker* (1995), discusses MacEwen's preoccupation with memory, culture and identity.

24 Noman was first published in 1972; *Noman's Land* followed in 1985.

cultural identity is something we must recognize or imagine within ourselves. He tells a reporter that swimming across the lake was the only way he knew how to come home, and adds, "There is another country, you know, and it's right inside this one."

TRACING TORONTO'S LITERARY GENEALOGIES

Like Robert Charles Wilson in "The Inner Inner City" and Gwendolyn MacEwen in *Noman's Land*, this book seeks to map the city within the city. Its journey begins, as Michael Ondaatje suggests it must, with the imagined city that must be navigated before the real city can truly be seen. Charting the imagined city requires a circuitous descent into the urban labyrinth, but in return it offers the most tremendous reward: a sense of the shape, character and scope of Toronto literature, and, perhaps for the first time, a certainty that Toronto is a city that lives richly in the imagination. Our journey into the imagined city begins with a search for its origins, which may be traced back much further than we have come to expect. Still, we begin with Toronto's most familiar literary landmarks because, like pottery sherds scattered at the entrance to an archaeological dig, they provide the first clues to the treasures concealed in the layers below. If a city's literature offers an archaeology of its history, topography, commerce and culture, then the visible city is only the tip of the tel.

Perhaps the most familiar of Toronto's literary landmarks is Ondaatje's *In the Skin of a Lion*—a work exploring the complex and sometimes contradictory interplay between city dreaming and city building—whose 1987 publication literary critic Anderson Tepper credits with having given Toronto its literary voice.[25] But if we dig just a little deeper, we begin to uncover a rich trove of literary works half-exposed beneath a thin layer of cultural detritus. Literary scholar Sophie Levy suggests that a "consciousness of the city" begins to "manifest [...] in the work of its writers" in 1968, the year Dennis Lee's poetry sequence *Civil Elegies* first appeared, a series of lyrical meditations on Toronto that won the Governor General's Award for Poetry in 1972.[26] Similarly, poet and literary scholar Stephen Cain attributes the rise of a genuinely local literary culture to a "new generation of writers" buoyed by the "nationalistic spirit of post-Centennial Canada" and the emergence of the Toronto-based publishing houses Coach House and Anansi.[27] Indeed, following an example

25 Tepper, 12 December 2005.
26 Levy, 2001.
27 Cain, 2002. Coach House Press had its origins in 1963-64 when Stan Bevington, a printer, began producing ephemera and chapbooks; Bevington was joined by Victor Coleman in 1967. Dennis Lee and David Godfrey followed closely, setting up House of Anansi the same year.

set earlier by poet Raymond Souster, whose Contact Press published some of the earliest work of Margaret Atwood, Michael Ondaatje, bpNichol and David McFadden,[28] the two presses supported emerging and established Toronto writers—among them Douglas (George) Fetherling, Ted Plantos, bpNichol, Margaret Atwood and Michael Ondaatje—with anthologies like *T.O. Now: The Young Toronto Poets*[29] and *The Story So Far*.[30]

It is true that the Centennial period produced many groundbreaking Toronto works. *The Meeting Point*, the first novel in Austin Clarke's "Toronto Trilogy" exploring the struggles of West Indian Torontonians in a hostile, racist city, was published in 1967.[31] *Cabbagetown*, Hugh Garner's well-known novel about class conflict in Depression-era Toronto, first appeared in its complete form in 1968, a year before *The Edible Woman*, Margaret Atwood's famous first novel challenging traditional gender roles, was published by McClelland & Stewart. In that same year McClelland & Stewart also issued Scott Symons' then-controversial homoerotic Toronto satire, *Civic Square*, as 800 or so typed manuscript pages signed and sealed with ribbon in a large blue box. Seemingly all at once, literary works exploring the challenges of race, class, gender and sexuality in a rapidly changing city met with enthusiastic readers eager for literary innovation and probing social analysis. But Centennial celebration aside, 1967 is ultimately an arbitrary date, one that risks consigning decades of Toronto literature to prehistory. Indeed, Cain acknowledges that the kind of Toronto literature appearing after the late 1960s was "different" from what preceded it rather than having materialized out of nowhere, adding that this transformation had been "fermenting for many decades previously." If this is the case, then what imaginative terrain did Toronto writers traverse prior to 1967?

The earliest imaginative representations of Toronto do not originate in written works at all, but rather in First Nations oral narratives, including those giving Toronto its name. Popular claims that "Toronto" is a Huron (Oendat)

---

28 In the introduction to *Blues & True Concussions*, Michael Redhill's 1996 anthology of emerging Toronto poets, Dennis Lee credits Raymond Souster's Contact Press with "the greatest feat of talent scouting in our literature." *New Wave Canada*, published by Contact Press in 1966, featured early work by Victor Coleman, George Jonas, David McFadden, bpNichol and Michael Ondaatje. Lee notes that Souster also published early work by Margaret Atwood, George Bowering and Gwendolyn MacEwen, confirming his status as one of Canada's great discoverers of literary talent.

29 Edited by Dennis Lee, *T.O. Now* (1968) featured the early work of poets who went on to literary success, among them Greg Hollingshead, Doug Fetherling and Ted Plantos. A generation later, Lee's anthology was the inspiration for *Blues and True Concussions* (1996), a "follow-up" anthology edited by Michael Redhill and featuring a subsequent generation of emerging Toronto poets, notable among them Christian Bok, R. M. Vaughan and Kevin Connolly.

30 *The Story So Far* (Coach House) appeared in six annual instalments between 1971 and 1979, and featured local as well as international voices.

31 Clarke's "Toronto Trilogy" includes *The Meeting Point* (1967), *Storm of Fortune* (1973) and *The Bigger Light* (1975).

word meaning "the place of meeting"[32] are disputed by geographer Alan Rayburn, who in "The Real Story of How Toronto Got Its Name," harnesses compelling historical, cartographic and linguistic evidence to argue that Toronto (originally Tkaronto or Taronto) is a Mohawk phrase meaning "where there are trees standing in the water." This phrase seems aptly to anticipate Toronto's glittering lakefront towers but in fact referred originally to a canoe route from Lake Ontario providing passage to Tkaronto, a narrowing of Lake Simcoe (formerly Lac de Taronto) where stakes were driven into the water to create fish weirs at an ancient fishing spot declared a national historic site in 1982.[33] Like so many cultural diasporas that have followed—or perhaps like MacEwen's amnesic Noman—Tkaronto emerged from the wilderness, migrated toward present-day Toronto, forgot its name, adopted the new language and learned to fit in. Now, however, the name Tkaronto is being rehabilitated, in one instance through a compelling 2007 film called *Tkaronto* exploring urban aboriginal identity in contemporary Toronto.[34]

Toronto's recorded literary history dates back nearly four centuries. In *Toronto During the French Regime*, historian Percy J. Robinson carefully sifts fact from fiction in accounts prepared by the region's French colonizers dating from as early as 1615. In *Literary Images of Ontario*, William Keith traces imaginative English-language accounts of Toronto to diaries and correspondence dating as far back as the 1770s, observing, "By a happy chance we are favoured with continuing literary impressions of Toronto from its very beginnings as an English settlement—even, indeed, a little before those beginnings." Strictly speaking, the narratives Robinson and Keith reference (including diaries, letters, emigrants' guides, maps and colonial reports) were intended as realistic rather than literary accounts, but, as Robinson points out, early maps and colonial reports were often conjectural and sometimes simply made up. Similarly, Keith observes that texts such as Elizabeth Simcoe's diaries mingled

---

32 The view that Toronto means "the place of meeting," a long-standing popular interpretation, is regularly traced to historian Henry Scadding's *Toronto of Old* (1878: 74-75), an etymology Scadding expanded upon in "Etymology of Toronto: Why I prefer 'Place of Meeting" To "Trees in the Water" as the Probable Meaning of the Word "Toronto," an impassioned speech delivered before the York County Pioneer and Historical Society in 1891 and subsequently printed in pamphlet form to ensure the widest possible distribution of his interpretation.

33 Historian Percy J. Robinson explicates this history in detail in his excellent book, *Toronto During the French Regime, 1615-1793* (1933; reprinted 1965). Robinson also offers a thoughtful assessment of the etymology of Toronto, identifying at least four meanings—"place of meeting," "trees in the water," "fish-spearing lake" and "lake opening or door"—before concluding that the matter would remain an open question until further evidence came to light. It is here where Rayburn enters, half a century later, with new cartographic and linguistic evidence supporting the Mohawk "trees in the water" etymology.

34 *Tkaronto* (2007), written and directed by Shane Belcourt.

fact and fantasy drawn from English, French and First Nations narratives of the region.

Keith also suggests that a distinctly Torontonian sort of poetry emerged during the Rebellion of 1837. The verses depicted a city among whose inhabitants civic sentiment was often as much a matter of currency as conviction. Historian John S. Moir's *Rhymes of Rebellion* includes several dozen of these works, published mainly in newspapers of the era, in which the line "famed Toronto Town" appears as a familiar refrain. These narratives, useful more as historical texts rather than for their literary merit, nonetheless provide an important record of the heated sentiments that surrounded the rebellion, a formative event in Toronto's history.[35] They also underscore the importance of political satire in a city whose fortunes have always failed or flourished according to the will of its powerful elites. Indeed, political relations in the later part of the century spurred several satirical works, perhaps chief among them journalist and social reformer T. Phillips Thompson's *The Political Experiences of Jimuel Briggs*, a hilarious, illustrated send-up of leading public figures and policy initiatives of the day.[36]

Satirical journalism aside, one of the earliest fictional representations of Toronto is John Galt's 1831 work, *Bogle Corbet*, a frontier novel depicting, in passing, the city then known as York as rough around the edges, although exhibiting an early appreciation of social diversity. Indeed, a character encountered during a brief sojourn at a Front Street hotel adjures Galt's protagonist to settle among migrants of mixed background, asserting, "[S]ociety never betters itself without new ingredients," and adding, "[W]here emigrants of different degrees and trades mingle, they do well, and everything about them becomes promising."

Toronto's literature oeuvre appears to have taken solid root by the 1880s, by which time a market had been established for locally set works like Graeme Mercer Adam and Ethelwyn Wetherald's *An Algonquin Maiden* (1887), Annie Savigny's *A Romance of Toronto* (1888), John Charles Dent's *The Gerrard Street Mystery and Other Weird Tales* (1888), Edmund Ernest Sheppard's *A Bad Man's Sweetheart* (1889) and Thomas Stinson Jarvis's *Geoffrey Hampstead* (1890). Novels set in Toronto were common by the turn of the century, and even a partial list suggests their rapidly expanding scope: Robert Barr's *The Measure of the Rule* (1907) depicts 1870s Toronto as a town poised between outpost and urbanity; Frederick Nelson's futuristic "novel," *Toronto in 1928 A.D.* (1908),

---

35 The 1837 Rebellion has also inspired contemporary literary works, among them Dennis Lee's *Civil Elegies* (1968; 1972) and Rick Salutin's play *1837: William Lyon Mackenzie and the Canadian Revolution* (1976).

36 Thompson, 1873. See also Ramsay Cook's examination of Thompson's satirical journalism in *The Regenerators: Social Criticism in late Victorian English Canada* (1985).

was modelled on early speculative fiction and sold as a souvenir at the 1908 Canadian National Exhibition; in Suzanne Marny's *Tales of Old Toronto* (1909), outdoor spaces like the bustling markets and the rural Don Valley function as necessary counterpoints to the interior confinements of Victorian society; the portrayal of wild Indian warriors and upright French officers in George F. Milner's *The Sergeant of Fort Toronto* must have thrilled Anglo-Saxon readers when it first appeared in 1914; and Augustus Bridle's *Hansen: A Novel of Canadianization* (1924) sets Toronto at the centre of its author's vision for a country unified across culture and class.[37]

Many of these works are valuable more as cultural or historical documents rather than for their literary merit, although their descriptions of Toronto offer considerable amusement to a contemporary reader. In *An Algonquin Maiden*, for example, a courting couple debates the visual appeal of 1880s Toronto while traversing its wintry streets:

[P]resently Rose remarked upon the beauty of the town. Even in his love wrapt state the idea struck Allan as slightly absurd.

"Where do you find it?" he asked in amused perplexity, looking at the little wooden houses and shops, the meagre beginnings of a city that as yet had no time to be beautiful, and noted the vile mud with which the streets were thickly overlaid. "Though, of course," he added, "there is scarcely anything to be seen save darkness, and that element is strictly necessary to an appreciation of the beauties of 'Muddy Little York.'"

"Oh," exclaimed Rose, "don't you see the lights flashing in the windows, and in every little muddy pool on the street? Think of the concentrated life in these little human nests set against the vast wilderness. Look at those faint yellow rays mingling with the slanting lines of snow, with the deep woods and dark sky in the distance. If it isn't beauty it is poetry."

A Romance of Toronto offers similar verisimilitude in its depiction of the city. Written in the florid language of the late Victorian era and set principally in the pastoral suburb of Rosedale, Savigny's novel describes Toronto as

a fair maiden with many children, whom she has planted out on either side and north of her as far as her great arms can stretch. She lies north and south, while

37 While original editions of these works are difficult to locate, contemporary reprints and electronic editions have become available in cases where copyright has entered the public domain. An extensive inventory of Canadian literary works published during this period is found in Lewis Emerson Horning and Lawrence J. Burpee's *Bibliography of Canadian Fiction* (1904). Also see J. Castell Hopkins' survey "Canadian Literature," published in *Annals of the American Academy of Political and Social Science* (1913).

her lips speak loving words to her offspring, and to her spouse, the County of York; when she rests she pillows her head on the pine-clad hills of sweet Rosedale, while her feet lave at pleasure in the blue waters of beautiful Lake Ontario.

The Measure of the Rule, set in 1870s Toronto, depicts the city as a bustling capital of commerce, at least as viewed by a recent arrival from a rural Ontario township:

> After dinner I went out to view my newly-acquired kingdom. The clear-cut moon had risen glittering and cold, and seemingly so near as to be neighbour to the city and part of its municipal lighting scheme. The streets presented all the splendour of an Arabian tale transplanted north; the shops were ablaze with light; the pavement thronged with an effervescent people. The street was musical with the tinkle of silver-tongued bells, and alive with the swift motion of spirited horses and gliding sleighs. This capital was a city of hilarious youth, with the riches of the world displayed behind sheets of plate-glass, transparent as curtains of dew.

By the assessment of the city's own writers, a single century after having wrestled the first rough-walled structures from the wooded wilderness, Toronto's European colonists had built the city into a thriving economic, political, cultural and even creative capital.

Perhaps the most prominent markers of Toronto's growing literary reputation were well-known works by two internationally regarded writers, naturalist Ernest Thompson Seton and Hemingway protegé Morley Callaghan. Generations of readers around the world familiar with Seton's widely translated *Wild Animals I Have Known*, first published in 1898, may not be aware that several of these animal stories, including "Silverspot, the Story of a Crow" and "Redruff, the Story of the Don Valley Partridge," are set in Toronto's ravines. This work, alongside Seton's *Two Little Savages*, an account of a young boy who makes himself at home in the Don Valley, prompted Germaine Warkentin to describe Seton as "the first writer to make the life of the ravines his subject."

Similarly, Toronto novelist Morley Callaghan found early success among American readers with *Strange Fugitive*, an internationally bestselling 1928 novel describing the moral unravelling of its bootlegger protagonist, a man chafing against the confines of provincial Toronto. Contrary to claims that setting a novel in Toronto has always been the kiss of death to American publishers, Callaghan's New York publisher boldly announced *Strange Fugitive*'s Toronto setting on the book's dust jacket.[38] Curiously, although *Strange Fugitive* was an American bestseller, it sold poorly in Canada: one Toronto newspaper,

---

38 *Strange Fugitive*'s 1928 Scribner's dust jacket text reads, "Morley Callaghan, a young Canadian, has aroused admiration in literary circles [....] This is his first novel. It is the story of a young workman in Toronto, Canada..."

the *Mail and Empire*, sniffed that while the book might be "a success in New York," it was "not quite the thing" for Toronto: "it was, in other words, too frank, too French, too Russian, or too something or other."[39] Still, arguably marking the end of Toronto's formative literary period, *Strange Fugitive* is considered one of the earliest "gangster novels"[40] and has also been described by literary scholar Justin Edwards as "Canada's first urban novel."[41]

From the 1930s onward it was *de rigueur* for writers to set novels in Toronto. One such example, Patrick Slater's[42] *The Yellow Briar*, was a bestseller that remained in print for two generations following its first appearance in 1933 before finally fading from view in the early 1970s.[43] Like Barr's *The Measure of the Rule* and Milner's *The Sergeant of Fort Toronto*, Slater's novel takes a historical approach, narrating the city through the eyes of a young boy whose family, in flight from the Irish famine, had landed in Toronto in 1847. Describing a town where "hammers rang early and late, in all directions, cracking up frame dwellings and lodging places," Slater vividly invokes Toronto at a crucial moment of its history:

> In 1847, there was plenty going on in Toronto to fill a young lad's mind and keep his face agape. We had come from drippy Donegal where, in the little pockets and quarter-acre patches, "the pratties grow so small they have to eat them skins and all." Toronto seemed to me a stirring, big town; and things were in a constant commotion. There were brawls aplenty for the seeing, and startling street fires by night. Then, too, there were the public hangings. Adventure bunted into a fellow round any corner; and there was lots to eat.

Viewed through an ethnographic lens, Slater's novel provides an interesting counterpoint to historians' descriptions of Toronto in this era, which have generally advanced a progressive, even triumphalist account of the city's political and economic development.[44] There is something of a Horatio Alger narrative

---

39 Quoted in White, 1993, and Edwards, 1998.
40 Dubro, 2004. See also Sypnowich, 1970.
41 Edwards, 1998.
42 "Patrick Slater" was a pseudonym adopted by the novel's author, Toronto lawyer John Mitchell. In a lengthy biographical essay on Mitchell published in the novel's 1970 printing, Dorothy Bishop described Mitchell's extensive use of published and archival source materials on Toronto history in the preparation of *The Yellow Briar*, and claimed that Mitchell was the first novelist to tackle the cholera epidemic in 1940s Toronto and its devastating impact on the Irish immigrant population.
43 Kenneally, 2005. *The Yellow Briar* was reprinted regularly in the 1930s and 1940s and was brought back into print by Macmillan in 1970. A print-on-demand edition has recently become available.
44 One notable example of triumphalism in accounts of Toronto's history is Victor Russell's anthology *Forging a Consensus: Historical Essays on Toronto* (University of Toronto Press, 1984). Two of Toronto's best-known histories—Henry Scadding's *Toronto of Old* (1873) and Eric Arthur's *No Mean*

evident in *The Yellow Briar*, too, but the novel also describes public hangings, devastating fires and a typhus epidemic that decimated the city's Irish population.

Still, curing Toronto's literary amnesia is more than a historical undertaking, and as such requires more than a simple inventory of works set in Toronto. Such a record can gain provenance only when early fictions are seen as antecedents for contemporary ones—that is, when we start paying attention to Toronto's literary genealogies, looking for preoccupations, motifs, even characters and neighbourhoods that recur across genres and time periods. At this point things cannot help but get really interesting.

Cabbagetown, Hugh Garner's classic novel of working-class, Depression-era Toronto, for example, is familiar to most readers via the Ryerson Press version published in 1968. *Cabbagetown* described the deplorable living and working conditions endured by the inhabitants of what Garner called "the largest Anglo-Saxon slum in North America." But this was not the novel's first appearance: it had been published in abridged form in 1950 by White Circle, a pulp imprint of Collins Publishing that produced disposable fiction sold at newsstands and bus stations. The original *Cabbagetown*, a crime thriller culminating in the violent death of its petty-thief protagonist, was very different from the probing analysis of social conditions most readers encounter in the subsequent version.

Garner also published another pulp novel called *Waste No Tears* (subtitled "The novel about the abortion racket") in 1950 under the pseudonym Jarvis Warwick, reportedly referencing the seedy Warwick Hotel on Jarvis Street, where Garner stayed during some of his legendary alcoholic binges.[45] Most notable for their depictions of Toronto's "skidrow," Garner's early works (perhaps themselves distillations of the "gangster" style pioneered by Callaghan in *Strange Fugitive*) seem directly to anticipate subsequent literary explorations of poverty and violence in Toronto's "skidrow," including Ted Plantos's derelict-populated *The Universe Ends at Sherbourne & Queen*, Peter Lonergan's Orwellian *Leslieville* and Michael Holmes' alternately salacious and savage *Watermelon Row*. These later texts—and the Toronto they describe—cannot truly be appreciated without an awareness of the socio-economic, historical and literary milieus that produced them.

Michael Redhill's acclaimed 2006 Toronto novel, *Consolation*,[46] is, like Anne Michaels' *Fugitive Pieces* and Michael Ondaatje's *In the Skin of a Lion* before it, credited with awakening interest in Toronto's historical origins through literary

---

City (1964; reprinted or reissued regularly thereafter)—also depict a relentlessly progressing city.
45 Sward, 1982.
46 Winner of the Toronto Book Award in 2007 and long-listed for the prestigious international Man Booker Prize in the same year.

engagement with its landscapes and the images they evoke (photographic in the case of Ondaatje and Redhill; cartographical in Michaels' work). But literary efforts to historicize the city date at least as far back as the eighteenth-century journals and letters of colonial administrators and political poetry of the 1830s. For example, fictionalized accounts of Toronto's history were so interesting to readers that novelist Isabelle Hughes was able to publish four volumes of her "Toronto gothic" Telforth saga[47] linking a fictional Kingsway family's fortunes to the city's progress from the 1830s forward. Subsequently, Hugh Hood's twelve-volume Proustian saga, *The New Age*,[48] grounded many of its analyses of Canadian culture and identity in the city among several generations of another fictional Toronto family. In particular, three volumes (*The Swing in the Garden*, describing 1930s Toronto as viewed through the eyes of a young boy growing up at the working-class edge of Rosedale; *Reservoir Ravine*, a novel of the University of Toronto's University College in the 1920s; and *Black and White Keys*, a war novel contrasting the city's complacency against the horrors of the Holocaust in Europe) elevate Toronto to the status of character, vividly depicting the interplay of the city's landscapes and the Goderich family's ambitions.

Another undeservedly forgotten mid-century Toronto novel whose shadow looms across this city's contemporary fiction is Phyllis Brett Young's *The Torontonians*, first published in 1960. Apparently the first novel to feature Toronto's modernist City Hall (then under construction) on its cover, *The Torontonians* was an international bestseller in its time and reprinted in international editions for nearly a decade. Until literary scholars and the author's daughter pressed for its republication in 2007, *The Torontonians* had been almost entirely forgotten. And yet the rapidly changing city Young depicts—beset by sprawl, rapid redevelopment and a veritable revolving door of cultural and architectural changes—seems an apt representation of Toronto today. More provocatively, Young's subversive proto-feminist novel may be seen as a direct precursor to Margaret Atwood's 1969 novel, *The Edible Woman*, which invokes startlingly similar landscapes and social conditions and whose female protagonist finds equally idiosyncratic solutions to her sense of social confinement. Whether such connections are inadvertent or intended, they deserve notice as evidence that Toronto's literary genealogy stretches back further and is much more tightly interwoven than we have come to think.

Indeed, when tracing the genealogy of Toronto novels it is impossible not to be struck repeatedly by their thematic connection to current works. Gwendolyn

---

47 Hughes' Telforth saga consists of *Serpent's Tooth* (1947), *Time in Ambush* (1949), *Lorena Telforth* (1952) and *The Wise Brother* (1954).
48 *The New Age* consisted of twelve volumes published between 1973 and 2000, the year of Hood's death.

MacEwen's "mythopoeic" voice, for example, echoes strongly in Darren O'Donnell's *Your Secrets Sleep with Me*, whose Toronto is represented as a lonely adolescent. While in *Noman's Land* MacEwen describes Torontonians as "so lonely they didn't even know it, maybe even lonelier than me," O'Donnell seems to add, "and speaking of the city—it is, in fact, a teenage city, pubescent, a little nervous; masking shyness with a performance of aloofness; snooty but universally so and born of an unawareness of just how beautiful it is. [...] it's an ugly beautiful city; a shy city; a city that has a hard time saying hello to acquaintances. A sad city. A lonely city."

The Jewish protagonists of John Miller's *A Sharp Intake of Breath* and David Bezmozgis's *Natasha and Other Stories* have a great deal in common with Jacob Grossman in Henry Kreisel's 1948 novel, *The Rich Man*, as immigrants struggling to make a place for themselves in the perplexing and seemingly impenetrable social terrain of Protestant Toronto. The polyphonic, multi-racial city Dionne Brand renders in *Thirsty* and the lyrical currents shared among the black storytellers appearing in Karen Richardson and Steven Green's anthology *T-Dot Griots* have literary origins in Austin Clarke's searing analyses of racial subalternity in Toronto. As MacEwen writes in "Sunlight at Sherbourne and Bloor," "the present is the logical outcome / Of all points in the past, and that building going up across the / street has been going up forever. Everything we do now contains the / seeds of its own unfolding."

THE CITY AT THE CENTRE OF THE MAP

Even as it traces Toronto's literary genealogies, this book seeks to accomplish something more than inventory thematic dimensions of this city's literary culture. It also argues for a profound shift in how we write, read and think about Toronto. This task requires sustained and thoughtful engagement with the city's realities as well as its ideals, its challenges and strengths, its dreams, its differences, and above all an appreciation of its perpetually emergent qualities. Toronto's ongoing struggle to recover from its cultural amnesia provides the perfect opportunity to determine our own identity and cultural principles, to decide—at long last—what Toronto really stands for. We might begin by acknowledging that the truest representations of Toronto are found not in official plans, tourism campaigns or corporate bids for "world class" status but rather in the unflinching commitment of writers to imagining Toronto as it is and might become. The city's literary texts offer an ideal medium for such reflections not only because of their depth and diversity but because they represent the only reliable map to the city within the city, the city at the centre of the map.

The secret, then, to Toronto's identity isn't to be found in the relentless building and rebuilding of its structures, in civic self-aggrandizement nor in its inhabitants' disquieting and unceasing quest for visceral entertainments, but in our connection to (and displacement from) the city's subterranean terrain, our own half-buried past and half-articulated dreams. And how do we learn to remember who we are in this city? We keep reaching for something, looking for a map that will lead us reliably into the deepest recesses of the city within the city. Like MacEwen's Noman, we seek signposts—the vast and sweeping architecture of the CN Tower, the familiar cadences of ancestral accents, the shadow of the viaducts across the ravines, the glittering marquees of discount stores and strip clubs, a sudden uprushing of pigeons above a subway grate—that will help us navigate the unmarked pathways toward the inner inner city. It is only as we tell stories about it that the city begins to grow solid around us.

Imagining Toronto seeks to interpret Toronto literature against the backdrop of the city itself. It traverses the unyielding grid of the city's streets, descends into the murk of its ravines, rides a hundred rickety high-rise elevators and broods in a dozen streetcars stranded in traffic, all while eavesdropping upon the textual conversations of its writers. It looks closely at the images and experiences that recur most hauntingly in literary works, and asks: what versions of Toronto are these authors trying to convey, and why do they write them? What is it about Toronto that prompts such a diverse outpouring of literature? What images and experiences haunt the city's literary muse? What stories remain unwritten, and when—and how—will they be told?

It is time, now, to venture into the city within the city. Imagine standing on the Bloor Viaduct with Toronto's familiar landmarks laid out before us. Far beyond the bridge's luminous veil, the CN Tower blinks in the distance; beside it the Bay Street towers rise like glittering monoliths. Below us the Don River flows as it always does, sodden with debris and murky with effluvium. Along the Parkway the traffic moves in sinuous slow motion and the rail corridor sings its silent metallic tune. There is a set of wooden steps leading down over the side, and as we descend them, the great bridge yawns above us like a mouth, stretched open as if straining to speak. Between broken glass and stinging nettle are graffiti obscured by sumac, their messages as inchoate as paintings on the wall of a cave. We descend until we lose our bearings, until the landscape merges with the base of the bridge, and the sounds of trains, traffic and the river grow almost indistinguishable from one another. We have reached the city at the centre of the map: let us begin.

– 2 –

THE CITY AS TEXT

ARCHAEOLOGIES OF MEMORY

The city lies in the broad basin of the lake bed as if cradled by an ancient hand. Beyond the buried shoreline of a vanished sedimentary sea, and beneath the beds of rivers that reach through it like fingers, are the limestone remnants of its Quaternary geology laid down in layers, like pages of the city's past. As Toronto poet Anne Michaels writes in *Skin Divers*,

> There is no city that does not dream
> From its foundations. The lost lake
> Crumbling in the hands of brickmakers,
> The floor of the ravine where light lies broken
> With the memory of rivers.

The city is bound to landscape, its narratives cartographical, and it is only by traversing its texts that we might find the forgotten signposts that will help us regain our bearings and remember who we are.

In *Consolation*, a novel about the city's relationship with its buried past, Michael Redhill describes Toronto as "the city walking on water." The contemporary waterfront has been pushed 240 feet beyond the original shoreline by landfill; above it the downtown towers loom like trees standing in the invisible water, the organic meaning of the city's name brought to life in concrete and glass. Submerged in the original harbour and buried forty feet beneath a sports arena under construction, or so the novel's protagonist insists, is the wreck of a ship in whose hold rests a rusted case containing dozens of photographic plates, a complete visual record of the city in 1856.[49] The power of these images—evidence of whose existence remains as ephemeral as the lost city they document—is arresting. Buried just out of reach, they embody tensions between development and destruction that have resulted in the methodical obliteration of entire eras of Toronto's civic history, tensions that seem rooted in a peculiar ambivalence about the city's origins. At the same time, in a city where so much has been lost to memory, the images offer the promise of recovery, as if redemption might be derived even from the story of their existence. As *Consolation*'s protagonist observes, "There is a vast part of this city with mouths buried in it [....] Mouths capable of speaking to us. But we stop

---

49 *Consolation* is based on historical fact: a nearly complete visual record of the city in 1856-57 was indeed commissioned in an ultimately unsuccessful bid to have Toronto named the permanent capital of the Province of Canada. The images produced, of which only twenty-five survive, are the earliest photographs of Toronto known to exist. These images are reproduced and their providence explained in depth in *Toronto's Visual Legacy: Official City Photography from 1856 to the Present* (Lorimer, 2009).

them up with concrete and build over them and whatever it is they wanted to say gets whispered down empty alleys and turns into wind. People need to be given a reason to listen."

A reason to listen lurks beneath nearly every surface of the city. For poet Eirin Mouré the listening is literal. In *Sheep's Vigil by a Fervent Person*, Mouré invokes the secret sound of the city's buried creeks, flowing invisibly under parking lots and pavement in sinuous slow motion toward the lakeshore.[50] Perched above a sewer grate, poised between presence and absence, Moure wonders at this proof of the persistence of water and writes, "In this way I'm alive. / I'm the Discoverer of Nature" before concluding that, like the city itself, "Nature is fragments without a whole. That's the great mystery."

Another mystery of the city's fragments is their capacity to evoke constellations of existence larger than themselves. In *Soul of the World*, a meditation on the meaning of time, poet Christopher Dewdney describes a late-summer sunset that illuminates the south wall of his Toronto home and etches in golden light the imprint of a kitten's paws immortalized in century-old brick. The unexpected appearance of these traces of the past moves Dewdney to measure the lifespan of a kitten against the longer legacy of the bricks and to muse, "All these indelible imprints, like footprints in wet concrete, are a permanent record of transient events." Visiting the Don Valley Brickworks, an abandoned factory[51] where the bricks used to build thousands of Toronto homes, including his own, were once baked from clay and crushed limestone quarried from the side of the adjacent ravine, Dewdney senses the city's history swirling around him and comments, "It seemed then that time leaked like a mist out of the limestone around me. It seeped out of the prehistoric clay and lingered over the ponds. There was something moody, desolate and marvelous about the abandoned buildings with their empty windows. The architecture of the old factory seemed emblematic of another time, another place, an evening

---

50 In *Emerald City: Toronto Visited* (1994), John Bentley Mays inventories many of Toronto's buried streams, including Mount Pleasant Creek, Rosedale Brook, Castle Frank Brook, Russell Creek and, perhaps most famously, Taddle Creek (in whose memory the arts magazine *Taddle Creek* is named) and Garrison Creek. Many other waterways, some unnamed, lie tightly channelized or buried beneath the city's streets—until a storm surge brings them to life and they burst through the pavement, opening sinkholes capable of consuming vehicles whole. In recent years city planners and environmental organizations have suggested that some of these creeks might yet be restored to the surface, although high costs, a century of city-building and political inertia make such a result unlikely in the city core. Still, in the inaugural issue of *Taddle Creek* (December 1997), Alfred Holden observes optimistically, "It's such a Toronto thing to do. You take something beautiful, make it wretched, and bury it. Then, a hundred years later, recognizing both error and opportunity, you dig it up and make it bloom."

51 Evergreen, a charitable foundation that holds stewardship of the Brickworks in conjunction with the Toronto Region Conservation Authority, has begun converting the buildings into a cultural centre. The majority of the quarried lands has been transformed into parkland.

almost a century ago when a kitten walked over wet bricks and looked up to watch the swallows."

It is a compulsion of cities to consume themselves, to demolish and build over their most iconic edifices in an unceasing quest for civic greatness that sometimes seems indistinguishable from cultural nihilism.[52] As *Consolation*'s protagonist observes of Toronto, "this whole place erases itself every day." In *Fugitive Pieces*, Anne Michaels' powerful novel weighing the brevity of human history against the vast span of geological time, a professor of geography and his young protege traverse the Don Valley intending to visit Chorley Park, the Lieutenant Governor's storied estate, perched high above the ravine like a fortified citadel. Reaching their destination, they are astonished to discover the mansion has been demolished: "We emerged from the scrub of the ravine into the garden and lifted our heads to emptiness. Chorley Park, built to outlast generations, was gone, as though an eraser had rubbed out its place against the sky." In stunned disbelief the elderly geographer asks his younger companion, "How could they have torn it down, one of the most beautiful buildings in the city? Jakob, are you sure we're in the right place?" Wearily, familiar since childhood with the consequences of cultural erasure, Jakob replies, "We're in the right place, koumbaros. ... How do I know? Because it's gone."

If Toronto's ruins are not as grand as Roman amphitheatres or Abyssinian tombs, they are no less poignant. Upper Canada's first parliament buildings, reduced to rubble and buried under a car wash.[53] Garrison Creek, once the largest watershed between the Humber and Don Rivers, degraded to a sewer, its bridge entombed beneath landfill and garbage.[54] Millennia-old Aboriginal settlements, their archaeological wealth of cultural artifacts bulldozed by developers and scattered to the wind.[55] Even the much maligned Gardiner Expressway is a standing ruin, half-demolished, its brutal, elegant arches lining the waterfront like orphaned mastodons.[56]

---

52 William Dendy's *Lost Toronto* (2nd ed., 1993) traces the regrettable loss of much of the city's nineteenth and early twentieth century architectural heritage. Dendy writes, "No one envisaged, when each one was being built, the ultimate fate of the building, or charted—as often happens today with new high-rise office buildings—the date on which it would be considered obsolete and consigned to the wrecker. [...] As living, cared-for, respected elements in the ongoing life of Toronto they would have provided a touchstone for the development of the twentieth-century city." Similarly, in *Toronto's Lost Villages* (1997), Ron Brown writes, "the older a city gets, the newer it seems to look."

53 Dieterman and Williamson, 2001.

54 Reeves, 2007; see also Mays, 1994.

55 Williamson, 2008.

56 In *Concrete Toronto*, architect Calvin Brook evokes the Gardiner Expressway's primordial beauty and argues that its greatest challenges arise not from the placement or design of the expressway itself but rather from the need for sympathetic use of the lands under and around it. ("The Gardiner Expressway," in *Concrete Toronto: A Guidebook to Concrete Architecture from the fifties to the seventies*, ed. Michael McClelland and Graeme Stewart, Coach House Books).

If anything has the capacity to mitigate these losses, it is the vanished city's way of insinuating itself into our narratives of the present. As *Consolation*'s protagonist tells his fiancée in hope of alleviating the grief she feels for her father, a historian whose death by drowning is a powerful metaphor for the contemporary city's indifference to its past, "He's alive in a thought you're having [....] There are some things you can bring back." In *Fugitive Pieces*, Anne Michaels reveals how quickly the city's past can be conjured to life through the invocatory power of gestures and words:

> With a few words (an incantation in Greek or English) and the sweep of his hand, Athos sliced a hill in half, drilled under the sidewalk, cleared a forest. He showed me Toronto cross-sectioned; he ripped open cliffs like fresh bread, revealing the ragged geological past. Athos stopped in the middle of busy city streets and pointed out fossils in the limestone ledges of the Park Plaza Hotel or in the walls of a hydro substation. "Ah, limestone, accumulating one precious foot every twenty-five thousand years!" Instantly the streets were flooded by a subtropical salt sea. I imagined front lawns crammed with treasure: crinoids, lamp shells, trilobites.

In this sense, Toronto's writers are archaeologists of memory, dredging the city's subterranean layers for fragments that flesh out the city's contemporary form and give shape to its present-day preoccupations and ambitions. It is through these fragments that the city reveals itself: the angle of light between buildings, an overheard conversation, the memory of water flowing beneath pavement. As Gwendolyn MacEwen writes in *Noman's Land*, "The past was the secret and mysterious city, the city within the city, the city of the alleyways and swimming pools and the city of the lakeshore. And the lake, which cared nothing for time, would often cast up strange relics of the future, as well as the past, upon its shores."

And this is how we make our way into the city within the city: by travelling downward, like dowsers drawn to the scent of water. Only then, once we have pressed our hands into limestone layers and listened to the earth speak, will we be able to regain our bearings and travel upward, blinking as we emerge from subterranean shadow into the illuminated grid of the city's streets. And as we navigate the city at the centre of the map, we realize that we, too, are part of the story, crafting new narratives of Toronto even as the city swirls and eddies around us like a buried river brought back to life.

RAVINE CITY

From the air Toronto appears flat, a city rising almost imperceptibly above the impassive mirrored surface of Lake Ontario. At closer proximity, however,

Toronto reveals itself to be a city of inverted mountains,[57] its terrain striated and stretched apart by ravines, deep glacier-etched river valleys that bisect the city like the lines on a human hand. For all the ways they have been altered—buried, bridged, polluted, paved over—the ravines remain Toronto's most prominent geological feature,[58] carving the city into neighbourhoods and interrupting the rectilinear progress of the urban grid. At the same time, the ravines define more than Toronto's topography: they are the repository of the city's memory and the symbolic seat of its conscience, a tangled warren of nightmares and desires played out in subterranean shadow. Descending into the ravines is like touring the urban subconscious, a labyrinth of the city's secrets exposed to sudden view.

Referring to the powerful draw of the city's ravines, novelist Hugh Hood describes Toronto as "a city where sooner or later you find yourself going down into a dark place in the ground." Maggie Helwig expands on this perspective in her acclaimed novel *Girls Fall Down*, portraying Toronto as a city that, for all its ambitions of corporate and cultural ascendency, is most deeply preoccupied with its subterranean layers:

> It is a city that burrows, tunnels, runs underground. It has built strata of malls and pathways and inhabited spaces like the layers in an archaeological dig, a body below the earth, flowing with light.

Margaret Atwood, without doubt the most prolific chronicler of the city's ravines, writes that "to go down into them is to go down into sleep, away from the conscious electrified life of the houses. The ravines are darker, even in the day."[59] These descriptions of the ravines invoke contrasting images of darkness and light, underscoring the contradiction at the heart of the ravines: they are at once enigmatic and illuminating, perilous and inviting, forbidden and

---

57 The image of Toronto as a city of inverted mountains has become one of its principal leitmotifs. In *Toronto Places: A Context for Urban Design*, Canadian architect Larry Richards refers to Toronto as "San Francisco upside down" (Baraness & Richards, eds., 1992), Journalist Robert Fulford expands on Richards' description in *Accidental City*, averring that "the ravines are to Toronto what canals are to Venice and hills are to San Francisco" (1996). In 2003 the City of Toronto elevated this aphorism to policy status, quoting Fulford in literature accompanying its Ravine Protection By-Law (City of Toronto, 2003),

58 Naturalist Murray Seymour refers to the ravines as "the hidden country." His book *Toronto's Ravines: Walking the Hidden Country* (Boston Mills Press, 2000) explores six of Toronto's major ravine systems in cartographical, cultural and ecological detail through thirty-four self-guided walking tours. See also *Toronto Rocks: The Geological Legacy of the Toronto Region* (Fitzhenry & Whiteside, 2004), in which geologist Nick Eyles argues that Toronto's ravine systems "provide one of the best geological records of the last 135,000 years in North America."

59 Quoted in Sullivan, 1998.

irresistible. Like the city itself, the ravines ply all their paradoxes at the same time, and it is precisely their incongruity that makes them so central in its literature.

The appeal of the ravines seems strongest among children, especially those seeking to escape an urban existence that is painful, abusive or otherwise alienating. The earliest literary work to express this attraction is naturalist Ernest Thompson Seton's *Two Little Savages*, a turn-of-the-century novel sprinkled liberally with woodlore, structured around the narrative of a young Toronto boy who withdraws to the Don Valley early one spring, drawn by an ageless wilderness he has discovered at the edge of the city:

> Oh, what a song the Wild Geese sang that year! And yet, was it a new song? No, the old, old song, but Yan heard it with new ears. He was learning to read its message. He wandered on their trailless track, as often as he could, northward, ever northward, up the river from the town, and up, seeking the loneliest ways and days.

In Barbara Gowdy's novel *The Romantic*, a parallel yearning draws Louise, a young girl who deals with maternal abandonment by retreating to one of the city's eastern ravines, where she spends the afternoons in a small shelter built of branches tied together with lengths of yarn she has unravelled from one of her absent mother's sweaters:

> In the tee-pee, among sticks of sunlight, I sort through my stone collection and feed Jell-O powder to black ants. Sometimes, overhead, I hear a faint whine I think must be the clouds gliding by. Then there are moments of silence so absolute I am convinced I hear the ants' footsteps; it is a tinkling sound, as if they wore bells on their ankles. When I lie with my ear to the dirt floor, the tunnelling of the worms is distant thunder. All around me pine trees cross out the view. I am at the heart of an impenetrable fortification. Safe.

But if the ravines are spaces of silence and solace, they are also caverns of change. In Richard Scrimger's novel *Into the Ravine*, three boys decide to navigate the length of Scarborough's Highland Creek on a raft they have built themselves. During a journey reminiscent of Huckleberry Finn's cruise along the Mississippi, the boys make friends with a homeless dwarf named Ernesto, who joins them on their journey and summarizes the social anthropology of the ravines, describing its appeal to children like themselves:

> They come down in the morning and stay all day, season after season, catching, climbing, growing—creating worlds where they make the rules. You three know

what I'm talking about. Except that you're almost too old for the ravine, aren't you? You've already left your own part—the part you know. The creek is your childhood, and you are following it to where it ends."

After narrowly evading a terrifying creature known as Bonesaw and almost inadvertently solving a major crime, the boys and Ernesto part ways. As they watch their empty raft float away on the moonlit surface of Lake Ontario, the boys realize the truth of his prediction: that their adventure has marked the culmination and conclusion of their childhood and that their journey down the ravine has been, quite literally, a rite of passage into adolescence.

While in Seton's, Gowdy's and Scrimger's narratives the ravines are places for play and discovery, to many parents the city's ravines are symbols of pollution and peril, rumoured to harbour disease and colonies of vagrants. Set in the early years of the twentieth century, Barbara Nichol's poignant children's story, *Dippers*, evokes the tensions arising from the forbidden appeal of the ravines:

> Mother used to say to us, "Now, you girls don't go down to that river." The Don River was right there. Mother always thought something bad was going to happen. But you could go swimming down at the river and the boys could go fishing.

But where Nichol emphasizes the innocence of childhood exploration, in "The Ravine" poet Elana Wolff channels a more suggestive image of the ravines, alluding to their proto-sexual significance in the lives of young girls:

> And in the soft mythology of memory,
> gully triumphant.
>   Intractably tied to the tail end of girlhood.
> Damp gash where
> trilliums peeked like summer solstice fairies
> and were snatched.

In Wolff's poem, the "damp gash" of the ravines is a metaphor for the female body that connects this gendered landscape unmistakably to the possibilities and perils of adolescent sexuality. If the CN Tower is Toronto's largest phallic object, then the ravines are clearly its female corollary.

Wolff is not the only writer to connect the city's ravines to the female body. But where Wolff remains ambiguous about the consequences of their corporeal power, Margaret Atwood represents the ravines unmistakably as sites of victimhood and predation. In *The Edible Woman*, Atwood's first published novel, a woman follows her lover into an unfamiliar tributary of the Don Valley and is startled when he leads her to the edge of the Brick Works, the vast chasm of its quarry spilling out before them at the bottom on the ravine. Unsettled by the sudden appearance of this unexpected netherworld, a jarring metaphor for the unanticipated implications of her affair, Atwood's protagonist reflects, "It seemed wrong to have this cavity in the city: the ravine itself was supposed to be as far down as you could go. It made her suspect the white pit-bottom also; it didn't look solid, it looked possibly hollow, dangerous, a thin layer of ice, as though if you walked on it you might fall through." Marian flees the ravine but is unable to evade its consequences, and finds the shallow, sheltered life she has imagined for herself sliding away like clay crumbling from the edge of the quarry.

In *Lady Oracle*, Atwood foregrounds descriptions of the uncultivated terrain of the ravines with accounts of social cruelty and the threat of sexual molestation. Joan, Atwood's protagonist, is sent weekly by her mother across a particularly unkempt section of a nearby ravine despite its dangerous reputation:

> My mother was terrified of this ravine: it crawled with vines and weedy undergrowth, it was dense with willow trees and bushes, behind every one of which she pictured a lurking pervert, an old derelict rendered insane by rubbing alcohol, a child molester or worse.

Perhaps inevitably, one afternoon in the ravine Joan encounters a man who exposes himself to her, then bows graciously and hands her a fistful of daffodils. While unsettling, this encounter is not frightening: Joan knows already that the real danger of the ravine is not the spectre of molestation but rather the bullying she endures from a group of older girls her mother insists she accompany across the ravine for safety. Choosing Joan as the target of their animosity, the girls exclude, then taunt and finally decide to tie Joan to a bridge that crosses the deepest part of the ravine, where they abandon her as bait for the "bad man" she had encountered the week before. Long minutes later Joan is rescued by a man who unties her and accompanies her out of the ravine. Joan is never able to decide whether her rescuer was the same man who had exposed himself to her, but she understands indelibly the capacity of the ravines to encourage or lend cover to the feral appetites of those who are drawn to their terrain.

Atwood revisits the feral invitation of the ravines in *Cat's Eye*, describing a young girl found murdered in the ravine below the Don Valley brickworks:

This girl is our age. Her bicycle has been found near her. She has been strangled, and also molested. We know what "molested" means.

What "molested" means, Atwood makes clear in the novel, is that the assault is understood to be the girl's own fault, for riding her bicycle into the ravine, presumably alone, and perhaps also for wearing the white angora sweater with a fur collar and pom-poms described in lurid detail in newspaper reports of the crime. The incident is deeply troubling to Elaine, Atwood's protagonist, who observes,

> I have long since dismissed the idea of bad men in the ravine. I've considered them a scarecrow story, put up by mothers. But it appears they exist, despite me.

The incident disturbs memories of Elaine's own traumatic encounter in the ravine, an incident she has managed very nearly to repress. Nonetheless, like a cold wind coursing through the ravine, the girl's death "stirs up something, like dead leaves."

Although girls are, in literature as in life, disproportionately likely to be the victims of sexual violence, boys who wander into the city's ravines are not invulnerable. The middle-aged protagonist of Paul Quarrington's novel *The Ravine* blames his alcoholism, his failed marriage and his stillborn literary career on "the incident," a partially repressed memory of having been sexually attacked, alongside his brother and a boyhood friend, in a wooded ravine just below the suburban community of Don Mills. After struggling and failing to understand a trauma so horrifying it has haunted his adult life, Quarrington's narrator concludes simply, "what happened down in the ravine has fucked us over profoundly. Look at Norman! He's a goddamned priest!" In the end, he comes to terms with the assault after realizing, with the help of his fellow victims, that what matters is not the memory of the assault itself but rather how to deal with the ravine he has carried around inside himself throughout the intervening decades.

If these narratives are taken literally, in Toronto's ravines cast their long shadow over so many unspeakable acts that at times their wooded slopes seem littered with the bodies of brutalized victims. In Maureen Jenning's Victorian detective novel, *Let Loose the Dogs*, a man stumbles into a ravine near Yonge Street to sleep off a drunken stupor and learns, upon awakening, that he has been charged with the murder of a rival found bludgeoned to death in the nearby creek. The homeless protagonist of Rosemary Aubert's mystery novel *Free Reign* discovers a severed hand in the little garden he tends in a remote tributary of the Don River. In Jill Edmundson's crime thriller *Blood & Groom*, a man is found shot to death in the scrub just below Rosedale Valley Road; the leading suspect is his jilted former fiancée.

What is it about the ravines that makes them the location of so much imagined violence—far more, in fact, than occurs in them in real life? Are the ravines themselves dangerous, the urban embodiment of the "nature the monster" thesis Margaret Atwood outlines in her influential 1972 book of Canadian literary criticism, *Survival*?[60] Alternatively, do narratives of their malevolence reflect the long-standing separation of culture (the realm of reason, order, civilization, masculinity and the mind) and nature (the domain of passion, disorder, savagery, femininity and the body) in contemporary Western thought?[61] Novelist Timothy Findley suggests an alternate reading in *Headhunter*, writing about a woman murdered in a Rosedale ravine while her neighbours and even her husband stand by in silent complicity:

> Sarah departed the house at eleven-thirty. The moon was shining. This was October 28th. She wore her best woollen coat and scarves and a pair of heavy boots. She carried a walking stick and a flashlight. On her head she wore a tall, brown hat made of felt. In her pocket, there was a sandwich. She had been gone no more than half an hour when her screams and their echoes began to rise up through the mists—and they lasted a full five minutes. Several men and women went rushing to the hilltop and onto the Glen Road Bridge overlooking the ravine—but none went down to assist her. When the last of her cries had been issued, many birds flew up from the trees through the darkness, after which silence fell. It was only then that Lilah's father called the police.

As Findley's narrative underscores, it is the not the ravines that are evil, but rather we who project our own desire and darkness upon them. Lilah's mother is killed *in* the ravine but not *by* it: the agents of her death are people, including those who stand by and do nothing to help her.

If the ravines are sinister spectres in the minds of some Toronto writers, for others they are places of solace and release. In "The Other Goldberg Variations,"

---

60 In *Survival*, Atwood argued that the principal tropes in Canadian literature revolve around the intersecting themes of survival and victimization amid a hostile landscape. According to her thesis, violence—even between people—is ultimately a natural phenomenon. Despite the decades that have elapsed since its publication, and despite Atwood's insistence that the book was never intended to provide an authoritative opinion on Canadian literature, *Survival* remains one of the most prominent works of Canadian literary criticism.

61 Dualistic thinking is considered characteristic of Western culture since the Enlightenment, although dualisms (culture/nature, male/female, mind/body, etc.) are both older and common in many cultures. For a history of the culture/nature divide in Western thought, see ecologist Neil Evernden's *The Social Creation of Nature* (1992).

poet Maggie Helwig channels Toronto's famously reclusive composer, Glenn Gould, when she intones,

> Knowing
> that I could walk seventeen miles through a ravine
> in the heart of Toronto, and never
> directly see the city
> is of some comfort.[62]

A similar comfort exists for the homeless gardener in Rosemary Aubert's *Free Reign*, a disgraced former judge who has retreated to a remote section of the Don Valley to bear out the shame of his fall from grace. After drifting among rundown rooming houses and finding occasional shelter in the ravines, eventually he simply remains there. On one of his infrequent returns to the city's streets, Ellis describes the various moods of the river valley, his walk culminating along the stinking stretch of the Don near its channelized mouth, surrounded by decaying factories and the remains of an abattoir still spilling its miasma into the river decades after having been closed. He finds solace even in this derelict landscape, which mirrors his own capacity for persistence in the face of ruination and exile:

> I loved the river even here. I loved how dark it was, how it held its secrets with the dignity of the damned. I loved how grass and even small trees managed to sprout out of the concrete that held it captive. [....] I loved the sounds, even if they were the sounds of man rather than the sounds of nature. I loved the rattle of the old bridges as the streetcars went over them. I loved the lap of the water as it licked at concrete. I loved the wind in the slim weeds that grew between the railroad ties. I even loved the sound of the rush-hour trains, the buzzing traffic, the sound of my own feet on the asphalt path. I think what I really loved in those moments when I was cupped in the hand of the city was life.

Neither quite natural nor completely urban, the ravines offer a reprieve from a city whose entire horizon can seem hemmed in by high-rises and transmission towers. Sometimes the relief they offer is temporary, as it is for Foster, one of the protagonists of Catherine Bush's novel *Minus Time*, who describes once having run away from home to live in the ravine below Don Mills:

---

62 Helwig, 1989. In 1979 Glenn Gould wrote and narrated an episode called "Glenn Gould's Toronto" for the Canadian Broadcasting Corporation's *Cities* series. Helwig's poem is an homage to Gould, appearing to draw from and expand on some of the film's passages.

"When I was thirteen," Foster said quietly, "I ran away from home and lived in the ravines by myself for over a week. I was thinking about it because of the leaves, because it was just this time of year. Actually I caused kind of stir. I was called the ravine boy in the news, I had my picture in the paper, and afterward the police were kind of freaked out that they hadn't been able to find me. I started out in Wilket Creek Park and made my way down, south of the Science Centre. Down toward the Don Valley Parkway. I was really lucky that it didn't rain. I had a sleeping bag and I'd brought food and I was careful because I didn't want to be found. … [A]fter a week I got bored and lonely, and I figured my parents had had a chance to really miss me and even think I was dead, so I made my way to a supermarket parking lot and convinced a woman to drive me home."

For Foster one week in the ravines was long enough, a temporary distraction from the troubles of his teenaged life.

Others, however, seek a more permanent break from their urban existence. Margaret Atwood's Booker Prize–winning novel, *The Blind Assassin*, opens with the death of one of its principal characters when her car tumbles over the St. Clair viaduct into the Vale of Avoca in midtown Toronto:

Ten days after the war ended, my sister Laura drove a car off a bridge. The bridge was being repaired: she went right through the Danger sign. The car fell a hundred feet into the ravine, smashing through the treetops feathery with new leaves, then burst into flames and rolled down into the shallow creek at the bottom. Chunks of the bridge fell on top of it. Nothing much was left of her but charred smithereens.

Although ultimately the death is ruled an accident, Atwood's narrator understands the bureaucratic sleight-of-hand required to make it so. Even before the necessary inquest, a police officer who informs her of the death leaves little doubt about its true nature:

He said the tires may have caught on a streetcar track or the brakes may have failed, but he also felt bound to inform me that two witnesses—a retired lawyer and a bank teller, dependable people—had claimed to have seen the whole thing. They'd said Laura had turned the car sharply and deliberately, and had plunged off the bridge with no more fuss than stepping off a curb. They'd noticed her hands on the wheel because of the white gloves she'd been wearing."

Despite witness accounts, mechanical evidence and measurements taken at the death scene, the social taboo of suicide makes just enough room for the narrative that Laura's death was nothing more or less than a tragic accident.

While the suffering of those who propel themselves over the edge of the city's ravines ends shortly after they do so, the difficulties faced by their families have often just begun. In Phyllis Brett Young's *The Torontonians*, the mother of one of the protagonist's friends jumps to her death from the Sherbourne Street bridge over the Rosedale Ravine, leaving behind a young daughter who must cross that very bridge every day for years afterward. A similar challenge confronts the protagonist of Paul Quarrington's *The Ravine*, consigned to pass the spot where his father's car had slammed into an abutment of the old Diamond Bridge over the Don River near Don Mills. Having concluded that the death was a suicide, Quarrington's narrator—struggling to deal with his own traumatic history with this same ravine—comments, "It is not insignificant to me that my father died while crossing the Don River. My father died going through the ravine." In Dionne Brand's *What We All Long For*, a young woman walks regularly along the Bloor viaduct near a spot once frequented by her mother, who loved it, she said, because it reminded her of home, "except for the bridge, except for the traffic, and except for the winter." After her mother leaps to her death from the twenty-first floor of a nearby St. Jamestown apartment, the long view from the viaduct is all her daughter has left. A similar loss permeates the pages of Claudia Dey's novel, *Stunt*, in which a young woman searching for her missing father recalls one of his early suicide attempts:

> You told me once that you nearly killed yourself but that at the last moment God saved you. You knew that you had to die outside the house so as not to scar us forever, so you called a taxi and you opened the passenger door, noose already looped around your shoulder. 'Rosedale Ravine, man.' You planned on hanging yourself from a 130-year-old tree in the place you found most beautiful in the city.

Stepping out of the taxi after a difficult journey in dense fog, Sheb walks along a path that leads him not into the ravine but, uncannily, back to his home instead, where he proclaims a faith in miracles. Despite this claim, before long Sheb abandons his young daughter at the edge of Lake Ontario, leaving her to spend nine surreal years reconstructing the fragments of her father's life before realizing that he had returned to the ravine that night to hang himself, his body found dangling from the oldest tree in the Rosedale Ravine a day later. And in the horror of that realization is the irony of a remembered conversation:

> 'Don't leave me again.'
> 'I won't.'
> 'Promise.'

'I promise.'
'Promise.'

If suicides are often a shocking mystery to surviving family members, an inescapable (if sometimes impenetrable) logic informs the timing, means and especially the place of death. In her short story "Midnights on the Bloor Viaduct," science-fiction author Leah Bobet describes the peculiar appeal to the despondent of the Bloor Viaduct, reportedly the site of over 400 suicides[63] since its completion in 1918:

> Winter turned into spring, and on the news they talked about Seasonal Affective Disorder and suicide rates, and how they were building a suicide prevention net on both sides of the Bloor Viaduct to keep the jumpers from jumping. The commentators scoffed at the project: the net might keep them from jumping there. They would jump onto the subway tracks and out the windows and off the buildings and from other, farther bridges. You couldn't stop someone who really wanted to die.

Bobet's narrator is herself a jumper, albeit one who realizes in mid-fall that she is capable of flying when the sensation of wings exploding in her chest buoys her above the ravine floor and she comes to rest on one of the viaduct's girders amid a confusion of pigeons. Contained in this revelation is the contradictory motive underlying so many suicide attempts: the desire not exactly to die, but rather to be released from the anguish of an existence that has become an unbearable burden. The impassive depth of the ravines offers the promise of oblivion and a kind of absolution; jumping is the ultimate surrender to something larger than the self.

That the ravines are larger than the self is at the root of their significance in the city's literature. They are the city's archives, their layered geology an open vault housing not only our wish to remember but also our desire to forget. In *Fugitive Pieces*, Anne Michaels describes the ravines as an invitation to escape the present by slipping backward through geological time:

> Like diving birds, Athos and I plunged one hundred and fifty million years into the dark deciduous silence of the ravines. Behind the billboard next to Tamblyn's Drugstore we dipped into the humid amphitheatre of a Mesozoic swamp, where massive fronds and ferns tall as houses waved in a spore-dense haze. Beneath a parking lot, behind a school; from racket, fumes, and traffic, we dove into the city's sunken rooms of green sunlight. Then, like andartes, resurfaced half a city away.

---

63 A variety of sources report this figure, including the Schizophrenic Society of Ontario, whose lobbying led to the erection (1997-2003) of the Luminous Veil, a suicide prevention barrier along the Bloor Viaduct.

For Michaels' protagonists, both survivors of war who have suffered great losses, the vast scale of geological time compressed in the layers of the ravines is a source of tremendous solace. The sheer immensity of geologic time dwarfs human history, reducing even the most monstrous atrocities to a few artifacts scattered among stone. As Jakob observes, "[T]hese weekly explorations into the ravines were escapes to ideal landscapes; lakes and primeval forests so long gone they could never be taken away from us [....] [T]he way Athos saw the world, every human was a newcomer."

Where Michaels emphasizes the temporal enormity of the ravines, in *In the Skin of a Lion*, Michael Ondaatje stresses their spatial vastness, describing them as gulfs that dwarf even the huge viaducts that knit their edges together. "Where does the earth end?" Ondaatje asks, invoking a workman who swings from the scaffolding of the Bloor Viaduct guiding pieces of the growing bridge into their metal moorings and once, famously, rescuing a nun blown over the side by grabbing her out of thin air. Years later he flickers and fades in archival photographs, reduced to a spectre against the massive undercarriage of the bridge:

> Even in archive photographs it is difficult to find him. Again and again you see vista before you and the eye must search along the wall of sky to the speck of burned paper across the valley that is him, an exclamation mark, somewhere in the distance between bridge and river.

A silhouette among shadows, he nearly vanishes, too, in the larger narrative of the viaduct, a story favouring the prominent public figures who dreamed the bridge into being. Nonetheless, having left his mark on the material structure of the viaduct, having become legendary among the bridge workers, Nicholas Temelcoff is embedded in the history of the bridge as deeply as a rivet pinned into steel.

As Michaels and Ondaatje suggest, we are as much a part of the history of the ravines as they are of ours. Contemporary Torontonians, too, are reminded of this every time a culverted creek surges beyond its banks and opens sinkholes in city roads,[64] every time a row of houses lists because its basements are built on landfill, and every time the Don Valley Parkway is flooded during a summer rainstorm. As John Bentley Mays observes in *Emerald City*, "the river will let us use its ancient flood plain, but on its own terms."

And if this is a source of solace as well as a challenge to the city's sense of

---

64 In 2005 and 2009, massive sinkholes appeared along Finch Avenue between Jane and Dufferin streets after heavy rains caused culverted streams (Black Creek in 2005; the West Don in 2009) to overflow their banks. The repairs took months and cost millions of dollars and reminded Toronto residents of the primordial power even of the city's buried waterways.

itself, then perhaps this is why so many narratives return to the event of Hurricane Hazel, the devastating 1954 storm that reclaimed the city's ravines[65] and has etched itself indelibly onto the city's texts. Anne Michaels, for example, writes vividly in *Fugitive Pieces* of the way the storm reduced entire neighbourhoods to mere artifacts washed up on the banks of the Humber River:

> In the bank, four wooden knobs, evenly spaced: excavate an inch or two and the legs of a chair will emerge. A few feet downriver, a dinner plate—perhaps with the familiar and ever-popular blue willow pattern—sticks out of the bank horizontally like a shelf. You can slip a silver spoon out of the mud like a bookmark. [...] Hidden beneath the grass, all around you, the wide, silent park is studded with cutlery.

Michaels' depiction is only one of many retellings of the hurricane that, like narratives of other storms and other floods, recur in the city's literature like an undertow. Memories of the storm have prompted at least two children's stories: Steve Pitt's *Rain Tonight* and Eric Walters' *Safe as Houses*. In a recent adult novel, Mark Sinnett's *The Carnivore*, Hurricane Hazel foregrounds an emotional storm that capsizes a couple's marriage.

In "Shale," a short story throughout which the Humber River lurks like a familiar stranger, its banks treacherous and lined with fossil-filled shale, Antanas Sileika considers the impact of Hurricane Hazel on a boy whose young friend, Patsy, is swept away when her parents refuse to leave the home they have built stubbornly on the banks of the rising river. While half the street Patsy lives on washes away, David and his father escape across a railway trestle in the middle of the storm:

> The wind was high down the river valley, and I could tell when we were over the water. It was roaring somewhere beneath us and I could feel the trestle tremble whenever something heavy hit one of the pillars. [...] Strange sounds came out of the darkness below us, shrieks of wood against concrete and a pinging noise as if a metal cable was flapping in the wind. At times I thought I could hear voices.

For weeks afterward the river disgorges concrete and twisted metal. David looks for signs of Patsy's house, but the river has shifted within its banks and he cannot know whether any of the ruins he sees are hers, so utterly has the neigh-

---

65 Jim Gifford's *Hurricane Hazel: Canada's Storm of the Century* (Dundurn, 2004) describes the storm's devastating effect: eighty-one deaths, 4,000 families left homeless, entire neighbourhoods washed away, bridges, roads and public infrastructure destroyed, and tens of millions of dollars in property damage. Many of Toronto's contemporary city planning regulations, particularly those governing construction on flood plains, were adopted as a result of Hurricane Hazel.

bourhood been erased from the river's geomorphology. Months later, after the bridges have been rebuilt and much of the rubble hauled away, David returns to the river and sifts through silt and shale looking for them, digging, he says, for fossils.

While Toronto's fierce storms give the city's rivers a chance to reclaim lost territory from human transgressors, literary accounts of these calamities also afford opportunities for redemption or growth. In *Free Reign*, Rosemary Aubert's homeless protagonist uses his hard-won knowledge of the river's habits to help rescue more than thirty people from underneath the Bloor Street Viaduct during a sudden storm, reminiscent of the 1954 hurricane, that rapidly floods the city's valleys and roads. In Margaret Atwood's story "Hurricane Hazel," the storm metaphorically foregrounds the "atmospherically supercharged" end of a teenaged relationship. Dimly aware of having escaped from a liaison that would have drowned her as surely as the rising river, the young narrator observes,

> The morning after the hurricane, I had only the sensation of having come unscathed through a major calamity. [...] I had wanted something more like tragedy. Two people had actually been drowned there during the night, but we did not learn that until later. This is what I have remembered most clearly about Buddy: the ordinary-looking wreckage, the flatness of the water, the melancholy light.

But if Atwood's narrator has hoped for a more symbolic wreckage, perhaps the river, tiring of being hemmed in by culverts and gutters, has as well. As the prolific Toronto poet Raymond Souster suggests, "the rain is only the river / grown bored, risking everything / on one big splash."

Nature-culture dualities that portray nature as monstrous or vengeful have traditionally addressed the suffering of people, bereft and uncomprehending in the face of nature's uncontrollable rage. However, while stories and poems about Toronto's ravines during Hurricane Hazel employ similar devices emphasizing human loss and contrasts in scale (such as pinpoint lamps wavering in the storm-torn darkness, or Michaels' striking archaeological image of fragile dinner plates sunk into riverbanks), they are also structured as morality tales, suggesting, for example, that those trapped by rising water have contributed to their own misfortune by building on the floodplain and remaining there even after being warned that hemmed-in waterways inevitably breach their banks. Atwood and Souster suggest more pointedly that only the most visible wreckage will force us to pay heed to the city's rivers. As Michaels writes in *Fugitive Pieces*, "The closest we come to knowing the location of what's unknown is when it melts through the map like a watermark, a stain transparent as a drop of rain."

TORONTO THE WILD

In "The Lights Keep Changing," Toronto poet Paul Vermeersch writes about a city pigeon, "[u]ndistinguished from the million others / roosting quietly in the city's details," who wanders into traffic and is clipped by a passing car. Dragging a broken wing, the bird staggers in the street until it is vaporized by a cube van speeding through the intersection. The pigeon's death goes unlamented and nearly unnoticed in a city where "nothing comes to a halt / but one grey bird, and the lights keep changing."

Although we have come to think of cities as belonging wholly to the cultural domain, Toronto is populated increasingly by creatures we would once have considered wild. Alongside animals who have traditionally lived among humans, undomesticated wildlife have also made places for themselves in the interstices of the city. Racoons (a species noted Don Valley naturalist Charles Sauriol once predicted would become increasingly rare due to habitat destruction) have colonized urban garages and attics and are among the city's most successful scavengers, easily defeating the devices residents employ to secure their garbage bins. Virginia opossums, once thought to be extinct north of the American border, show up regularly on back porches where they are sometimes mistaken for oversized rats. In 2008 a black bear wandered into a residential area east of the city, eluding wildlife agents until it was captured a few blocks away from a suburban shopping mall.[66] A few months later, a coyote snatched a pet chihuahua from a Beach-area backyard, spurring some residents to demand that city officials hunt the creature down and shoot it.[67] Many Torontonians willingly endure being doused in dog slobber, buy bells and mirrors for pet parakeets and outrageously pamper their jaded cats, but these accounts suggest that our tolerance for wild creatures, grudging at best, turns rapidly to revulsion or terror whenever they are perceived to threaten the sanctity of the urban sphere.

In Timothy Findley's *Headhunter*, starlings are identified incorrectly as the carriers of sturnusemia, an AIDS-like virus sweeping the city. In response, death squads are dispatched, gassing and burning birds in the trees where they roost. Stray cats and unleashed dogs are shot on sight because, as natural scavengers, they are considered hazards due to the risk of "sanguinary contact" with the birds. In truth, the sturnusemia virus is the result of a genetically engineered virus that escapes from a lab. It has nothing to do with birds, who are simply convenient scapegoats, chosen to distract attention from the government's inability to control this man-made virus without compromising the

66 "Black Bear Captured in Pickering," *Toronto Star*, 28 May 2008.
67 "Dog Owners Defend Coyote After Dog Killed," *Toronto Star*, 23 February 2009.

profitability of its biomedical research interests. Even the vaccine, imposed on the public by government fiat, is ineffective and offered merely as a placebo against civil unrest.

If we are tempted to view Findley's novel as mere fiction, it is worth considering the scores of cattle slaughtered at the very suggestion of bovine spongiform encephalopathy, the millions of chickens incinerated in efforts to control the spread of avian flu, the sudden collective aversion to pork in the wake of the recent H1N1 "swine flu" pandemic. If this is not evidence enough, consider the ways we dispatch mice—rumoured carriers of hantavirus—with poisons that cause them to die silent but agonizing deaths under the refrigerator or behind the microwave, or with glue traps that do not actually kill but trap their victims in terror and misery until they finally suffocate or starve to death. Similarly, raccoons, known to be carriers of roundworm and rabies, are expelled roughly from attics and outbuildings, as are squirrels, whose feces can transmit histoplasmosis infection. Even Canada geese have become targets for elimination because their droppings mar the aesthetics of urban parks and are claimed to contaminate the city's water supply.

In *Girls Fall Down*, a novel exploring the city's response to disease, Maggie Helwig vividly describes the effect an ordinary pigeon has on medical staff when it unwittingly flies into a Toronto hospital and huddles in an empty room. Seen as a "disoriented disease vector, potential reservoir of avian flu, West Nile, any number of other infections," the pigeon's appearance invokes rage in a staff member who attempts to dispatch the terrified bird using any tool capable of doubling as a weapon:

'Just let me kill the fucker!' an orderly in a mask and industrial gloves was shouting, grabbing for the pigeon as it leapt from his hands, its wings slicing upwards. [...] The orderly ran at the bird with a canvas bag and it veered up again, greeny-white shit falling into another orderly's long hair. 'Jesus!' she screamed, her hands flying up.

The pigeon began to spiral, high out of reach, and the orderly dropped the bag and picked up a mop, began stabbing the wooden handle at the bird. 'Open a window!' someone else called. 'Open a window, let it out!'

Eventually the bird is driven out through a window, accompanied by shouts of "Kill it, kill it, we have immuno-compromised patients in here!"

Why do urban wildlife—including creatures we encounter every day—elicit such a disproportionate response? Perhaps it is their very proximity that alarms us. In "Feral Cats in the City," an essay discussing urban residents' conflicted relationships with domestic and stray cats, geographers Huw Griffiths, Ingrid Poulter and David Sibley argue that a "dialectic of desire and disgust" dominates urban attitudes toward animals, particularly "those animals which transgress the boundary between civilisation and nature." This view is similar to a sentiment expressed by French philosopher Bruno Latour, who observed in *We Have Never Been Modern* that western culture "purifies" ontological categories by eliminating objects that call their separation into question. Urban animals, being neither quite natural nor completely urban, rupture our careful separation of culture and nature. In short, they are a threat. They are the city's ultimate Others, reflecting our inability—despite our protests to the contrary—to come to terms with difference, even among species.

Even the animals we profess to love and protect are under threat in cities, especially when efforts are made to return them to "natural" settings they may never have known. Gwendolyn MacEwen's story "The Demon of Thursday" serves as a telling cautionary tale, describing the consequences for a family of buffalo let loose from their enclosure in the High Park zoo, only to wander the city streets in fear until they die of shock, fatigue and "horrible, unwanted freedom." As MacEwen's protagonist observes, "They were born in captivity; what could be worse than this excruciating freedom?" A parallel problem arises when we try to rehabilitate animals who have abandoned (or been abandoned by) the domestic realm. In 2009 a man caring for a feral cat colony near the Scarborough Bluffs was reportedly ordered by City officials to purchase a license for each animal.[68] Failing to do so, they intimated, would result in the destruction of the colony, a strange punishment for animals who have become homeless due to neglect or abandonment. Filmmaker Justine Pimlott's documentary *Cat City*—which features the Bluffers Park cat colony and its caregivers—opens with an observation, attributed to Gandhi, that "the greatness of a nation and its moral progress can be judged by the way its animals are treated." The City's response to Toronto's feral cat population suggests we have a long way to go.

The protagonist of Bill Cameron's novel *Cat's Crossing* is a housecat who, suffering from an ailment, smells a healing plant miles away and slips away from its suburban Toronto home to make a long, perilous journey to the lakeshore. The cat's distressed owners, perhaps more wealthy than wise, announce a $2 million reward for the cat's safe return and the entire city is thrown into a frenzy by would-be rescuers who resort to fraud, arson, violence and blackmail in efforts to cash in on the prize. In doing so, they confirm an observation made by an urban werewolf in Kelley Armstrong's Toronto novel *Bitten*—media descriptions of human malfeasance as "savage" or "animalistic" are unfair to wildlife. As Armstrong's protagonist retorts, "Show me the animal that kills for the thrill of watching something die. [...] Only humans kill for sport."

---

68 "Fur Flies over Bluffers Park Cat Colony," *Toronto Star*, 19 June 2009.

If there is any way to resolve the essential contradiction that underpins Torontonians' response to urban wildlife, it will only come about if we relax our compulsion to rigidly separate culture from nature. Rather than coddling house cats and recoiling at raccoons, maybe we should try to encounter Toronto's wild creatures in their territory and on their terms. One space where such a thing seems eminently feasible is at the derelict edge of the city's ravines. In her story "Rock Dove," Alissa York describes a six-year-old child who rescues a sparrow that has flown against the window of a house, hiding the bird in her bedroom while it heals:

> That bird turned me furtive. I stole a shoebox from Mama's closet, ripped up turf in the yard's back corner, even raided the next-door bird feeder like a greedy jay. I walked on cat's feet in my bedroom, and waited till I could hear Mama washing dishes or saying the rosary before I dragged the box out for a peek. Three whole days passed before the sparrow was strong enough to beat its wings against the cardboard lid. I might've been young, but I knew there was only one thing to do.

Releasing the bird as soon as it is well enough to fly, York's protagonist begins a lifelong pursuit of rescuing injured birds who come to her almost as if they recognize her as one of their kind. York extends this narrative in *Fauna*, a novel in which a rundown wrecking yard between Dundas and the Don Valley Parkway doubles as a wild animal shelter whose denizens rescue rabbits, hawks, raccoon kits, coyotes and almost every other kind of urban wildlife, mending their own broken lives by caring for the city's creatures.

An even more striking place where we might resolve some of these contradictions is the Leslie Street Spit, a narrow promontory stretching five kilometres into Lake Ontario just east of downtown Toronto. Despite having been built almost entirely out of construction debris and remaining an active dumping zone, the spit provides habitat for hundreds of species of plants and birds and a wide variety of wild animals, its remarkable biodiversity owed to an unusual combination of human activity and natural processes. In *Toronto the Wild*, Wayne Grady explains how the intersecting trajectories of city-building and wildlife movement created such a richly populated preserve:

> Begun in 1959 as a project that had some vaguely hopeful connection to the St. Lawrence Seaway (more ships would be coming to Toronto, so we needed more docking space), the spit is really nothing more ambitious than a huge landfill site protruding five kilometres out into Lake Ontario. But by 1980, it had been

colonized by 278 species of plants, from wild grasses and sedges to full grown trees and shrubs. How did all these plants get there? Many of them were trucked in with the construction waste, as bulldozers cleared former residential districts to make room for businesses, but most of the plant seeds must have travelled the way seeds are supposed to travel: borne on the wind, washed ashore by the waves, deposited in bird droppings—some 200 species of birds have also been seen on the Spit at one time or another—or stuck to the fur of animals or the socks, pant cuffs, or boot soles of us human vectors.

Going on to inventory some of the more unusual plants and animals who have come to populate the spit (among them an alkali grass normally found only in salt marshes, a plant Grady speculates has thrived on salt-laden snow dumped by city crews during the winter), Grady sums up by concluding, "Leslie Street Spit is a great place to go to get an idea of what would happen to Toronto if the city were allowed to run wild."

Not everybody is pleased at the prospect of the spit being taken over entirely by birds, of course. In Paul Quarrington's *Whale Music*, one character deftly summarizes both sides of the ongoing debate over the fate of wildlife populations deemed to be out of balance with the urban order:

I'll tell you the best and the worst thing about Toronto, Des. The best thing is that it's got more seagulls than anywhere in the universe. We got billions and billions of the little dudes. There's this place called the Leslie Street Spit, and you can walk down there and see nothing but gulls. And I like to do that, don't ask me why. And the very *worst* thing about it is that everybody thinks this is a big problem. They say that seagulls are stinky, smelly birds, and people want to poison all the gull eggs and turn snakes and mongeese and hawks loose on the Spit. And when I hear people talk like this, I get mad. I think, hey, slime-bucket, if these seagulls are so bad, why did God make so fucking many of them?

Graeme Gibson extends this theme in *Gentleman Death*, describing landfilling practices that have methodically destroyed the habitat of night herons and woodcocks, leaving the spit dominated by hardy species willing to nest and feed almost anywhere:

It's only the gulls that resist. Seventy thousand nesting pairs of ring-billed gulls. Sleek, mean-eyed as street-fighters, and prolific, they fill the air with flight and noise. In wheeling raucous flocks they descend upon the city's garbage, they perch in the rigging of pampered sailboats and shit all over them.

Still, a wide range of wildlife has managed to make use of even the most in-hospitable terrain, and it is this persistence in the face of adversity that attracts Gibson's narrator to this unkempt promontory of land:

> Although the city is full of ravines and hidden tracks it is here, to the Spit, that I'm drawn for solace. Year by year the former have become simpler and tidier, with chipped bark jogging paths, with directional signs and picnic tables on mowed grass. On the other hand, colonized by almost three hundred species of plants and refuge to innumerable other creatures from jack-rabbits to an occasional beaver, the Spit has grown wilder and ever more complex.

Sitting on a pile of rubble near the end of the spit, Gibson's narrator senses a ghostly visitor, a snowy owl who has travelled from the distant tundra to stare impassively into the eyes of a man struggling to come to terms with his own mortality. Musing, "If it was the cranes that inspired humankind to make letters, our first alphabet, the owls taught us silence and melancholy; it is from them we learned how peace is inextricably bound up with sorrow," Gibson's narrator settles back against the stone on the spit's windswept landscape, this melancholy refuge where two lonely creatures can find peace and silence.

THE LIMINAL CITY

In *Emerald City*, John Bentley Mays describes Toronto's liminal spaces—the city's derelict port lands and waterfront, and its alleys, ravines, vacant lots and abandoned industrial sites—as "thinking places" where it is possible to gain enough distance and perspective to reflect upon the city's relationship with its landscape and our own place in the cosmos. In the "subtle melancholy" of these spaces, Bentley writes, "one can disappear completely from the crush and rattle of urban existence" and consider mortality, fate, faith and the exigencies of time.

Liminal is an old dictionary word meaning "threshold." But a threshold, as Toronto author Gary Michael Dault writes in *Cells of Ourselves*, is always more than an entrance:

> Thresholds, though wider than the idea of doors, share their role as repositories of desire and temptation. What is opened at a door? Onto what landscapes of the imagination does a threshold gaze? Gaston Bachelard has written that a door is an entire cosmos of the half-open. A threshold is perhaps, by extension, a cosmos of the already half-understood.

As a formal concept, liminality may be traced to the work of twentieth-century anthropologist Victor Turner, who studied rites of passage such as birth, adolescence, marriage and rituals of death.[69] Describing the liminal phase as a state of being "betwixt and between," Turner explored not only social ceremonies but also transitional spaces such as passages, peripheries and places of pilgrimage. These locations, he argued, are important spaces of transformation and reflection but also embody the unknown, and as such, represent mystery and danger as well as life, death, growth and change.[70] If Toronto is a city of sharp edges that grate against one another like tectonic plates, its liminal spaces knit the rough edges of the city together, buffering its boundaries and marking transitions between the punctual, predictable Toronto we think we know and the feral, disordered or supernatural city we have always suspected exists alongside it.

Toronto's most resonant liminal landscape is the long edge of Lake Ontario that sighs and clutches at the city's foundations like a sibilant stranger. Although nearly all of the city's landscapes have been shaped by alluvial processes, Toronto has turned its back on the contemporary waterfront and the city is laid out and lived in as if it were landlocked. In his novel *Dirty Sweet*, John McFetridge describes the city's waterfront as dominated by a row of "highrises blocking out Lake Ontario in front of them, like the city was embarrassed to have a waterfront. Somewhere under the expressway and between warehouses was 'historic' Fort York." Still, the lake haunts our memories and dreams. It floats perpetually at the edge of our vision, and if we turn and look, or if we listen only a little, it returns to us as reliably as a wave bringing in weeds or waterlogged wood. Whenever the city pauses—in the long moment before sleep, in the stillness between streetlights, before the first breath of every birth—it is possible to hear lake sounds: the high-pitched ping of halyard shackles hoisted against a main mast, the low reverberation of an island ferry, the sough of winter wind scraping across an open expanse of ice, the ceaseless suck of water nursing at the city's foundations. As Michael Redhill writes in *Consolation*, "The lake often had this kind of presence in the city, a visual primacy that made one feel encroached upon, even if—especially if—a person turned his back on it."

Toronto did not always turn its back on Lake Ontario: the sheltered natural harbour was, in fact, one of the principal reasons given for establishing an

69 See Turner's "Betwixt and Between: The Liminal Period in Rites de Passage" (1967). Turner's studies of liminality extend the work of anthropologist Arnold van Gennep (see van Gennep's *The Rites of Passage*, published in English in 1960).

70 See also Turner's *Dramas, Fields, and Metaphors: Symbolic Action in Human Society* (1974) and *Image and Pilgrimage in Christian Culture: Anthropological Perspectives* (1978). Literary analyses of liminal space have relied significantly upon this work.

English settlement at this location.[71] As local historian William Kilbourn declares in *Toronto Remembered*, "Toronto was born of the water." Toronto's harbour, cradled by a long peninsula severed from the mainland during a violent storm in 1858 that created the Toronto Islands, offered more than safe anchorage for lake vessels: it also provided a visual focus for the growing town. In *More Than an Island*, historian Sally Gibson observes that "for all the residents of York and Toronto right up to the time when the railways and then the highways cut the city off from the waterfront, the lake with its harbour and its island was a source of endless fascination." Describing homes and public building edifices built to face the water, Gibson adds, "the lake was the great natural element dominating York. The lake and the Peninsula, like the mountain in Montreal, provided the focus for the town."

In *The Swing in the Garden*, the first volume of an epic, Proustian saga tracing the circuitous genealogy of Canadian nationalism, novelist Hugh Hood emphasizes the central role the lake and its connecting waterways have played in Toronto's history and suggests that the surest route into the soul of the contemporary city begins with an excursion down to the waterfront:

> "Down to the docks" led deeper and deeper into city life, into the essential Toronto of pickup and delivery and redistribution of wealth into parceled-out units in small tankers. [...] For all of recorded North American history, Toronto has been "the Carrying Place." That narrow forefinger of sand curving out from Ashbridge's Bay and Cherry Beach, cut off from the mainland by the Eastern Gap—those two trickling streams now dirtied, dammed, nearly destroyed, our Don and Humber—this excrement-laden bay, these polluted beaches, are the scenes of aboriginal commerce unimaginably ancient. Before historical time begins in North America the carrying place was and is.

Although waterfront rail lines and urban expressways have long since replaced the harbour as the city's major shipping and receiving routes, the busy commercial

---

71 In truth, the story of Toronto's location is nearly as complicated as the origin of its name. In 1615 the French established a trading post and later a fort near the base of the Humber River at the terminus of a long-standing portage, the Toronto Carrying-Place, to Lake Simcoe. More interested in defence than trade, in 1793 the English, under the governorship of John Graves Simcoe, established a new settlement adjacent to the natural harbour formed behind the long sandbar of the Toronto Islands. A defensive stronghold York was not (it was twice occupied and burned by American invaders), but a rapidly expanding bureaucracy calculated to support York's bid to remain the seat of government helped ensure the town's continued prominence and growth. Cynics might argue that similar calculations continue to define Toronto today. Early descriptions of Toronto in this era are found in *The Diary of Mrs. John Graves Simcoe* (covering the period 1792 to 1796), John Howison's *Sketches of Upper Canada* (1821) and Anna Brownell Jameson's *Winter Studies and Summer Rambles in Canada* (1838). Eric Hounsom's *Toronto in 1810* (1970) provides an illuminating account of the city's earliest decades as an English settlement.

marinas, crowded urban beaches, lakewater filtration infrastructure and ongoing condominium construction boom reflect Toronto's origins as a maritime city and its continuing orientation toward the lake. Every time we take a sip of tap water, shiver in the climate-controlled chill of a downtown office tower or watch a rainstorm round the western curve of the lake, we are reminded of its significance to the city. As Chris Chambers writes in "Greatest Hits of Drinking Water" (from *Lake Where No One Swims*,) "I saw it moving north somehow defying gravity / through an underground grid, a network of pipes, / like a system of locks beneath streets; / the hydrating veins of Toronto." As Chambers suggests, long after we turned our collective backs to it, the lake has continued to move through us, nourishing and replenishing the city with its water.

In *The Measure of the Rule*, Robert Barr describes a nineteenth-century visitor's first impression of a city whose horizon was still dominated by the islands and the immense curve of the lake:

> I stood for a moment, and gazed down past the Union Station to the great lake upon whose shore the city stood. To the eye it was as expansive of the ocean, for in the clearest day no man can see to the other side. Motionless it lay, and sailless; frozen, and pure white with the wreathed snow that covered it to the horizon. Along the water front rose innumerable masts of ships locked in the iron grip of winter. A mile or more away a curved island partially enclosed a bay that faced the city, and the surface of this bay, dark as slate, was of smooth, clear ice, from which the wind seemed to have swept every vestige of snow.

For Barr's protagonist, the frozen lake is a wonder of winter and a reason to revel in his new city, but for others the lake is a reminder of all they have lost or left behind and a stark symbol of their sense of having been cast ashore at the very edge of a seemingly impenetrable wilderness. In her famous indictment of 1830s Toronto, unhappy camper Anna Brownell Jameson described Toronto as a

> little, ill-built town on low land, at the bottom of a frozen bay, with one very ugly church, without tower or steeple; some government offices, built of staring red brick, in the most tasteless, vulgar style imaginable; three feet of snow all around; and the gray, sullen, wintry lake, and the dark gloom of the pine forest bounding the prospect; such seems Toronto to me now. I did not expect much; but for this I was not prepared.[72]

---

72 Anna Brownell Jameson's unflattering depiction of Toronto may be attributed at least partly to a projection of her internal psychological state. Reportedly summoned to Canada to shore up her estranged husband's position as Chief Justice of the Province of Upper Canada, Jameson found her-

A similar sentiment pervades Michael Redhill's contemporary novel *Consolation*. His protagonist, a pharmacist-turned-photographer enduring his first winter in Canada in 1855, finds that the town's position, pressed into a narrow wedge between the forest and the frozen lake, produces in him an almost unbearable tension:

> He remembered freshly his first glimpse of the city, as the ferry came around the western side of the island that lay off its shore: a vision of spires and yellow brick and white stone set against a wall of trees. And from that distance—even as the ferry bore down on Brown's wharf at the foot of Yonge Street—the seeming feebleness of the little twists of smoke and steam rising from different buildings, Lilliputian industry while all around it raw nature went on about its effortless business. *Who thinks of making a city in the rough?* he'd thought, seeing the place for the first time, and he knew from the expressions on the faces of the newly arrived that this was the wondering thing that occurred to everyone that made landfall here.

Hoping to make sense of his own reasons for making landfall, near the end of a difficult winter Hallam returns to the harbour, a place he has avoided for fear it will elicit the unbearable urge to return to England—an impulse he has taken such care to suppress—and stands rapt in the terrible beauty of the frozen lake:

> Hallam continued to the base of Brown's wharf and stood there surveying the expanse of frozen lake. There was slurried water where ships' hulls made contact with the ice, tied up at their wharves and scratching at the element like animals in cages. Spring would come now—one could feel it in the air. Out into the dim light, the lake lay pale and off-white, encased in its icy sheath like a plate of tin covered in crystalline silver. Lunar caustic, that substance which drank light. Hallam stood before that expanse, a shiver of joy and fear in his muscles, looking at a giant photograph being made by stars.

Like a confrontation with mortality, the lake elicits in Redhill's protagonist the dual urge toward flight or fight. Ultimately it is Hallam's recognition of this landscape's absolute otherworldliness—an otherworldliness mirroring his own sense of dislocation and exile—that grants him the courage to stay.

In *The Dominion of the Dead*, literary scholar Robert Pogue Harrison argues that the liminal edge between land and water is a site of existential tensions,

---

self abandoned and alone in the frontier city in the middle of winter. After enduring a single winter in Toronto and touring the province's rural regions the following summer, Jameson returned to England and produced *Winter Studies and Summer Rambles in Canada*, first published in 1838.

particularly those pertaining to life, memory, oblivion and death. In his reading of western literary texts, the sea is the enemy of both land and life, breaking upon one and severing the other with implacable indifference. If land is the repository and ultimately the ossuary of culture and history, the ocean is an abyss, a vast but unnavigable underworld that swallows everything familiar and leaves nothing but waves in its wake. Harrison observes:

> In the eschatological imagination where such visions are born, earth and sea belong to different, even opposing orders. In its solidity and stability the earth is inscribable, we can build upon its ground, while the sea offers no such foothold for human worldhood. No doubt that is why the sea, in its hostility to architecturally or textually imprinted memory, often figures as the imaginary agent of ultimate obliteration.

He concludes that the ocean's most remarkable quality is its unearthliness. Metaphorically fathomless—beyond visualization, memory, even conception—the sea is the earth's sublime, its Other. It is the eternal symbol of the loss of the self.

In popular mythology Toronto's ravines are narrated as places of molestation and murder, but in the literary imagination it is the lakeshore where the city has its most meaningful encounters with mortality. Some of these encounters are markedly macabre, reflecting the waterfront's attraction to suicides eager for oblivion or killers anxious to abandon the evidence of their crimes, while at other times the lake serves a more sacramental purpose as the site of memorial ritual. Often it offers a little of both.

Redhill's *Consolation*, for example, opens with the suicide of its protagonist, a man dying of amyotrophic lateral sclerosis who steps off the back of the Hanlan's Point ferry into the breach between the city and its inland sea, his death by drowning a metaphor not only for the suffocating progress of his disease but also of the city's submersion of its own history:

> He holds tight to the lash-post and shimmies around to the front of it, drinking the moist air in ecstatic gulps. The vague slopings of the deck are transmitted to his brain as an optical illusion: the city pitching up gently and subsiding, up and down, his sense marvellously lulled. Water moving under the boat. Sky, city, blue-black lake, city, sky. The peaceful sound of water lapping the hull. He lets the swells help him forward and up. More air against him now, his thin windbreaker flapping, his mouth full of wind, the sound of a long, deep breath—

With the city dissolving into thin air before him, the harbour rising, welcoming and finally consuming him, David Hollis's death is a liberation from personal suffering that manages also to serve as a symbolic indictment of the city's cultural amnesia. But not all deaths—not even all chosen ones—offer this same quality of release. In *Consolation*, Redhill also relates the story of another man who, more than a century earlier, had hanged himself from a windmill at the water's edge during a late winter storm, unable to bear the exigencies of his life in the frontier city:

> The man had made himself a noose and slipped it over his head, then tied the other end onto a heavy gaff that he eventually managed to jab through a passing mill blade. No one wanted to speculate how long he'd stood in the wind-thrashing dark, throwing the end of his life into the air, hoping to lash it to the elements. To imagine how determined he was on death would be to invite thoughts of where one's own limit lay. What if there was, in every person, a threshold beyond which only death could sate you? After succeeding, the suicide spun in a small circle around the centre of the windmill, and wilted there for three days, a ghoulish figure in the squall, seen in the distance through the snow, rising and falling like a marionette.

Redill's lurid description underscores the eschatological aspect of the lake edge, its endless horizon a threshold between the longing to live and the lure of oblivion.

In *The Robber Bride*, Margaret Atwood describes a suicide who casts himself into the lake near the Scarborough Bluffs, despondent over a failed affair. His wife, waiting grimly for news, is not surprised when the police recover her husband's boat and eventually his body from the forbidding water:

> Where Mitch is, is in Lake Ontario. He's been there a while. The police pick up his boat, the *Rosalind II*, drifting with sails furled, and eventually Mitch himself washes into shore off the Scarborough Bluffs. He has his lifejacket on, but at this time of year the hypothermia would have taken him very quickly. He must have slipped, they tell her. Slipped off and fallen in, and been unable to climb back on. There was a wind, the day he left harbour. An accident. If it had been suicide he wouldn't have been wearing his lifejacket. Would he?
>
> He would, he would, thinks Roz. He did that part of it for the kids. He didn't want to leave a bad package for them. He did love them enough for that. But he knew all about the temperature of the water, he'd lectured her about it often enough. Your body heat dissipates, quick as a wink. You numb, and then you die. And so he did.

Unable to bear the combined burden of failure and the weight of his wife's forgiveness, Mitch seeks an end in the chilly embrace of the lake.

One of Canada's most famous literary suicides, the death of Boy Staunton in Robertson Davies' *Fifth Business*, also occurs in Toronto's harbour:

[A]t about four o'clock on the morning of Monday, November 4, 1968, his Cadillac convertible was recovered from the waters of Toronto harbour, into which it had been driven at a speed great enough to carry it, as it sank, about twenty feet from the concrete pier. His body was in the driver's seat, the hands gripping the wheel so tightly that it was very difficult for the police to remove him from the car. The windows and the roof were closed, so that some time must have elapsed between driving over the edge and the filling of the car with water. But the most curious fact of all was that in Boy's mouth the police had found a stone—an ordinary piece of pinkish granite about the size of a small egg—which could not possibly have been where it was unless he himself, or someone unknown, had put it there.

After considerable speculation, in *The Manticore*, a subsequent volume in the Deptford Trilogy, Davies' readers learn that Staunton, overwhelmed by the pressures of public life, had expressed a desire to escape them. His interlocutor, a hypnotist of great talent, acknowledges having contributed to the man's death but insists that he had not murdered him. Instead he argues that Staunton's wish, like that of many suicides, was nothing more or less than an inchoate desire to be released from burdens that had become unbearable. In this sense, Staunton's long drive off the short pier has the air of leaping into the abyss, surrendering all control and even the self to the elements, to the cosmos, to oblivion. As Magnus Eisengrim observes, later, he had no choice but to allow Staunton to "dree his weird"—that is, at the long edge of the lakeshore, to submit to his fate.[73]

And what of those who are left behind to make sense of our loss and grief? The lake serves us, too. *Consolation* is silent on the subject of what David Hollis's family does with his body after recovering it from the contemporary lake—one imagines it suspended, like ashes stirred by the air, or buried like the ship he had sought, under the footings of the Union Arena—but other literary works emphasize the lake's role as a receptacle for cremated human remains, a watery way station between earth and eternity.[74] In Margaret Atwood's *The Robber Bride*, three women board an Island-bound ferry on a blustery Remembrance

---

73 The death of Boy Staunton is a plot device that helps drive the narrative of the entire Deptford Trilogy. This trilogy—the most widely read of Robertson Davies' works—consists of *Fifth Business* (1970), *The Manticore* (1972) and *World of Wonders* (1975). All three books engage at length with Toronto, among other settings in Canada and Europe. *Fifth Business* remains Davies' best known novel, owing largely to its ubiquitous presence in high school courses on Canadian literature.

74 Contrary to claims to the contrary, made mainly by representatives of the funeral industry, there is no blanket prohibition against scattering cremated human remains in Ontario. According to the Ontario Ministry of Consumer Services, "any individuals or families who wish to scatter the cremated human remains of their loved ones on Crown land and Crown land covered by water in Ontario can do so," although mourners are encouraged to obtain permission before scattering ashes on private property.

Day, intending to scatter the ashes of Zenia, their shared adversary, over the deepest part of the passage:

> The three of them stand at the back of the ferry as it churns its way through the harbour, outbound towards the Island, trailing the momentary darkness of its wake. From the mainland they can hear, faintly, the sound of bugles, and of muffled shots. A salute. The water is quicksilver in the pearl-coloured light, the wind is slight, cool, but mild for the time of year, the month. [...] Month of the dead, month of returning, thinks Charis. She thinks of the grey weeds waving, under the poisonous, guileless water, at the bottom of the lake; of the grey fish with lumpy chemical growths on them, wafting like shadows; of the lamprey eels with their tiny rasping teeth and sucking mouths, undulating among the husks of wrecked cars, the empty bottles. She thinks of everything that has fallen in, or else been thrown. Treasures and bones.

When Charis heaves the container of ashes over the rail, it splits in a jolt of blue light and smashes into pieces, strafing the water with shards of pottery and ashes that drift in the ferry's wake like liquid smoke. Shocked but not entirely surprised, the women interpret this flash of fury as Zenia's final expression of malice. But even if this has been the case, the lake insulates them from it, the waters dispersing and perhaps even purifying the sinking remains of their rival.

A similar watery undertaking occurs in Gordon Stewart Anderson's beautiful, poignant novel *The Toronto You Are Leaving*. A man whose lover and longtime friend has died at the height of the AIDS epidemic travels by ferry to the Toronto Islands to scatter his ashes. Aboard the ferry he holds his arms aloft to ward off the pollution and disease of the city as the vessel crosses from the cultural to the natural realm:

> David stood on the upper deck in the stern, legs and arms spread, hands braced against the wood of the rail, and faced back towards the heaving water, the carnage of the gulls and the towers of the city. It was his place to hold all of that at bay, to make the signs that mark the passage from one world to another—beyond the glistening waters of the harbour.

Making his way to a narrow beach at the apex of the island, David walks west along an avenue of trees worn smooth by wind and water, performing a meditation of peace and purification at each station before reaching his destination:

> He spent some minutes there, drinking in the vigor of the Primeval. Lake Ontario at this spot was innocent of pollution, refreshed by currents that swung along

the shore from the east. Those currents had built the Islands, gouging materials from the sandstone bluffs of Scarborough to deposit there, a sacred offering to the people of Toronto, a sacred trust—which David felt obliged to honour and keep. [...] The grove was a most sacred place. A screen of poplars, beeches and willows (among the most primitive of trees) shielded a strip of pure red sand, running down into the water on two sides. Ancient trunks, half in the water and half out, worn bare of bark and smoothed by the caress of countless waves, marked the limits of the *sanctum sanctorum*. The water that washed this strip of sand was the purest water on the islands. This was the point where the current ran closest to the land.

Wading waist-deep into the water, David pours his lover's ashes out onto the lake, where the heavier fragments sink into the red sand while the rest are carried away by waves. Then he turns away, bereft, to confront the urban morass and his own mortality.

Neither entirely land or water but containing elements of both, the Toronto Islands are a fitting site for memorial rituals because their fluctuating sands reflect the fleeting passage of life, buffeted by storms of fortune and bracketed by the permeable border between the here and the hereafter. Literary representations of the islands underscore these unsettled qualities, evoking islands strung along the lakeshore like beads broken from a ravelled string and washed about according to the whims of wind and water. In *Stunt*, a surreal novel in which obsession and loss appear doubled and wavering, like light reflected upon wind-swept water, Claudia Dey evokes the violent natural forces that formed the islands:

Toronto Island is a sandspit. From above, it appears as a collection of rocks smoothed flat for luck by a nervous hand. Marbled by water, it is composed of fourteen islands in total, the archipelago coming together in a thick hook shape at its western end. The island was formed over the course of 10,000 years. After the Scarborough Bluffs were bullied into being by the last ice age, Toronto deaf under a kilometre of ice, the bluffs were carried by wind and currents to form a peninsula. The night of April 14, 1858, a storm broke the peninsula's neck, separating it from Toronto for good and founding the island. It was, like so many things, born out of a natural and lengthy violence.

Where Dey anthropomorphizes the natural processes that created the islands, in *The Swing in the Garden* Hugh Hood emphasizes the economic activities of dredging and filling that have produced the offshore landscape familiar to contemporary Torontonians:

The geography is simple enough. What are called the Toronto Islands are really a low sand spit formed by the curve of the shore of Lake Ontario, the feed of water and mud into Toronto Bay from the Don and Humber Rivers, and the prevailing winds and movements of water along the shore. This spit juts westward from what is now called Cherry Beach, and was deliberately severed by dredging in the nineteenth century, to form the Eastern Gap. [...] [T]he Eastern Gap was man-made, the sole justification for the isolated distinction of these three communities, much as the English Channel insulates Britain as England, Scotland, Wales. And just as the Channel Tunnel project has for over a century excited fear among certain islanders that their cherished distancing from European affairs might be destroyed, so the slow filling-in of the Eastern Gap by movement of wind and water has sometimes threatened to allow the Toronto Islands to revert to what they were when Colonel Simcoe and his lady arrived on the scene from Niagara-on-the-Lake—a mere peninsula without the splendid isolating channel to protect, distance, distinguish.

As Hood goes on to explain, local politicians, land developers and civil engineers have long sought—albeit with only partial success—to put their stamp on the very sands that have shaped so much of Toronto's identity.

Despite the efforts that have transformed the islands from a series of wind-swept sandbars into a robust atoll complete with an airport, public utilities and an urban water park, the lake continues to have its way with them, and a series of seawalls and regular dredging are required to maintain the islands in their current configuration. Moreover, the "splendid isolation" enjoyed by island residents has always been something of an illusion, given their hundred-year fight to secure and defend land leases against politicians' plans to turn the entire land mass into a public park.[75] As Hood suggests in *The Swing in the Garden*, island residents have also struggled to distinguish themselves from seasonal visitors whose primarily recreational presence has often overwhelmed and threatened to undermine their own more permanent tenure:

It took time to become accepted as a true islander. A summer's residence wasn't enough, or even two or three. Twenty summers might qualify you but the real ticket of admission was winter residence, going to primary school there, riding the *Ned Hanlan* or the *Geary* from the Filtration Plant on frozen winter mornings to work or school in the city, playing euchre or rummy in the small smoke-filled cabin below the waterline in the bow and hearing the ice crashing against the plating,

75 Sally Gibson's *More Than an Island* (1984) offers the most complete document of the long tug-of-war between island residents, tourists, entrepreneurs and municipal politicians.

arriving at the John Street tugboat dock to walk along the frigid quayside to the streetcar stop at the foot of York Street, that was to be a true initiate, something of a participant in extremely esoteric rites.

Finally, the islands' changeable character is exemplified most vividly by irresolvable disagreements about how many there are. In his 1953 essay "Bohemia on the Bay," novelist Hugh Garner insisted there were eighteen, a claim supported, at least in principle, by a 1947 land-use plan representing the islands not as they were but as City planners hoped they might become. Two decades later, Hugh Hood wrote in *The Swing in the Garden* that "eleven tiny islands" cling to a long sandy "peninsula" separated from the mainland by the Eastern Gap. A generation later, Claudia Dey states simply in *Stunt* that there are fourteen islands, a number that seems accurate enough provided Ward and Centre Island are counted separately despite denoting opposite ends of the same parcel of sand. Ultimately, however, uncertainty about how many islands there are remains part of their mystery and charm, reinforcing their stature as what Hugh Garner calls "four miles of foreign territory" immediately adjacent to the familiar city.

Despite questions of number, size and position, the islands have remained attractive to generations of Torontonians seeking an escape from the pressures and pollution of the city or the weight of their own lives. As early as 1884 local historian Charles Pelham Mulvaney highlighted the islands' popularity as "a celebrated health resort" and seasonal habitation, adding that "[i]n later years, as the city grew wealthier and more populous, the Island became not only a sanitarium [sic], but a popular place of summer residence; neat cottages, bungalow-like Bohemian dwellings of all shapes and dimensions, and comfortable aristocratic villas lined the shore facing the lake and bay." Commenting on the islands' attraction to visiting day-trippers, Mulvany asked,

Who in Toronto is not familiar with the busy bustling scene of the steamer's arrival, the large-sized vessel freighted with its well accommodated crowd of pleasure-seekers, the tiny half-decked steamer, no bigger than a man-of-war's launch, also with its load of passengers, who seem fearless as the vessel rolls and dips almost to the water's edge? [...] At the landing is another crowd of holiday-makers waiting to inspect the new arrivals. On the sands are bare-legged lads and lassies digging with wooden spades, building sand castles, and wading in the shallow water. Under the trees and on the hotel porticos are bevies of young ladies, glorious in summer bonnets and holiday costumes. The place is evidently to Toronto what Coney Island is to New York.

Perhaps unsurprisingly, in the same way that Coney Island aroused indignation among American moralists, so too did some of the pastimes popular on the Toronto islands outrage the sensibilities of local martinets. Historian Mary Louise Adams, evaluating the moral discourse underpinning social perceptions of the islands, cites turn-of-the-century social chronicler C. S. Clark as exemplary of the set of social reformers hell-bent on spotting sin behind every sand dune, quoting his concern that any wakeful lurker could catch numerous couples "en flagrante delecto" near the strand on any warm Saturday night. Several decades later, in "Bohemia on the Bay," novelist Hugh Garner derided the islands as "that jerry-built demi-paradise of the deserted, defeated and demi-mondaine," and described its residents as "belong[ing] to a half-world that includes chronic alcoholics, wife and husband deserters, beachcombers, dead-beats and spinsters-on-the-make."[76] Garner (himself a chronic alcoholic who lived on Centre Island for several years in the early 1950s) added that "[n]obody ever knows what is going to happen next on the Island, and that is part of its charm"—an oblique reference, perhaps to having contracted hepatitis after a storm inundated the island's septic tanks and polluted the residents' drinking water in the spring of 1953.[77]

In *Summer Island*, a memoir of his Toronto Island boyhood, Phil Murphy confirms Garner's claim that almost anything can—and does—happen on the islands, but emphasizes the darker undercurrents. His episodes, interwoven with vivid descriptions of the islands' idyllic qualities—the constant backdrop of "lake water lapping with low sounds by the shore" (a line borrowed, incidentally, from Yeats), boisterous games lasting late into the night, the pleasant paradox of camping in comfort—proceed almost unvaryingly to an unhappy conclusion. A crow shot and left suffering in the bushes, two suicides, the death of a family cat, the unravelling of a marriage and the constant shadow of war. In the end, it seems, the very qualities that draw people to the islands sometimes prove their undoing, particularly for people unable to reconcile their pastoral surroundings with the city's inevitable intrusions. The islands offer only a temporary escape.

A similar subtext permeates Hugh Hood's *The Swing in the Garden*. His young protagonist, revelling in the sand and waters of the islands, remains conscious of the family's reason for being there. Nearing bankruptcy as the Depression drags on, his parents have come to Centre Island to manage a rundown hotel, the Lakeview, having chosen this line of work not only for the income but because it will provide shelter as well. In the background, too, are the looming conflicts that will precipitate World War II and, ultimately, end their sojourn on the islands.

---

76 Garner, 1964. "Bohemia on the Bay" was first published in *Saturday Night* magazine in 1953.
77 See Steuwe, 1988.

In Helen Humphreys' novel *Leaving Earth*, a young girl growing up near Hanlan's Point watches two women circle the lake in a small biplane, hoping to set a world record for endurance flying in August 1933. Isolated by poverty—her father maintains the carousel at the island amusement park; her mother is an itinerant fortune teller—and her half-Jewish heritage, Maddie's feelings of alienation increase when her mother is attacked by anti-Semitic thugs. Idolizing the pilots circling endlessly overhead, Maddie becomes convinced that one of them is her real mother when a note reading "I love you" drifts down from the sky. Like many Torontonians during the Depression clinging to any reason for hope, Maddie's fantasies of escape revolve around the airplane, its solipsistic flight path signalling both the prospect and paradox of flight.

As Murphy's, Hood's and Humphreys' narratives suggest, for much of their history the islands were less a luxury resort than a landing place for Torontonians unable to maintain a cottage "up north" or, in some cases, even afford to live on the mainland. In *Leaving Earth*, Humphreys summarizes the itinerant social history of the islands:

> Once there were Native encampments on the eastern side the islands. In the 1800s, city dwellers came across in boats to set up tents and small cottages for summer use. Gradually a tent community evolved and ferries began regular crossings of the bay. By 1933, the only summer tent community left is on Ward's Island and, of the one hundred or so families who live on the islands year round, most have some form of wooden cottage and live on Centre Island, Hanlan's Point or the western bar. There is a grocery store on both Hanlan's Point and Ward's Island, but residents depend largely on the services of Centre Island's Manitou Road. Here can be found a butcher, grocery stores, a bank, drugstore, dairies and restaurants—including the pricey, elegant Pierson Hotel and the cheaper Honey Dew, which sells hamburger and frankfurter sandwiches.

Two decades later the Municipality of Metropolitan Toronto began expropriating leases and tearing down homes as part of its plan to convert the islands into parkland. Islanders fought these changes (successfully, at least for the small enclave of sought-after residences remaining on Ward and Algonquin islands), but by the early 1960s many homes had been abandoned or rented out by residents unwilling to repair dwellings they expected to lose at any time. Among these new residents were poets, performers, painters and other artists attracted to the islands not only for their primordial qualities but also because the rent was cheap. Rosemary Sullivan writes in *Shadow Maker*, her biography of poet Gwendolyn MacEwen:

In the early sixties, the houses on the island were mostly summer homes, cheap and insubstantial clapboard, sided in insulbrick. Little money was spent on renovations since it was assumed the city would one day expropriate the properties for a public park. [...] The island was a place for cultural refugees, many of them artists who came because it was cheap—the rent was usually fifty dollars a month. Islanders could look back across the water at the city skyline and feel they had stepped out of civilization into some kind of sylvan wilderness. But the price was that in winter, with the fierce winds sweeping in off the lake, one froze to death. The bedroom walls would be covered with ice and space had to be made for the mice driven in by the cold.

In "Animal Syllables" MacEwen, who lived on Ward Island during a short-lived marriage to fellow poet Milton Acorn in the early 1960s, evokes the conditions that gave rise to Sullivan's observation:

I have begun to repair the house, having put it off for ages, deciding which aspect of it was most in need of repair.
    Of erections, how few are domed like St. Peter's? I ask myself (Melville), as I hammer nails into the tottering walls.
    Are there too many realities? I ask, as several of the nails fall out. [...]
    Then I begin to bring the outside in, that the house might be a small, select museum of the world. In the summer I bring driftwood, shells, flowers. There is no key to this place and, in a sense, no door. There is free passage in and out. Already small weeds shoot up between the floor and the wall.

Margaret Atwood extends MacEwen's invocation in *The Robber Bride*, describing a woman (a protagonist some commentators have suggested was modeled on MacEwen) drawn to the islands because they mirror her own translucent permeability:

They moved into this house in late spring, and from the very first Charis knew it was right. She loved the house and, even more, she loves the Island. It's infused with a vibrant, brooding, humid life; it makes her feel that everything—even the water, even the stones—is alive and aware, and her along with it. Some mornings she goes out before daybreak and just walks around, up and down the streets that are not real streets but more like paved bicycle paths, past the dilapidated or spruced-up former cottages with their woodpiles and hammocks and patchy gardens; or else she just lies on the grass, even when damp.

The islands also offer an escape from the city, a place Charis prefers to view from a distance:

> From here on the Island, the city is mysterious, like a mirage, like the cover on a book of science fiction. A paperback. It's like this at sunset too, when the sky turns burnt orange and then the crimson of inner space, and then indigo, and the lights in the many windows change the darkness to gauze; and then at night the neon shows up against the sky and it gives off a glow, like an amusement park or something safely on fire. [...] Charis would rather look at the city than go there, even at dusk.

The problem with the islands, Charis is dismayed to discover, is that the retreat they offer is temporary: life, even urban life, intrudes inevitably, dissolving her diligently maintained serenity just as a storm sucks away the vulnerable sand that forms the islands' frail foundation.

Most contemporary visitors to the islands are day-trippers: holiday-goers unable to snag an invitation to a cottage in the Kawarthas, gay men staking out territory beyond the reach of bashers and social disapprobation, and harried families whose quests for an afternoon of pleasure are often heavy with an air of frustrated indolence. In *The Toronto You Are Leaving*, for example, Gordon Stewart Anderson's narrator describes a motley assemblage of passengers waiting to board the island ferry who seem more like refugees fleeing a war zone than vacationers in search of amusement:

> Mothers and their babies complained of the heat; old women with feet twisted from years of wearing high heels; teenagers in ragged cutoffs, oversized T-shirts and caps on backwards, slick ghetto blasters blaring; earnest environmentalist trendy types with long hair and bicycles; cyclists in muscles, spandex, helmets and wrap-around sun glasses; children in packs of twenty or more, tended by harried day care workers; homosexuals who had taken the wrong ferry on the way to their 'secret' beach. David watched them all, and tried to avoid being pushed, shoved aside or trampled upon.

After an afternoon of rushed revelry, island visitors must pack up and return to reach the docks in time to board the final ferry back to the mainland or risk being stranded overnight. In *Stunt*, Claudia Dey's protagonist describes a scene that resembles the aftermath of a mass evacuation:

> Lake Shore Avenue cuts through the island, from its eastern to its western point. I follow it. My boots are the only percussion against the pavement. Otherwise it is completely abandoned. No trucks. No bicycles. No geese. Its surroundings too. Dirt and scrub and sky. A scrupulous minimalism. I am a fleck between civilizations. Shot from a cannon, wandering a land that I do not know. I pass the fire

station, the fountain, the public washrooms and the lockers checked orange and blue. I can smell the charcoal and the meat from the day's picnics. A sunbather's blanket lies crinkled in the sand. A ball. A harmonica. A shoe sideways in the grass. Did everyone have to tidy all at once and leave in a hurry? Was there a great rush, and they had to run, dropping their things and only half-dressed? Or maybe everyone is hiding.

Left behind on a debris-strewn stretch of sand, however, Eugenia discovers a secret close-kept by the islands' semi-permanent residents and the few visitors who trace their paths during the off-season: in the stillness between seasons, in the deep silence broken only by the cries of gulls and the continuous rhythm of waves collapsing against the piers, there is room enough to release a lifetime of care. This is the islands' deeper draw.

In the shadow of a lagoon, Eugenia—Stunt, her father calls her—plies a private carnival, tying a rope the thickness of a noose between two trees and attempting to walk along it. Falling repeatedly, cutting herself on concealed glass, she steps again and again into the abyss until finally, buoyed between memory and muddled hope, she reaches the other side:

> Around me, there is only the white puff of cottonwood seeds, floating like shrunken clouds. I am thousands of feet in the air and I am suddenly a giant. In the silence, I hear a line snap. It is the line between us. The one that bound me to you. *Snap*. And with that snap, a mysterious pool takes shape. It does not have any echo or reflection. It is indifferent. It is aloneness. Finally, aloneness.

Like the mourners who consign loved ones' ashes to the sand and water, Eugenia learns to let go of the search for her father, watching the memory of him shimmer and fade in the water. The next time she steps out on a tightrope, it is stretched high above the city, fastened at the ends only by air. She walks across it and heads toward the islands, looking finally for herself.

In *More Than an Island*, Sally Gibson evokes the islands' appeal to seasonal visitors and semi-permanent residents from the Aboriginal era to the present, describing the islands' residents as "a cavalcade of characters from Canada's history," among them "summering Indians, buckskinned explorers, black-robed Jesuits and intrepid fur traders [....] Redcoated English soldiers and invading Americans, horseback-riding ladies and duck-shooting gentlemen, wretched commercial fishermen and pioneering hotel owners" who "left their footprints on the Island's sands, long before the Island became a popular resort for millions and a well-loved home to thousands down through the years." The islands have been many things to Torontonians—a "Bohemia on the Bay," a "place for cultural refugees," a retreat, a healing place, a place to hide, a home. But perhaps above all, the islands' value lies in their liminal position between land and water, culture and nature, being and whatever lingers beyond it. Without mountains to serve as an urban muse, the islands have become the city's sublime. Visiting the islands, valuing them, Torontonians experience something truly akin to transcendence.

In "Lagoons, Hanlan's Point," Raymond Souster describes the islands as "the antechamber / of a slowly waking world," a perspective evocative of the islands' liminal position at the edge of the lake. In "Animal Syllables," a prose poem appearing in her 1982 collection *Earthlight*, Gwendolyn MacEwen suggests, further, that the islands are made up of "shorelines of souls," lying thick on the beaches like shells. Invoking the islands' metaphorical and material impermanence in the city's memory, their way of vanishing and reappearing beyond the wind and wake, MacEwen adds, "We fold in upon ourselves like the waves, we fold under, falling in and out of the world's vision."

LITERARY INTERSECTIONS

In his classic book, *No Mean City*, Toronto architectural historian Eric Arthur judges Alexander Aitkin's 1793 survey of York—ten oblong blocks stretching north and west from the corner of what are now Front and Berkeley streets—to have been "indescribably mean and unimaginative," describing it as "a plan with which we have had to cope for almost two hundred years and with which posterity will have to deal with till the end of time."

A vastly expanded version of Aitkin's grid, adopted by Governor John Graves Simcoe as the nascent settlement's plan, provides structure to the contemporary city, which is still composed almost entirely of orderly lines and concessions spaced like cartographical clockwork. It is, in fact, difficult to get lost in most parts of Toronto because traveling in any of the cardinal directions will almost invariably take commuters to one of the city's major intersections, arrayed in rows as easily recognizable as stations of the cross.

Critics of Toronto's grid point out its insensitivity to major topographical features like the ravines and rivers that once bisected the city at regular intervals. They are quick to claim that the grid symbolizes both a colonial imperative and a civic malaise dating back to Toronto's earliest origins as a European settlement. What critics of the grid overlook, however, are the tremendous advantages rectilinear streets have conferred upon Toronto. For two hundred years the grid has accommodated Toronto's tremendous growth while keeping the inner city walkable, liveable and accessible to public transit. Moreover, far from being insensitive to Toronto's natural topography, streets like Spadina and Avenue Road that crest the ancient shore of Lake Iroquois provide un-paralleled vistas of the city sloping toward the contemporary lakeshore, while viaducts connecting the east-west spans of Bloor-Danforth over the Don and Dundas Street West at the Humber River are gateways into Toronto's geologic past. Finally, any person who spends time exploring Toronto quickly becomes familiar with the many districts that deviate from the grid, Rosedale's laby-rinth streets being only one well-known example. In the older parts of the city, such variations almost always signal a shift in topography and, as such, con-nect the city to its ravines and the ghosts of its watercourses. Like everything else about Toronto, the streets are hybrid, neither quite culture or nature but a complicated amalgam of everything they touch.

Neither featureless nor inorganic, Toronto's streets animate the urban inte-rior, bringing movement to the city like sinews or a corporeal map of ligaments and limbs. In *Signal Fires*, Christopher Dewdney invokes the city's organic qualities, writing:

> The streets are vast crystalline
> networks, linked luminescent organisms proliferating to
> the horizon.

Ronna Bloom draws a similar analogy in "The City," describing streets as bodi-ly metonyms, their intersections traceable upon well-travelled flesh:

> I am going out all the exits on the highway
> at the same time. Mapping
> a leg to a shoulder, a memory to a hill, a blue vein
> to an arm. Cross
> sections of past. Yonge Street meets
> Bloor north of Piccadilly Circus
> like a skin graft. Major intersections
> cross the body.

Adding, "the city / calls to my voices, my limbs," Bloom's narrator responds to the invocation of streets, beckoning her to explore whatever lies beyond them.

In "On City Streets and Narrative Logic," literary scholar Steven Winspur notes that literary intersections in works of fiction signal narrative movement and provide meeting points between lines of plot. Far more than standing in as the passive "topoi of the text," Winspur argues that they also serve as onto-logical thresholds, textual invitations to travel between "the city here and now" and the "elsewhere."

No writer exemplifies this invitation better than bpNichol, whose long poem, *The Martyrology*, signals its psychogeographic purpose in the opening stanzas of Book V and overlays a Chaucerian landscape upon the streets of contemporary Toronto:

> here
>> ere i begin
> among the streets & houses stand around me
> How Land over the bridge
> (du pont) to Daven's Port
> & in between a sea (mer)
> Wal
>> Full tragedies are played[78]

Interspersing the names of well-known Annex streets (Howland, Dupont, Davenport, Walmer) among his lines, Nichol plays with language and landscape in ways that make his mythopoeic discovery of the city a kind of pilgrimage, accompanied by saints, dragons and perilous voyages along the ancient lakeshore. Nichol's use of medieval language, his mythologically resonant lines and the epic scope and heroic structure of the poem transform the familiar streets of the Annex into an imaginative landscape where anything—an ocean voyage, a conversation with the dead, a romantic affair between streets—becomes possible. In "In Tens/tion: Dialoguing with bp," poet and literary scholar Steve McCaffery suggests that Book V of *The Martyrology* is as much a spatial as poetic text, referencing cultural theorist Michel de Certeau's comments on the "mythic experience" of the metaphorical city before observing,

> [Nichol's] dominance of spatiality seems guaranteed by the presence of fragments rather than wholes. Juxtapositions, collisions, slips, spaces, twists, gaps...these seem the figures of a rhetoric of space which determines *The Martyrology* as a literary object. The work's refusal to assume a panoptic stance and the deliberate eschewal of totality and closure also suggest its consideration as a major text of space rather than a poetic journal of lived time.

In this way we might think of *The Martyrology* as a paracartographic guidebook, a skeleton key to the city within the city. And indeed, as Nichol muses, "i found a map lead me / thru Toronto's streets / into another reality."

---

78 Nichol, 1982. The first two lines of this volume of *The Martyrology*—"a road / a rod"—allude directly to Nichol's use of the poem as pilgrimage. "Rod" (also "rood") is a measure of distance and is also the Old English word for "cross."

Since Nichol, psychogeographic street maps have become a trope in Toronto literature. In *james i wanted to ask you*, Michael Holmes suggests that the city's principal thoroughfares may be navigated and even evaluated according to their distinctive personalities:

> here's the longhand of smiles
> on queen street
> (not the accountable
> algebraic smiles
>
> of bay street not the bisecting
> lingual smiles
> of bloor not even
> a gloss on
>
> the hard lupine smiles
> of yonge street)
>   just plum lips
> bust up on
>   pulling you
>   in

Similarly, in her long poem "Alphabet City," Lynn Crosbie traces an equally idiosyncratic terrain, mainly along Bloor, College and Queen, her descriptions of misadventure always underlain by an aura of heartbreak. In another poem, "Geography," Crosbie describes walking along College near Grace Street, toward an apartment where her friend, poet Daniel Jones, had once tried to kill himself:

> It is arduous, approaching Grace. You must continue, trace the narrow
>   lines of its map, and be
> prepared. To draw the blade neatly,
>
> divide your wrists into continents. Rivers are created, tributaries,
>   fault-lines—
> geography's red and blue relief, where forgiveness lies remote
> and uncharted.

Years later, a subsequent suicide attempt succeeds, and Crosbie is left to walk the haunted streets, *"without plan, / without direction, incomprehensible and monstrous."*

Every street in Toronto has a story, and many of the city's streets—among them the "Mink Mile" on Bloor near Bay, and the various villages (Chinatown, Corso Italia, Greektown, Little India, Little Malta, Little India) that cluster along the Danforth, Dundas, Gerrard or St. Clair—help define the neighbourhoods they serve, but two arteries—Yonge Street, long considered the city's commercial core, and Spadina Avenue, a street that has harboured so much of Toronto's cultural history—stand out in ways that transcend the local, so much so that they have become definitive of Toronto itself.

Despite the contemporary city's size and sophistication, Torontonians remain rather quaintly prone to promoting self-aggrandizing myths designed to bolster civic self-image while concealing a neurotic sense of insecurity. One such myth, repeated in stories and city guides and even carved for posterity into the concrete sidewalk outside the Eaton Centre, revolves around the claim that Yonge Street is the longest street in the world.

Perhaps Torontonians are not to be blamed for this particular conceit. In *The Canadian Guide-Book*, published in 1891, Charles G. D. Roberts attributes this assessment of Yonge Street to an Englishman, journalist and noted bombast George Augustus Sala. Frederick Young repeats Sala's claim in his 1902 memoir, *A Pioneer of Imperial Federation in Canada*, and adds as evidence an anecdote from Henry Scadding's *Toronto of Old* confirming the street's reputation:

> A story is told of a tourist, newly arrived at York, wishing to utilize a stroll before breakfast by making out as he went along the whereabouts of a gentleman to whom he had a letter. Passing down the hall of his hotel, he asks in a casual way of the book-keeper: 'Can you tell me where Mr So-and-so lives? (leisurely producing the note from his breast-pocket wallet). It is somewhere along Yonge Street here in your town. 'Oh yes,' was the reply, when the address had been glanced at, 'Mr So-and-so lives on Yonge Street, about twenty-five miles up!'

For his part, Scadding suggests only that Yonge Street stretched, at its full length, from the lakeshore to Penetanguishene, a claim in keeping with Governor John Graves Simcoe's desire to establish a secure inland connection to the province's interior.[79]

Yonge Street's claim to be the longest street in the world was encouraged by a complex cartographical calculus in which its various components, aggregated as Highway 11, extended nearly 2,000 kilometres to end near the northeastern tip of Lake Superior. The *Guinness Book of World Records* did recognize Yonge Street as the longest street in the world from 1965 until as recently as

---

79 Scadding [abridged by Armstrong], 1987. A more complete history of the street's origins is found in F. R. Berchem's book *The Yonge Street Story, 1793-1860* (McGraw-Hill Ryerson, 1977).

1998, but (following a re-examination of naming conventions and in light of the road's many discontinuities) has since assigned that honour elsewhere.

Although Toronto no longer stakes much of its identity on this particular claim, Yonge Street's storied length remains a shadow in the city's literature, drifting periodically to the surface like a legend shared among elders. In *Raymond and Hannah*, Stephen Marche introduces Yonge Street using the same sort of language nineteenth-century visitors might have employed to describe a colonial city boldly (if clumsily) carving itself out of the trackless wilderness:

> Yonge Street starts uncertainly behind the twisted veil of the Gardiner Expressway. From the mangled touristy waterfront it struggles north, out of the weakling suburbs. Gathering force, it pushes through the industrial hinterlands, past breweries and plastics manufacturers, and by rivers beside nickel smelters and their warehouses. Then the wilderness raises its darkness. The mixed forests jut up. Smashed animal corpses litter the road, sustaining the ravens. Under its bridges flow rivers and streams too numerous to name or to remember. Yonge Street runs 1897 kilometres north and west to end in the practical anonymity of Rainy River on the Ontario-Minnesota border.

The irony underpinning Marche's quasi-heroic tone loses its subtlety in Kristen den Hartog's novel *The Perpetual Ending*. Young twin girls visiting Toronto for the first time are struck by the chaos and filth they encounter while walking downtown, and in an anxious effort to impress her daughters, whom she has transported unwillingly to this unfamiliar city, the girls' mother recites Yonge Street's claim to fame. "This is the longest street in the world," she tells them, adding, in response to their complaints about the noisy, filthy streets, that "Toronto might just be the cleanest city in the world."

Despite Lucy's optimism, the girls find Toronto's claims to cleanliness lying crumbled in the gutters of Yonge Street, mute testament to the unacknowledged death of yet another urban legend: Toronto's reputation for order.

In Joyce Marshall's 1957 novel, *Lovers and Strangers*, a young architect deplores Yonge Street's tawdry streetscape, considering its rundown storefronts an affront to his notions of engaged urbanity:

> At the corner of Yonge and Bloor he paused for a moment, glancing south. God, he thought, how does one ever get used to such an insanity of ugliness? He'd come from the several little towns of his childhood with a bright dream of City, had found instead this untidy sprawl, snugged against a long curve of Lake Ontario, spitted on Yonge Street, the city's principal shopping street and its main artery

79

to the north. From the gasoline tanks and coal-dumps of the lakeshore, the street presents almost without interruption a tawdry hodgepodge of shops and offices, each with its one- or two-storeyed dusty-windowed loft, a jungle of telegraph poles and overhanging street signs, at night a leaping madness of varicoloured neon.

Like a planner fixated on progress, he imagines razing the entire Yonge Street strip to the ground and transforming the trip into a monument to mid-century modernism:

Long ago in the middle thirties, when he had time and only time, he had drawn a plan for a new Yonge Street, then built a scale model of the plan. Every stick and brick he had demolished to make a street of more than twice the width with a boulevard of grass and trees. No skyscrapers—a more leisurely style for this more leisurely city—skyscrapers were for lower Bay Street and its sidestreets. Yonge was to have block-long buildings of crushed limestone, none more than eight storeys high. Every three or four blocks a corner park. The strip of reclaimed fill below the tracks was to be landscaped, and the rise from the ravine to St. Clair was to be all terraced rockeries.

In a telling testament to Yonge Street's tawdry persistence, Marshall describes the fate of Roger's earnestly crafted scale model, a source of amusement among his colleagues and friends:

Then one hot waiting August night in 1938, Ted brought around an old set of German soldiers. Pre-1914, unfortunately, but he'd painted little swastikas on the tin hats. They'd have to do. With a certain wry solemnity they'd ranged them up their broad beautiful Yonge Street and then Roger, as proprietor, had set a match to the whole thing. Everyone had grown a little quiet, he remembered, because the metal figures dwarfed not only the trees but the buildings—just a dozen it took to reach from the waterfront to Queen—and the flames raised scarcely a blister on the pre-1914 paint.

Roger's frustrated dreams of a beautified, boulevarded Yonge Street have been shared by subsequent generations of planners and politicians anxious to swing the municipal wrecking ball. As William Kilbourn elaborates in *Toronto Remembered*:

Yonge Street has cast a shadow over many of Toronto's nobler aspirations. It is an affront to planners, engineers, efficiency experts, moralists, aesthetes, epicureans and history buffs. [...] To dedicated boosters of Toronto, Yonge Street is an outright offence. A few years ago the director of the National Gallery of Canada described it as "400 outhouses leaning up against Eaton's." Nathan Phillips, whose career on city council spanned five decades, called it "a disgrace to a city the size and importance of Toronto," but he never managed to change it.

Yonge Street is remarkably resistant to change. Even as canyons of condominiums that have come to dominate the streetscape above College and Yonge-Dundas Square make a daily mockery of the public realm, Yonge remains quintessentially Torontonian, its commercial strip still dominated by discount dollaramas, red-carded restaurants, seedy sex shows, second-hand bookstores and a storefront Scientology mission.

As some parts of the downtown core grow increasingly sterile, many Torontonians have grown nostalgic for Yonge Street's seedy strip. In *Sex and Character*, a fictionalized memoir of his wayward youth, F.G. Paci's narrator, a twenty year old from Northern Ontario eager to experience city life in late 1960s Toronto, sums up the street's appeal:

> The Yonge Street strip was my favourite haunt. I liked strolling up and down the garish neon emporiums and fast-food outlets, the leather shops and dirty bookstores with the movie booths in the back. There were jazz and rock bars jumping with music. There were triple-bill theatres plastered with gaudy posters where derelicts and bums could sleep in the afternoons. There were strip bars advertising nude women by the breast-load. On any night I could catch the Hare Krishna devotees banging on their bongos and chanting. Scientology girls stood at the corners, ready to befriend and indoctrinate with their deceptively winsome smiles. Hawkers and pedlars set up shop beside the store fronts and clogged the sidewalks, selling their watches and leather goods. Street kids and panhandlers and prostitutes slunk in the doorways, ready to pounce.

Adding, "It was a place where I could be anonymous amongst the social misfits and misbegotten, those who had slunk so low in life they had nothing else to hide," Paci evokes Yonge Street's reputation as a place to let off steam. In "Prodigal Son Returns to Yonge Street," poet David Donnell gives voice to a similar wistfulness, intimating that by pulling the plug on Yonge Street's tawdry spectacle, what we risk losing is no less than the city's soul:

> O my elegant street of pimps and whores and thugs,
> the fastest growing metropolis in North America
> has gutted you and trashed your storefronts. [...]
> there is nothing left of you now but a long street of toilet paper

that everybody has wiped their hands on and left nothing, nada,
not even themselves, not even their address, not even their legend.

Still, perhaps Yonge Street will have its revenge. In the spring of 2010 the front facade of a commercial building under renovation at the corner of Yonge and Gould collapsed, spilling bricks and debris into the intersection. Given its location immediately across the street from the gutted remains of Sam the Record Man (an iconic Canadian music retailer whose famous sign—two giant vinyl discs lit up like a spinning strobe—was unceremoniously removed in 2008 amid public protest after the property was acquired by Ryerson University), it is tempting to imagine the building's collapse as a protest, a refusal—and perhaps even a warning that Yonge Street will not go gently into that good night.

Like Yonge Street, Spadina Avenue is principally a commercial strip, but where Yonge has derived its identity directly from the business of buying and selling, Spadina is defined by the generations of immigrants—most prominently Jews and Chinese, but also British, Hungarian, Vietnamese and Caribbean—who have lived, worked, worshipped and shopped in its tenements, workshops, synagogues and stores. No other street in Toronto is immersed as deeply in the city's cultural history, and no other street is a more visible symbol of how much the city owes to its immigrants—nor bears in every brick evidence of how hard they have worked to establish themselves.

In the introduction to Rosemary Donegan's *Spadina Avenue*, Rick Salutin suggests that the street is set apart even by its name, commenting on the Spadina's Ojibway etymology[80] and observing,

Many Toronto street names (and other local features) imply that the city is still the preserve of modern descendents of groups like the United Empire Loyalists or the Family Compact. [...] Spadina, though, reminds almost everyone that they're newcomers in a place where all non-native Ojibway-speakers have only recently arrived. It's an equalizer.

Adding, "Maybe that's why wave after wave of immigrants have felt comfortable on Spadina," Salutin goes on to inventory Spadina's varied history as a hub of Jewish settlement, a nucleus of political mobilization (most notably labour activism in the garment industry and the fight against the Spadina expressway), a place for public diversions (among them the lost, lamented Victory Burlesque

---

80 Spadina is derived from an Ojibway word, spelled "espadinong" (according to Leonard Wise and Allan Gould's book *Toronto Street Names*) or "ishpadinaa" (according to Eric Arthur in *No Mean City*), which refers to a rise of land.

and the El Mocambo nightclub) and, most recently, the centre of the city's largest Chinatown. Along the way, Salutin adds, Spadina has also appealed to Toronto's Hungarians, Blacks, hippies, homeless, draft dodgers, drinkers and poets.

Although Salutin suggests that immigrants have historically felt comfortable on Spadina, the street's association with a succession of narrowly defined segments of the city's population has also made its reputation something of a mixed blessing. For all the advantages of living among familiar faces and enjoying a common cultural language, an ethnic enclave starts to resemble a ghetto when residents begin to feel hemmed in by outsiders'—or community members'—expectations of them. In Dionne Brand's *What We All Long For*, the daughter of highly educated Vietnamese refugees reduced to running a Spadina restaurant describes the consequences of cultural expectation:

> The restaurant became their life. They were being defined by the city. They had come thinking that they would be who they were, or at least who they had managed to remain. After the loss of Quy, it made a resigned sense to them that they would lose other parts of themselves. Once they accepted that, it was easy to see themselves the way the city saw them: Vietnamese food.

For Tuyen's family, Spadina symbolizes dispossession and a profound *loss* of identity, a wound compounded by finding themselves subsumed within a hegemonic model of cultural diversity. Brand adds, "Neither Cam nor Tuan cooked very well, but how would their customers know? Eager Anglos ready to taste the fare of their multicultural city wouldn't know the differences."

Being part of an identifiable cultural community can be a tremendous source of comfort—although such tight-knit familiarity might also be said to breed its own form of cultural contempt. The narrator of John Miller's novel *A Sharp Intake of Breath* describes a Depression-era Jewish community centred on Spadina that resembles a closely knit but rather vicious small town:

> My parents were avid readers of the morning newspaper. One newspaper, the *Toronto Mail and Empire*, they read to keep track of their class enemies. Others, they read because of political interest or because the writers spoke to our community. The communist weekly *Vochenblatt* and the daily *Yidisher Zshurnal*—the Hebrew Journal—were in this category, though I believe they also read these two to see who was the latest person to be denounced. The Yiddish press was vicious and retributive and heaven help you if you were on the other side of their graces. Reading those papers satisfied a ghoulish fascination: who would be torn to shreds *this* week? Whose character would be assassinated ruthlessly? My parents read these denunciations, clucked, and shook their heads, but they kept going back for more.

Isolated within the larger city but passionate about Jewish identity and local and international labour politics, Toshy's family revels in such muckraking not only because it is a way of participating in the political, social and spiritual conversations of their community but also because it gives them a sense of control over the narrative of what it means to be Jewish and working-class in Toronto.

A generation later, when the protagonist of Helen Weinzweig's *Basic Black with Pearls* revisits the Spadina Avenue of her youth, she experiences a similar, if more subtle, sense of social judgement. Stepping into a bakery dressed like a middle-class matron of means, she is surprised to be recognized as a *landtzman*:

> I circled the small store, pretending to be making up my mind, all the while edging towards the rear, where I had seen a doorway screened off by a faded red velvet drape. Even though her eyes never left the newspaper, I sensed the woman was taking my measure. I wished I had on a printed rayon dress with a clean printed cotton apron over it, as she was wearing. I regretted being dressed in my black dress, the tailored tweed coat, the pearls. If you have grown up in these streets it is the act of a traitor to return smelling of expensive perfume and sporting the costume of another class.

Her efforts to pass as an Anglo are undone when she asks for "a quarter of the Russian black." Smirking with silent triumph, the storekeeper bends to fulfill a request she knows only a local would know to make. Exposed, Weinzweig's protagonist acts out against the storekeeper, spilling bread and tipping out the contents of the cash register until, resigned and perhaps relieved to be recognized and back in familiar territory, she sits down and chats with the woman about the serialized story in the current edition of the *Jewish Daily Forward*.

Later, walking along the wide avenue, Weinzweig's protagonist considers Spadina's strange contradiction: that each new immigrant population reprises many of the experiences of the previous one, making Spadina a palimpsest not only of itself but of the whole city's cultural history. It is this observation that helps her come to peace with her own fractured past: the realization that her history, too, is preserved in the bricks and businesses:

> On Spadina again, caught in the downpour, against which I did not lower my head, crossing block after block along a route taken a hundred years ago by colonial soldiers marching to Fort York. I was not interested in this street as history. Nor were the Chinese and Portuguese and West Indians, I thought, who all about me were hurrying to take shelter. Their expressions were the same as ours when

we arrived on this street: a look that was empty of the past and that suffered the present. But their eyes gleamed as if reflecting the future that was visible all about them—a future of sturdy clothes and well-stocked stores and motor cars. Even in the rain I could see what appeared to be new shops and buildings were only facades over the old: larger windows, bright tile, some stone work. I felt my past had not been erased, just covered over and given new names in other languages.

Matt Cohen echoes this sentiment in "Spadina Time," a story whose narrative reads like a well-worn memory that repeats itself in a shifting loop, emphasizing something new each time:

What do you do all day, Harold asked.
    I walk around.
    There was a girl here to see you.
    She wore a sweater and slacks. Standing beneath the streetlamp in early summer she tapped her toes on the pavement and waited for him. He memorized the angle of her neck, the way she laughed with the passerbys and leaned against the lamp post as if it were her house. She was carrying a straw bag and the handles were bound together by a red scarf. They walked up Spadina to the reservoir, turning around to see how far they had come, tangling themselves up in everything that hadn't happened.

Later, someone else—perhaps Spadina itself—asks Cohen's narrator, "What have you been doing lately?" and he replies, "I sit under the tree over there and meditate on the white light of my memory of you."

A generation later, Alice Burdick's poem "Spadina Way" suggests that a similar sort of memory loop continues to animate Spadina. Writing, "This desire to see so much is inherited, / passed from each previous generation," Burdick summons a multi-sensory impression of wind-blown wicker, rotting vegetables, car stereos and cultural contradictions:

A cold wind blows down Spadina today. Straw baskets
and prisoner-made plastic utensils must be tied down gently but firmly
with shiny pink ribbons, looped into bows. I swear I saw
three Rabbis eat spring rolls with relish. [...]
A man runs cockeyed through the streets at dawn.
He slaps a hand high-five and jumps over a big puddle.
In a darkened shop window a starving cat watches a mouse
gnaw an avocado. The man blows a mouth organ onto the window
and a shadow of steam spreads briefly. The avocado drops

and rolls under the cash register. Man high-fives the windowpanes and slumps onto collapsed cardboard.

Writing that Spadina "[m]ust be like religion, / a calling one should not resist," Burdick employs language that is both surreal and faintly spiritual to invoke Spadina's chaotic mix of culture and commerce, underscoring its centrality in Toronto as the Avenue all other streets are measured against.

In his memoir, *Typing: A Life in 26 Keys*, Cohen refers repeatedly to Spadina as Toronto's "cosmic spine." Appropriately, after his death from cancer in 1999, a park at the corner of Bloor and Spadina was renamed Matt Cohen Park. And here, at the centre of Cohen's—indeed, of the city's—universe, anyone can sit under a tree on benches provided for the purpose, and "meditate on the white light" of our memories of Cohen, of Spadina, of Toronto.

WHAT MOVES US

When asked to contribute to Toronto's sesquicentennial celebrations in 1984 by writing something on the theme "What moves you about Toronto," poet Irving Layton responded succinctly with a short piece beginning, "What moves me about Toronto is the TTC."[81]

The Toronto Transit Commission isn't the only thing that moves people about the city, although nearly 2.5 million Torontonians take public transit every day. Toronto is also a city of drivers: *Toronto Life* magazine reported in 2008 that Toronto is the fourth most congested city in North America, with commuters spending an average of seventy-nine minutes trapped in traffic every day.[82] Taking some of the load off the city's roads and rails are the more than one million Torontonians who cycle, among them tens of thousands who commute regularly to work by bike.

Most of the time, commuting is boring, a tedious hour or two during which travellers enter a kind of spiritual suspended animation. Periodically, however, something jars us out of our stupor: a pileup on the 401, a subway suicide, a tractor-trailer gearing down behind our ten-speed. Then the stories come out, and small wonder so many of them are about fear. But there is beauty, too, in the liberty one can experience while riding fast on a bike, or the power of possession that goes along with owning a car. This is what moves us most.

Travelling on the Bloor-Danforth subway line in a train rumbling over the Prince Edward viaduct is a surreal experience. Swaying between stations,

---

81 See "Varied Hues," quoted in Betts, 2006.
82 See Phillip Preville's article, "Toronto's Traffic Time Bomb," in the February 2008 issue of *Toronto Life*.

shuddering in the darkness of the tunnel, the train suddenly bursts into bright air, floating as if airborne high above the Don Valley. At moments like this, when a passenger can appreciate that the subway does far more than carry passengers from one end of the city to the other, it transports Torontonians from one reality to another.

In his long poem *The Subway*, Philip Quinn describes trains and tunnels using neurological terminology, suggesting that like dendrites and nerve endings the trains shoot passengers like messages all over the city:

the hard drive hisses, pulses with a green light
the Go signal

the reptilian, a wondrous, jostling synaesthesia
in an already crowded station

sibilant subtitles on a slippery stand-up stage

the brain stem, a bursting flower [...]

The city's skyscape bites down
A syllogism filled with chewed vescicles

A former cell occupied by one, now joined together in a six-car jelly
    that twitches

While the engine pumps itself up
While the brain engorges itself

I spread myself all over the interior of this map

In Quinn's subterranean Toronto, stations are synapses, subway cars are electrified axons and the scraps of paper that billow and burn in the tunnels are fragments of memory that flicker long after their bearers have gone. Darren O'Donnell brings this metaphor to the city's surface in *Your Secrets Sleep with Me*, describing the streetcar tracks as the city's most vital, if misunderstood, lines of communication:

If you lay your ear on the tracks you can tune into many of the different conversations that are happening on the various streetcars, the talk reverberating down into the seats, into the wheels, then shaved and sent spinning into the tracks which zip them back and forth, up and down the city's streets. The loudest of the conversations manage to reverberate themselves further, up from the rails into the wheels of other vehicles, further, even, into the bodies of the passengers.

Of course, there's always the hint of menace in the wires. O'Donnell continues, "A little boy had once been lulled to sleep by the bustle, his tiny ear pressed to the rail, a contented smile secure on his face, when a streetcar sheared off his head."

O'Donnell is not the only writer who detects menace in the rods and rails. For the young protagonist of Kristen den Hartog's *The Perpetual Ending*, subways are frightening not only because they are dangerous but because they are crowded, dirty and claustrophobic:

[W]e stand on the long platform with the crows, looking across like into a mirror. Even down here there are too many people. We can never get away from them. Most of them are rushing, unhappy, traveling alone. On either end of the platform is a black hole, who knows where it takes us? I see a mouse flit, maybe a rat. Something lives everywhere, in all the corners. Living underground, traveling underground, roofs pressing down.

The noise comes first, not like a real train. And then it bursts through the hole, long and dull silver, causing wind that stops our breath, moving too fast to stop but stopping anyway, everyone rushing toward it. Lucy gripping my elbow, pushing me through. Where are you? My heart flutters strangely, a butterfly in there. Could we get caught in the doors?

Similarly, in *Basic Black with Pearls*, Helen Weinzweig attributes her narrator's unease to a feeling of being confined underground, having given up control to the anonymous (perhaps insane) operator of a machine moving much faster than walking speed:

Subways, tubes, metros—I am always uneasy in a steel car under the ground, afraid the automatic doors will not open, or afraid that the automatic doors will open in a dark passage too narrow for escape. We sit with fists clenched. I concluded that in a subway, because flight is impossible, we prepare to fight.

Exiting the subway and surfacing near a streetcar transfer, she feels an odd relief and considers its cause:

I was happy to surface and get out at Dundas Street. From the corner I watched a streetcar six blocks away come waddling towards us. It stopped with all its doors open. We embarked in a leisurely manner. The conductor was calm, straightening out transfers against the palm of his hand while answering questions. We pushed gently against one another until seats were found. On a streetcar I feel safe. Every two blocks I have a choice of staying on or leaving. I pull on a cord overhead and the conductor is alerted to my intentions. I have but to step down one step at the exit and the doors fly open.

Regular riders might take issue with Weinzweig's idealized description of streetcar travel. Still, the relief at not being underground, at not having to deal with the trickling tremor of a terrorist attack, a cave-in—or something unimaginably worse—is what causes some passengers to stick to the surface routes.

In Tanya Huff's urban fantasy novel *Blood Price*, a man stands on the empty subway platform at Eglinton West subway station, waiting for a late-night train and tantalizing himself by daydreaming about spectres he imagines skulking in the darkness between stations:

He wandered down to the southernmost end of the platform and peered into the tunnel. No signs of lights, but he could feel wind against his face and that usually meant the train wasn't far. He coughed as he turned away. It smelled like something had died down there; smelled like it did at the cottage when a mouse got between the walls and rotted.

"Big mother of a mouse," he muttered, rubbing his fist against his nose. The stench caught in his lungs and he coughed again. It was funny the tricks the mind played; now that he was aware of it, the smell seemed to be getting stronger.

And then he heard what could only be footsteps coming up the tunnel, out of the darkness. Heavy footsteps, not at all like a worker hurrying to beat the strain after a day's overtime, nor like a bum staggering for the safety of the platform. Heavy footsteps, purposefully advancing toward his back.

Enjoying the transient terror of anticipating something where logic tells him nothing can possibly be lurking, Ian keeps his back to the tunnel until something shambles onto the platform and rips out his throat in the middle of a scream. Attacked by a demon dwelling in the city's subterranean spaces, Huff's hapless young man fulfils the secret dread harboured by many passengers who peer nervously into the darkened tunnel: that maybe there really is something living in there.

Not all threats in the subway system are supernatural. In Graham Mc-Namee's young adult novel *Acceleration*, a teenaged boy fleeing a murderous youth runs desperately into Wilson Station, seeking shelter in the brightly lit confines of the station. Hoping to elude his pursuer by escaping on the next train, Duncan limps onto the platform only to find the tunnel empty and

89

no train in sight." His attacker approaches him on the platform, casually but menacingly, and cruelly checks him onto the tracks—just as a train lumbers out of the tunnel:

> I stumble and fall off the edge of the platform, hitting the tracks hard and knocking what little wind I had left out of me. My eyes refuse to focus. All I see is two blurry white eyes coming toward me. There's a rumbling sound that seems to come at me from all directions. The tracks vibrate under my back, and my last active brain cells tell me that those aren't eyes I'm seeing, shining from the dark.

As Duncan tries to climb up, his assailant kicks him again. Driven by adrenaline and terror, Duncan grabs Roach and pulls him onto the tracks as well, and they tumble and struggle as the train thunders toward them:

> The last thing I see is Roach staggering to a standing position, his glasses gone, holding his hands out blindly. He moves to try to escape to the northbound tracks. Then there's the scream of metal as the train brakes. Sparks fly, and my scream joins the train's. I think I hear other voices screaming too, from above.
>
> Impact. Blinding pain. The world goes black, and I'm falling a very long way, getting smaller and smaller, carrying our screams down with me.
>
> Then nothing.

With this chilling description, McNamee puts a frightening spin on many Torontonians' unspoken fears of subway pushers, giving any rider good reason to stay well clear of the yellow line at the edge of the platform.

> More often, the scenes that play out on subway platforms are more prosaic, if no less heartbreaking. In Gordon Stewart Anderson's *The Toronto You Are Leaving*, a young man who has just learned that his lover has been unfaithful rushes into the subway system and takes a train blindly, not knowing or caring where it is headed.

Only after the train crosses the Bloor Viaduct does David realize he has traveled in the wrong direction to a part of the city he does not recognise. Berating himself, suspecting that having taken the wrong train symbolizes his loving "the wrong sex, the wrong people," David gets off at Greenwood Station, where he paces the platform restlessly, daring himself to step into the path of an oncoming train:

> A train was coming, pushing along its plug of air, and he went back against the wall. He slumped against the tunnel wall as if he loved it, staring at the red front

of the train. He could see the little box where the driver sat, waiting for the crazy and the queer to confess they couldn't live. He longed to see some righteous, monstrous face, but he couldn't make out the face until the train was close. He knew he was playing a game with himself, but he was terrified something inside him might say, 'So you think this is a game, do you?' And he would jump.

Shaken, Anderson's protagonist walks out of the station intact, but not everybody steps back from the breach.

In Crad Kilodney's story "Girl on the Subway," a young man notices a woman sitting on the train looking unusually sorrowful. When they both get off at York Mills Station, some instinct causes him to keep the woman in sight, and when he sees her approach the edge of the platform he approaches her and asks her not to jump. Kilodney's narrator convinces the woman to leave the station with him although, after a surly exchange on Yonge Street, she jumps into a passing taxi heading back in the direction they had come from. Still, he believes he has prevented a suicide until a friend suggests she might have returned to the station and jumped anyway. Consternated, he argues against the prospect:

"Well, I haven't read anything in the papers about a suicide on the subway."

"You wouldn't in any case. The transit commission has a strict policy of never acknowledging them. They feel the publicity would only encourage it."

"I didn't know that."

"It's true. I know somebody who works for them. There's an average of one suicide or attempted suicide per week on the subway. Nobody ever reads about them in the papers." He let out a deep breath. "Anyway, you did the right thing."

Torontonians may remain largely in the dark about subway suicides,[83] but in *21 Hotels* Michael Holmes supplies more graphic detail than most Torontonians would care to hear about their medical aftermath. His narrator, an orderly working the midnight shift at a Toronto hospital, processes the remains of a holiday-season jumper:

This one time, working midnight Emerg admitting, two cops shuffled in ahead of these Paramedics wheeling a big red bundle on an old squeaky gurney. Some-

83 Historically the TTC has refused to publicize suicide attempts in the system, concerned partly that doing so would inspire copycat jumpers, but in 2009 the TTC began to release such data in accordance with a ruling under the Municipal Freedom of Information and Protection of Privacy Act. In "Priority One: Suicides on the Subway Tracks—How Many, How Often and How to Stop Them," published in the August 2010 issue of *Toronto Life*, Rachel Giese offers a sobering assessment of suicide (and survivor) rates, people's reasons for jumping and the impact of suicides on TTC staff.

thing vaguely gory about the way the splattercloth was bunched up and over like a large makeshift belljar. They weren't laughing the way cops laugh in hospitals ... relieved, at least, that it's not their misery. And they didn't make eye contact, or say much of anything. It was December 23rd, the coroner couldn't spare the staff or hearse, so they were escorting the pieces of this guy into a narrow corridor filled with beat up drunks and broken legs and heart attacks. This is not an urban myth: more people kill themselves in the subway during the two weeks before Christmas than at any other time of year. Sometimes they get mangled between the wheels and rails and literally get diced to bits. Often it's like a blender, a Margarita.

And what of the aftermath, not only for those who must clean up the gore and gristle, but for the surviving family members and friends? In *What We All Long For*, Dionne Brand speculates on some of the consequences:

> A man once jumped in front of a subway train, embracing his three-year-old son. What it must have felt like to be held like that, simultaneously clasped to a bosom and thrown against a devastating object. Why had he taken the boy with him? [...] The next week Carla saw the funeral on the television news. What a mess he'd caused—now a lot of people had to put things right, had to mourn him, to bury him, to pick out his funeral clothes, carry his coffin, weep for him.

Only the suicide can know why he jumped, but the truth is that subways are lonely places, and sometimes for the despondent the train's irrevocability is an irresistible draw. And who among us can say we have never thought, even for a moment, what it would be like to jump from the platform and be swept away?

For many lonely Torontonians, however, public transit is a source of solace, a way to feel belonging even despite the city's daily alienations. The protagonist of Pat Capponi's novel *Last Stop Sunnyside*, a psychiatric survivor who lives in a Parkdale rooming house inhabited by outpatients like herself, describes a journey by streetcar as soothing:

> I love the Queen streetcar. Even now, in its elongated, accordion-like dorm, it beats every other bus, every other route the TTC has to offer. I know people who spend all day riding back and forth, if they can cadge a ticket. When you don't have a life, it's a way of connecting, feeling a part of the world, and there's so much to see, briefly framed through the wide windows: bums panhandling, giggling children and their harried mothers, posturing teenagers, bemused tourists, all caught up in their own movements, their fleeting concerns.

It is at moments like this, when the warm press of bodies or the lulling motion of the train or the tram puts passengers halfway into sleep, that we can imagine another side of the city. Perhaps this is why Gary Michael Dault writes in his lovely vignette, "Branch Line,"

> a leaf fell onto the floor
> of the subway car
>
> all the passengers
> looked up at
> the metal grill
> the ceiling
>
> every one of them
> expecting to see the sky

In this moment, perhaps only for as long as it takes to pick up our commuter bags or close the book we've been reading between stops, transit becomes something transcendent.

FAST CARS, SLOW LANE

There are many ways of getting around a city like Toronto, and despite the accessibility and ease of public transit and the pleasure and adrenaline of biking, Torontonians remain wedded to their cars. This is not only a suburban phenomenon, nor a conceit confined to middle-class Torontonians who spend weekends bathing and buffing their BMWs. The people in Toronto who rely most on cars are those who drive them daily to distant factory jobs, praying the transmission will hold out, that Finch Avenue will not suddenly pop another pothole, that there will be parking at Price Chopper, that owning a vehicle will somehow mean they have arrived in a city otherwise determined to wall them out.

In Austin Clarke's story "Doing Right," a Barbados-born parking enforcement officer practises his profession with such dedication that he tickets the Premier, the Attorney-General and a prominent Member of the Provincial Parliament for parking infractions. Other West Indians in Toronto come to see him as a kind of ambassador—until he is reassigned to the predominantly black neighbourhood of Oakwood and St. Clair and begins ticketing the cars of other Caribbean immigrants with even greater zeal.

A wry story of turnabout? Or a probing analysis of postcolonial cultural dynamics in a Toronto where race and identity politics seethe beneath the surface of the superficially tolerant, "multicultural" city? Clarke argues the latter in his introduction to *Nine Men Who Laughed*, writing that his black male characters live "under a smear of self-doubt" at the periphery of a city that resents their presence and numbs them into accommodation. And indeed, Clarke's protagonist mitigates his own oppression by distancing himself from the West Indian community, referring to his neighbours as "you people" and chortling to a friend, "I ticket fifty more bastards, mainly Wessindians."

A precursor to this story is Clarke's "The Motor Car," in which Barbadian-born Calvin Kingston labours and saves to buy a new Galaxie, fantasizing about the admiration and envy his new car will elicit. As it turns out, he cruises the streets only to find that "not one blasted West Indian or black person in sight to look at Calvin new car and make a thing with his head, or laugh, or wave," and parks in front of his boarding house to indifference and silence, even though he "stoop down and play he looking at the tires, give them a little kick with his shoes to see if they got in enough air, look under the car to see what the muffler look like, and things like that, only he know full-well that he don't know one blasted thing bout motto-cars except to wash them off, or that yuh does drive them."

In both of these stories, cars foreground social relationships in which race, class, power and subalternity are deeply ingrained. In "Doing Right" the protagonist is reduced to public servitude within a white bureaucracy and, because he cannot take his frustration out on his oppressors or the fellow West Indians he grows to hate being identified with, instead he targets their cars, taking hollow pleasure in threatening their most visible possessions. Similarly, commenting on "The Motor Car" in Noah Richler's *This Is My Country, What's Yours: A Literary Atlas of Canada*, Clarke points out that Calvin seeks to identify with the dominant culture by obtaining the very object—an expensive car—that whites accept as a symbol of material success. But as Clarke observes, "The thing about possessions [...] is that you are successfully an owner of material things only if people recognize them as your precious possessions, and what really disillusions Calvin is that when he brings home the new car, nobody is there to see him exude his pride of ownership. [...] Calvin is robbed of that, in the same way he is robbed of his ambition."

The above observations should give some hint that the cultural politics of cars are not only social but spatial as well. Clarke's characters move restlessly through the city, between boarding houses they will never own and transient jobs where they remain outsiders. It is hardly surprising, then, that cars loom large as symbols of success: they are visible, achievable and, above all, portable. As such, they become tools for transforming the liminal urban spaces Clarke's West Indians inhabit.

For example, in "Doing Right," Clarke observes that "Wessindians accustom to parking in the middle o' the road, or on the wrong side, back home. And nobody don't trouble them nor touch their cars. And since they come here, many o' these Wessindians haven't tek-on a change in attitude in regards to who own the public road and who own the motto-cars." In Toronto, the roads are the only spaces where Clarke's West Indians are able to assert what literary scholar Batia Boe Stolar describes in "Building and Living the Immigrant City" as a "rural" or "native-soil" use of space. Their efforts are undermined, however, by a functionary who, by ticketing their haphazardly parked cars with hostile zeal in a bid to distinguish himself from fellow "Wessindians," takes away even this opportunity for self-expression.

Other writers, too, invoke cars as visible symbols of their characters' efforts to navigate a city cleaved by social divisions and spatial exclusion. In Toronto literature, taxi drivers are nearly invariably visible minorities—Pakistani doctors, Sikhs with tech degrees, Africans escaping genocide—a theme brought subversively to life in Ansara Ali's *The Sacred Adventures of a Taxi Driver*. Ali's narrator transforms his ceaseless movement through the city's streets into a spiritual journey reflecting his unique perspective on the city's movements and its cultural landscape. New to the country and unable to secure any other kind of work because he is deemed underqualified, overqualified or lacking sufficient Canadian experience, he applies for a job as a taxi driver. His interview is a surreal experience that grants him early insight into the solipsistic experience of actually being behind the wheel:

> "Let's see, do you have ten years' driving experience?"
> "Ten years? I've only been in the country ten days."
> "Ten's the requirement. Years, days, what does it matter to me? Ten's good enough."
> "But..."
> "Do you know every single street in this city?"
> "Not a single street."
> "That's good enough for me, too. That's how I started. You're hired."

Twenty years later, Ali's narrator considers what being a taxi driver has cost—and gained—him:

> O Toronto, City of New Beginnings, it was thee who made it possible for me to play a new round in the old game, the game of life. It was you who gave me rank, position, profession, albeit the meanest of ranks, the humblest of positions, the lowliest of professions. It was not much, but it was something. And it was better than nothing. By it I came to know your moods, even thy pulse, and thy ways,

even thy highways and byways. For did you not make me Taxi Driver? And my taxi and I, were we not allowed to roam freely within your gates to pick up lessons like bouquets from your field of many flowers?

For Ali, liminality is liberating, even transcendent. Unlike others who remain fixed in place by social or economic standing, he is spatially untethered and therefore able to perceive the city as an organic, fluid whole. He transforms the city by flowing through it, his taxi conveying not only passengers but understanding and meaning.

While many see cars as reflections of taste and wealth, selfish luxuries in this era of heightened ecological consciousness, for many Torontonians—labourers who commute to distant and shifting job sites, newspaper deliverers cruising the streets before dawn, taxi drivers—cars remain a simple necessity. And for those who (like Austin Clarke's protagonists) are excluded from the conventional spaces and symbols of possessions and success, cars are something more: an entry point, a symbol of arrival, a vehicle enabling them to penetrate the city's social and spatial barriers.

URBAN ARCHITEXTS

The Aboriginal meaning of Toronto's name—"where there are trees standing in the water"—is an apt metaphor for the glittering towers that gird Toronto's downtown core, anchoring the city to the lake edge like oaks in a sacred grove. One of the city's most beautiful spaces, the Allen Lambert Galleria at Brookfield (formerly BCE) Place, channels this metaphor directly through its design, a six-story atrium buttressed by massive pillars that branch out at their tops like boughs in a forest canopy.

The urban forest is Toronto's predominant architectural metaphor. In "House of the Whale," Gwendolyn MacEwen describes the city's bank towers as steel replicas of Haida totem poles. When her protagonist, one of the thousands of Aboriginal construction workers hired for their willingness to work at heights, climbs the steel framework of a bank building under construction, he feels it shudder like something animated and alive:

> I went up, and the cold steel felt strange against my skin and I sensed long tremors in the giant skeleton of the bank, and it was as if the building was alive, shivering, with bones and sinews and tendons, with a life of its own. I didn't trust it, but I went up and up and there was wind all around me. The city seemed to fall away and the voices of the few men who accompanied me sounded strangely hollow and

unreal in the high air. [...] The next day I imagined that the bank was a huge totem, or the strong man Aemaelk who holds the world up, and I started to feel better."

Catherine Bush invokes similar imagery in *Minus Time* when her protagonist, a young woman who has fled the city in search of perspective, finds familiar silhouettes in the wooded landscape and muses, "Among the trees on the southern horizon rose something that could have been a smoke stack or a tower, or perhaps it was simply a branch, a tree trunk that had grown in the shape of a tower."

Even where writers resort to other metaphors, they are quick to suggest that the city's buildings are animated by a kind of natural magic. In "House of the Whale," one of MacEwen's protagonists suggests to the other that Viljo Revell's modernist City Hall is poised to give birth to one of their spirit ancestors:

> We walked past City Hall and I asked you what the little concrete bubble was for.
> 'Why, that's the egg, the seed,' you said.
> 'Of what?'
> 'Why, Lucas George, I'm surprised at you! Of the *whale*, of course! Come on!'
> 'Looks like a clam shell to me,' I said. 'Did I ever explain to you where mankind came from, Aaron? A clam shell, half-open, with all the little faces peering out.'

In *Born with a Tooth*, Joseph Boyden's narrator makes a similar, albeit more sinister, observation about the Skydome under construction, its walls rising "as if they were being pulled by magic from the tired skin of the earth":

> That this huge building was round as a medicine wheel was no surprise to him. Nothing in the world existed without a reason. He stared up at the white dome roof, curved like an egg, curved like something he could still not quite figure. The big sign on the other side said in blue letters as tall as a person that this was a stadium, a dome for men to play in and for spectators to cheer. For the last two months Painted Tongue had felt an ugly fear, a wolf spider, creeping up his back. All fear made no sense, and this was no different. Painted Tongue was afraid of the day the men would finish construction, of the day they would pack up their tools and leave this new thing completed. Maybe it was the falling and the pills that were now helping him to recognize just what it was the men were building. His gut tightened in awe and fear.

Realizing that the domed stadium resembles a giant turtle rising up at the edge of the water, Painted Tongue fears the new world it portends.[84] Like

---

84 In one version of the creation story, various animals push mud onto the back of a turtle to make a place for Sky Woman to give birth to twin sons. One son, named for the trees that hold up the sky,

Yeats's rough beast, slouching toward Bethlehem to be born, Painted Tongue dreads the new world opening up before him because he knows it will be as sharp and unyielding as the city itself. By evoking the entities that animate Toronto's public buildings, Bush, MacEwen and Boyden align themselves with a long-established literary tradition dating at least as far back as the classical Greeks, whose orators memorized long speeches by imagining walking through large buildings whose walls were alive with their narratives and arguments. The city's public buildings—its libraries, museums, universities, storied commercial spaces like Honest Ed's, centres of government like City Hall and Queen's Park, points of entry like Union Station or the blinking beacon of the CN Tower—are far more than mere settings for human activity. The names of Canadian cities carved into the cornices of the Great Hall at Union Station, the strobe of the marquee at Honest Ed's, the pod-like elevators in the Toronto Reference Library, the weighty facades of the city's museums and university buildings and the perpetual presence of the CN Tower all contribute directly to Torontonians' experiences of those places and the meanings assigned to them. As Mark Kingwell writes in *Concrete Reveries: Consciousness and the City*, "Concrete is the stuff of dreams. It is the world itself coming into being. And the city fashioned of it, those hard streets and unsmooth precincts, is the site where our dreams can take up their concrete contours."

UNION STATION

In an era when many people think of trains as a quaintly outdated mode of travel, Toronto's Union Station continues to serve twice as many passengers as Pearson International Airport, making it Canada's biggest transportation hub and one of the busiest stations in the world. More than 65 million travellers pass through Union Station every year. Although most—particularly local riders taking the subway or regional commuters heading home by GO Train—do not pass through the station's beautiful Beaux-Arts concourse but rather remain cloistered in the station's thundering bowels, this massively colonnaded temple of travel has remained the city's symbolic entrance since its grand opening in 1927.

In literature, travel by train tends to symbolize an inner or outward journey toward wisdom and maturity. A train station, then, is another kind of liminal space, where the traveller remains in psychological or spiritual limbo, having

nurtures and shelters all other living things. His brother, named for the hardest sedimentary stone, causes destruction wherever he goes. One day the brothers battle over the island. Although the son named for the trees that hold up the sky is victorious, he can only banish his brother to live on the back of the turtle, where he lies in wait for new opportunities to bring destruction to the island.

neither quite departed nor arrived because some revelation or jolt of recognition has yet to manifest itself. As a result, for the traveller anticipation is always mixed with melancholy because, in the end, every journey also represents the loss of something: innocence, a sense of rootedness, the familiar face of home.

In *Basic Black with Pearls*, Helen Weinzweig evokes this fear of leaving something—or being left—behind:

> Outside the Union Station images come to me of my war-time voyeurism at sixteen, when I went on Saturdays and Sundays and holidays to watch the tearful partings and reunions. I remembered especially the children. They hovered near a parent, their eyes bright with fear. They pretended pride of luggage, saying they would watch it, served by an intuition that where there are possessions there is home; that they would not be left behind so long as they stayed close to the suitcases.

The problem with possessions, however, is that they may easily be lost or stolen, and in this sense the apprehension Weinzweig's children experience is well-founded. Howard Akler gives further expression to this hazard in *The City Man*, a novel about a gang of pickpockets who frequent Union Station during the Depression, seeking out easy targets for petty larceny. Viewing ticket-buyers and tired travellers as easy marks, a man and woman work in tandem, guiding likely victims into the poke like cattle being led to the slaughter:

> Each minute this morning hangs perilously, like long cigarette ash. She flicks her wrist. Grey flakes fall onto the grey marble floor. All around her is the click-click of shoes and dollied steamer trucks that rumble in the rotunda of the Great Hall. Her eyes are steady. Watching intently the line of suckers at the ticket window and the bills that emerge one by one from their pockets. The first is a fiver, the next two are singles. She smiles. Sees clearly now the corner of a ten-dollar bill and leans forward, budging the moment when they will begin to head her way. She takes another drag. Tendrils of smoke curl around her hand.
>
> Here they come.

Even as the city police close in on their action, the pair continue to work the station, motivated by a combination of habit and the thrill of outwitting even bigger marks. Almost always the victims have no idea they have been targeted, nor do they realize until later—long after the train has left or they've hailed a hack on the street outside the station—that they've been robbed of their watch or wallet. Only an aura of loss remains, drifting like cigarette smoke through the limestone columns of the Great Hall.

The losses Union Station presides over are not only material ones. In Hugh Garner's 1951 novel *Present Reckoning*, a soldier discharged at the end of World War II steps through the doors of Union Station into a city that seems not only indifferent but largely uninhabited:

> The wartime excitement lingered, but the war had ended the day before with the unconditional surrender of Japan. The wide station doors that had gobbled up the youth of the city for six years would soon begin to spew them forth again, but now, on this morning, the act of regurgitation had hardly begun, and only a few lonely and bewildered young men came through the station doors and looked askance at Civvy Street that they had left so eagerly years before.

For Garner's protagonist, Union Station represents both irrevocable rupture and a tedious sameness. After six years in transit, nearly every city looks the same, and by the time Tom Neelton returns to Toronto his contempt is nearly complete. For months he hangs around his old haunts and tries to reconnect with a woman he had known before going overseas, but he cannot seem to find a way back to the city he once thought he knew without destroying either it or himself and, in the end, he returns to Union Station to try his luck somewhere—anywhere—else.

A parallel transience inhabits the protagonists of Anne Michael's *Fugitive Pieces*. A Polish Holocaust survivor and his guardian, a Greek geographer who rescued him from the ruins of Europe, arrive like many thousands of others before and since, hoping to disappear into a city war has never entered:

> From the great limestone hall of Union Station, with its many tracks and tunnels, train passengers from the transatlantic docks at Montreal poured into the Toronto street. [...] There was a small crowd at the doors of the station, but from that one busy point, the city stretched deserted, like overflowing darkness beyond a small pool of lamplight. The travellers dispersed into taxis and, within minutes, even the wide plaza outside the station was empty.

As travellers vanish into its many crevices, the city seems deserted, except for Jakob and Athos who remain standing in front of the city's open gate, uncertain how to move forward and unable to go back.

The young protagonist of Rabindranath Maharaj's novel *The Amazing Absorbing Boy* gives the people who feel this sense of ceaseless exile a name: refugees. Riding the subway because there is nowhere else he can go, one afternoon Samuel lands at Union Station on a whim:

I got off there because I didn't want to return early to our apartment and so followed a rush of people out of the train and into the Union building. And the minute I entered the big hall all my loser feelings dropped off. Everybody was walking and walking and moving and moving in a long, never-ending stream. Some had briefcases, and others were dragging suitcases behind them like boxy puppies. Maybe they were leaving the city or going for a vacation or just returning from their jobs, but all this constant motion made everything feel temporary.

Feeling oddly at home in this transitional space, Samuel makes a habit of returning to Union Station, which, he reflects, "reminded me of those Star Wars bars with all sort of strange aliens sitting right next to each other and not noticing all the snouts and fish faces and extra eyes and antennae right on the opposite table." After he attends a seminar for immigrants at the Toronto Reference Library and then in the street is given a leaflet advocating for refugee rights, Samuel decides that these are the people he has been looking for at Union Station:

Refugees. I wondered how many people wandering around here were refugees. Was there some way to detect them? Something in their clothes or gestures? What about the Ethiopian man sitting by himself? He was too well dressed and had an expensive briefcase besides. The woman from India with a dot on her forehead? She looked too fat and happy. The pink stooped man wearing an old coat and hat? He might be too old. I changed benches and focused on another group. The seminar woman said they lived like ghosts and I imagined them, just like the Flash, vibrating at a special frequency that made them mostly invisible.

Having no way of knowing whether any—or all—of the people he encounters in Union Station are refugees, Samuel concludes that nearly everyone passing through the station is in flight from something.

In Paulette Jiles' novel *Sitting in the Club Car Drinking Rum and Karma Kola*, a man pursues a woman through the bowels of Union Station, neither of them sure whether it would be preferable for her to make or miss her connection:

Why wait for the baggage claim to mangle your bags when you've got an escape to make? She's up the stairs like a kamikaze homing pigeon, and he's right after her. Double takes as perfectly innocent travellers coming down the escalator get bumped aside by a fleeing paperhanger, a skip-tracer in pursuit—only he just wants to tell her goodbye. He wants to tell her he's going to join her. He might say he'll share the story if only she'd stay in it. He wants to get out of the way of the point of view. He's going to say he'll write home and say *Wish you were here* on a tacky postcard of the CN Tower.

But for this picture-postcard image to come true, either the woman will have to stop moving and confront whatever has kept her running between cities and the stories she has told about her life, or the man will have to start. As the perpetual stream of people passing through Union Station suggests, that might be a difficult thing to manage. In "Union Station," an essay appearing in Marc Baraness and Larry Richards' book *Toronto Places*, Katherine Govier describes Union Station as a theatre of endless departures, adding, "What is left? Footsteps on the stone floors. Echoes, which populate this space more than anything else. The announcer's disembodied voice high in the ceiling. The large, white-faced clock, at almost human height, which moved, and moves on."

SCENES FROM A LIBRARY

Martha Baillie's episodic Toronto novel *The Incident Report* is organized around 144 events narrated to have occurred in and around an imaginary library located in a real Toronto neighbourhood. Although the "incident reports" derive their structure from statements meant to document serious library-related offences ranging from theft to threatening conduct, the novel describes a far wider range of idiosyncratic activities engaged in by library patrons and staff, making Baillie's narrator a keen observer of the private preoccupations that play out in public places.

Despite their unexciting reputation, libraries are among the city's most intriguing public spaces. Far more than mausoleums of meaning, their dusty shelves sepulchres for rows of decaying tomes, libraries are stages for many kinds of human drama. Baillie describes library patrons who tuck religious tracts into books, hide beer cans in the piano, pleasure themselves with decidedly unerotic reading material or deliver silent orations to invisible audiences. Her most poignant episodes, however, are descriptions of distressed patrons who seek solace in the library's secluded environs. One afternoon, for example, Baillie's narrator observes a dishevelled library patron who walks in wearing an infant strapped into a snuggly. Concerned for the well-being of the baby, the librarian watches the patron—"a young woman pacing, talking under her breath, her thick socks falling and her hair a tangled nest"—until, near closing time, she sees into the snuggly and realizes the heartbreaking reality of the situation: "There was no infant. Only crumpled clothes stuffed in a snuggly."

At a time when churches lock their doors and charities have begun to keep banker's hours, urban libraries have become daytime shelters for the city's dispossessed, particularly those who are isolated, elderly, homeless, bored, lonely and have nowhere else to go. In Stephen Marche's novel *Raymond and Hannah*, a graduate student encounters an emaciated elderly man who passes the daytime hours in the rarefied confines of Robarts Library at the University of Toronto:

> Time has curved him like a hockey stick, and he has to use two crutches to keep his glacially slow movements somewhat steady. Distinct urine stains overlap in patches on the front of his pants. He smells. He shakes. Still, every day the old man climbs to the newspaper room on the library's fourth floor. There he scribbles letters to whatever editorial boards he happens to be angry with that day. Somnolently, disgustingly graceful, he departs when his work is done five or six hours later, and he may as well be a ghost, a stone rattling in Raymond's brain cage, a dream dreamt by someone in his place.

The man is so omnipresent that Raymond has come to think of him as "the elder, the ultimate reader, the daemon of Robarts Library."

Idiosyncratic behaviour in the city's libraries is hardly limited to patrons who wander in from the streets. The protagonist of Alana Wilcox's novel, *A Grammar of Endings*, is a librarian who begins to scribble in library books, as if by doing so she can rewrite the ending of a failed relationship. More curiously, in Timothy Findley's *Headhunter*, a clairvoyant employee at the Rosedale Public Library discovers how little power she has over her ability to raise the dead when, during an evening seminar, she inadvertently calls forth an arsonist who sets the library on fire. Despite Lilah's frantic efforts, much of the collection is lost, although she does manage to save copies of two Canadian classics—*Roughing It in the Bush* and *Life in the Clearings*—whose famous protagonist, Susanna Moodie, remains a grateful, ghostly presence in Lilah's life thereafter. Months later, while sitting in the newspaper reading room at the Toronto Reference Library on a snowy winter afternoon, Lilah inadvertently releases Joseph Conrad's infamous villain, Kurtz, from the pages of *Heart of Darkness*. Ignoring Lilah's commands that he return to the book, Kurtz strides out of the reference library to wreak havoc upon the city.

Unlike Kurtz, however, some protagonists seek nothing more than the comfort of being pressed between the pages. In Rob Budde's novel *The Dying Poem*, an obscure Toronto poet enters the empty Metropolitan Library an hour before its planned demolition by explosives and sits down in an empty reading room, three favoured volumes spread out around him:

> They recovered his ruined body almost twenty-four hours later. It was twisted and torn and only barely held together in places. When they uncovered him, his left

arm was miraculously raised above his head into the tonnes of rubble. Stretched straight up, his hand seemed to be reaching to touch something. Or as if to catch something lost in that chaotic last moment.

A book was lodged in his chest.

Recovered from the rubble, his death deemed a suicide, Henry Black leaves behind a life even more mysterious than the manner of his death. A filmmaker producing a documentary about Black's enigmatic life and death considers the poet's posthumous notoriety and concludes, "Such is the sacrifice for poetry."

"All books are a conjuring," writes Findley in *Headhunter*, referring to the capacity of literature to call forth the most powerful of human passions. But if books have magical qualities, then libraries are warehouses of the fantastic, waystations between the familiar city and the surreal streets so many Torontonians—particularly the poor, isolated, homeless or mentally ill—inhabit. It is a small wonder that public libraries attract so many strange goings-on, given their reputation as places where you can do almost anything you want—read, write, sleep, meditate, pray and even invoke the dead—just as long as it's quiet.

UP AGAINST CITY HALL

Every weekday, thousands of Torontonians step off the subway, lock up their bikes, nudge their way into parking spots and push past buskers and beggars to enter the complex of civic real estate containing Viljo Revell's City Hall and its sandstone shadow, the sprawling Romanesque Revival building designed by iconoclast architect Edward James Lennox, currently used as a courthouse and colloquially known as Old City Hall. Anchoring these public buildings is Nathan Phillips Square, a large paved plaza named after the mayor who motivated Toronto's first great experiment with architectural modernism. Presiding over the square are the curved towers of City Hall and the pod-like ovum of its council chambers, sometimes said to look like an unblinking eye or a pair of hands, but in truth resembling nothing so much as two bewildered penguins standing guard over an ostrich egg.

In *Stroll: Psychogeographic Walking Tours of Toronto*, urban explorer Shawn Micallef calls Nathan Phillips Square "a sacred civic space, perhaps the finest concrete manifestation of peace, order and good government in Canada." Emphasizing the square's role as a public space, Micallef adds,

> During the day, it's enjoyed by seemingly everybody: scores of office people, wayward hippie girls with back-packs twice as big as they are, lobbyists on cellphones, some homeless folks on the periphery and a constant stream of people crossing

the square on their way to City Hall. Crossing the square is a ceremonial march: you're forced to regard City Hall from afar and approach it on foot—it's huge, but you can walk right in.

Micallef goes on to compare Nathan Phillips Square to a classical Greek agora, containing "all the elements of a formal public space that became a civic living room." Micallef's enthusiasm for the square—one of the few public spaces in downtown Toronto, he points out, that "respects the right and need of citizens to gather"—is unmistakable, but not everyone shares his optimism.

In "Tale of Two Cities, " Irving Layton derides Toronto as a city preoccupied with sex and money, the long litany of its lust and greed culminating in Nathan Phillips Square:

> At Bloor and Bay
> I open my plastic bag
> for the golden rain to fill
> FALL golden coins FALL FALL keep FALLING
> dazzle and daze me with your meticulous shine [...]
> Holy Holy Holy Holy Holy
> and I sink with my bag
> under the floor of striptease joints
> where the sad men paste their eyes
> between the jittery cheeks of young girls
> to leave them for blue assholes
> and walk out blind in the noonday stare
> carrying their genitals in briefcases
> to Philips Square where all around them
> men and women are falling in a steady drizzle
> from the tall taller tallest building
> in a race with the golden rain to the pavements

If Layton considers unrestrained avarice a symptom of the city's spiritual malaise, Scott Symons is convinced it is the only possible cure. In *Civic Square*, his controversial homoerotic send-up of Toronto Toryism, Symons refers to Nathan Phillips Square as the "Anti-Hero" and "Anti-Body" not only of his book but of Toronto itself, a place without a Place:

> [T]he pickets gone we stroll instead through Osgoode backs New City Hall (and Old beyond) with open rink skate to music and the Archer, Moore's handiwork, stands narrowbone for all this square I noted as we entered here there was no focal

point instead it sucks me in as opens up spins head (makes gay!) lightweight until Old City Hall anchors in my open-up the New is half-ass while Old is Founding Father's Fallus

we need them both by God the one is cuntass that the other fulfills

Ultimately, Symons concludes, the only cure for High Toryism is to be fucked gloriously in the ass and, that accomplished, he and his lover watch the hated square dissolve and vanish, its reflecting pool dissolving into mudflats and alderbrushes.

More recently, in *Consolation*, Michael Redhill describes the new City Hall and its civic square as a place that is at once ludicrous and faintly menacing:

The cab left them at the bottom of Nathan Phillips Square on Queen Street. [...] Two hundred metres to the east was the red-brick old city hall, downgraded now to a traffic court. It had been deemed unsuitable for the city of the sixties, which had built itself something that looked like a broken ice-cream cone with a tumour in the middle. The plaza was made up of wide, square concrete panes floating over an unseeable depth. The inch-wide cracks between the panes suggested that they were movable, that if you stood on the wrong one, you'd be sucked down into a tar pit that flowed under city hall.

Intimating that getting sucked into the affairs of city council is akin to falling into a bottomless pit, Redhill characterizes the City Hall complex as cold and uninviting, an experience his protagonists confirm almost as soon as they open the heavy wooden doors and enter its mausoleum-like interior.

In *Civil Elegies*, undoubtedly the most well-known literary evaluation of Toronto's civic ambitions, Dennis Lee describes Nathan Phillips Square's unfulfilled promise, his long poem a paean to missed opportunities and moral cowardice in a city that has always stopped just shy of its own becoming:

I sat one morning by the Moore, off to the west
ten yards and saw though diffident my city nailed against the sky
in ordinary glory.
It is not much to ask. A place, a making,
two towers, a teeming, a genesis, a city.

Toronto has not managed to fulfil even these modest ambitions, Lee adds, challenging the myth of Mackenzie's famous rebellion by calling it "the first / spontaneous mutual retreat in the history of warfare." Describing the square as haunted by the ghosts of our civic forbears "still / demanding whether Canada will be," Lee notes that in the midst of this unfulfilled promise,

The spectres drift across the square in rows.
How empire permeates! And we sit down
in Nathan Philips Square, among the sun,
as if our lives were real.
Lacunae. Parking lots. Regenerations. [...]
[G]enerations of
acquiescent spectres gawk at the chrome
on American cars on Queen Street, gawk and slump and retreat.
And over the square where I sit, congregating above the Archer
they crowd in a dense baffled throng and the sun does not shine through.

The only resonant object in the square, Lee maintains, is Henry Moore's *Archer*, a large bronze sculpture that fills the void with tension, like a bow bent back so an arrow can seek its mark. *The Archer*, Lee writes,

Was shaped by earlier space and it ripples with
Wrenched stress, the bronze is flexed by
Blind aeonic throes
that bred and met in slow enormous impact
and they are still at large for the force in the bronze churns
through it, and lunges beyond and also the Archer declares
that space is primal, raw, beyond control and drives toward a
living stillness, its own.

These same forces—tectonic, aching, endless—forge cities and nations, but only if we remember the passions they arouse in us long enough to act on them.

In "The Man in the Moore," one of the stories in *Noman's Land*, Gwendolyn MacEwen finds a similar resonance in *The Archer*. Her protagonist, an amnesic searching for his memory in the city without a past, finds that the sculpture sparks something in him:

'I have the most extraordinary feeling that I *know* this thing,' he thought, and then realized that he had spoken aloud, for a bum who was sitting on a nearby bench got up and joined him in scrutinizing the sculpture.

'You like this thing?' he asked. 'I don't like this thing. Nobody likes this thing, they just get used to it, that's all. Piece of crap, if you ask me.'

'I mean I feel like I *know* it, it's almost as though I've been inside it, you know? I'm the only man in this city who's seen it from the *inside*. [...]I kid you not, my dear man. You see, yesterday I remembered something. It's not much, but it's a start. See down at the bottom where it says H. NOACK—BERLIN? Well that's the name of the foundry in Germany where they cast Moore's stuff—and I was there. Yes, I was there sometime in the sixties, I remember it now. I visited the foundry, and since I knew something about welding, one of the workers let me crawl in through the square hole in the piece and weld a couple of seams inside.'

'You mean it's hollow?' asked the bum.

'Of course it's hollow. [...] God, I remember it like it was yesterday.'

'You mean you were literally inside it? Like in real life?'

'I was. And I remember workers left things like cigarette butts and coffee cups inside. I left a ball point pen in there; it fell from my shirt. I can't prove it to you, but if they ever opened this thing up they'd find the pen in there. A red pen. A Parker.'

As if in answer to Lee's declaration that "it is time to honour the void," MacEwen's protagonist recalls having probed the sculpture's hollow interior and seen what was inside. In this sense Noman is better off than the city he inhabits: at least he knows he is amnesic. But to return to Lee, if the square, like the sculpture—like the citizens of this city—is indeed empty, it is the kind of emptiness that invites us to fill it with something, a myth we can believe in, some meaningful part of ourselves. It becomes possible to share Micallef's optimism about City Hall and the square that anchors it: it's huge, but you can walk right in.

TORONTO'S TOWER OF BABEL

In the ancient city of Babylon, or so a very old story goes, a great tower was built by a civilization whose people wanted to communicate directly with the gods. Angered at this arrogance, the gods caused the people to speak in different tongues, ending their collaboration and scattering the tribes across the land. Unable or unwilling to work through their differences, the people did not realize the tremendous gift they had received. The great tower fell into ruins.

The CN Tower is Toronto's Babel. Completed in 1976 as a telecommunications tower, for a generation it was the tallest tower in the world and is still viewed as a symbol of technological and architectural ascendency. Rising high above the city, gleaming in sunlight, glowing at night, it is the world's most visible urban muse. In *Accidental City: The Transformation of Toronto*, Robert Fulford calls the CN Tower a "concrete pencil," adding, "It redraws our local map, rewrites our memories of Toronto." This is an especially apt metaphor, one that points toward the ways Torontonians narrate our experiences of the Tower, representing it variously as a passive backdrop, an empty vessel, a "monument to nothing," a phallic symbol, a spirit tree and a beacon of light, tolerance and hope.

Even when we turn our backs upon it, the CN Tower remains a sly presence in our photographs and narratives. Its shadow glides ceaselessly across our memories of the city like the second hand of time. The tower is always there in the corner of our gaze, a visible totem to the ways we inhabit and imagine the city. Far more than simply a phallic object or an architectural monument, it marks Toronto's paracartographic origin point, standing at the very intersection of the city's axes, where all the coordinates resolve to zero. The tower is Toronto's tallest tale, resonating like a frequency between the real and the imagined city and joining them into fragments of a textual map of Toronto that is continually redefined and redrawn.

Despite its visual prominence, from the beginning the CN Tower posed difficulties for Torontonians uncertain about its symbolism. In "Six Months of the CN Tower," Pier Giorgio Di Cicco writes,

> it goes up, & one knows time has passed.
> it flashes at us now. the streets fall
> into it, as if to say, this is what
> it all comes to. it fools us / sometimes
> people talk about it, up here.
> it reminds us of what it takes up
> place for / an absence / something to
> occupy us.

To Di Cicco, the tower is a symbol of spiritual ennui and cultural emptiness, a monument to materialism that fails to bring transcendence because the preoccupations it commemorates are worldly ones.

Gwendolyn MacEwen extends this reading in *Noman's Land*, calling the CN Tower "a monument to nothing, a space-ship that would never have lift-off, a rocket without a launching pad." Similarly, in "Tower and Dome," poet Diana Fitzgerald Bryden suggests that the tower symbolizes nothing so strongly as the aching proximity of fantasy and frustration, describing it as "—that unplunged hypodermic— / a bubble of thin air." Tellingly, to Bryden the tower is revealed most plainly when low-lying winter clouds roll in off the lake and reduce it to a headless stump.

In *Outage*, a novel about the cultural costs of technological compulsion, Bruce Powe measures the CN Tower—"a landmark where no one lives or stays"—against Middle Eastern minarets designed and used to "establish a pathway like a funnel between the earth and sky, between humankind and the invisible." In contrast, any messages emanating from the tower are inchoate, too convoluted or confused to be understood:

This tower is a source of ghostly voices, turbulent speech, stray notes, and static, an infinite variety that may bear no single message, only the enticements and variations of energy, complex and nomadic, a stir and sound more enigmatic than any structure that we could make.

This is the tower's central enigma: it can stand for anything—or perhaps nothing at all.

Daniel Jones suggests the latter in his infamous, scatological poem, "Things That I Have Put into My Asshole." Inventorying objects his narrator has sodomized himself with, ranging from the organic—"[s]aliva and semen and butter and baby oil, / tongues and thumbs and fingers of women"—to the architectural—"the intersection of Bathurst and Queen, / Honest Ed's Warehouse, / Hamilton Ontario"—Jones's poem culminates in an outrageous performance of *objektsexualität* as his narrator is penetrated by the CN Tower. Announcing, "I came all over Bay Street, / as the world's highest disco, / rotated upon my prostate," Jones declares the tower even more completely spent:

> It lies limp on the frozen surface
> of Lake Ontario.
> You can barely see the tungsten bulbs
> spelling 'Eat a lobster'
> through the film of K-Y jelly.
> GO FREE TORONTONIANS!
> The small sacrifice
> of a very large asshole.

Deflated and drained of its power, the tower collapses, liberating the citizens of Toronto from its omnipresent phallic silhouette and freeing them to fill the horizon with their own stories of the city.

Since Jones, the image of a toppled CN Tower has become something of a trope in Toronto literature. In *Your Secrets Sleep with Me*, Darren O'Donnell suggests that the CN Tower is too derelict an image to represent the city when, early in the novel, a tornado topples the tower into the lake. More shocked than Toronto's citizens are the other downtown buildings, who wonder whether the collapse of the tower should be considered a consequence of hubris or a suspected suicide:

> As the structure formerly known as the world's tallest freestanding lies in the lake waiting for news of a better day, there's heated talk among the other buildings, a debate that rages around whether the tower can't get up or won't get up. The

smaller, older buildings all seem to agree that it can't but won't, while some of the bigger bank buildings claim that won't is the same as can't, that a loss of will is a loss of will and once the juice is gone the juice is gone, you might as well use the thing as the first leg in a walkway connecting to America.

Civic leaders consider the fate of the tower, uncertain whether to rebuild it or transform the structure into something new. Some are content to leave it lying in the lake, while others, citing civic pride and national identity, argue that the tower should be resurrected. Ultimately, however, while the tower's collapse engenders feelings of loss and displacement, the empty horizon also represents an opening, an opportunity to revisit the intentions of the tower's original designers. O'Donnell writes,

> It has become a symbol of what's possible for that teenaged city, for that youthful country. It's a gracefully designed monstrosity, conceived at a time when to be a citizen of that sprawling nation was to be just on the verge of happening.

No longer pinned down by the power of the tower's presence, Torontonians are free to play, to protest, to speak truthfully for the first time, to listen, to love and even, as one protagonist does, to levitate above the city unimpeded by the tower, viewing Toronto from every possible perspective before unravelling among the stars.

Perhaps this dreamed-of destruction would not be necessary if only Torontonians could learn to decipher the tower's essential riddle. But decoding its blinking message is a challenge even to the generation of Torontonians who have grown up in its shadow. In Catherine Bush's *Minus Time*, a young girl watches the tower transform the city's horizon, measuring its seemingly inexorable progress while perched in the back seat of her parents' car:

> The road dropped away in front of us, the whole city spread below us, the gray concrete stump that was the beginning of the CN Tower visible in the farthest distance. The Tower was going to be the tallest freestanding structure in the world, with a huge communications antenna at the top. [...] We had watched the tower being built: Each time we drove over the steep hill on Avenue Road it had grown a little bigger, one cement block set on top of another, until sections of its enormous radio antenna were being lifted into place by helicopter. *A new age in communications is born*, a voice on the radio had told us.

Two decades later the tower—and its role as a giant radio antenna—develops a more personal and poignant significance for Helen when it becomes the closest possible point of contact with her mother, an astronaut circling the earth every ninety minutes during a record-breaking space endurance mission. To celebrate the new record, civic officials have decided that the city's lights will be dimmed—all except for those on the tower, which will glow and pulse as the world's tallest freestanding structure becomes a satellite link-up to the space station. Asked to participate in the spectacle, Helen is disturbed not only to learn that her private communications with her mother will become part of a public broadcast, but at the deeper contradiction of contact that would deny any prospect of corporeal intimacy. In a clarifying moment of refusal, she leaves the city entirely and drives to a remote part of the province where, lying in the darkness beside a silent lake, she can see both the tower and the space station passing overhead. And it is only in this way that she feels she can reach her mother, at a remove that acknowledges the unbearable distance between earth and space and the efforts made to bridge it.

As Bush's novel suggests, the CN Tower is a symbol less of size than of distance. This latter meaning, if of secondary importance to many native-born Torontonians, is certainly not lost of newcomers to the city. In M. G. Vassanji's *No New Land*, the CN Tower serves as a blinking beacon to Nurdin Lalani, an immigrant who addresses an outsider's silent questions to it from his apartment window high above the Don Valley. The tower's presence as a destination, even a deity, is evident throughout the novel:

> From their apartment, through the living-room window and the balcony, the Lalanis could see, penetrating through a mass of foliage in the distance, the top of the CN Tower blinking its mysterious signal. In rain or shine, a permanent presence in their lives, a seal on their new existence, the god-head towards which the cars on the parkway spilled over, from which having propitiated they came racing back.

Like many newcomers to Toronto, the Lalanis map their new city between two poles: at the north, their apartment in Don Mills, and to the south, the inscrutable tower, the only other familiar structure in the city. Even across the divide of roadways and ravines, Nurdin is certain the tower hears his adjurations. To visitors he describes the tower as a god, albeit a mysterious one. But just as he is unable to penetrate the city's racial barriers or grasp the incomprehensible subtleties of its bureaucratic dialects, he cannot translate the message the CN Tower blinks in response to his silent questions, the "coded message he could not understand."

The CN Tower is the origin of Nurdin's mental map of the city, the site of navigation and reckoning. At the same time, it reflects his position as an outsider, excluded by colour, custom and some whispered undercurrent in the city's language. Like everyone in the city, Nurdin orients himself toward the solid presence of the tower, but the tower orients him as well, marking him as an Other and putting him in his place. Always visible, yet remote and impenetrable, the CN Tower is a potent symbol not only of the oceans Nurdin has crossed to arrive in Toronto, but also of the great distance that remains ahead of him.

Still, if there is any possibility of bridging such cultural divisions, the CN Tower—the one part of Toronto everybody can see and interpret in their own way—is the city's most likely meeting point. Nalo Hopkinson's speculative novel *Brown Girl in the Ring* represents the CN Tower as a beacon that connects two worlds, its energy ultimately suffusing the apocalyptic city and suggesting the possibility of spiritual cleansing and renewal. Hopkinson's Toronto is riven by poverty and by roadblocks raised by the satellite suburbs intent on severing themselves from the inner city, which has become a poverty-stricken, gang-infested war zone. Hopkinson maps the city as "a cartwheel half-mired in muddy water, its hub just clearing the surface." The CN Tower is the axis of this mired cartwheel, occupied by a criminal gang that dominates the decrepit downtown and uses black magic to pillage and poison the city. Ti-Jeanne, the granddaughter of a Caribbean spiritualist and healer who lives in the former visitor's centre at Riverdale Farm, is roused to resistance when Rudy, a shadow-catcher, steals her grandmother's heart to sell it as an organ transplant for the province's ailing premier. Calling the orishas—all the oldest ancestors, the ones who can carry her prayers to the God Father—to the CN Tower to break the duppy bowl in which Rudy has imprisoned the souls of murdered citizens, Ti-Jeanne realizes that tower contains power of its own:

> She remembered her grandmother's words: *The centre pole is the bridge between the worlds.* Why had those words come to her right then? Ti-Jeanne thought of the centre pole of the palais, reaching up into the air and down toward the ground. She thought of the building she was in. The CN Tower. And she understood what it was: 1,815 feet of the tallest centre pole in the world. [...] For like the spirit tree that the centre pole symbolized, the CN Tower dug roots deep into the ground where the dead lived and pushed high into the heavens where the oldest ancestors lived. The tower was their ladder into this world.

Ti-Jeanne calls up toward the heavens and down into the earth for all the ancestors and all their children to come to her aid. The pole sways and throbs with the cadences of their drumming and the thunder of their multitudinous voices. A furious storm breaks over the tower, dissolving the dark duppy magic and ushering a healing sunrise across the city.

This image of ancestral voices swirling around the tower is repeated in Hédi Bouraoui's novel *Thus Speaks the CN Tower*,[85] only where Hopkinson introduces the collective spirits of her protagonist's Afro-Caribbean ancestors rising from the underworld, Bouraoui channels the ghosts of Toronto's Aboriginal inhabitants—those who built the tower as well as those who walked the landscape long before there was ever a city on the lake. Bouraoui's narrator is the CN Tower itself, recast as a graceful, feminine quasi-deity who watches over the city and treats her triangular base as a symbol of the three founding people of Canada as well as an emblem of national unity and cultural tolerance. The tower also serves as the setting for a variety of intersecting cultural negotiations involving, among others, an Aboriginal construction worker who caps the tower's summit and proceeds to leap from its pinnacle, a beautiful Anglo-Saxon executive who hires and fires according to inscrutable whims, an educated Sudanese reduced to running the tower's elevators, a pair of conniving French Canadians who plot the tower's destruction and a mad poet who scribbles cryptic notes and crumples them in the tower's stairwells. With a nod to Nietzsche's *Thus Spake Zarathustra*, Bouraoui argues that the tower is a paragon of human possibility, a bellwether that embodies not only Torontonians' worst motives but also their best impulses. Attesting that "[f]rom my summit, I do nothing but beam words. I capture them, but especially transmit them," Bouraoui's tower describes a spontaneous assembly at her base that, unlike most protests, is a celebration of free speech:

> The Torontonians arrived from every direction in aprons, blue jeans, shorts and swimsuits. Under a hot sun, they brandished hundreds of placards. [...] The slogans overlap, each one claiming to be original in the Canadian stream: "The Time of Scorn is over," "The Era of Dignity has arrived." Each one chooses to express himself with a different choreography. An Indian declaims, in the holistic art of Kathakali which is, simultaneously, masked theatre, dance, song, tied to mystery: "At troubling moments, you must plunge in," "All Good Things belong to the Creator, the Effort must be man's." Souleyman waves a banner with a Mali proverb: "Wish good luck to others, so that you will have your own luck," an Amazigh: "Man is made of alfalfa, you must break it to twist it." The Toronto polyphony vibrates with multiple accents

Revelling in this "enthusiastic assembly without frontiers," the Tower muses,

---

85 Originally published in French in 1999 as *Ainsi Parle la Tour CN*, Bouraoui's novel was short-listed for the Ontario Trillium Book Award and won the Prix Afrique and the Prix Christine Dumitriu van Saanen in 2000.

In my workshop tongues of rock and language of crystal, steel words and gripping phrases of mortar are conjugated ... No voice has been ignored! All are invited to take up the challenge. Of a height never attained. Instead of stifling the dissident voices, Toronto tries to harmonize them. In the manner of the Moose-Spirit. To the hardworking enterprise of the Jews the mercurial Italian is grafted. And at the heart of this warm chorale other voices are mingled: Portuguese, Spanish, Caribbean, Latin American ... restoring Latinity to its first harmony. The latter, in all its dignity, dialogues with Anglo-Saxon which gets a grip on itself, instead of yielding to the temptation of the stratified neo-colonial dance, doesn't sell off any of its cardinal points, reintegrates the waves of pride. Thus it invents my body baptized as a Tower.

As Bouraoui's novel indicates, far from being a "monument to nothing," the CN Tower is a lightning rod for free expression and a potent symbol of both struggle and achievement.

Despite the diversity of these literary renderings, nearly four decades after its completion one wonders whether the CN Tower can possibly retain any of its magic. Since the 1970s Toronto has become a far more cosmopolitan city—residents are more likely to peer down upon the tower from airplane seats than ride an elevator 346 metres to its windswept observation decks. Satellite transmissions have supplanted many of the tower's telecommunications capabilities, portending a time when technological advances will render the tower functionally obsolete. More critically, when the Burj Khalifa skyscraper in Dubai officially surpassed the height of the CN Tower upon its completion in 2009, local critics were quick to deride the CN Tower's rapidly fading claim to be the tallest freestanding structure in the world.

As recently as 2010, *The Guinness Book of World Records* has continued to list the CN Tower as the world's tallest tower, although other structures, among them the Guangzhou Tower in China, soon seem destined to surpass it. Still, in many ways Toronto can afford to have the CN Tower usurped by record-breaking structures in other cities. At one time the CN Tower was the centre of our identity, a signal that Toronto had achieved something worthy of the world's notice. In 1976, the year the tower was completed, it was possible to see the edge of the city from the tower, which was visible from virtually every part of Toronto as well as the surrounding countryside. In the intervening decades, however, Toronto has grown well beyond the tower's gaze and, accordingly, perhaps we can afford to be gracious to the tower's usurpers— especially those like Burj Khalifa, because what is Dubai but a city much like Toronto was in 1976: brash, youthful, a work in progress, eager to make its mark and thereby prove itself a "world-class" city.

Torontonians who declare themselves bored with the CN Tower or consider the skyline cheapened by its presence would do well to consider the fate of the World Trade Centre in New York. Until September 11, 2001, many New Yorkers considered the Manhattan skyline to have been marred by the massive edifices of the World Trade towers. Since the towers were destroyed in the 9/11 terrorist attacks, one of the most poignant representations of New York has shown up in artists' renderings of the Manhattan skyline, a gap showing between the buildings like a pair of missing teeth—but with the silhouette of the missing towers still reflected in the water.

– 3 –

THE CITY OF NEIGHBOURHOODS

THE POETICS OF WALKING

In *Toronto: An Illustrated History of Its First 12,000 Years*, historian Ronald Williamson describes a set of 11,000-year-old human footprints reportedly uncovered in the clay under Lake Ontario by city workers digging a water-supply tunnel near Hanlan's Point in 1908. The find includes more than one hundred footprints, including those of a child, representing a small group appearing to walk in the direction of the contemporary lakeshore.[86]

Eleven millennia after these earliest Torontonians made their mark on the local landscape, we continue to engage most meaningfully with the city by walking, our own ephemeral passage measured by shadows on the sidewalk and patterns in the dust. It is only on foot, in fact, that we are able to find our way into the city within the city, because its guideposts—invisible openings to unnamed alleyways, vernacular landscapes of front-yard fountains and back-yard bocce courts, shifting densities of cats and dogs, and subtle variations in porch pillars between one neighbourhood and the next—are discernible only at the speed of walking. In *Wanderlust: A History of Walking*, essayist Rebecca Solnit suggests that "the mind, like the feet, works at about three miles an hour"; she goes on to describe walking as one of our most primordial activities, an observation that connects us to Toronto's forbearers, the group of hunters and gatherers whose footprints were once preserved in the 11,000-year-old muck under Lake Ontario.

In "Walking Off the Map," a 2006 essay describing Toronto's contemporary culture of urban explorers, John Bentley Mays writes, "They are all walkers, and their tread along the city's streets is intent and focused. We see them moving at the pace of dowsers looking for streams buried beneath the pavement; and dowsers they are, these seekers for the fugitive urban imaginary in the solid matter of the city." Evoking journeys motivated by "curiosity about what lies behind locked gates, under manhole covers, down disreputable alleys," Mays suggests their movements may be traced to an intellectual genealogy mapped and remapped by *flâneurs*, Situationists, psychogeographers and public-space activists.[87] But in showing that the city is better understood as a

---

86 See Williamson, 2008; also Leslie Scrivener, 23 November 2008. "The Enigma of Lake Ontario's 11,000-year-old footprints," *Toronto Star*.

87 Readers interested in psychogeography in Toronto are directed, first, to Shawn Micallef's excellent book, *Stroll: Psychogeographic Walking Tours of Toronto* (2010), and to its forerunners, John Bentley Mays' *Emerald City: Toronto Visited* (1994), Harry Bruce's *The Short Happy Walks of Max MacPherson* (1968) and Henry Scadding's *Toronto of Old* (1873;1878). More broadly, the psychogeography movement has its roots in the Lettrist International and Situationist International societies active in 1950s and 1960s Paris: an influential work of this era is Guy Debord's "Theory of the Derive," first published in *Internationale Situationnist* in 1958. The Situationists held that seemingly

series of parallel universes rather than lines on a grid, these excursions reveal something far deeper than Toronto's cartographical quirks. The walkers Mays describes are dowsing not merely for the city but for the city's stories. Unfolding like maps across the vivid terrain of the urban imagination, these stories are the vital linchpin connecting city dwellers to what cultural theorist Michel de Certeau calls the "poetic and mythic experience of space."

In *The Practice of Everyday Life*, de Certeau refers to "the long poem of walking" as a series of rhetorical strategies expressed in physical space: at street level the body turns, detours and returns in the same way a phrase manifests, inverts and completes itself on the printed page. In this sense walking is at once lyrical and vividly metaphorical: we leap ahead, retrace our steps, omit passages, take shortcuts, lose ourselves, experience surprise and become open to discovery. In short, we walk in the same way we read—and for that matter, write.

At the same time, our movements through the city are more than merely textual recreations of urban life. As de Certeau adds,

> If it is true that *forests of gestures* are manifest in the streets, their movement cannot be captured in a picture, nor can the meaning of their movements be circumscribed in a text. Their rhetorical transplantation carries away and displaces the analytical, coherent proper meanings of urbanism; it constitutes a "wandering of the semantic" produced by masses that make some parts of the city disappear and exaggerate others, distorting it, fragmenting it, and diverting it from its immobile order.

Ultimately, the deepest meanings of the city are inscribed not only in individual texts but are inherently interstitial, the outcome of invisible interactions between people and narrative paths that intersect, contradict and complete one another. The city's stories nearly infinite in their variety.

Performance scholar Mike Pearson and anthropologist Michael Shanks extend this metaphor in their groundbreaking, interdisciplinary book, *Theatre/Archaeology*, describing walking as

> a spatial acting out, a kind of narrative, and the paths and places direct our choreography. This regular moving from one point to another is a kind of mapping, a kind of narrative understanding. Paths link familiar places and bring the possibility for repeated actions. Different paths enact different stories of action. Walking is like a story, a series of events, for which the land acts as a mnemonic.

---

aimless walking represented a radical insubordination to capitalism.

In Toronto, the city of neighbourhoods, this mnemonic is especially important because so many of the city's landscapes—the tawdry excess of the Yonge Street strip, the Kew Beach boardwalk, shade-dappled lawns in the Kingsway and the wind tunnels at King and Bay—are brought to life most vividly when they are walked across, argued over and generally animated by the embodied performances of urban life. As Chinese-American geographer Yi-Fu Tuan points out in *Topophilia*, his famous analysis of human engagement with the physical landscape, we perceive space and give meaning to place by measuring it against the scale of our own bodies. In this sense it becomes clear that it is not only at the speed of walking but at the scale of the lived body that cities—and their stories—become truly legible. Even when our walking appears aimless, we play with the city's narratives, rewriting them with every step.

But how do we make sense of our movements across Toronto's temporal, spatial and social terrain? How do we translate this "wandering of the semantic" into a collection of coherent narratives of the city? In an essay exploring literary representations of one of Toronto's most storied neighbourhoods, the Annex, literary scholar and poet Stephen Cain argues that an engaged urban poetics can transform everyday encounters with place into larger narratives that tap directly into the city's mythological well. Explaining the need for poetry that does more than merely describe or commemorate the city, Cain writes,

> I seek a poetry that is vital, alive in responding to the city dynamically and dramatically, and one that urges its readers to move off the page to create meaning in the poem—and constructs a meaning that is activated only when the reader has engaged with the city in a like manner. A poetry that rereads the streets, the signage, the geography and cultural atmosphere of Toronto in its very structure. That is, not a poem *about* the Humber River, but a poem that attempts to *become*, in its rhythm, language, sound effect, the Humber. Not a poem *describing* walking through Kensington Market, but a poem that *creates* the psychological experience of walking in Kensington through verbal dissonance, register shifting, typography and juxtaposition.[88]

Introducing the work of Canadian cultural innovator bpNichol, whose multiple-volume poetic epic, *The Martyrology*, engages at length with the Annex,[89] Cain shows how Nichol evokes the neighbourhood's mythos by metaphorically

---

88 Cain, 2006. Among other works, Stephen Cain is also the author of *Torontology* (2001), a collection of poems not so much about Toronto as inspired by an extended engagement with the city's social and spatial terrain.

89 bpNichol's *Martyrology* is a long poem published in nine parts by Coach House Press between 1972 and 1992. In the *Martyrology* (as in the rest of his prodigious output) Nichol reinvents nationhood, identity, politics, reality and the nature of faith while redefining poetic style and structure.

deconstructing street names to evoke the city's primordial landscape of buried watercourses and the ancient shore of Lake Iroquois lapping at the edge of Davenport (which Nichol renders as "Daven's Port") Road. Cain then undertakes a psychogeographic jaunt through the Annex using spatial references in *The Martyrology Book V* as a guide, reporting that "what emerges is an accidental arousing of latent memories and half-forgotten experiences that suddenly gain new significance."

As we travel further into the city within the city, our own latent memories and half-forgotten experiences stirred by literary evocations of local landscapes, we begin to respond with our own stories, new narratives that alternately coincide with, challenge, add colour to and reconsider the experience of place. And if we travel far enough, eventually we will reach the part of the city where, as Gwendolyn MacEwen writes in *Afterworlds*, "Nothing remembers its name because / It has become its name."

THE CITY OF NEIGHBOURHOODS

In an essay published in David Macfarlane's anthology *Toronto: A City Becoming*, philosopher Mark Kingwell writes that Toronto is "not a city in the modern sense of a unified whole." Describing Toronto as "a linked series of towns held loosely together by the gravitational force of its downtown core,"[90] Kingwell argues that Toronto has no "normative or mythic" centre, "no single agora or narrative." He has it half right: this city *is* a loose agglomeration of small towns—but it is precisely this feature that gives Toronto much of its identity.

Almost before the ink was dry on John Graves Simcoe's 1793 town plan,[91] Toronto's residents had already begun to segregate themselves into districts carved up according to culture or class, and many of Toronto's most distinctive neighbourhoods—among them Yorkville, the Annex, Forest Hill, Parkdale and the Junction—had their origins as autonomous towns and villages whose existence was predicated in part upon their spatial and social separation from Toronto. Even after having gradually been annexed, absorbed or amalgamated

90 In describing Toronto as a city without a metaphysical centre, Kingwell engages in some cartographic sleight-of-hand. Nearly all large cities—London, New York, Paris, Los Angeles and San Francisco in particular—have become sprawling agglomerations of individual communities characterized by distinct identities and intense local loyalties that come close to equalling and sometimes trumping their connection to the metropolitan centre. Still, as Michael Redhill's protagonist observes in *Consolation*, "it's only overwhelming if you try to take it all in at once."

91 Earlier plans for Toronto (which Simcoe renamed York) exist, but Simcoe's 1793 sketch was the first to incorporate the elongated rectangular grid upon which the contemporary city is based. This and other plans for the city are beautifully arranged and contextualized in Derek Hayes' *Historical Atlas of Toronto* (2008).

into the central city,[92] many of these communities have retained their distinct identities. Perhaps this is why, nearly fifteen years after a massive, final amalgamation absorbed the cities of York, North York, Etobicoke, Scarborough, the Borough of East York and the old boundaries of Toronto into what is colloquially known as the Megacity,[93] Toronto's municipal code remains a clumsy pastiche of local by-laws and the City has not yet adopted a comprehensive zoning by-law to replace the forty-three zoning codes inherited from formerly autonomous municipal entities.

Novelist Hugh Garner once described Toronto as "a score of cities joined together by geographical propinquity."[94] In their popular 1965 song "Toronto the Good," satirical folk performance act the Brothers-in-Law lampooned Toronto, deriding it as a place where "an antique administration drags on / like a bunch of small villages rolled into one."[95] In *Raymond and Hannah*, novelist Stephen Marche characterizes Toronto as a city where "the streets proceed tiresomely through the neighbourhoods in which each house tries to be more ordinary than the next." Where Marche sees ceaseless banality, however, Margaret Atwood senses something sinister in Toronto's repetition of architectural styles, cadences of red brick, long rows of identical verandahs and narrow front walks. In *Cat's Eye*, Atwood's narrator returns to Toronto after a long absence and finds the city essentially unchanged despite its surface veneer of glittering cosmopolitanism: "Underneath the flourish and ostentation is the old city, street after street of thick red brick houses, with their front porch pillars like the off-white stems of toadstools and their watchful, calculating windows. Malicious, grudging, vindictive, implacable." Still, for most Torontonians, the city's distinct neighbourhoods are sources of comfort and belonging,

---

92 Toronto owes its present boundaries to a series of annexations and amalgamations dating to the nineteenth century. The eponymous Annex was annexed in several bursts between 1883 and 1888. Rosedale was absorbed in 1887. Parkdale was annexed in 1889. The Junction—also known as the Town of West Toronto—joined Toronto in 1909. Forest Hill remained a separate village until 1967, when it was annexed along with the Village of Swansea in the west end. Toronto's most controversial annexation—imposed by the Province in the face of vigorous opposition from local residents—was the merging of York, East York, North York, Etobicoke, Scarborough, the regional Municipality of Metropolitan Toronto and the former City of Toronto into a single megacity in 1998.
93 In 1997 the Province adopted legislation to amalgamate the member cities of the Municipality of Metropolitan Toronto into a single tier of government, and effective 1 January 1998, the present boundaries of the City of Toronto—stretching from Lake Ontario to Steeles Avenue and from Etobicoke Creek to the Rouge River—came into effect. This amalgamation, enacted against the will of Toronto-area residents and despite a prolonged filibuster in the provincial legislature, remains controversial, although no serious effort has been made to dissolve the Megacity subsequently. Indeed, a variety of proponents have argued that Toronto should become a separate province with new powers under the Canadian Constitution.
94 Quoted in Mann, 1970.
95 "Toronto the Good" appears on the Brothers-in-Law's sophomore album, *The Brothers-in-Law Strike Again* (1966), as well as a variety of greatest-hits compilations.

places where it is possible to retreat from the frenzied pace of Toronto's twin preoccupation with commerce and traffic.

In 2009 the *Toronto Star* published a map of Toronto identifying more than 170 of the city's known neighbourhoods.[96] Describing the patchwork of neighbourhoods as "part of our mental geography," the newspaper pointed out that Torontonians' passion for our most local environs is steeped in our particular history as well as the desire to belong to an identifiable social community that functions at the human scale. This impulse to belong is so important to Torontonians that real estate agents regularly stretch informal neighbourhood boundaries to tap into their perceived cachet, a phenomenon that has given rise to "West Kingsway," "South Annex," "East Riverdale" and the cartographically confusing "Bloor West North."

Toronto's neighbourhoods are distinguished by local history, architectural character, cultural composition and, perhaps above all, their sense of separation from the amorphous mass of urbanity that has grown into North America's fifth-largest city. They are also delineated by topography: ravines, rail lines, arterial roads and commercial concentrations that serve as bridges as well as boundaries between the city's residential enclaves. But if these distinctions seem neutral or sociologically inconsequential, it must be acknowledged that Toronto's neighbourhoods are also divided by class—socio-economic boundaries that partition the city as firmly as if a fence had been erected between them.

Populated largely by racialized minorities and recent immigrants, low-income neighbourhoods like Regent Park and the Jane-and-Finch corridor have become informal ghettos, their residents isolated by social discrimination and geographical determinism. In *Poverty by Postal Code*, a 2004 report prepared by the United Way, a young Regent Park resident tells an interviewer, "When you apply for a job you never say you're from the Park. One of my friends got a job at a bank but he didn't put his address. You have to lie so they don't think you're a thug." This experience is echoed in Graham McNamee's young adult novel *Acceleration*, set in Toronto's Lawrence Heights, an area known as "the Jungle" only partly because of its labyrinthine streets. Having grown up enduring the social stigma of living in public housing, McNamee's narrator counters the reputation of his neighbourhood as a breeding ground for gangbangers and welfare bums:

> Don't get the wrong idea. It's not like the projects you see on TV, with drive-by shootings, Chihuahua-sized rats, and kids falling down elevator shafts. The Jungle

---

96 "The Star unveils unique map of neighbourhoods. *Toronto Star*, 8 March 2009.

is just a worn-down kind of place where the kids run wild and herds of cats live out back by the garages. It's right on the edge of an industrial wasteland—factories, a steel mill and a strip mall a couple blocks down. Some kids at school call the place Welfare Towers, which is a lie. People here work. Most of them. They're just not rich.

When Duncan realizes a nearby construction site will soon accommodate middle-class condominiums, he tells a friend who comments, cynically, "Who's going to buy a condo next to the Jungle? I mean, what a view!" Familiar with the Jungle's reputation, Duncan responds, "I'm sure they'll put a barbed-wire fence around the new place to keep us out."

Still, it is not only poor and racialized Torontonians who sometimes feel walled in. In "Ghetto of the Mind," an essay appearing in William Kilbourn's anthology *The Toronto Book*, journalist Erna Paris articulates the sense of confinement experienced by young women growing up in the "uterine closeness" of Forest Hill:

> Our lives in the Forties and Fifties were insular and "unreal"—unconnected to the WASP reality of Toronto, unconnected to the rural reality of Canada. We knew almost nothing beyond the Village, the downtown department stores where we'd sometimes wander on Saturday afternoons and charge clothes to our fathers' accounts, and the bits of northern Ontario where we summered and wondered at the people who stayed there after Labor Day.

Novelist Sharon Abron Drache expands on this narrative, describing Forest Hill as a "golden ghetto" in an eponymous collection of short stories about young and middle-aged women who find themselves chafing against the constraints of Forest Hill's tight-knit Jewish community. They and their parents or husbands may have striven to establish themselves in material comfort in this exclusive enclave, but those efforts have not made it any less confining.

Whether comforting or confining, Toronto's neighbourhoods help define our sense of urban identity. Laid out along the city's streets like knots in a storyteller's cord, Toronto's most distinctive neighbourhoods are recognizable less for their architecture or the size of their dwellings than for the stories that emerge from their streets. In contrast to the deep-seated social indifference widely supposed to characterize the contemporary urban condition, people in Toronto neighbourhoods are drawn together by the shared experience of blackouts, break-ins, bedbugs and broken elevators, grinding poverty, inherited wealth, shocking deaths, mysterious disappearances, skyrocketing rents, soaring real estate values and, perhaps above all, the awareness of belonging to physical and social spaces that have lent themselves to local mythologies.

A REQUIEM FOR THE ANNEX

In *The Annex,* an illustrated history of the distinctive Toronto neighbourhood bounded informally by Avenue Road, Bloor Street, Bathurst Street and the CPR line just north of Dupont Street, Jack Batten profiles more than a dozen prominent writers who have contributed to the Annex's literary reputation, among them Morley Callaghan and his son Barry Callaghan, Katherine Govier, Dennis Lee, Gwendolyn MacEwen, Marian Engel, Margaret Atwood, Sylvia Fraser and bpNichol. Describing the Annex as "the most literary section of Toronto," Batten quotes Robert Fulford as having observed that "late at night, if you listen closely, you may pick up one dominant sound: the clicking of word-processor keys. The impression that writers sometimes outnumber houses is not always false."

While undeniably accurate in a historical sense, Fulford's observation has an air of nostalgia when read in the context of the contemporary Annex. Nearly all the writers Batten identifies are dead—two of them, Matt Cohen and Gwendolyn MacEwen, have Annex-area parks named in their memory—and most of the other authors have long since left the Annex and no longer reference the neighbourhood in their works. In *Toronto: A Literary Guide,* Greg Gatenby describes Katherine Govier's well-known story, "Brunswick Avenue," as "the Bible of this street," but the story—a parable about an ambitious group of artists and writers who outgrow their neighbourhood—is crafted as a reminiscence of a corner of 1970s Toronto that no longer exists. When Govier's narrator returns to her old stomping grounds a decade later, she reflects upon her reasons for leaving, musing, "There was nothing wrong with Brunswick Avenue except that we had lived there too long." Like a small town that cultivates until it cloys, by the late 1970s the Annex has done all it can for Govier's protagonists—they must go elsewhere to grow creatively, or stay and become stagnant.

In the introduction to the twentieth-anniversary edition of *Fables of Brunswick Avenue,* Govier (who lived on Brunswick Avenue for seven years while starting out as a writer) revisits Brunswick as an author and finds it irretrievably altered:

> Giving the street one last, longing look, I strive to feel the ghosts of the elders of the community: Matt Cohen, Marian Engel, Elizabeth Smart. I can't, not today. [...] My *New Grub Street* is not entirely gone, but it has been gentrified. One part of it is even going to be some kind of archive, some perfected version of itself, where successful and aging former residents of Brunswick Avenue will have a doorman, parking, and new tiles.

Gentrification has brought far more than architectural change to the Annex, and even if they wanted to live in one of Brunswick Avenue's distinctively gabled mansions, few aspiring authors could afford the rent, let alone carry the costs of a mortgage as previous generations of writers have done. Jack Batten emphasizes this point in "The Literary Annex," noting that "while many writers on the prosperous end of the scale, mostly those in journalism and other nonfiction forms, have continued to make the Annex their neighbourhood of choice, younger writers seeking garret accommodation have bypassed it in favour of less pricey areas of the city."

Still, for half a century the Annex was Toronto's creative centre, housing scores of writers and inspiring dozens of representations of life—both real and imagined—within its twenty square blocks. As Rosemary Sullivan writes in *Shadow Maker*, her biography of Gwendolyn MacEwen, "The Annex was defined against the mainstream. [...] The Annex had flair. It felt like a downtown cross-section where several worlds met." Why was the Annex such a creative hotbed? Some of this productivity may be attributed to its proximity to the University of Toronto, where many Annex residents studied or taught. The university has traditionally fostered literary societies and provided opportunities for publishing creative work, and many prominent Annex writers— among them Atwood, Cohen, Lee and David Helwig—got their start teaching courses, writing and performing in university theatre productions or contributing to student literary journals.

An equally important consideration was that the Annex was an inexpensive place to live. In *The Annex*, Jack Batten explains the powerful appeal of cheap housing:

> For MacEwen and for writers of every sort—novelists, poets, journalists, authors of biographies and other works of nonfiction—the Annex has been a welcoming home during much of its existence. This was particularly true in the decades following the Second World War, the reason largely being that, along with the Bohemian atmosphere that writers such as MacEwen found congenial, the Annex price was right. Rooms and small flats in the neighbourhood houses came at a reasonable bargain for young writers at the beginning of their careers, and for those who made successes, the purchase price of Annex real estate stuck close to the affordable level.

Katherine Govier says a little more about the kinds of characters attracted to the Annex during this period:

> Our neighbours were like us, striving photographers, potters, film-makers, and graduate students in English or biology; a would-be actress who baked plasticine

toys in her oven to sell at subway stops. Livings were put together from part-time teaching, grants, odd-jobbing. Everyone was involved in rounds of submissions, auditions, applications; there were never any openings. We had all come from someplace else, and the city seemed to be a conspiracy to keep us out.

And so, in second-floor flats and attic apartments, contending with rattle-paned windows, leaking radiators and manipulative landladies, an entire generation of Toronto writers took up residence amid the Annex's decaying grandeur and prepared to make its mark.

Despite the size and architectural opulence of many of its homes, built mainly by wealthy industrialists and businessmen between 1890 and 1910, the Annex remained in decline from the Depression until "white-painters" began buying up and renovating its grand edifices in the 1970s and '80s. Although the Annex had a certain enviable cachet at the turn of the century, it could never compete with Rosedale or the escarpment of land above Davenport Road that eventually became Forest Hill Village, and so, a generation after its grandest edifices were built, the Annex slid into a long decline. In *The Torontonians*, Phyllis Brett Young puts a topographical spin on the area's loss of standing:

> Julia and Ned's house was one of those old, three-story houses on Admiral Road built at the turn of the century when everybody had been so certain that residential Toronto would, following a tradition established by the ancient Egyptians, grow westward towards the prevailing wind. That Toronto society should instead have climbed the hill that cut across the city from east to west was a blow to a great many people who had overlooked the fact that social climbing is not necessarily limited to metaphorical heights.

The impact on the Annex was profound: by mid-century many of the gracious homes once occupied by wealthy industrialists and their wives had been broken up into small apartments or rooming houses occupied increasingly by the city's teeming masses of immigrants, including large numbers of Europeans displaced by war. One of *The Torontonians'* protagonists, a wealthy Moore Park housewife who had grown up in the Annex during the twenties and thirties, drives through the once-familiar streets with a friend and is dismayed to observe how greatly it has changed:

> It had been a mistake to show Susan the house on Elmdale Avenue. Susan, very naturally, had seen exactly what there was to see, a row of large, dingy boarding-houses with garbage cans at the kerb. It was odd how you could tell, just from looking at the outside of a house, that it was a boarding-house. Even the maples,

which had once been so lovely, were now too big for the street and cast a perpetual gloom over it even at high noon. She had tried to tell Susan what it had been like in the past, but it had been no good. Susan had understood that it had been unlike what she saw, but that was as far as her understanding could go. Even memory, clear as it was, wavered in the face of that drab scene, and Karen herself had avoided Elmdale Avenue after that. This was not a difficult thing to do, because she no longer knew anyone who lived in the Annex.

During an era in which social standing in Toronto had as much to do with where one lived as it did with economic class, race or even religion, Karen's declaration—that "she no longer knew anyone who lived in the Annex"—was tantamount to a sweeping rejection not only of the entire district but of anyone who would live there as well.

Hugh Garner's 1962 novel *The Silence on the Shore* describes life in the post-war Annex as a geometry of dingy rooms in rundown boarding houses. His protagonist, Walter Fowler, the editor of a small trade magazine whose wife has just left him, approaches a seedy house where he has arranged to rent a room and casts his eye over its shabby facade:

The house was like its neighbours, a tall austere old family dwelling, probably with steep staircases for skivvies to climb. It was a house that had grown too big for the families of the present, and too private in its shouldered intimacy with those beside it for the modern suburbanite. With a few eccentric exceptions all the houses on Adford Road and nearby streets had become the living quarters of semi-transient roomers, whose familial connections were as ephemeral as their connections one with the other.

Walter's fellow roomers, a deeply impoverished French-Canadian family, a compulsive drinker, a Polish refugee and several university students, live together in quiet desperation, uncertain whether any of their trajectories will be ascendant or irrevocably downward. Appropriately enough for the Annex, Garner's protagonist is a frustrated novelist who takes comfort in the hope that his austere surroundings might stimulate creative work.

The rooming-house residents of Garner's novel preface a period beginning in the mid-1960s when the Annex began to recapture some of its former cachet. This time, however, the neighbourhood's faded Victorian charm and proximity to the university and changing downtown made it appealing to students, faculty and, increasingly, the aspiring writers who made the neighbourhood into the Literary Annex. At the same time, however, simply living in the Annex was no guarantee of creative accomplishment—a hard lesson for some residents, particularly those who carried the costs of investing too many creative, personal or political expectations into a single neighbourhood.

In *The Streets of Summer*, a novella set in mid-1960s Toronto, David Helwig describes the appeal of the Annex's faded grandeur to his protagonist, a graduate student determined to spend the summer living in one of the bighouses north of Bloor:

> John Morris had always liked the part of Toronto just north of the University, and today he had come there straight from the station. He had just come back from a week spent at home, and now he put his suitcase down and looked around him. The houses he saw were big old brick structures with bay windows and doors surrounded by stained glass. They were relics of an age when homes were as ponderous as the fat, black queen, deeply rooted in the ground, built to crush the family into unity. Many of them had now been broken up into apartments or boarding houses for the transient population that inhabited this part of the city.

Musing that "even the air smelled cleaner up here than it did below Bloor Street," John rents a room in a home on Prince Arthur and settles in, hoping to finish his thesis, recapture his lost youth and perhaps foster a romance with one of his housemates, a willowy woman whose lithe presence he considers part of the good fortune of living in the Annex. His new environment, however, produces complications of its own and within a few weeks John realizes the Annex is not entirely the idyllic neighbourhood he has imagined it to be. His attractive housemate Sonya, a German war refugee, turns out to be a troubled manipulator whose boyfriend, a struggling actor, ends up diving to his death from the balcony of one of architect Uno Prii's distinctive Annex highrises, his body arcing to the ground in monstrous parody of the building's curvilinear frame.

Another frustrated writer who hopes to find inspiration in the Annex is the protagonist of F. G. Paci's novel *The Rooming House*. Paci's narrator, a young university graduate who works for Adanac Press, a nationalist, left-wing publishing house, spends his days copyediting proofs and reading the slush pile and his nights writing feverish experimental fiction inspired mainly by his experiences in an Annex rooming house:

> The rooming-house was a few blocks north of the university in the Annex on a tree-lined street of large Victorian homes, most of which had been converted to student residences, frat houses and a few communes with psychedelic facades. It was actually a double-house, with two open verandahs bordered by brick columns and wooden steps. [...] I constantly wrote about Milly—and the other residents of the rooming-house, using elaborate and pretentious metaphors that sought to

unravel what I believed were the complexities of their lives. I'd use expressions like "the path toward lucidity" and "the power of drama" and "the loss of God."

As the rejections slips pile up, a prominent editor refuses to nominate him for an arts grant and he is laid off from his publishing job, Mark wonders whether the universe is conspiring against him. After Dennis Lee declines to take on one of his tortured manuscripts—gently suggesting the young man learn to write himself out of "the straightjacket of clichés and derivative language"— Mark begins to realize that although his sojourn in the Annex has granted him considerable knowledge and even a little wisdom, his struggle toward maturity and bid to reconcile the disparate parts of his character will gain traction only if he leaves the neighbourhood.

Although the Annex has long remained a centre of publishing activity and a kind of halfway house for aspiring writers, literary representations of the neighbourhood have taken on a decidedly eschatological tone. It is almost as if the Annex embodies creative tensions—particularly those arising between artistic idealism and the pragmatic demands of living and working—that can be resolved only through pathos. If the Annex is an artist's retreat, its quiet streets and shaded gables conducive to creative output, the escape it offers is ultimately illusory, like living in a dream one must eventually wake up from.

In "Sibelius Park," Dennis Lee invokes an Annex so deeply steeped in his personal, publishing and political narratives that it becomes difficult to walk through its streets without feeling haunted (or judged) by his own past:

> Walking north from his other lives in a fine rain
>   through the high-rise pavilion on Walmer
> lost in the vague turbulence he harbours
>   Rochdale Anansi   how many
> routine wipeouts has he performed since he was born? [...]
>   Drifting north to the street-storey
> turrets and gables, the squiggles and arches and
> baleful asymmetric glare of the houses he loves
>   Toronto gothic

Similarly, in *The Martyrology* bpNichol summons the Annex's "ghost geography," referring to friends living and dead as if their very identities are imprinted upon the neighbourhood's streets:

> walked today west thru snow   across Dupont
> frozen streets/seas   thot then of Kit James

dead this past year
caught myself (briefly) wondering
'what's Kit doing?'
But he is done [...]
Spadina
    a dirt road
trucks rumbling north for the subway's construction
underground
        underworld
under wal
    mermur
murmer
    mer made memories
white world of whispered presences
(Kit?)

Kath MacLean invokes an equally poignant past in "for a cappuccino on Bloor," recalling her Annex childhood as a place where "our voices play / themselves out in the streets one / after the other." Returning to Toronto as an adult, she digresses among the familiar streets, musing,

here are the empty alleys
houses with the same blank look [...]
    (by the cafe window i tell you
    where the street people live
    show you my house in the Annex
    the ghosts i've left behind

and imagines herself remaining among them, staying as a stray cat, "a small grey shadow / you see from the corner of her eye."

The "small grey shadow" who haunts the Annex most vividly is, of course, Gwendolyn MacEwen, brought briefly back to life in Desi Di Nardo's poem "Rainbird in the Annex." Di Nardo's narrator, a poet herself, describes the contemporary Annex as inhabited by the spirits of her literary predecessors whose voices and scent and even clothing continue to drift through the rain-dappled streets:

I make my way to MacEwen's salient red door
to catch some remnants of her
a faint scent lifting into old familiar skin

her unbendable pronounced lightness absorbed by sky
deliquescent words lost to the sun
her cordless poetry smothered by wind
I float on
forgetting why I came and
become caught in Atwood's wide-brimmed hat
I nestle in
and burrow seeds
surrounded by other flight

Di Nardo's narrator suggests there is room for other spirits to enter the Annex like birds, building new nests of words and seeding new creative synergies, but in truth the Annex has become a literary mausoleum.

In *Local Matters*, an anthology of essays emerging from an online community connected with Dooney's restaurant—a place he refers to as "the closest thing Toronto has to a literary café"—Brian Fawcett suggests that the Annex accommodates a unique combination of cultural producers and consumers: writers, restaurateurs, shopkeepers and provocateurs. Still, he worries that there might be "a point somewhere in the not-so-distant future when Bloor West will cease to be a specific dynamic place and will become another unlocated strip mall." Despite the invasion—"the Virus," Fawcett calls it—of corporate franchises into the Annex, the neighbourhood retains many of its familiar waystations and watering holes. Dooney's is gone, a victim of the Annex's relentlessly shifting social demographics, but the old Country Style Hungarian restaurant remains, almost unchanged since the 1960s, on Bloor just west of Howland. The Future Bakery, on the south side of Bloor across from the immortal Brunswick House, is not one of the Annex's original hangouts but has been there so long even Katherine Govier cannot recall what preceded it. Still, in the Literary Annex there has been a marked shift from production to consumption.

The Future Bakery, a place Govier describes as "remarkable in that every single person seated in it is writing," is emblematic of this change. In *Satellite Dishes from the Future Bakery*, Michael Holmes conducts what amounts to a 'pataphysical séance with bpNichol, writing, "i am a shifter / an uncomfortable text / a moratorium" and adding

the chora flowing
into lives not mine not being
lived tho i have i now
being alive

and having you reading me
                    a community
i went to with my side bared
not as the truth the tru th
definite as the saint trust is
the precise chronology
                    marking tracing
yer temp(orality (knot mine butt yers)

By writing what he calls a "my(th'o)logical history," Holmes exemplifies the irony of the Future's name: people may still write at the Future, but, like satellites beaming signals from the furthest reaches of the galaxy, they are listening mostly to the past.

Steven Heighton further illustrates the shift toward literary consumption in *The Shadow Boxer*, a novel about a young fighter who abandons boxing to pursue a literary career:

> Eddy and Sevigne are in the Future Bakery, a sprawling, echoing, sun-filled cafeteria in the Annex. Side by side on high stools they look out through retracted windows over a railed-in patio full of young people drinking and smoking. An anorexic woman with thanatic make-up and cyan spiked hair sits sketching in the margins of *A Brief History of Time* as if illuminating a manuscript; at separate tables two sallow, edgy college boys smoke rolled tobacco and scribble severely in notebooks. Now and then they glance up at the street—twinned profiles bristly and soulful, mutually unaware.

Sevigne's discomfort is mirrored by the protagonist of Warren Dunford's novel *Soon to be a Major Motion Picture*, who describes a coffee shop across the street from the Future as an alternative hangout for those for whom writing has become a kind of performance:

> The main attraction of the place is the jumble of rickety tables outside where all the neighbourhood intellectuals come to bask in the sun and sip espresso. You see a lot of people hunched over notebooks, presumably at work on the Great Canadian Screenplay.
>
> Personally, I think it's pretentious to write in public.

These descriptions are a far cry from the protagonists of Katherine Govier's "Brunswick Avenue," who write in solitude and come out only to decompress or commiserate, or the narrator of Frank Paci's *The Rooming House*, who pounds away on a portable Remington typewriter in the perpetual twilight of his rented Annex room.

Some of the differences between these generations of writers may be chalked up to cultural and technological shifts: a desire, perhaps, to connect with other writers in public places or to seek inspiration from realistic rather than idealized surroundings; technological advances, certainly, have made writing a more portable activity. The biggest difference, however, is that in many ways the Annex has become a bedroom community, the sort of place, as Bert Archer says about Toronto, where "people live, not a place where things happen." These days most Annex residents are well-paid professionals: lawyers, doctors, university professors. The dwindling number of houses broken up into apartments are still inhabited by students and, yes, aspiring writers, but for the most part even the writers who live there no longer write about the Annex. In truth, most of the twenty- and thirty-something writers who bring their notebooks and laptops to the Future Bakery and a dozen other Bloor Street patios live elsewhere, and do the bulk of their writing in—and about—other parts of the city.

The protagonist of Margaret Atwood's *The Robber Bride*, a historian who spends her days researching and writing about war, considers her Annex home a retreat, a place to escape from the challenges of the outside world:

> At the street corner Tony turns to look back at her house, as she often does, admiring it. Even after twenty years it still seems like a mirage that she should own such a house, or any house at all. The house is brick, late Victorian, tall and narrow, with green fish-scale shingles on its upper third. Her study window looks out from the fake tower on the left: the Victorians loved to think they were living in castles. It's a large house, larger than it looks from the street. A solid house, reassuring; a fort, a bastion, a keep.

The narrative action in Atwood's novel occurs all over the city—Queen Street, the University, the Toronto Islands, downtown offices—but not in the Annex. In this respect the novel might be thought of as a requiem for the Annex, a benediction that bestows the gift of narrative upon the other parts of the city.

KINGS OF CABBAGETOWN

Dating to the late 1840s, when Irish immigrants flooded Toronto in flight from the potato famine and a series of epidemics, Cabbagetown is one of Toronto's oldest and most curiously bifurcated neighbourhoods. Once famously described as "North America's largest Anglo-Saxon slum,"[97] since the early 1970s much of Cabbagetown has been transformed by gentrification into an affluent neighbourhood inhabited mainly by professionals, artists, executives and media consultants. At the same time, other sections of Cabbagetown and its environs, including Regent Park, St. Jamestown and Moss Park, have experienced entrenched poverty and are perceived as inner-city ghettos. This contrast is likely one reason why the boundaries of Cabbagetown are tightly contested.

In *Cabbagetown Store*, a memoir of his Cabbagetown boyhood published in 1953, journalist J. V. McAree writes that Cabbagetown is neither a legal entity nor a title appearing on any survey but rather a name that was "was applied to that part of Toronto lying south of Gerrard Street, north of Queen and east from Parliament Street to the Don." Adding, "[c]laims to have been citizens of Cabbagetown put forth in later years by persons living beyond these boundaries have been properly disallowed and resented," McAree fires the first salvo in the battle over Cabbagetown's boundaries. Hugh Garner—Cabbagetown's most prolific chronicler—defines similar territory in his novel *Cabbagetown*, describing the inclusion of other areas (including regions to the west of Parliament or north of Gerrard) as "an error."

In their 1971 book *Working People: Life in a Downtown Neighbourhood*, a cultural analysis of the Cabbagetown area documenting a period when gentrification was beginning to alter the district's physical landscape and social terrain, James Lorimer and Myfanwy Phillips point out that Cabbagetown's boundaries reflect meaningful class dynamics and are therefore best understood as being both spatially and socially fluid:

> People in Toronto who do not live there generally call it "Cabbagetown." Respectable residents object on the grounds that Cabbagetown is a name which refers to the area to the south of Gerrard Street, the Anglo-Saxon, working-class, low-income Toronto neighbourhood most of which was demolished to make way for the Regent Park-Moss Park public housing projects. In fact, however, most city residents use the name to refer to Toronto's Anglo-Saxon, working-class "slum" areas, and probably if they have thought about it would realize that Cabbagetown in their sense of the term moved north, south and then west as its original area was demolished.

For their part, Lorimer and Phillips decline to use the name "Cabbagetown,"

---

97 Hugh Garner gave Cabbagetown the dubious sobriquet "North America's largest Anglo-Saxon slum," repeating the phrase often and with evident pleasure. The label appears in his introduction to the 1968 edition of *Cabbagetown* and is repeated on the first page of his 1970 novel *The Sin Sniper*, also set principally in Cabbagetown.

acknowledging its "abusive" and pejorative connotations. Instead, they call the area "east of Parliament."

In *Cabbagetown Remembered*, published little more than a decade later, George Rust-D'Eye repeats some of this history but, significantly, bows to "the recent tendency to apply the name to the area north of Gerrard Street." Published in 1998, Penina Coopersmith's *Cabbagetown: The Story of a Victorian Neighbourhood* completes the inversion of Cabbagetown's boundaries: in the book's foreword, Rust-D'ye pops up again, asserting simply that "[t]oday's Cabbagetown" represents the area north of Gerrard Street. The old boundaries of Cabbagetown receive scant mention, apart from Coopersmith's assertion that "[i]t was in the wake of the demolition of the old Cabbagetown and the urban renewal of the 1960s, that today's Cabbagetown pulled itself together and carved out a new identity." Indeed. Far be it for the residents of "today's Cabbagetown"—now a Heritage Conservation District—to associate themselves too closely with memories of "the largest Anglo-Saxon slum in North America" or the public housing projects, like Regent Park, that replaced it. The boundaries of today's Cabbagetown—just like the boundaries of old Cabbagetown—have everything to do with socio-economic class.

In *Cabbagetown*, the district's most iconic rendering, Hugh Garner's narrator describes returning home to Cabbagetown, with its small, mainly run-down houses and scattered neighbourhood stores—"shoe repair shops, dirty little grocery stores, broken biscuits, Salvation Army salvage store, taffy apples, tinsmith's supplies, used clothing; second-hand, third-rate, the purveyors to the poor—":

> He was now in familiar territory. This was his neighbourhood, dotted with the homes of his neighbours and friends. The street names greeted him with long-known familiarity—Sackville, Parliament, Taylor, Oak, Sumach, Sydenham—old names given to them at their christening when the area was a suburb of a much younger city. Now that they too were old they wore their aristocratic-cum-sylvan names like a harridan with flowers on her hat—jaunty, past caring, but clinging to something that was part of what might have been.

Garner's protagonist, a sixteen-year-old who drops out of school to support himself and his indigent, alcoholic mother, finds employment with a grocery wholesaler, but loses his job as the Depression deepens. Finding only transient, low-paying work, he grows increasingly class-conscious as he notices the Depression's disproportionate effect on already poor areas like Cabbagetown.

Despite feeling beleaguered by his increasing destitution, Ken remains faithful to Cabbagetown, leaving only to ride the rails across the country like

tens of thousands of other men in a fruitless search for work before returning to care for his mother and tend to their rented Cabbagetown row house.
His neighbours, however, are not so loyal when confronted with prejudice
against their neighbourhood. One of Ken's friends, a young man who hopes
to insinuate himself into a better part of society, grimaces and cringes at being
identified with Cabbagetown:

> He hated the neighbourhood, and especially the backyard squalor that was typical
> of its streets. He also hated the noise of the hordes of children, and the dirt and
> stupidity of most of its inhabitants. More than anything else he hated his address,
> even though his own family's house was not as shabby as the ones around it. He
> particularly hated having to live in Cabbagetown.

Asked by a prominent Torontonian he hopes to impress what part of the city
he hails from, Ken's friend Ted replies "the East End" rather than admit he lives
in Cabbagetown. His interlocutor, a man with Fascist sympathies who claims
to be interested in "urban blight and social questions," responds,

> "I saw some real eyesores down in that section of the city, places that really needed
> cleaning up. Take that slum neighbourhood north of there, Cabbageville is it—?"
> "I think so," Theodore said.
> "An eyesore. People living in filth and squalor. A regular breeding place for
> disease and discontent. It should be burned to the ground. Do you know the place
> I mean?"
> "Oh, yes, sir. I've been through it."
> "I feel bad about it; it gives our city a bad image. It's costly too, why nearly
> half the families are getting welfare assistance. Think of it! If it weren't for the
> economic panic I'd recommend that it be razed and a low-cost housing develop-
> ment built in its place. Of course just now our hands are tied, there simply isn't
> any more of the taxpayers' money to be squandered on philanthropic projects.
> The people down there wouldn't appreciate it anyhow. I heard of a recent housing
> development in England where they found the people using their new bathtubs
> for coal bins. Can you imagine that!"

This kind of commentary is, of course, the core of the social narrative that led to
the bulk of Cabbagetown being razed in the late 1940s and replaced with Regent
Park, Canada's first social-housing experiment. If this derogatory conversation
seems an exaggeration, it is worth noting that the producers of *Farewell Oak Street*,
a 1953 documentary film about Regent Park, took considerable care to show view-
ers that Regent Park's residents did *not* use their bathtubs as coal cellars.

In the 1968 edition of *Cabbagetown*, Garner describes the redevelopment as "a godsend to ex-Cabbagetowners," adding that it reduced reliance on social assistance and benefitted "new generations of Cabbagetowners [who] had money and jobs, which most of those who came before them had not." An irony of Regent Park is, of course, that the housing experiment was troubled nearly from the beginning. Many of the changes imposed on the neighbourhood exacerbated the poverty and social isolation they were designed to eliminate. As early as 1963—only four years after the second phase of Regent Park was completed—the Metropolitan Toronto Housing Corporation acknowledged that the project's design (which obliterated Cabbagetown's familiar grid of streets and replaced the district's two-story row houses with modernist townhouses and cruciform apartment blocks) was flawed, observing for future reference, "It is the authority's view that such housing projects should, whenever possible, merge with the surrounding residential areas and not be readily identifiable," and adding, "It, surely, is clear that a blending of income groups is required to establish a suitable basis for an integrated community."[98]

That Regent Park has never been well integrated with the rest of the city is underscored in Mark Thurman's *Cabbagetown Gang*, a novel about a group of teenaged boys who fight, explore and get into minor trouble like kids everywhere—except that they do so in an asphalt jungle. As Thurman's narrator observes,

> Broken bottles. Hmmm ...broken glass, glass here, glass there, glass everywhere in the parking lot, on the sidewalks, all over the concrete and tar. It's like a desert of shiny bits of broken glass. Regent Park. They should change it to Glass Park, or Concrete Park, Tar Park, Kid Park: Regent-Glass-Concrete-Tar-Car-Kid-Park.

In Rabindranath Maharaj's novel *The Amazing Absorbing Boy*, a teenaged Trinidadian boy sent to Canada to stay with his father finds himself living in Regent Park at a time when the City is embarking upon yet another social-housing experiment, this time hoping to replace the community's decrepit townhouses and apartment buildings with a mixed-income development. Handed a notice about the planned transformation, Samuel ignores it until the implications begin to sink in:

> I read the sheet in the elevator. It seemed that Regent Park was going to be demolished and its residents placed elsewhere. All of a sudden I felt real happy. Maybe me and my father would move to a place similar to that described by Sporty, and

---

98 Quoted in architect Chris Warden's *The Real Cabbagetown History*, n.d. Available at http://chat. carleton.ca/~cwarden/projects/rp_history.pdf.

there we would start over and get to know each other as father and son. He might even resume his inventions. And perhaps years later a passerby would glance at our house and say, "That is where Samuel and his father used to live. Father was an inventor and the son was a college student."

Recalling an acquaintance's declaration that "dreams couldn't find a place to grow in the city because there was too much concrete," Samuel remains indifferent to the eviction, musing, "I had never thought of Regent Park as a community, maybe because living with my father encouraged me feel it was a place to escape from." Still, when a neighbour who spends her days rallying residents against the demolition complains, "Just imagine that I have to start over again at my age. With strangers on all sides. That is nastiness. Real nastiness," Samuel realizes that Regent Park *is* a home to many of the other residents and considers the possibility that Regent Park, or some other place in Toronto, could become home to him, too.

That Regent Park has been a home to many of its residents is exemplified in an anonymous memorial poem painted on the wall of one of its buildings slated for demolition:

Rest in peace our family and friends
You left us with nothing but pictures
And memories and mothers left empty
Rest in peace our family and friends
Our broken hearts cherish the moments
You brought us together to share an emotion
Till we meet again[99]

In the same way that writers like Garner felt compelled to pay homage to a version of Cabbagetown that has long disappeared, Thurman and Maharaj find a similar obligation to represent Regent Park as something more than a failed experiment in public housing but rather as a neighbourhood where real Torontonians live.

Regent Park isn't the Cabbagetown area's only failed housing experiment. In the late 1960s a series of high-rise apartment towers called St. Jamestown was built along Wellesley Street, intended for upwardly mobile young professionals. St. Jamestown first appears in the city's literature in Margaret Atwood's *The Edible Woman*, as the apartment of her narrator's fiancé, Peter, who lives in a model apartment in the under-construction complex. Atwood

---

99 Author unknown. Thank you to Sumeet Ahluwalia for photographing and sharing this work.

describes the neighbourhood simply as "a run-down area, nearly a slum, that is scheduled to be transformed over the next few years by high-rise apartments." This dismissive view was the prevailing sentiment in an era when urban renewal—as had been done in Cabbagetown south of Gerrard—meant razing and replacing entire neighbourhoods.

St. Jamestown remained a swingers' retreat for only a few years before gradually becoming another low-rent housing complex, appealing to immigrant families who could not afford to live anywhere else. A generation later, although peripatetic efforts are made to foster community and beautify the grounds, the towers of St. Jamestown have become symbols of inner-city poverty. In *How Happy to Be*, Katrina Onstad describes an immigrant woman who moves into a St. Jamestown apartment in the hope of establishing herself in the new country:

> With five hundred extra dollars from the government and a job cleaning offices at night in the Bay Street financial district, Mercy and Maria got a bachelor apartment in a sky-rise in St. Jamestown, a collection of towers with optimistic names: the Halifax, the Vancouver, the Montreal. St. Jamestown was built in the Seventies so swinging singles could live downtown and walk to work, but the white professionals only stayed a few months, edged out by groups of immigrants bringing their families one by one from far away, all to live together in apartments no bigger than a bus. The families—big, loud, always working—lived side by side with the gangs and junkies who wandered over from Regent Park. They stayed in St. Jamestown for years, and every single time she entered its teeming corridors, Mercy thought, St. James, brother of John, disciple of Jesus.

St. Jamestown also appears in Toronto literature as the apartment building Carla's mother falls to her death from in Dionne Brand's *What We All Long For*, further reinforcing the sense of misery experienced by many of its residents.

As for Cabbagetown itself, even as Hugh Garner described it as an Anglo-Saxon slum, the parts of the neighbourhood not submerged beneath public housing were already beginning to change—although for a time the familiar conditions persisted. In "Living in Toronto," Al Purdy describes Cabbagetown as a scene of unmitigated dereliction, calling it "a maze you see into / but don't comprehend" and adding,

> Living in the fortunate slums
> near Parliament Street in old Cabbagetown
> among the drunks and Italian workmen
> there was always a monster-stench
> lurking the Shop for Crippled Civilians :

watching from 19th century houses
choosing a victim from drunk and sober
in rain or slush on Parliament Street

In his novel *Cabbagetown Diary*, Juan Butler describes Allen Gardens in similar terms, describing it as "a place to go if there's no show at the movies":

> It's a slum park, and by that I mean a city block of grass, trees, benches, a drinking fountain and a hothouse beside the public toilets, full of plants and flowers—all that right in the middle of the worst slum in Toronto. The people in Cabbagetown (they say Cabbagetown got its name because the first people to come here were Irish, whose love of boiled cabbage and potatoes is second only for their love of booze) all flock to the Gardens when the midday heat starts driving them out of their grimy little rooms, and one by one in the afternoon the place is so full you can hardly see the grass you're stepping on.

Parts of Parliament Street—and indeed Allen Gardens—retain some of their derelict flavour, but by the early 1970s it was clear that all that remained of the old Cabbagetown neighbourhood—the area north of Gerrard—was beginning to gentrify. The novel that best captures Cabbagetown's transitional moment is Tim Wynne-Jones' detective novel *The Knot*. Of early 1970s Cabbagetown, Wynne-Jones writes,

> Cabbagetown was a strange hybrid of a community in the urban core of Toronto. It wasn't more than a mile square. The streets were narrow and tree-lined, and the architecture Victorian in style, if not uniformly in vintage. Whatever else it was, it was old and quaint and well-situated. It had become a slum when the middle class had fled to the suburbs but now it was undergoing a renaissance as a new middle class flooded back into the city's heart. The houses, grand or ramshackle, row or detached, were being resuscitated. The results were mixed: some fine homes were artfully reclaimed to a serviceable beauty, grander homes refurbished to something of their erstwhile splendour, and some less noble shacks given a glamour far exceeding their original value. Propped and stayed, their faces lifted like vain dowagers, the ersatz competed with the splendid, and pretension sidled up to good taste hoping to be mistaken by the uninformed.

Wynne-Jones points out that this was not accidental or happenstance, adding, "Cabbagetown wasn't merely housing, it was something of a movement spearheaded by the historically minded, the community spirited and, not least of all, the speculatively shrewd."

Wynne-Jones also gives some sense of the cost for Cabbagetown's long-standing residents, who found themselves confined to increasingly small pockets of apartments and rooming houses before being shifted out of their neighbourhood entirely, moving to its ungentrified fringes along Parliament or Sherbourne or moving into the high rises of Moss Park and St. Jamestown:

> Amidst the hurly-burly, the poor watched from their shabby porches what was, they thought, their indigenous land reclaimed from the oblivion of Skid Row, and which was now suddenly threatening them on every side. It was a neighbourhood in flux; welfare and well fed living side by side. [...] Handsome folk shared the sidewalk willy-nilly with winos and panhandlers. It was a microcosm of the city; a cell in all its stages of vitality and decay.

At the same time, gentrification did not move forward all at once. In David Type's 1984 play, *Just Us Indians*, a protagonist looks around her at a neighbourhood in transition and judges just how much—and how little—it has actually changed:

> The houses are startin' to get all fixed up. They all got dogs and cats are their kids are as sassy as they come. But I see the Passifumes and the McIntires and the Eye-talians down the street, with their run-down porches and their insul-brick walls, underneath all this new stuff. I put up that insul-brick myself. There, see is? Course it's all fallin' apart now. Front yard full of weeds. Can't grow a damn thing...and there usta be elm trees all along here too. You know, sometimes I feel like I'm the last living thing here.

A generation later, it is difficult to find evidence of Cabbagetown's working-class roots. Even the single-story workers' cottages have been tarted up, embellished in some cases with a second-story steel-and-glass addition. But Cabbagetown is far more than a collection of quaint Victorian brick homes designed to appeal to the upwardly mobile: somewhere lurking in a layer of grime beneath the floorboards is the old Cabbagetown, identifiable by the twitch of a starched lace curtain in a front window, or the faint but unmistakable scent of cabbage growing somewhere in a neighbour's backyard.

CULTURAL TOURISM ON COLLEGE STREET

College Street is the closest Toronto gets to the Old Country. Resolutely European, it is one of the few downtown districts that have managed to withstand periodic onslaughts of cultural popularity and, after the commotion dies down, return recognizably to its former condition. In the introduction to *College Street, Little Italy*, publisher Denis De Klerck and poet Corrado Paina describe College Street as "Toronto's renaissance strip," not only because it is an important site of cultural production or because it has defied the odds to remain a vibrant urban community, but because—with its street cafés, espresso-fuelled politics and religious processions—it is Toronto's last link between the Old World and the New.

De Klerck and Paina trace the beginnings of College Street's "Little Italy" identity to the early 1980s, when city councillor Joe Pantalone and broadcaster Johnny Lombardi fostered local institutions to forestall neighbourhood decline, but Italians lived along College Street long before the neighbourhood developed its distinctive cultural character, living alongside Jews and, later, Portuguese in homes many of them built from the foundations up. In his novel *The Secret Mitzvah of Lucio Burke*, Steven Hayward depicts College Street as the centre of a nascent Italian community in the 1930s:

> Michelangelo's Garage, where Lucio works, is located at the intersection of College and Clinton Streets, in the part of the city where most of the Italians live and the cheapest boarding houses are. Nearly all the boarders in the Clinton houses are male, unskilled labourers from the south of Italy who have come to Canada to work laying bricks or spreading tar on roads or digging ditches. [...] But there are more than boarding houses on Clinton Street. There are other houses, half finished or barely started, belonging to men who plan one day to bring their families to Canada. These houses are for the most part only basements, with tarps for roofs and cinder floors. On Sundays the men who own them can be seen in their backyards, turning over the soil, planting and watering. This is the one thing that all the houses have in common, no matter how picked over their insides. Their backyards have been transformed into tiny fertile provinces, growing tomatoes and garlic, onions, *lattuga romana*, radicchio, green peas and snow peas and the hairy, sweet *tortarello* cucumbers that come from Bari and are really a kind of melon.

In "College Street, Toronto," Gianna Patriarca invokes a similar landscape, describing the convoluted passage that brought Italian men and, later, their families, to the College Street area:

> For my father it began in 1956
> in the basement of a Euclid Street
> rooming house
> with five other men
> homeless, immigrant dreamers

bordanti
young, dark
handsome and strong
bricklayers
carpenters
gamblers [...]
then the exodus
of wives and children
trunks and wine glasses
hand stitched linens in hope chests
floating across the Atlantic
slowly
to Halifax
To Union Station
To College Street.

On narrow side streets north and south of College, immigrant families crowded into houses well or poorly built, the familiar and the foreign interweaving until sometimes they wondered who they were and feared for who they might become.

Still, along College Street even anomie could become a source of solace. In Anne Michaels' novel *Fugitive Pieces* a Polish war refugee ventures into the immigrant neighbourhood west of Bathurst Street: a lonely man singing the songs of his homeland—all he has left of it:

> One evening I walked up Grace Street, a summer tunnel of long shadows, the breeze from the lake a cool finger slipping gently under my damp shirt, the tumult of the market left blocks behind. In the new coolness and new quiet, a thread of memory clung to a thought. Suddenly an overheard word fastened on to a melody; a song of my mother's that was always accompanied by the sound of brush bristles pulling through Bella's hair, my mother's arm drawing with the beat. The words stumbled out of my mouth, a whisper, then louder, until I was mumbling whatever I remembered. [...] I looked around. The houses were dark, the street safely empty. I raised my voice. "Foolish one, don't be so dense, don't you have any common sense? Smoke is taller than a house, a cat is faster than a mouse...."

Walking along darkened streets filled only with the sound of his voice, Jakob realizes, belatedly, that he is singing to an audience of strangers:

> Up Grace, along Henderson, up Manning to Harbord I whimpered; my spirit shape finally in familiar clothes and, with abandon, flinging its arms to the stars.

But the street wasn't empty as I thought. Startled, I saw that the blackness was perforated with dozens of faces. A forest of eyes, of Italian and Portuguese and Greek ears; whole families sitting silently on lawnchairs and front steps. On dark verandahs, a huge invisible audience. [...] There was nothing for it but to raise my foreign song and feel understood.

Despite having little in common but their shared foreignness, Jakob and his silent audience feel a little more at home in this neighbourhood where mutual strangeness makes them equals.

By the late 1970s the area De Klerck and Paina describe as having resembled a Mediterranean village was beginning to change. In *College Street*, a memoir of his Toronto boyhood, Olindo Romeo Chiocca describes College Street in this period as "a contradiction between the old and new," adding,

College Street is cafes, Italian shoes in windows, skinned rabbits on hooks, the scent of garlic and onions, and the old world men and women fading from the scene. It is wind-proof hair, all-black clothing, scattered music, pierced tongues, and an overlapping of Italian cultures trying to blend in with the elusive, never-quite-defined Canadian culture. The inhabitants, strollers, and posers carry old world attitudes and hopes for their children: calloused hands, swollen egos, large dreams, and soft gloves that grip the steering wheel of Daddy-bought Ferraris.

But even the changes Chiocca observes pale in comparison to the contradictions that come to define the College Street community in the 1990s.

When a revitalized Bar Italia opened in the early 1990s, it became College Street's literary hotspot and helped transform the neighbourhood's image. In Daniel Jones' story "In Various Restaurants," the restaurant becomes a backdrop to tortured conversations, social avoidance and literary posturing:

Inside the Bar Italia it is dark and crowded. There is the sound of many people talking all at once and of billiard balls striking other billiard balls. Two writers I know stand leaning against the bar drinking espresso. I manage to pass without them seeing me. [...] I ask Nicola if she minds if I smoke. She says she does not mind. I always ask and this is always what she says. The waiter comes and places two menus on the table. I order a *latte macchiato*. Nicola asks for a glass of water and pushes her menu to the side of the table. I order the salmon salad—*insalata di salmon, patate nuove, cicoria*. Nicola asks for the same. The way she pronounces the words, in her precise English accent, makes it sound like something different, something I wish I had ordered as well.

Russell Smith is credited with having written—and set—parts of novels and several short stories—including "Chez Giovanni'—in a thinly fictionalized Bar Italia. In Smith's versions of College Street bars, the tables, the staff and particularly the women are elegant and gleam with unfulfilled promise, much like College Street itself. By the mid-1990s College Street seemed in danger of turning into a parody of itself, a point Sarah Dearing emphasizes in her novel *Courage My Love*. New to the city, Dearing's narrator ventures into Little Italy hoping to obtain the proper ingredients for an authentic Italian meal. Disappointed, she complains,

> Little Italy doesn't live up to its quaint street signs and boot-shaped lights. The types of shops I'd anticipated are absent and it is little more than a street of trendy restaurants. Where are the friendly greengrocers and butchers? The women in black gossiping on the sidewalk?

Wandering into Bar Italia, she asks the waiter, plaintively, "Are there any other ethnic neighbourhoods, specific ones, and real, not just theme parks like this?" At the same time, Philippa is complicit in having contributed to College Street's theme-park atmosphere, sustained principally by Anglo-Saxon Torontonians like herself who are eager to cloak themselves in the neighbourhood's zeitgeist: before leaving her Yorkville condominium to travel to Little Italy, Philippa invents an Italian name for herself—Felipitta—and dons a Benetton dress, the only item in her closet that sounds remotely Italian.

The perils of College Street becoming a parody of itself are outlined more powerfully in Corrado Paina's poem "Open College," a vision of his neighbourhood turned into a giant sidewalk café serving caffe e latte, gelato and gnocci alla Romana to Anglo tourists from other parts of the city:

> they could close off the area
> like in Rome
> and put tables
> in the streets!
> the summer is different on College
> and the distant sirens
> belong
> to the city
> on College bells are ringing
> on College firetrucks are a civic event
> on College they know you [...]
> along College

the pantograph of a streetcar
tears through the viscera of the sky
hunks of watermelon
bits of pistachio ice cream
scraps of tomato
and threads of parmesan and pecorino
rain
upon the tables of College

But Little Italy is a neighbourhood that has retained its identity. Long-standing institutions like Café Diplomatico and Bar Italia have survived and will retain their local flavour long after the poseurs have moved on. Describing Little Italy in *How Happy to Be* as "the latest neighbourhood to moult its immigrant past and make way for sommeliers and organic grocers," novelist Katrina Onstad acknowledges its tenacity, adding,

Five years ago, this street was mostly textile shops and Portuguese bakeries. Then neighbourhood bars where old men congregated for satellite soccer gave way to lounges with neon signs, then lounges went out of fashion and became clubs. Still, the Portuguese women hold their ground, displaying buttons and zippers in their windows while next door a gourmet delicatessen features kumquats and gooseberries in theirs.

Gianna Patriarca reinforces this point, musing,

the Italians are almost all gone
to new neighbourhoods
modern towns.

My father is gone
Bar Italia has a new clientele
Women come here now
I come here
I drink espresso and smoke cigarettes
From the large window
that swims in sunlight
I think I see my father
leaning on the parking meter
passionately arguing
the soccer scores.

TEXTURES OF KENSINGTON MARKET

If every Toronto neighbourhood has a story, then Kensington Market is where the narrative refuses to be confined to the page. Like a cluster of pigeons, the Market's stray voices erupt outward to scatter and coalesce, muttering greetings in a hundred tongues, bargaining, hectoring, laughing and weeping. It is true that there is stillness here, but even the night is alive with breathing.

Kensington Market has always been on the verge of turning into something else, and this was true even a century ago when the neighbourhood's streets—named in homage of its Anglican founders[100]—first began to resonate with the guttural inflections of Yiddish in an area already being referred to as "the Jewish Market." It must be added that the overlapping iterations of Kensington Market that have embedded themselves in the city's cultural imagination did not even begin in the Market's current location, well-known as the area bounded by College, Spadina, Dundas and Bathurst. The true origins of Kensington Market are found in a nearby slum district once known as the Ward.

St. John's Ward, a municipal district once bounded by College and Queen streets on the north and south and Yonge Street and University Avenue on the east and west, was segregated from the rest of the city by culture as much as by class.[101] In a 1913 magazine essay called "Toronto's Melting Pot," Margaret Bell refers derisively to the "seething, sweaty centre" of the Ward with the "Hebrew disorder" of its "garish" shops, the "slatternly decay" of its "tumbledown houses," the "dirty little wretches" who play in its streets and the "unintelligible muttering" of its residents.

Even sympathetic visitors were repelled by the filth and crowding in the Ward, and considered its decrepitude an affront to life and health. In Barbara Greenwood's children's story *Factory Girl*, a young woman ventures into the Ward to enquire after a fellow garment worker who has inexplicably been absent from the sewing floor. When she reaches the dwelling she encounters a scene that appals and horrifies her:

> Katya turned into a side street, then, with an anxious glance at Emily, down a
> narrow alleyway between two apartments. The stench of overflowing privies filled

---

100   Jean Cochrane's book *Kensington* (2000) traces the story of the Denison family, who owned and developed much of what subsequently became Kensington Market. Many Market-area streets, including Denison, Bellevue, Robert and Lippincott, are named after the Denison family and its connections.

101   For historical and social perspective on Jewish identity in the Ward and Kensington Market, see Stephen Speisman's *The Jews of Toronto: A History to 1937* (1979) and Gerald Tulchinsky's *Taking Root: The Origins of the Canadian Jewish Community* (1992).

Emily's nostrils. She began breathing through her mouth. This was even worse than the smell in their own lane. They came out of the dark into a patch of light. There was a tiny yard filled with debris—a legless chair, a wheel from a cart, a mattress sodden with something that gave off an acrid smell, a jumble of rusting iron rods. [...] "Magda there." Katya pointed to what appeared to be cellar steps leading down to a small landing. Then she turned and darted away.

At the bottom of the cellar steps, behind a doorway lodged open beside a reeking chamber pot, Emily discovers a dank, almost unfurnished dwelling occupied by her motherless co-worker and five younger siblings, one lying sick and coughing on a mattress on the floor.

Sympathetic to what he saw as the suffering of the Ward's inhabitants, in the early phase of his career as an artist, Group of Seven member Lawren Harris ventured regularly into the Ward and produced dozens of sketches and paintings of the district's ramshackle houses, lath exposed and stucco peeling around broken windows with sagging shutters, offering what literary scholar Gregory Betts describes in *Lawren Harris in the Ward* as "one of the earliest glimpses of urban poverty in Canada." An occasional poet, Harris also wrote texts that Betts suggests should be read alongside the paintings themselves because of the way they flesh out and give form to the paintings' stark, representational quality. In one poem Harris writes,

In a part of the city that is ever shrouded in sooty smoke,
And amid huge, hard buildings, hides a gloomy house of
Broken grey rough-cast, like a sickly sin in a callous soul.

Harris anthropomorphizes this decrepit building strenuously, describing broken chestnut trees that "stand / wearily before it, subdued by a bare rigid telephone pole" and window shutters that "sag this way and that like dancers / suddenly stopped in aimless movement." The single note of levity—or perhaps it is merely madness—is produced by a front door that "smiles, and even laughs, when the / hazy sunlight falls on it— / Someone had painted it a bright gay red." In another poem Harris invokes the moral response the Ward seems to demand of its visitors, asking,

Are you sad when you look down city lanes,
Lanes littered with ashes, boxes, cans, old rags;
Dirty, musty, garbage-reeking lanes
Behind the soot-dripped backs of blunt houses,
Sour yards and slack-sagging fences? [...]

THE CITY OF NEIGHBOURHOODS

Are you sad?
Are you like that?

Another visitor who looks into the Ward's littered lanes and is sympathetic to the humanity he finds there is the protagonist of Augustus Bridle's 1924 novel, *Hansen*. A Scandinavian immigrant encountering Toronto for the first time, Olaf Hansen emerges from "the human fly-trap known as the Union Station" and is confronted almost immediately with the city's contrasts, chief among them the presence of a seething slum behind the formidable stone structure of City Hall:

> [O]n to University Avenue, so broad and sweeping under its elms that he was puz-
> zled to behold on the east side, rows of rickety shacks which seemed popping with
> queer people. He let himself digress here into what was evidently a large slum in
> which ramshackles on the street edge were screens for tumbledown tenements
> behind; where banana vendors, street-pianos, bearded patriarchs, Irishwomen,
> Billingsgaters, slouchy negroes, senoritas and swarming juveniles jostled in a cos-
> mopolis of humanity—the famous St. John's Ward.

Hansen asks a resident of the Ward—an immigrant like himself—for help in securing a bed and a meal before realizing the gravity of his error and leaving the Ward to seek lodgings in a more respectable part of the city. Still, he finds himself drawn unaccountably to the Ward, whose residents he sees engaged daily in vital acts of city-building. Indeed, their stories and struggles come to influence his university studies and subsequent political career as a national-ist who considers Canada's most stalwart citizens to be those who fell the for-ests, till the soil, survey the continent—and create new lives for their families in urban slums like the Ward.

Despite the sympathetic response of visitors like Harris and Hansen, most Toronto residents avoided the Ward, a district that social reformer Mary Joplin Clarke claimed was "generally regarded by the respectable citizens of Toronto as a strange and fearful place into which it is unwise to enter even in daylight."[102] Arguing that a combination of social and racial prejudice lay at the heart of the Ward's reputation, Clarke added, "The danger that lurks in these crowded streets is not always clearly formulated in the minds of those who fear it, perhaps it is the dagger of an Italian desperado of which they dream—per-haps the bearded faces of the 'Sheenies' are sufficient in themselves to inspire

---

102   Quoted in James, 2001; see also Betts, 2007. Mary Joplin Clarke was a social worker at Central Neighbourhood House, a community centre serving impoverished residents of the Ward; Clarke made these observations in a 1915 essay called "Life in the Ward."

terror—but at any rate the fear remains and probably it could best be analyzed as Fear of the Unknown."

But if the Ward was a source of fear among most respectable Torontonians, it was attractive to bootleggers, hustlers, con artists and the city's dissolute, who seemed to recognize something of themselves in the Ward's crooked corridors. The protagonist of Morley Callaghan's 1928 novel, *Strange Fugitive*—a work crime writer James Dubro has called "the first of the modern gangster novels"[103]—is a restless man who chafes at the confines of his domestic life and finds himself drawn to the corner of Yonge and Albert streets, where he loiters among the preachers and pickpockets at the perimeter of the Ward. One night, having lost his job and walked out on his wife, he decides spontaneously to rob a bootlegger and set himself up in business in the Ward, crossing a boundary that is as much moral as it is geographical.[104] In the Ward—or so it seems to Harry—the ordinary rules no longer apply, and he revels in the amoral unreality of his life and his rising prominence in the city's underworld until, perhaps inevitably, a gangland gunfight brings him down in a hail of bullets.

Given how sharply Callaghan contrasts the Ward, a warren of "Chinese merchants, chop-houses and dilapidated roughcast houses used for stores," with the practically pastoral topography of Harry's abandoned marriage, it is tempting to infer, as many contemporary commentators did, that the Ward exerted some dark power over the city, ensnaring upright citizens with its alien alchemy. But if the Ward was the white, middle-class city's Other, it should be understood not as the "respectable" city's opposite, but rather as its visible shadow. In many ways the Ward was a projection of characteristics deemed incongruent with the public image of Toronto the Good, even if in truth it was as much a part of the city's character as Orange parades, church picnics and prohibition. Nonetheless, even as "respectable" Torontonians patronized the Ward's speakeasies, brothels and burlesque halls, and provided reliable trade for bootleggers like Harry Trotter, as Steven Hayward makes clear in *The Secret Mitzvah of Lucio Burke*, ultimately the neighbourhood was understood best simply by its contrast to Toronto the Good: "The city's policemen and judges and magistrates and lawyers and most of its doctors and every one of its mayors are members of the Orange Order. The rest of the people are pressed into a dirty corner of the city called the Ward [...] where the Italians and Jews live—the wops and the kikes, as they are mostly called by most of the city."

---

103   See Dubro's introduction to the 2004 reissue of *Strange Fugitive*.

104   A number of critics have commented on the moral topography of Callaghan's novels; see, for example, Dennis (2000), Edwards (1998), Woodcock (1972).

Despite being "pressed into a dirty corner" of Toronto, the Ward and its residents loomed large in the city's imagination until mid-century. One of the district's biggest problems was its visible persistence.[105] Disturbed that slum conditions continued to define the area even in the 1950s, in "City Hall Street" Raymond Souster described the Ward as "an open sore on the face of God":

O this courtyard never changes,
  it's still the same dirt, same rot, same smell,
  same squirming, crawling tenement, tin-roofed sweat-box
on the lower slopes of Hell.

Perceived as "a cancer of the modern civic organism" and a threat to Toronto's self-image,[106] inevitably the Ward became a target for commercial redevelopment and civic improvement projects destined to eradicate it. In 1909 a section of the Ward was demolished to make room for a new general hospital, and a surging real estate market during subsequent decades propelled the rapid conversion of speculative slum holdings into lucrative commercial properties in Toronto's expanding downtown core.[107] Even a significant increase in owner occupancy in the remainder of the Ward did not stem the tide for long. During the Ward's long decline, its residents moved west toward Spadina Avenue, where many of them worked in Toronto's garment industry. At the turn of the century the bulk of Toronto's Jewish population had been concentrated in the Ward, but by 1931 Kensington Market was home to 80 percent of the city's Jews.[108] Between 1947 and 1955 the City acquired and finally expropriated properties in the south end of the Ward—by then known as Toronto's first Chinatown[109]—to build Viljo Revell's City Hall, and after that the Ward was no more.

Near the end of his examination of Lawren Harris's paintings and poetry engaging with the Ward, Greg Betts acknowledges that although "[t]here is nothing left of the Ward [...] the neighbourhood survives in spirit in Kensington Market." On the whole, unlike representations of the Ward (which focused mainly on its slum conditions or examined cultural and class conflict occur-

---

105 By the early twentieth century, the Ward had housed destitute Torontonians for well over a generation. In *Toronto: Past and Present*, C. Pelham Mulvany referred to the Ward as being "of unsavoury appearance and repute" and went on to describe even its better streets as being "occupied by dingy and rotten wooden shanties, the dens of Jewish old clothes sellers and recipients of stolen goods." (1884)

106   See Duffy, 2001; Purdy, 1997.

107 Dennis, 1995.

108 Cochrane, 2000.

109 Yee, 2005. Yee notes that Toronto now has at least half a dozen "Chinatowns," including concentrations in the Gerrard and Broadview area and in Scarborough, Markham and Richmond Hill.

ring within its boundaries),[110] depictions of Kensington Market have typically emphasized its community-mindedness and sensual qualities.

Something else that has survived in spirit are outsiders' perceptions of the Market as a foreign place in the middle of the familiar city. In Lauren B. Davis's novel *The Stubborn Season*, a young gentile woman visits the Market to look for a man who knows something about her missing uncle, lost among the thousands of men who have travelled across the country looking for work during the Depression. Arriving at College and Spadina and feeling lost and out of place, Irene reflects on her sudden feeling of foreignness: "[I]t was just a mile or so from her own house, but it could have been on another continent completely." Asking for directions to Baldwin Street, she walks tentatively into Kensington Market for the first time:

> Soon she was in the midst of the market area. It was a narrow, labyrinthine network of streets and alleys. Even in the cold air, the smells were so strong she could taste them on her tongue. Chickens and rabbits and pigeons in cages, fish and rotting garbage, cooking cabbage and meat. The little tilting houses were pushed right up to the sidewalk, which was covered with pickle barrels and half-frozen rotting lettuce leaves and a steaming pile of what might have been chicken guts and newspapers written in an odd squiggly script.

Entering Kensington Market for the first time, outsiders like Irene found the neighbourhood a shocking departure from the staid streets of Anglo-Saxon Toronto. To Market-area residents, however, Kensington's accents and odours were harbingers of home in the midst of a hostile city.

In his 2007 novel, *Baldwin Street*, Alvin Rakoff inventories some of the objects that brightened Kensington Market even in the Depression-darkened city:

> The red of radishes. The green of Granny Smiths. The lime of limes. The orange or oranges. The yellow of squash. Pale cabbages. Dark aubergines. Purple marrows. Beet root reds. Violet plums. [...] The beiges of earthenware bowls from black-brown to delicate cream. Pots. Pans. Aluminum or enamel. Cups. Saucers. Dishes. Porcelain or fine china. Glasses. Tumblers. Pitchers. Basins. Nuts. Beans.

---

110 Lawren Harris's Ward poems and Barbara Greenwood's *Factory Girl* both emphasize the Ward's more derelict qualities, while Stephen Hayward's *The Secret Mitzvah of Lucio Burke* and John Miller's *A Sharp Intake of Breath* focus more on cultural identity and the community that developed even in the face of anti-Semitism and economic inequality. Notably, Harris and Greenwood's works were written or are set in the early part of the century, while Hayward and Miller's novels describe Ward conditions in the 1930s, reflecting relative increases in stability (if not always prosperity) enjoyed by Toronto's Jews.

Barley. Chick peas. Combs. Brushes. Brooms. Mops. Undershirts. Undershorts. T-shirts. Trousers. Pants. Shorts. Jeans. If we ain't got it, lady, we get it for you, lady. What colour you want?

Seeming almost to anticipate external judgements levelled at the Market, Rakoff adds, "Baldwin Street was a mass of colours. Not organized. Not neatly planted arrays. Not row on row of pristine perfection. As with the front of other peoples' houses. Not here. But higgledy-piggledy. Random. Colours. Bombarding the eye. Colours."

Chaotic and colourful, Kensington Market was, even during the Depression, a tightly knit community connected through family affiliation, enterprise and the rituals of *Erev Shabbos*. If there is an Old Testament quality to literary representations of the era, it is because family lineage was highly pertinent to residents' lives. In Shirley Faessler's story "Henye," a genealogical summary precedes and informs the narrative:

When Chayelle came to us as stepmother I was six years old. We lived in rooms over the synagogue on Bellevue Avenue; and Yankev with his wife, Henye, and their daughter, Malke, who was a dipper at Willard's Chocolates and engaged to be married to a druggist, lived around the corner from us on Augusta Avenue. Their youngest son, Pesach, lived with his wife, Lily, in the upstairs flat of his father's house. Their other four sons were domiciled with their wives and children around and about the city.

Alvin Rakoff underscores the importance of lineage in his story "Names," invoking the surnames of Kensington's prominent families:

Goodbaum and Mandelbaum and Birmbaum and Applebaum. The names of Baldwin Street. What names! Names to rejoice in. Names to celebrate. Goldberg and Hershberg and Bloomberg and Rosenberg. And just plain Berg. Altman, Lieberman, Grossman, Goldman [...] Gelman, Simon, Levinson, Liebovitz, Brodsky, Sroka, Starkman, Salem, Seiden. And more. Mel Lastman became Mayor of Toronto. Joe Berman founded Cadillac Fairview. Arthur Kruger was Dean of Arts and Sciences at the University of Toronto. Frank Gehry, architect, renowned worldwide. Baldwin Street boys. Alumni of the ghetto.

Kensington Market's identity, Rakoff suggests, was derived from the names of the families who ran its businesses, attended its shuls and looked out for one another in its alleys and byways. When at mid-century the names began to change—"The Ostroffs became the Owens. Givertz became Givens"—it meant the Market had changed as well. If the Market had always seemed exotic to Anglo-Saxon Torontonians, by mid-century it began to seem foreign to Toronto's Jews, many of whom had moved to North Toronto to become middle-class inner-suburbanites.

Artist Joe Rosenthal and author Adele Wiseman capture this change in their 1964 collaboration, *Old Markets, New World*, which pairs sketches and text to evoke childhood memories of the Market. Observing that Canada's Jewish markets had, even by the early 1960s, developed a "strangeness" about them, Wiseman notes, "It is the strangeness of the past persistent, the past persisting into a future which probably has no place for it." Turning to Toronto's Kensington Market in particular, she adds,

> But most of the market dealers were of a generation that is gradually passing away. And the customers were mainly fairly recent immigrants and those of us who like to drop in on the past, occasionally, when we have time.

Still, any wistfulness in Wiseman's reminiscences is tempered by an appreciation of the present, and she concludes, "But if the markets, as we knew them, are doomed to disappear some day, the old market men will be the last to mourn. They did not bring up their sons to stand all day long in the cold, blowing on freezing knuckles, nor to stand wiping the steam from their eyes in the day-long heat."

From the 1960s onward, particularly as Portuguese, West Indian, South American, Chinese and Vietnamese specialty stores began to replace many of the Jewish businesses, Kensington Market became something of a tourist attraction, a chance for Anglo-Saxon Torontonians to encounter the exotic in their own city. Writers engaging with the Market, particularly those who encounter it as tourists, have responded increasingly to its aesthetic and sensory qualities, representing the Market's sensual splendours—its textures and smells in particular—as peculiarly corporeal metaphors for cultural diversity. In "Kensington Market," poet Raymond Souster invites visitors to

> examine fruits and vegetables
> as you would the breasts
> of a woman taken
> to bed for the first time

Souster is not the only poet who emphasizes the carnal qualities of Kensington Market's carnival atmosphere. In "Varied Hues," Irving Layton suggests that the Market seduces those who are drawn toward its depths:

O those lovely black corrupt olives. Nowhere else have I seen such generous ones winking at me with the moist eyes of a thousand Fatimas. I lost my heart to them on my first visit and haunt the place ever since. Fondly, I gaze at them and the crowds diverse as the maps of the world. They also hunger for sensations only this fabulous realm can gratify.

In "The Piscatorial Sonnets," Michael Holmes mythologizes the Market's origins as a sexual congress transacted midway between the Mediterranean and the Middle East, where, amid "[t]he market-place diurnal, the wafting notes of spice; / this is where father desert and mother sea / couple."

In suggesting that the Market's main appeal lies in the unmistakably sexual invitation it offers to visitors drawn into its depths, Souster, Layton and Holmes attach themselves to a long-standing literary tradition that conflates the exotic with the erotic.[111] But if Kensington Market is the city's colonized body, an open-air brothel where not only fruit but culture itself is set out to be squeezed and sold, then who is the pimp and who is the procurer?

In *Emerald City*, John Bentley Mays describes Kensington Market as a carnival, invoking architectural historian Spiro Kostof's portrayal of city streets as improvised spectacles where encounters are unscheduled and performances always unrehearsed, places where memory meets desire, where it is possible—indeed necessary—to be at once invisible and archetypal. But to those tempted to view Kensington as a carnival of consumption or a spectacle of the flesh, Mays cautions, "The Market is no neat theme park of Shopping Past. It is a living, bruising, sweaty history."

Those who have lived that history are markedly ambivalent about Kensington's cultural cacophony and the chaotic warren of its streets. The narrator of Neil Bissoondath's novel *A Casual Brutality*—a medical student who has come to Canada to escape the chaos and filth of Salmonella, his tellingly named hometown in a country referred to as Casaquemada (for "burning house")—responds simply with disgust:

The pigeons strutted stiffly, collapsed in clucking confusion in their confining wire cages stacked one on the other at the edge of the sidewalk, their acrid excrement spilling and dripping like a thin grey gruel into the drain. The cheese stores, narrow, crowded, brash with blaring radios, emitted the rankness of age

111 See, for example, Irving C. Schick's *The Erotic Margin: Sexuality and Spatiality in Alterist Discourse* (Verso, 1999). Using examples drawn from fiction, anthropology and travel literature, Schick argues that "exotic" spaces are simultaneously segregated and transgressed through discourses of sexuality and power. As one of Toronto's most visible spaces where the familiar and foreign intersect, it is hardly surprising to encounter literary texts that both exoticize and eroticize Kensington Market's spaces and inhabitants.

and curdle. Outside the vegetable shops, quantities of discarded fruits and greens suppurated in the heat like miniature heaps of compost. [...] Kensington Market, with its air of international peasantry, with its hand-painted signs in Portuguese, Hindi, Italian, with its promise of French pastries, Jamaican meat patties, Jewish bagels, with its intestinal streets clogged by cars and vans, with its implosive hot-house atmosphere, was a disappointment.

Nor does Kensington Market hold any nostalgic appeal for Carla, one of the protagonists of Dionne Brand's *What We All Long For*, because it reminds her of a cultural heritage she is trying to evade:

On Saturdays Nadine, Carla's stepmother, would take her to Kensington Market, where laden with bags Carla would wait, her body in an impatient and resigned burning, as Nadine talked to the storekeepers, haggling an extra piece of fish, an extra lime, an extra pepper, mistrustful of the weighing of every item. [...] Carla stood waiting, her nose rejecting the smells, her throat gagging on rotten fish and rotten vegetables, her face turning away from the appalling blood stains on butchers' aprons at European Meats, her whole being wishing to be elsewhere.

Unlike her stepmother, who has embraced her husband's Jamaican tastes and habits, Carla is eager to get away from her father and everything (including everything about herself) he represents. Brands adds, "She considered her father's customs foreign, embarrassing oddities that she would try to distance herself from in public. [...] So overwhelming was the whole market that the taste in her mouth was sweet and sickly at the same time. She vowed never to come here when she grew up."

For others, however, the Market provides rare opportunities for reconnection. The protagonist of M. G. Vassanji's *No New Land* encounters a woman whose family he had once known in their hometown of Dar Es Salaam. She invites him to her Kensington Market apartment for tea, and Nurdin begins a clandestine, albeit chaste, affair with his countrywoman, each visit sweetened with gifts of fruit or bread from one of the Market's stalls. Like the Market itself, Vassanji writes, "[s]he seemed to understand him completely, and her responses were in a language, an idiom, a tone of voice that to him were perfectly empathetic."

Even strangers might find themselves speaking forgotten tongues in Kensington Market, drawn together in a place that both reinforces and salves their shared foreignness. In *Soucouyant*, David Chariandy describes a man and a woman who fall in love in the one part of the city where they both feel at liberty to act like themselves:

It was early one morning at the height of summer. Adele was walking through the congested lanes of the market, and she had passed vendors calling out to her from behind arrangements of plantain or dried shrimp or okra. She had glimpsed under a rude canvas tent three live chickens and a goat, their freshness unchallengeable. She felt alive in this place, attuned at once to dozens of different voices and smells.

All at once, careening through the market on a bicycle is the man Adele knows almost immediately will be her husband. As he trades barbs with shopkeepers and stumbles over a stray chicken, something about the way he moves and the subtle way he smells speaks to her across centuries of shared colonial history. Chariandy writes, "Something oily that saturated their skins, something sweet-rotten and dreaded that arose from past labours and traumas and couldn't ever seem to be washed away."

Still, in Kensington Market there is always a tension between legacy and aspiration. If the Market has long been a portal for those seeking entry, it is also a doorway most are relieved to exit. In an observation borne out by census data, John Bentley Mays observes, "Very few immigrants not forced by poverty to do so continue living in Kensington Market voluntarily," and adds,

> To my knowledge, the residents of the Market today are almost all recent immigrants too poor to do otherwise, university students playing poor, and a handful of sophisticated urbanists who, for some reason, *want* to live among the Market's racket and odours.

It is this very contradiction, however, that lies at the heart of Kensington Market's appeal to the condo buyers, graduate students, art-scene poseurs and Saturday-afternoon shoppers eager to sample what seems to them like a subculture. They are all seeking something authentic, even though the sidewalk-patio, loft-style, slightly sanitized version of Kensington they come to consume is precisely what puts the Market's authenticity in acute danger of disappearing.

And even these "sophisticated urbanists" who come slumming to Kensington Market seek to put their mark on it. In Sarah Dearing's *Courage My Love*, one new arrival, in flight from her bland Avenue Road life, seeks to impose order upon the market's chaotic landscape by reordering its streets:

> Her Kensington Market had been ordered in an efficient separation of products, and she labelled the main roads, for simplified reference, as Fish Street, Clothes and Vegetable Avenues. How much easier life could be if all streets had such utilitarian names; a person would always know precisely what to expect from an address.

But the Market has its own way of resisting such coercions, sometimes by transforming its intruders. Later, having renamed herself, having listened, loved, and laboured there, Philippa—who renames herself Nova in honour of her new life—learns to appreciate the market's organic splay, observing:

> Underneath, like all markets, it possessed an ancient rhythmic hum created from trade, community, basic needs met, marriages—or at least couplings—made. This same music turns to white noise at a modern mall, some special secret element removed by its enclosure or the attempts at convenience.

For all its noisy chaos, dry rot and dereliction, Kensington Market might be said to redeem the city. More than a cultural microcosm of Toronto, it is also a patch of unrestrained humanity that leaks out into the rest of the city and makes it live a little more fully. As Dionne Brand's narrator muses in her story "At the Lisbon Plate, "This is my refuge. It is where I can be invisible or, if not invisible, at least drunk. [...] The smell from the market doesn't bother me. I've been here before, me and the old lady. We know the price of things. Which is why I feel safe in telling stories here."

PARKDALE, SCUMMY PARKDALE

Parkdale is a study in contrasts: dowager mansions turned into rooming houses, renovated row houses with granite kitchen counters and a separate nanny suite, hip hotel lounges where goateed graduate students mingle with local winos, crumbling high rises tenanted by single mothers and psychiatric out-patients, and luxury condos marketed to the artists whose industrial lofts were torn down so they could be built. In *Stunt*, about a young girl who haunts the streets of Parkdale for a decade in hopes of finding her missing father, Claudia Dey encapsulates the neighbourhood's contradictions:

> We live in Parkdale, a village in the west end of the city of Toronto, made up of Victorian mansions that used to border the lake. Women with parasols and bath-ing suits down to their calves, women with consumption, walked the beach, Sun-nyside Beach. Now the highway sits on top of us, a beleaguered crown, turning Parkdale into a tired beauty queen. Feathers in her hair. Crinolines in a knot. She is grand. She is slumped. She is a rooming house with clapboard siding, transoms, cornices and turrets. Her voice is parched and playful. She is all invitation. She will take you in when nobody else will.

These incongruities do not make for unmitigated chaos, a point Gwendolyn MacEwen emphasizes in *Noman's Land* in a description of one of Parkdale's principal intersections:

> The craziest intersection in the city is where King and Queen and Roncesvalles meet in a mad jumble of streetcar tracks which have been ripped up and rearranged a hundred times in the past. Finally, somehow, one street subtly becomes another. It is hard to tell what happens exactly—Queen devours King? Roncesvalles surrenders to King? Anyway, it all sorts itself out, or braids itself together, depending on how you look at it.

It is in the same way that one Parkdale—the Parkdale of rooming houses and crack addicts, or the Parkdale of karaoke night at the renovated Gladstone Hotel—subtly becomes another. It is hard to tell where—or when—to draw the lines between them, but somehow the neighbourhood fits together even though Parkdale is the one part of Toronto that seems determined to travel in several directions at once.

In *Suburb, Slum, Urban Village*, a scholarly study of Parkdale in transition, urban historian Carolyn Whitzman argues that three dominant narratives have defined Parkdale since its residential streets were first laid out in the 1870s. Parkdale, she reports, was marketed as a residential suburb from 1875 until the early twentieth century, when media and municipal politicians began referring to the declining neighbourhood as a slum, citing industrial intensification and an increasing immigrant population as causes of its decay. Parkdale's decline accelerated in 1955 when many of its lakefront mansions were demolished and submerged under the Gardiner Expressway while others were converted into rooming houses or replaced with medium- and high-rise apartment buildings. Whitzman suggests that Parkdale has been represented as an "urban village" since the late 1960s, although she acknowledges its bifurcated image as a gentrifying area blemished by pockets of seemingly intractable poverty.

In reality, as Whitzman points out, Parkdale has always contained elements of all three narratives. From the beginning it was a mixed-use neighbourhood attractive to wealthy homeowners as well as transients and factory workers, meaning the "binary rhetoric" of suburb and slum has never been accurate. More recently, although Parkdale has for a generation been represented as an urban ghetto populated largely by crack-addled prostitutes and a dumping ground for deinstitutionalized psychiatric patients, residential property values have increased inexorably and an active residents' association doggedly opposes efforts to expand the stock of affordable housing in the neighbourhood. If unpacking these contradictory characterizations seems as challenging as navigating the serpentine intersection of King, Queen and Roncesvalles, it is helpful to consider that their antithesis—indeed their unifying element—is almost invariably a rundown, decrepit, slum-like Parkdale presented as a contrast class to the family-oriented "flowery suburb" or gentrified urban district dreamed of by city planners, developers and residential landowners.

Most Toronto neighbourhoods seek to capitalize on local assets such as their proximity to the ravines or the size and character of their dwellings, but in Parkdale it is the district's downward mobility that has made it hip. With a combination of dread and a perverse sort of pleasure, Toronto writers portray Parkdale as a seedy, sometimes violent corner of the city, cloaking themselves in its squalor like an abused or abusive lover one cleaves to out of habit or fear rather than any residual affection.

In "Parkdale," a semi-scatological performance piece made popular at '90s-era open stages, Cad Gold Jr. (aka Cad Lowlife) and collaborator Rob Siciliano (a well-known Toronto spoken-word artist who died of lymphoma in 2004) would shout,

> In Parkdale, scummy Parkdale
> A Junkie does a Fix
> Whores suck on dicks
> Asshole beats his wife
> Goof takes a life [...]
> In Parkdale, scummy Parkdale
> Drunks spend their welfare cheques on booze
> In a bus shelter
> someone take a snooze

A spiritual complement to "Parkdale" are the lyrics to Big Rude Jake's punk-rockabilly song "Cold Steel Hammer," whose narrator invokes Parkdale in abject language:

> The sun comes up like stink off a dumpster
> And Parkdale wriggles like a leech
> And somewhere on the corner of Hell's half-acre
> The morning comes and kicks me in the teeth

These performance pieces are joined by Trevor Clark's 1989 novella *Born to Lose*, whose protagonists include a thirty-something woman who turns tricks for spare change and an amoral graduate student who takes her in, unsure whether his attraction is rooted in sexual desire or the opportunity to wield power over her. To Graham, gazing down from his Queen Street apartment, Parkdale is a spectacle, supplying source material for a research essay or a story he might eventually write:

> Graham looked out the window and watched a man on the sidewalk apparently talking to himself. He considered the overflow of psychiatric cases who reportedly lived in local rooming houses as outpatients; he often passed people on Queen soliloquizing. He loved south Parkdale for its older Victorian houses, colourful array of characters, trees lining the side streets, trolley cars, the nearby lake, Sunnyside Beach, cats roaming the garbage cans, the numerous yellow police cruisers.

Graham thinks of himself as detached from his surroundings but ends up drawn into Parkdale's squalid dramas as inexorably as the cockroaches roving restlessly across his walls.

In Mike Morey's comedic novel *Uncle Dirty*, Parkdale is depicted in the early stages of gentrification, with pockets of refurbished homes sharing the transitional streetscape with unimproved hovels:

> Young couples making a double-barreled foray into wedlock and the real estate market had recently bought the two end units of the row house. The district of Parkdale was making the transition from a predominantly elderly and Polish neighbourhood to a youthful English one. Children were appearing on the streets for the first time in decades, giving the area a poly-generational aspect it hadn't known in forty years. Contractors' vans blocked the sidewalks and Volvos appeared in driveways. And amid all this restoration and renovation, number twenty-three remained the local eyesore. [...] Odie's porch had lately taken a turn for the worse, listing ominously and destroying the illusion that the structure was sound.

Bowing to neighbourhood pressure, Odie finally hires someone to fix the porch, but instead of buying wood from a lumberyard, the contractor steals the planks from nearby park benches—all stencilled "City of Toronto Parks and Recreation"—and hammers them to the rotting joists, inducing the street's entire homeless population to relocate to Odie's front porch.

More provoking is Sandy Pool's long poem *Exploding into Night*, which anthropomorphizes Parkdale as eyewitness to a woman's murder, its dumpsters and alleyways awash with broken body parts strewn like markers across a macabre treasure map:

Imagine it is early. On Dovercourt, the men
have retreated, finally back to whence they
came. Piss-stained alleys mute and desolate. A
woman scurries out from behind the onion-
domed church, picks through dumpsters
lined against the curb. Rupturing the deaf
sleep of the city. Light rises from the streets,
fume-like, half-afraid. [...]
On the street someone is screaming. You push
through the day, its difficult topography.

Writing, "What / the street sees is anybody's garbage," Pool finds Parkdale the
perfect counterpart to a narrative of death and violence.

Other writers apply a kinder and more critical lens to Parkdale. Chief among
them is anti-poverty activist Pat Capponi, who portrays Parkdale with considerable sensitivity in her novel *Last Stop Sunnyside*. Accounting for the neighbourhood's long slide into dereliction, Capponi writes,

A Parkdale address once held a certain cachet, due to its proximity to Lake Ontario
and the hugely popular Sunnyside Amusement Park, which had been a major
draw for thousands of Toronto families every summer. The area's more vocal and
politically active ratepayers and business associations complain that Parkdale has
been turned into a dumping ground for alcoholics, drug addicts, ex-cons and de-
institutionalized mental patients. But none of these groups was responsible for
Parkdale's decline. It was the exodus of the wealthy that started the rush to the
bottom, after the closure of the park and the building of the Gardiner Expressway,
which cut off easy access to the lake in the fifties.

Noting that "[i]n spite of all the hyperbole and invective, which tends to reach a
crescendo at public meetings, the streets are mostly safe," Capponi's narrator,
a psychiatric survivor living in a King Street rooming house, finds in Parkdale
both community and comfort:

As I walk up to Queen Street, I recognize that there are indeed times when the
neighbourhood feels like one big institution, an all-purpose holding facility for the
mad, the criminal, the simply poor. Judging by media coverage of the area, bodies
should be a foot deep in the streets, but on a sunny day like this, even the dealers
crowding the corners, jostling each other in their loud, competitive hawking to
passersby, seem inordinately cheerful, the tension that ages and scars their faces
gone for the moment.

Adding, "There's a tolerance here for difference, eccentricity, the less-than-legal that can't be found in other parts of the city," Dana refutes the monolithic narrative of Parkdale as an unmitigated morass of violence and addiction.

Located just outside the old boundaries of the Village of Parkdale a block east of Dufferin and Queen, the Gladstone Hotel is Parkdale's spiritual epicentre. Until its recent renovation into a hip hotspot hosting high-profile cultural events, with thirty-seven hotel rooms designed by local artists, for decades the Gladstone provided low-rent accommodation and served cheap booze to local brawlers. As poet Paul Goldberg once mused, "They call it the Gladstone / because people are glad they are stoned." In another spoken-word piece, Christian Christian finds the Gladstone a more menacing entity and imagines having been molested by it as a young child:

> I am frightened by the Gladstone. I am certain that it follows me home every Tuesday night & I suspect that it wants to kill me because I know too much. You see I believe I am holding repressed memories of having been sexually molested by the Gladstone when I was a small child. It was 1957 I think when it snuck away from its foundations in a terrible shaking mambo of gravel shooting, stone dusting sleepwalking perhaps induced by a spilling of beer in its tower.

If an imposing, predatory Gladstone was a potent symbol of the old Parkdale, it has also become a hallmark of stability in the midst of a changing landscape. In *Gently Down the Stream*, novelist Ray Robertson depicts the Gladstone, on the very cusp of its conversion to a hip nightspot, as an important part of Parkdale's legacy:

> I've walked by the Gladstone Hotel dozens of times, even sipped cheap draft beer there once or twice with Phil years before as a slumming undergrad. Downstairs, it's a cavernous beer hall looking out onto Queen Street through a large street-level window and dotted with Parkdale regulars nursing dollar glasses of Export, checking out their horoscopes and Biodex at the back of the *Sun*, and generally trying to beat back the gloom. Upstairs, there are small rooms for rent with a shared bathroom at the end of each floor and no electrical cooking devices whatsoever, please. Once upon a time an entirely different demographic, travelling salesmen and itinerant labourers of long-dead decades slept and socialized upstairs and down. Now, anybody who needs a place to fuck, shoot up, or spoon out their welfare check by the week calls the Gladstone home.

Robertson's narrator, an armchair philosopher who gets a job as karaoke-night doorman at the Gladstone, watches the neighbourhood change around him with increasing anger. Late one night, out walking his dog, he sees a sign advertising the "Legacy Lofts," offering luxury living "in a unique 19th century setting" and gets out a can of spray paint to vandalize it, a small act of resistance against corporate-driven gentrification.

The protagonist of Zoe Whittall's *Holding Still For as Long as Possible* offers a succinct assessment of the social costs and benefits of neighbourhood change in Parkdale. Noting, "there was a new form of uncertainty in the air [...] On the sidewalks I often kicked giant screws that had fallen from fast-rising construction sites," she adds,

> A hotel that used to provide the neighbourhood a certain visible sketch factor had been rebuilt into a boutique hotspot called the Drake Hotel, with a hipster happy hour and over-priced entrees. The first Starbucks. Residents had reacted as if someone had taken a big shit on their front porch. [...] Roxy organized walks around the neighbourhood trying to mobilize residents against the encroaching virus of progress. She was full of historical tidbits, and she rallied against the take-over. Me, well, I secretly hoped they really would build the rumoured Loblaws or Shoppers Drug Mart. Then I wouldn't have to stand between peed-pants man and boob-touch guy at the 1-8 items aisle at Price Chopper.

Like many residents, Billy is ambivalent about what change will mean for Parkdale. Unable to determine whether she prefers the "authentic" Parkdale or a newer, better-serviced version of it, she realizes that what she really wants is both. And in the end this is the most honest assessment of Parkdale: what works best for the neighbourhood is a vision that accommodates rooming houses alongside renovated single-family homes and makes room for crack whores as well as condos.

In the conclusion to *Suburb, Slum, Urban Village*, Carolyn Whitzman invokes political theorist Iris Marion Young in arguing that what Parkdale needs—indeed, what it does best—is to provide "the cardinal virtues of city life": social difference without exclusion, variety and diversity in land use, eroticism (the pleasure and danger of the strange and surprising), and publicity (the encounters with difference that are the hallmark of public space). If, as Whitzman argues, Parkdale has successfully resisted the images—suburb, slum and urban village—imposed upon it, then undoubtedly an important part of that resistance has been the production of narratives emphasizing "scummy" Parkdale's violent, abject, absurd, exclusionary and nostalgic qualities.

THE MASSEYS AND THE MASSES: SOCIAL AND SPATIAL ASCENDANCY IN ROSEDALE AND FOREST HILL

In 1952, when noted Canadian man of letters B. K. Sandwell quipped that "Toronto has no social classes— / Only the Masseys and the Masses,"[112] he articulated one of Toronto's most deeply held cultural conceits. In a city that compulsively asserts social equality among its citizens, Torontonians are paradoxically prone to venerating the city's elites, thus engaging in a kind of collective cognitive dissonance that has become a defining feature in literary representations of two of Toronto's most refined neighbourhoods, Rosedale and Forest Hill.

Ever since their streets were first laid out, residents of Rosedale and Forest Hill have made a virtue of their geographical and social elevation above the low-lying terrain housing the unwashed masses of the inner city. Rosedale's mansions are perched principally above a network of ravines that bound it on three sides; the enclave is further protected from incursion by a circuitous network of roads and bridges that help preserve Rosedale's air of privacy and prestige. Finally, along the north periphery of Rosedale runs a CPR line that, as journalist Harry Bruce once observed, "separates Moore Park from Rosedale, thereby helping to protect each one from the cultural contamination of the other."[113]

Forest Hill's distinguishing feature is its position immediately above "the Hill," a promontory of land rising above the former shore of Lake Iroquois that helps insulate its denizens from the prosaic affairs of the city below. In *The Torontonians*, Phyllis Brett Young explains the symbolic importance of the Hill to Forest Hill, Rosedale and the then-emerging community of Moore Park :

> [H]er life had been divided into two separate sections as definitely as the city was
> divided by the Hill which was far more than a simple geographical line of demar-
> cation. To live below the Hill was, metaphorically, to live on the wrong side of the
> tracks, and excusable only if your father was a professional man. Even when this
> was the case, it was not considered in good taste to *like* living below the Hill.

112 Quoted in Scott and Smith, 1967. The complete verse reads, "Let the Old World, where rank's yet vital, / Part those who have and have not title. / Toronto has no social classes— / Only the Masseys and the masses." There are multiple layers of irony in this aphorism, given that the Right Honourable Vincent Massey—on the occasion of whose appointment to Governor General Sandwell's lines were written—made significant efforts to distinguish himself from his family's wealth and power while relying on it to fulfil his political and cultural ambitions. See Bissell, 1981; 1986. The final lines of Sandwell's verse also appear in Phyllis Brett Young's *The Torontonians* (1960), in a passage describing the subtleties of social class in Toronto.

113 A well-known *Toronto Star* columnist and magazine editor, Harry Bruce undertook regular psychogeographic-style walks in many Toronto neighbourhoods and wrote about them under the pseudonym Max MacPherson. "Dawn Raid on Darkest Rosedale," from which Bruce's observation is drawn, appears in *The Short Happy Walks of Max MacPherson* (1968).

The protagonist of Eric Wright's novel *Smoke Detector* extends this analysis, averring that Spadina Road—one of Forest Hill's principal thoroughfares—should be thought of as entirely distinct from the long blocks of Spadina Avenue that most Torontonians associate with the polyglot spectacle of Kensington Market and Chinatown. The Hill is anthropomorphized as a social adjudicator, accommodating Torontonians who settle on its slopes according to their wealth and station. Musing, "The rich are different from us [...] they live in Forest Hill," Wright's protagonist goes on to define the social significance of Spadina Road as it rises the Hill:

> The village stands at the top of Spadina Road which has been one of the great caravan routes of upwardly mobile immigrants since the nineteenth century. [...] As Spadina Avenue crosses Bloor Street, it becomes Spadina Road and passes through an area inhabited mainly by respectable transients—students, "singles" setting up house for the first time—then it climbs north through a middle-class district until it crosses St. Clair Avenue and becomes for a mile or two the main street of Forest Hill Village. The village is synonymous in Toronto minds with the Jewish Establishment, although it was originally created by successful Anglos and still honours Protestant thrift in the shape of Timothy Eaton United Church, a cathedral blessed by the money of the successful shopkeeper to whom the church is dedicated.

The symbolic significance of the Hill receives further emphasis in *Crestwood Heights*, sociologist John R. Seeley's well-known mid-century study of a thinly disguised Forest Hill. Underscoring the importance of topography to the district's self-image, Seeley writes,

> The very name "Crestwood Heights" expresses to perfection the "total personality" of the community, particularly in its relation to the metropolis of which it is a part. That name suggests, as it is clearly meant to do, the sylvan, the natural, and the romantic, the lofty and serene, the distant but not withdrawn; the suburb that looks out upon, and over the city, not in it or of it, but at its border and on its crest. The name is a source of pride, a guide for differential conduct (to some degree at least), but first and foremost a symbol evoking deference. Crestwood Heights is bound inescapably to Big City by many ties, but the proximity of the heterogeneous metropolitan area provides chiefly a foil against which Crestwood Heights can measure its own superiority and exclusiveness, core of its communal identity.

From this physical and metaphorical perch above the city, Forest Hill has, as William French writes with false modesty in *A Most Unlikely Village: An Informal*

History of the Village of Forest Hill, "attracted attention and exerted influence out of all proportion to its size."

The chief distinction between Forest Hill and Rosedale has to do with the origins and vintage of their residents' wealth. Forest Hill was founded and remains favoured by entrepreneurs and highly paid professionals. To approving observers, this marks it as a community of self-made men and mavens. To a different breed of privileged Torontonians, namely those affiliated historically with Rosedale, it is unseemly *nouveau riche*. Where Forest Hill Villagers have by reputation been preoccupied with wealth and conspicuous consumption, Rosedaleans have, since the community's earliest days, been represented as fixated on lineage and rank.

In *Mary's Rosedale and Gossip of Little York*, a quasi-biographical narrative of nineteenth-century Rosedale personages, Alden G. Meredith describes an elderly York couple's visit to their recently married daughter's home in Rosedale using language that broadcasts their—and her—dynastic ambitions:

> They have come to pay a formal call upon their granddaughter Mary, who has, in her recent marriage, so nearly fulfilled their hopes and desires, when she chose for her husband young William Botsford Jarvis, High Sheriff of the Home district.

Mary is, of course, Mary Boyles Powell, the granddaughter of Chief Justice William Dummer Powell and his wife, Anne Murray Powell, both Loyalists descended from prominent American families. Mary gave Rosedale its earliest identity after naming her husband's large estate to honour the wild roses that grew prolifically around the house and grounds. For his part, William Botsford Jarvis was a leading member of the Family Compact who, in his role as sheriff, is credited with having quashed the Upper Canada Rebellion in 1837.

The contemporary protagonist of Kim Moritsugu's novel *The Glenwood Treasure* reinforces this focus on inherited status, underscoring Rosedale's separation from the city while emphasizing her family's pedigree within its exclusive ranks:

> In the mid-nineteenth century, when the city was a small grid of neatly laid out streets clustered around the harbour and named after kings, queens and English market towns, Rose Park was a wooded area ten miles away where rich people built country houses. By the turn of the twentieth century, once-isolated estates had acquired closer neighbours in newly constructed manors. Soon, roads were laid that linked Rose Park to its environs, and bridges were constructed across the ravines. With access came development, the building of more houses, many grand enough to confirm the neighbourhood's reputation

as an exclusive, moneyed enclave. Emphasis on old establishment money, of my father's kind.

Even more than its distinctive topography, it is this overlapping combination of connections—forged in the shelter of private schools, exclusive clubs and dynastic marriages—that separates Rosedale from the rest of the city. Still, Rosedale's borders are not entirely impermeable. Moritsugu's narrator adds:

> For every stretch of ravine-lot mansions with multiple car garages (and coach houses), there are a few blocks of modest, 1920s-era four-bedroom boxes. A short retail strip features railroad flats above the few stores. And here and there, on Rose Park's outer, lesser streets, are small, one-storey, never-renovated houses built as workers' cottages, some the size of a one-bedroom apartment.

Timothy Findley emphasizes this latter point in *Headhunter*, describing in eschatological tones Rosedale's gradual loss of grandeur, a decline his narrator attributes to socioeconomic shifts and the slow disintegration of many of the neighbourhood's dynasties:

> Olivia's childhood had been lived at the very heart of Rosedale. South Drive was Rosedale's aorta. (Its vena cava was Crescent Road.) But the ebb and flow of its life was sluggish now—constrained and ill at ease. Newcomers—bearing gifts of money but none of taste—had come to buy the old houses, divide them up and rent them piecemeal back to the descendents of those who had been the original owners. The rents were exorbitant and sometimes smacked of a slap in the face—but that's what you got for being born out of time. Your name was often all you had—and the memory of place—and the absent shade of trees cut down in your exile.

Whether as renters or owners, outsiders occasionally claim a corner of Rosedale as their own, although not always without awkwardness or enmity on either or both sides.

In Margaret Atwood's *The Robber Bride*, a brash businesswoman, the daughter of Jewish immigrants who grew up in a rooming house, reflects upon what living in Rosedale has taught her:

> Old money whispers, new money shouts: one of the lessons Roz thought she had to learn, once. *Keep your voice down, Roz*, went her inner censor. Low tones, low profile, beige clothing: anything to keep from being spotted, located among the pushing hordes of new money, narrow-eyed, nervous money, bad-taste money, chip-on-the-shoulder money. Anything to avoid incurring the amused, innocent,

milky and maddening gaze of those who had never had to scrimp, to cut a few legal corners, to twist a few arms, to gouge a few eyes, to prove a thing. Most of the new money women were desperate, all dressed up and nowhere safe to go and nervous as heck about it [...] Though by now she's been new money for so long she's practically old money. In this country it doesn't take long.

Driving through Rosedale in a subdued Mercedes Benz, Roz contemplates "the fake Gothic turrets, the fake Georgian fronts, the fake Dutch gables, all melded by now into their own curious authenticity: the authenticity of well-worn money." Mentally appraising their worth as she drives, Roz observes that her own position on Rosedale has softened: "Much as she used to resent these prim, WASPy, self-assured houses, she's become fond of them over the years. Owning one helps. That, and the knowledge that a lot of the people who live in them are no better than they should be. No better than her."

Not every outsider living in Rosedale is able to make peace with the neighbourhood. In Austin Clarke's story "Four Stations in His Circle," a Barbadian immigrant resolves to buy a house in Rosedale, and begins saving money toward a down payment from his paint factory and post office jobs. Selecting an auspicious house during regular forays on foot, Jefferson wanders onto its grounds to inspect the house, not realizing he has already been identified as an outsider, a threat the community is quick to repel:

Five years of hard work have brought him here, tonight, in front of this huge mansion. *I going have to paint them windows green; and throw a coat o' paint on the doors ... the screens in the windows will be green like in the West Indies ... I going pull up them flowers and put in roses, red ones; and build a paling, and build up my property value ...* and he goes up on the lawn and tries to count the rooms in the four-storey house. *Imagine me in this house with four stories! and not one blasted tenant or boarder!* But he cannot count all the rooms from the front, so he goes through the alleyway to look at the back, and the rooms in the back and [...] four men pounce upon him and drag him along his lawn, with hands on his mouth and some in his guts, and drop him in the back seat of the car.

Despite being arrested for wandering around Rosedale at night, Jefferson buys the first house that comes on the market and moves in, although he cannot afford furniture and finds the rooms so empty he draws pictures of book-filled bookshelves on the walls. Repeatedly mistaken for the gardener, one day he snaps and tells his vacuous neighbour, "Look, I own this, yuh! And the name is Jefferson Theophillis-Belle!" Even after invitations to garden parties begin to land in his letterbox, Jefferson continues to be haunted by voices from the past asking him what he is doing and who he thinks he is. Eventually, having lost the post-office job and having learned that his mother has died because he bought a house in Rosedale rather than send her money for an operation, he ceases to distinguish fantasy from reality and wanders from room to room in the middle of the night, dressed in a fine suit and making small talk with invisible guests.

In keeping with our equivocal attitudes toward social class, Torontonians are conspicuously ambivalent about whether it is noble or decadent to live in Rosedale. In Wayne Johnston's novel *Human Amusements*, a newly wealthy family tours the city looking for a bigger home in a better neighbourhood. Their shared sense of anticipation turns to discord as soon as Rosedale enters the conversation:

> "Rosedale," my father said. "Why in God's name would we want to live in Rosedale?"
>
> "What's wrong with Rosedale?" my mother said.
>
> "What's wrong with it? It's Rosedale, that's what's wrong with it," my father said.
>
> "Could you be more specific?" my mother said.
>
> "I'd feel out of place there." [...]
>
> My mother replied that not everybody in Rosedale came from long-established families. There were people here like us, she said, self-made people who had been poor starting out.
>
> "We were never poor," my father said.
>
> "We were poor," my mother said. "But so were a lot of people who live here. Or at least their parents and grandparents were."
>
> My father said that was doubtless one of the standard lines that real estate agents fed the *nouveaux riches* to make them think they could be happy in a neighbourhood like Rosedale.

Even among some Rosedale-area residents there is a careful reticence about identifying too deeply with the neighbourhood. The protagonist of Hugh Hood's *The Swing in the Garden* describes himself, rather strenuously, as having grown up on a "fringe street, a kind of attic of Rosedale:"

> When I told people later on that I'd grown up in Rosedale, they were always impressed and ready to concede me a class distinction that I'd never thought of asserting. If I identified the location as "north Rosedale" the mistaken identification didn't occur, because north Rosedale was in some degree the dormitory of the servants of the south.

Timothy Findley makes a similar point in his story "Stones." His narrator describes a series of social and spatial distinctions that divide the sort of people who belong in Rosedale from those who do not:

We lived on the outskirts of Rosedale, over on the wrong side of Yonge Street. This was the impression we had, at any rate. Crossing the streetcar tracks put you in another world.

One September, my sister, Rita, asked a girl from Rosedale over to our house after school. Her name was Allison Pritchard and she lived on Cluny Drive. When my mother telephoned to see if Allison Pritchard could stay for supper, Mrs. Pritchard said she didn't think it would be appropriate. That was the way they talked in Rosedale: very polite; oblique and cruel.

Over on our side—the west side—of Yonge Street, there were merchants— and this, apparently, made the difference to those whose houses were in Rosedale. People of class were not supposed to live in the midst of commerce.

Nor would people of class exaggerate their affiliation with Rosedale, a point Hugh Garner makes in *Death in Don Mills*. A young criminal being interrogated by the police, asked about the places he grew up, invokes his social-climbing mother's spatial pretensions:

We moved into a flat in Rosedale, on Standish Avenue, backed up against the CPR main line. It's not a *Rosedale* Street, Inspector, if you know what I mean. The rich people in their mansions lived farther south, away from the main line railway track and the constant noise of passing freight trains. But it was *Rosedale*, don't you see? That's what made it important to her.

To the young man's mother, living within reach of Rosedale—and all that Rosedale money—was tantamount to the fulfilment of a dream although, he adds revealingly, "We were evicted for non-payment of rent on Standish. We lived in an upstairs flat."

As these narratives suggest, despite the high price of entry (even the modest north Rosedale homes Hood describes now sell for well over a million dollars despite their proximity to the railroad tracks), Forest Hill and Rosedale are no more or less homogenous than any other Toronto neighbourhood. Even so, more than a few literary representations of each neighbourhood have a quality of caricature or even menace about them, indications that writers (from without as well as within) feel that Forest Hill and Rosedale deserve to be brought down a notch. There are, for example, a disproportionate number of murder mysteries set in both neighbourhoods, among them James W. Nichol's *Midnight Cab*, set partly in Forest Hill, and Medora Sale's *Murder in a Good Cause*, Warren Dunford's *Making a Killing*, Liz Brady's *See Jane Run* and John Moss's *Still Waters*, set principally in Rosedale. Jon Ruddy's *The Rosedale Horror* is a pulp-gothic tale about a haunted mansion and an evil dowager who does away with overly curious interlopers.

Other literary works take aim at hubris, particularly those pointing at Toronto's most outrageous display of private wealth: Sir Henry Pellatt's famous folly, Casa Loma. Completed in 1914 and ceded to the City by its bankrupt owner less than twenty years later, Casa Loma has since been a hotel, a nightclub and, most recently, a museum. In *Summer Island*, the memoir of his Depression-era Toronto boyhood, Phil Murphy manages to convey envy, admiration and scorn in a few sentences, asking, "[I]s there dancing still at Casa Loma?" and adding,

> I suppose there must be; that grand old fake castle, the white elephant that rears its architectural absurdities on the Toronto skyline, would have to be kept standing somehow—and it's not much use for anything else, is it? I mean, when you have this place with a room big enough to let a whole regiment sit down to dinner, what else could you do but hold dances in it?

Not every writer is as cruel toward Pellatt's folly, however. In the children's story *The White Stone in the Castle Wall*, Sheldon Oberman describes a young boy who finds a large stone in his garden and resolves to haul it all to way to Casa Loma, where he has heard Henry Pellatt will pay one dollar for every coloured stone brought to help build a wall around the castle. John hauls his stone all the way up Spadina Hill, not noticing that the rain has washed his stone and left it pure white. Realizing that all his work has been for nothing, John leaves the stone with the castle's gardener, who is actually Pellatt in disguise. Admiring the effort, Sir Henry buys the stone anyway and has it built into the castle wall.

Dennis Lee's children's poem *The Cat and the Wizard* suggests that magic continues to reside within those very walls, describing an itinerant magician who wanders the streets of Toronto looking for a place to call home, until one day in a Laundromat he meets a cat who lives in Casa Loma, "Waiting and waiting / For someone to call." The cat invites the wizard to stay in the castle, which he does, bringing his big bag of tricks with him. In this way, Pellatt's folly becomes the city's most exclusive homeless shelter.

Other satires, particularly those directed at Rosedale, are harsher. Rachel Wyatt's *The Rosedale Hoax*, for example, combines intrigue and satire to suggest that far darker currents lurk beneath the placid surface of Rosedale than might be expected. A young woman watches over the neighbourhood from a perch high in her parents' mansion and concocts fantasies that are not all that far off the mark:

> The long black car which parked occasionally in the early hours outside the Reverend Cline's was moving away. The orgy was over. The long howling scream had

been brief. An exorcism? Julie and Anna, wild friends of Jack Grope, had gone in heavily for exorcism and said it was peculiar but more satisfying than plain ordinary sex. Perhaps in the back garden a virgin had been sacrificed, although the scream did seem to come from across the road. The men who got into the car and drove away were probably satanic priests and the Reverend Cline merely a servant, a tool of theirs.

A few houses down the street, a philandering husband mistakes the paperboy's requests for payment as blackmail notices, while his wife, wandering around in his lover's dress (dropped off in error by the dry cleaner), wonders why, having followed all the dictates of her class and upbringing, her life seems to be falling apart:

> Long ago they had said it was all a matter of having the right china, stapled together perhaps but expensively right; a man would not wander away from a house where the pile on the carpet was deep, where the right accents were heard and no raucous music ever played and the cream and sugar were served separately on a small tray.

Challenged to gauge what has changed about Rosedale, she muses,

> England had lost its influence on Chellow Street in the last couple of decades. And Chellow Street had lost some of its security. The world Gerald Quinn and his friends had built was changing. Because they had closed their ranks and kept out all undesirables, whether people or ideas, they had thought themselves safe forever. But Johnson Quinn was not like his grandfather. The Moxfords had managed to slide their ugly wedge-shaped house in between the others. The garbagemen were now the dictators of times and arrangements. The dry cleaner was now delivering his goods at random. Before long, the mailman would be reading the mail to decide whether it merited delivery or not.

Martha attributes much of the neighbourhood's decline to the Moxfords, a couple who had "insulted the street by moving into it," but the greatest hazards are local ones. Her own husband cannot seem to keep himself from sleeping with the neighbours, and the Reverend Cline's regular trips to the Holy Land are merely cover for the smuggling of luxury goods. Nothing in Rosedale, it seems, is quite as it seems.

Scott Symons, Rosedale's controversial scion, stretches satirical representations of Rosedale—a community he depicts as populated by "the inner group of Toronto Big Boys, all Chinless Wonders, those buck-teeth, give away the marsupial mommysack they're in"—considerably beyond their natural limit in his novel *Civic Square*. Of Rosedale by blood, Symons takes upon himself the duty to inform Dear Reader (rendered as D.R. or Dearreader) of Rosedale's true character, writing,

> Rosedale that's right, D.R.—
>
> Where I write you now (WHERE ARE YOU?—you've never come back, nor even written—except after the party, to thank me). Back in Rosedale Heart of Pan-Canadian Snobland
>
> Residence-Royal of the Family Compact (filthy dirty snotty lucrative oligops!) That's us, remember? Club for Squares, and Cubes, and Civic Squares.
> Real Apex of the Vertical Damned Mosaic (which ain't, we're told relentlessly, fair to Passed-Over Methodists—timid bastards shouting sweetly "hey wait up for us, or we'll cut off your nuts")
> National Seat of the IODE (a bloody big seat, too, fur-lined, by Creeds out of HBCO)
>
> Social heartland of Canadianglicannity (Trinity College, B.S.S., U.C.C., as Finishing Schools—largely, aptly, for non-Anglicans; Anglicans don't need it) Rosedale, has everything going for it.
>
> Except the streets aren't straight, nor the brains.
>
> Is last hangout of 19th century Canadian Romanticism, unimpeached, as yet picturesque Canada. Still, Rosedale
>
> You can always count of an article or two a year, damning it. Laugh at the British Bourgeois Homes, conglomerated Gothic-Georgian Redbrick (unique in world; nowhere else quite like—must find out why, D.R.
> but the funny part, about Rosedale I mean, is that so many often now the very people who condemn it live here.

Symons' depictions of Rosedale culminate in a riotous, vulgar rendering of high tea at the Old Family Home. For a few moments all is calm—"the household all organized thus—the party running of itself, and the Usurping Teapourer Quashed, and Mother Defended—and thus all Rosedale in Order, and thus the Empire (and Canada too)—until Margaret, his grandfather's "once-upon-a-time Second Parlour Maid," objects to his long hair, shouting "That's disgusting'. And I suppose you go in for all that sex stuff too." Hissing into the shocked silence, "I should take the scissors to you," Symons' narrator replies, "You already have," noting (in a whispered aside to D.R.), "As my cock shrivels dead. And dies in the dregs of my Derby cup no longer Royal."

A decade later Symons again descended upon his loved and hated Rosedale to collect fodder for a 1979 *Globe & Mail* essay titled "The Cherished-Loathed

Rosedale Myth." Roaming his old neighbourhood's winding avenues and inviting himself for coffee at the home of an elderly acquaintance who has not seen him for years, with possibly unconsciously hypocritical innocence he asks his hostess, "What makes people *hate* Rosedale so much?" Adding, "It's strange, so many journalists and writers spend their lives attacking what Rosedale represents, then end up living...in Rosedale!" Symons goes on to describe the multiple facets of the Rosedale myth (some to which—although he does not admit this in the essay—he has contributed):

> Yes, Rosedale is a national asset, and a national whipping-horse. And in reality there are at least three different "Rosedales." There is the geographic Rosedale, whose quiet walks and trees and muted manorial architecture have just restored so much peace to me. Then there is the Rosedale which Rachel Wyatt lampoons in her pert novel, the Rosedale Hoax—the same Rosedale that looms like some dowager dinosaur, consciously or subconsciously, in so much current Canadian theatre. A Rosedale that any fool can attack, a suitable snob symbol for national lust-hate. [...] More important, there is that unrecognized Rosedale which continues to play a massive role in our national culture, via people of immense talent and personality.

Never mentioning (or perhaps even thinking of) his own satire of Rosedale, Symons instead invokes Dennis Lee's poem, "When I Went Up to Rosedale," quoting not from its most harshly critical lines ("A claque of little men / Who took the worst from history / And made it worse again") but rather from its closing quatrain:

> When I came down from Rosedale
> I could not school my mind
> To the manic streets before me
> Nor the courtly ones behind.

Arguing that Rosedale's "courtly streets" are what give the neighbourhood—and by extension Canada—its "decency and national sanity," Symons concludes that Rosedale represents "the difference between being merely housebroken, and being civilized," adding, "Canada both cherishes and loathes the 'Rosedale myth.' Yet without it, without its quiet embodiment of decent manners, and its sense of family and of historical continuity, we might be merely Americans."

YORKVILLE

Contemporary Yorkville, a gentrified district of expensive boutiques and luxury condominiums whose spiritual epicentre is the intersection of Bloor Street and Avenue Road, owes the bulk of its literary reputation to a brief bohemian period that lasted less than a decade but has inspired at least two generations of writers eager to pay homage to the memory of a neighbourhood once known as Toronto's very own Haight-Ashbury.

Incorporated in 1853 and annexed by the City of Toronto in 1883, Yorkville grew from a crossroads into a prosperous suburb before its fortunes declined in the years following World War I. Before Yorkville became a bohemian centre, it was a working-class neighbourhood of narrow streets lined with rundown row houses. In *Berryman Street Boy*, a memoir interwoven with watercolours and sketches of pre-war Toronto, Canadian art historian Paul Duval describes the Depression-era Yorkville of his youth:

> I spent my boyhood from the age of four growing up in Yorkville, then a slum area in the heart of Toronto. Yorkville's population, during the twenties and thirties, was mainly Anglo-Saxon, a mix of English, Scottish and Irish, split on religious grounds and joined by a blind bias against other foreigners. [...] Shortly after I arrived as the fourth of eight children, the family was living at 30 Berryman Street, in one of a row of four decaying plaster houses, through the broken, dirty white surfaces of which wooden lathes were exposed like ribs.

Noting that the three adjoining houses had already been condemned and boarded up by the time of his childhood, Duval comments that his first published work, a short essay and sketch printed in the *Mail and Empire* (a predecessor to the *Globe & Mail*), described the derelict character of his own neighbourhood. As the fourteen-year-old Duval wrote:

> "There are innumerable houses in our own metropolis that are not fit for human habitation and are actually endangering the lives human beings. Some of the aforementioned houses are situated right at the doors of our City Hall. The above sketch was made a few blocks north of the busy intersection of Bloor and Bay Streets. This is not, by any means, one of the worst examples of the terrible conditions of the slums today."

The accompanying sketch, which appeared alongside the article, was of the back of his own Berryman Street home, a transgression that Duval reports his mother was reluctant to forgive.[114]

---

114 30 Berryman Street has since been demolished and rebuilt or altered so completely as to be unrecognizable, and faux-Victorian town houses now line much of the north side of the street.

Despite this backdrop of not-so-picturesque poverty, by mid-century Yorkville was a neighbourhood in flux as its southerly streets, zoned increasingly for commercial use, began to house galleries and shops frequented by wealthy doyennes drifting north from Toronto's Mink Mile.[115] In the late 1950s and early '60s the city's beatnik subculture established a beachhead amid Yorkville's growing cluster of coffee houses as nearby Gerrard Village—Toronto's original bohemian district—began to be overrun by hospital expansions and commercial redevelopment. After the mid-1960s a shift in the cultural *Zeitgeist* made Yorkville a gathering place for aspiring musicians and social activists as well as disaffected young people attracted to its tune-in, drop-out vibe.

In Dorris Heffron's novel *A Nice Fire and Some Moonpennies*, a sixteen-year-old girl slips away from her Kingston home and hitchhikes to Yorkville at the height of its hippie era, where she hopes to score some "Mary Jane," a drug she has never tried but has learned about from a classmate. Upon arriving in Toronto, Maizie is surprised to discover not only how small Yorkville is—"In case you don't know it, Yorkville isn't really a "ville" at all. It's just a couple of little streets off Avenue Road really"—but how young its habitués are, adding "The big attraction in Yorkville of course, is the hippies. All the bare feet and long hair and beads. I was kind of amazed myself. I mean I hadn't expected them to be so *young*. Most of the hippies there were younger than me."Maizie's wide-eyed words are echoed in Don Lyons' *Yorkville Diaries*, when his fifteen-year-old protagonist, having drifted downtown from Etobicoke, encounters the district for the first time:

> What an out of sight street! And the whole time it's been right around the corner from the Mont Blanc and only a ten second walk from the Supertest. There's folk-singing coffee houses and rock clubs and antique stores. And all of them open at 1 a.m. The sidewalks on both sides of Yorkville were packed with a couple of hundred people. Didn't look like there was one person over twenty years old. Just smiling faces walking slow, nodding and moving shoulders to music pouring out of the clubs and the cruising car radios. Yorkville is a one way street with two lanes of traffic crawling along at 5 m.p.h., windows rolled down, everybody leaning out, popping fingers to the tunes and talking back and forth.

Restored nineteenth-century row houses at 32-34 Berryman Street do manage to preserve some of the street's remaining architectural character.

115 Toronto's "Mink Mile" is a high-end retail strip of Bloor Street between Avenue Road and Yonge Street. The phrase, whose alliterative qualities seem to have contributed to its curious persistence in an era when few wear furs, is used most notably in Phyllis Brett Young's *The Torontonians*, to denote a combination of economic and moral conceit and a sense of social separation from the city's undifferentiated masses.

In F. G. Paci's *Sex and Character*, a student at the University of Toronto, new to the city from Sault Ste. Marie, offers a similar assessment of Yorkville—albeit one with a hint of foreboding. Describing a scene that sounds straight out of Haight-Ashbury—coffeehouses, young people with painted faces "dessed in psychedelic designs in day-glo" sitting on street corners panhandling or shooting the breeze, he adds, "Stray dogs prowled everywhere, leaving mounds of shit in the middle of the sidewalk. I saw a hippie girl, barefoot and in a filthy calico dress, squish her toes in a mound of excrement and calmly scrape it off on the curb."

This faint foreboding, bound up in the suggestion that a more troubled Yorkville lurks behind the tourist-friendly facade, ratchets up in Juan Butler's *Cabbagetown Diary* in which a jaded young hustler from Allen Gardens visits Yorkville on a lark and characterizes it cynically as a gathering place for dissolute people who are either on the run or on the make:

> Teeny boppers—ten to fourteen-year-olds who make the street look like a nursery corner. Hippies sitting on the sidewalk or on the steps of houses, their blank faces disappearing behind a curtain of hair. Beads, bells, buttons, tied and pinned onto the blankets and rags they call clothes. High on speed, LSD, grass and anything else they can lay their hands on. Black with dirt. Broads and guys all looking alike. Incense in the air. Getting up to walk slowly a few feet down the street till they find a new place to sit down. Tourists taking photographs. Greasers looking for a fight—black leather jackets and boots—(most of them are from the suburbs). Cops walking in pairs while a paddy wagon waits at the corner of the street. College kids walking hand in hand and pretending they're part of the scene. A man and a woman with a photo in their hands approaching the hippies and asking them if they've seen their daughter who's only fourteen and who ran away from home last week with her girl friend who's fifteen.

A predator himself, Butler's protagonist knows that the worried parents he watches have reason to fear for the well-being of young daughters (and sons) drawn to an illusory image of Yorkville. Behind the spectacle—or so an increasingly concerned public, alarmed at media reports of drug cults and gang rape, has come to believe—lurks a darker and far more dangerous Yorkville, one not so easy to leave behind when the last coffee houses close shortly before dawn.

Don Lyons makes a similar observation in *Yorkville Diaries*, describing a well-dressed man and woman he encounters handing out photographs of their missing daughter, a young woman he already knows has changed so much they would not recognise her even if they saw her in the street. Yorkville's young runaways were not always innocents: one of the protagonists in David Helwig's story "Something for Olivia's Scrapbook, I Guess," for example, is a teenaged fugitive hiding out in Yorkville to avoid capture after allegedly stabbing her mother to death.

Still, an idealism persists in Yorkville among those hoping to make it as musicians or tap into the generational moment. In Ray Robertson's *Moody Food*, arguably the most even-handed fictional treatment of Yorkville, the Village is represented as a place attractive to young Torontonians eager to try on a few different selves for size before donning the conventional cloak of responsible adulthood:

> For anyone starting to let his hair grow long and wanting to hear some good music and maybe even check out some of that free-love action you'd read about going down in places like California, that would basically mean Yorkville, just north of Bloor Street. No more than three blocks in all, Yorkville was our very own city within a city, every street, alley, and low-rent hippie-converted building bursting with the sounds of loud music and the sweet smell of incense and overflowing with like-minded friendly, freaky faces. There was the Inn on the Parking Lot, the Riverboat, the Mynah Bird, the Penny Farthing—coffee shops and folk clubs, basically—where you could listen to Joni Mitchell and Ian and Sylvia and a million others no one has ever heard of since. Everyone drank lots of coffee and smoked plenty of cigarettes and you could play chess outside if the weather was nice and there was pot if you wanted it and all the girls, it seemed, were eighteen years old and tall and thin with the kindest eyes and long dark hair and none of them wore bras even if there really wasn't all that much love going on, free or otherwise.

Robertson's protagonist, a university dropout who works in a second-hand Harbord Street bookstore, is drawn into the Yorkville scene by his girlfriend, a singer-songwriter and social activist, and a charismatic American musician who deflects direct questions about his origins even after talking the trio into joining his folk-blues band. The rapid rise and drug-fuelled fall of Graham's band mirrors the ascent and decline of Yorkville itself: naive enthusiasm gives way to bad sex, biker gangs, uncontrolled drug use, political agit-prop and altercations with civic officials. Near the end of the novel, Robertson describes a profoundly changed Yorkville, one marked by paranoia, an undercurrent of anarchy and the constant presence of the police:

> Outside, Yorkville was gearing up for another hot August evening. Crowd buzz, honking cars, and the faint strains of the Byrds' "My Back Pages" floated through the opened patio doors. But no sirens or fists pounding at the studio door. Not yet.

The cops—Toronto cops—were out there, though; under the direction of city hall every weekend now parked a paddy wagon at the corner of Hazelton and Yorkville and strictly enforced an under-eighteen 10 p.m. curfew as a way of letting everybody know who was in charge.

Moody Food culminates in a street protest and a rooftop rock concert that ends in tragedy, events combining the very ingredients—music, drugs, self-expression and protest—that continued to define Yorkville even as they contributed to its downfall.

Yorkville's reputation as a menace to the civic order peaked in August 1967 when hundreds of Yorkville habitués marched south to City Hall and staged a series of widely reported sit-ins following a street demonstration in Yorkville that turned violent when the police intervened.[116] In *Moody Food*, Robertson's narrator summarizes the August 20 altercation simply as "the day Yorkville decided to strike its blow against the empire, and the empire struck back." Lyons expands upon this narrative in *Yorkville Diaries*:

Sunday night, August 20th: The cops came out of nowhere, with no warning. It was supposed to be a lark. Suddenly they're charging into us, kicking girls in the stomach, punching heads, tossing longhairs into three paddy wagons. [...] What got this rolling was around 3 a.m. a bunch of us, maybe 300, sat down on Yorkville Avenue, right in the middle of the street. We were goofing and clapping and even chanting: "Close our street! No traffic! Cars, no! People, yes!" Sara and Uta were playing catch. I was trying to pick up the girl next to me. And pow! We're in the middle of a stampede. Cop boots everywhere. They had a field day. Some of 'em were really digging it. Fucking creeps! Supposed to keep the peace, not smash it.

These events, which galvanized public opinion both for and against the Villagers, marked the moment when a variety of actors—politicians and city planners, tourists, street kids, commercial developers and biker gangs—stepped up their efforts to control, contain, colonize or capitalize upon the Yorkville scene.[117] By 1968, social agencies had begun to treat Yorkville as a triage point

---

116 The 1967 sit-in is also the focal moment of *Flowers on a One Way Street*, Robin Spry's NFB film about Yorkville. Don Lyons' *Yorkville Diaries* includes an extended imaginative account of this event and the summer that preceded it. For further reading on Yorkville's social and political history during the 1960s, see Stuart Henderson's *Making the Scene: Yorkville and Hip Toronto, 1960-1970*.

117 Henderson (2007). In *Yorkville Diaries*, Don Lyons surveys Yorkville's deeply contested political terrain, describing self-anointed activists (including Clayton Ruby, David DePoe and John Sewell) descending upon the Village to coordinate dissent. As Lyons' protagonist observers, "Larry said Yorkville was turning into a circus. Well, now it's complete. The clowns are here. Call themselves politically aware organizers. Say they're going to help us utilize our political potential. They use that

for the drugged-out and diseased, and, following a hepatitis scare in August, it became clear that the bloom had fallen from the flower.

The Village's final years are portrayed most luridly in John Reid's 1976 novel, *The Faithless Mirror*. A sort of *Pilgrim's Progress* in reverse, the book opens with a description of Yorkville as a calculated spectacle in which visitors and Villagers confront one another in an unspoken standoff:

> Night after night, cars waited on Bay Street to turn westward at Yorkville Avenue and inch forward, bumper to bumper, so that their passive occupants might view what newspapers, radio and television told them was there to see. Two blocks and half an hour later they reached Avenue Road and the one-way show was over; they bore away with them memories of an illusion made manifest: it was as though all who were present inhabited a void between two mirrors: print and the spoken word presented a false image to which those who came as tourists reacted, seeing the mirror rather than the reality. [...] The crowd had been told it was the place to be: it was there. The affluent and the habitué sat on the terraces of a number of coffee houses that offered ring-side seats to the nightly circus at fifty cents for a cup of coffee. Few of them recognised what they were witnessing. For up and down the street roamed hordes of teen-agers, in the approved uniform of hippiedom, who were here for the night, their stay limited by the hour of the last bus back to the suburbs. It was a masquerade, where rival groups of teeny-boppers mistook each other for the authentic phenomenon. But they were not merely wearing costumes; they were acting out for themselves a role.

With graphic accounts of suicide, sexual assault, social nihilism and the seduction of a priest, depictions that give the novel a sense of wrenching inexorability, Reid traces Yorkville's long decline, and the novel culminates in apocalyptic, even biblical descriptions of a ruined community of lost souls who self-destruct in almost unimaginable violence.

Although *The Faithless Mirror* has been criticized for its overwrought characterizations of the time and place it depicts, the novel reflected a sentiment, widely held even among Yorkville supporters by the latter part of the decade, that the scene had soured. The "festering sore" city politicians had decried now needed to be lanced. In 1969, having quietly assembled entire blocks of Yorkville real estate, a commercial consortium announced plans to redevelop parts of the district into a hotel, parking garage and high-rise residential

---

word a lot: utilize. Relevant is another favourite. The Diggers are okay. They'll help you with a place to stay, food, clothes, V.D. advice, but these new guys are dangerous. You start marching, yelling, throwing things and you give The Man an excuse to move in, bust heads and haul you away. Makes you wonder. Maybe it was The Man who sent the clowns in."

complex. Despite local opposition, the plans met quickly with municipal approval, and by 1970 Yorkville was over. [118]

Critics of gentrified Yorkville have claimed that the district's rapid transformation in the early 1970s was the result of a calculated, coordinated effort between municipal politicians, public health officials, city planners and a police force determined to reclaim Yorkville's streets for the use of Toronto's more respectable citizenry. [119] Upon closer examination, however, it becomes apparent that the neighbourhood's rows of quaint town houses, proximity to downtown and village-like character—the very qualities that brought beatniks, bootleggers, hippies and hangers-on to Yorkville—also attracted real estate speculators eager to cash in on Yorkville's cultural cachet and commercial promise. In one sense this sounds like a standard narrative of gentrification: artists and other representatives of the urban avant-garde "discover" and transform a promising but rundown neighbourhood before being displaced in turn by more affluent purchasers in a rapidly appreciating real estate market.

But even in its Bohemian heyday, "the Village" harboured the seeds of its own transformation, one in which artists, poets and privileged urbanites were active participants. [120] In the early 1960s ,Yorkville already housed a number of high-end boutiques and art galleries, and by the latter part of the decade these were sufficiently well established that a 1968 City planning report described the neighbourhood as "an enclave of interior decorators' and couturiers' shops [...] sidewalk cafes, coffee houses, art dealers' galleries, fine housewares shops, boutiques and gourmet restaurants." [121] If the City's spin might be interpreted as political wish fulfilment, literary representations of Yorkville reflect a district where high culture held its own alongside the long-haired, lowbrow hippie scene, in part because it preceded it by several years.

Set in 1967, Anne Denoon's *Back Flip* populates Yorkville with a cast of artists, gallery owners and patrons of culture, all jostling for position in a city clawing its way toward sophistication. An instructor at the College of Art, walking to his Yorkville-area apartment, contemplates the district's significance to artists—and their importance to it:

> Reaching Yonge Street, he headed north. In the early sixties, the avant-garde scene
> had been driven uptown to the rundown streets north of Bloor. Max had always had
> a nose for trends, and the Lurie had been one of the first galleries to open up there.

118 See Caulfield, 1994; Henderson, 2007; Mathews, 2008.
119 Ruppert, 2006; Henderson, 2007.
120 Caulfield, 1994; Bain, 2003; Ley, 2003; Mathews, 2008. In *Dear M: Letters from a Gentleman of Excess* (1989), art dealer Jack Pollock conveys something of the vibrancy of the Gerrard Village and Yorkville art scenes.
121 City of Toronto: 1968; quoted in Matthews, 2004.

That would have been in '62. [...] He passed Wellesley, beginning to tire on the last leg of his trek. All right, artists probably had it better now than he ever had. He was willing to admit that. There were more galleries, sure...but Yorkville was already getting chichi. And the young guys starting out today didn't know what they had missed. Oh man, oh baby, oh you kid, let me tell you sonny, *those* were the days.

If Denoon's narrator seems caught up in reverie, the nostalgia is even more palpable in David Lewis Stein's 1967 novel, *Scratch One Dreamer*. Returning to Toronto after four years away, a young man revisits the streets where he and his cadre of undergraduate colleagues had once gathered to drink and debate politics, religion and philosophy, and finds the neighbourhood irrevocably altered:

> God, how Yorkville Avenue had changed. Joe had to thread his way through the tangled crowds. Clusters of girls in striped blouses and Bermuda shorts jostled against him. They seemed so painfully young. Surely, Joe thought, we were much older, Boag and Grant and I, when we were in college. Boys lined the street, leaning against the parked cars, speculating on the girls as they trooped by. They wore blazers and windbreakers ornamented with university coats of arms, and some carried and strummed guitars. They made Joe feel abominably old and stale. [...] This street once belonged to us, he told himself. Our time still lingers in the high, Edwardian remains of the upper floors along Yorkville, in the dull red bricks, the sculptured cornices and the gabled roofs. Up there, untainted by these crowds and carnival lights, something at least remains of our Yorkville Avenue. Huge trees with branches that spread leaves like green rain clouds lined Yorkville then. We had a whole world on this street.

Only slightly older than the new crowd, Stein's narrator finds that revisiting Yorkville makes him feel implausibly ancient, unprepared to admit how quickly the scene has passed him by.

In *Cat's Eye*, Margaret Atwood conveys some sense of Yorkville's transition from its working-class origins to a Bohemian district and, later, into a gentrified, expensive shopping centre. Atwood's protagonist, an undergraduate student at the University of Toronto taking a life-drawing class at the "Toronto College of Art" around 1960, is seduced by her instructor, who takes her to his Yorkville apartment:

> Josef's apartment was on Hazelton Avenue, which was not quite a slum although quite close to it. The houses there are old, close together, with frumpy little front gardens and pointed roofs and mouldering wooden scrollwork around the porches. There were cars parked bumper to bumper along the sidewalk. Most of the houses were in pairs, attached together down one side. It was in one of the crumbling, pointy-roofed twin houses that Josef lived. He had the second floor.

Years later, a successful artist whose work is being shown as a retrospective in a Queen Street gallery (by the 1980s Queen Street having become Toronto's new bohemian centre), Elaine returns to Yorkville and strolls among the boutiques, absorbing the utterly changed landscape:

> I turn a corner, onto a side street, a double row of expensive boutiques: hand-knits and French maternity outfits and ribbon-covered soaps, imported tobaccos, opulent restaurants where the wineglasses are thin-stemmed and they sell you location and overhead. The designer jeans emporium, the Venetian paper knick-knack shop, the stocking boutique with its kicking neon legs. [...] I walk up the street, along to the corner. The next street is Josef's. I count houses: this one must be his. The front's been ripped out and glassed over, the lawn is paving-stone. There's an antique child's rocking horse in the window, a threadbare quilt, a wooden-headed doll with a battered face. One-time throwouts, recycled as money.

Like Stein's protagonist, Atwood's narrator cannot quite reconcile the new Yorkville with the seedy streets she had encountered in her youth. The antiques in the renovated window, ghostly artifacts of a bygone era, underscore her sense of displacement.

For Atwood's narrator, the old Yorkville is so deeply buried it is almost as if it had never really existed. This is a point Sarah Dearing emphasizes in *Courage My Love*, whose new-to-the-country narrator, realizing she has stepped into an antiseptic shell of a neighbourhood, muses, "Yorkville, the rental agent had told us, was once the hippie headquarters of Toronto, but not a hair of anti-establishment remains: no record shop, no musical blitz on the tastefully umbrella'd patios, each occupied by a mass of identical people." Unwilling to conform to Yorkville's empty aesthetic, Philippa abandons her bland husband and beige Cumberland condo and moves into a rented room in Kensington Market, a neighbourhood she considers better suited to her Bohemian spirit.

What Philippa doesn't know is that the aspects of Kensington Market that appeal to her most—especially the coffee houses and counterculture conversations—are precisely the features that had defined Yorkville in another era of the city's history. Philippa has not so much abandoned Yorkville as entered a version of the district as it might exist in a parallel universe. This, of course, is utterly characteristic of Toronto, known as the city of neighbourhoods not only because it has so many of them but because, like water moving in a convection current, the past or future of any given neighbourhood can be found just a few blocks over or a streetcar ride away.

– 4 –

THE MYTH
OF THE
MULTICULTURAL CITY

MUSIC FROM ELSEWHERE

At times it seems possible to navigate Toronto by sound alone. The city resonates with a discordant symphony of sirens, streetcar clatter, garbage trucks and
gunshots. Every intersection produces a distinct soundscape: rush-hour horns
reverberating against downtown towers, the circadian stillness of the city's ravines, sprinklers arcing over suburban lawns, the restless rhythm of traffic tracing the urban grid. Floating across this aural topography are the multi-layered
compositions of voices whispering, speaking, shouting and singing the city into
being. Crossing the city is like spinning a radio dial: static interspersed with
clipped tones, talk-show chatter, sales pitches and snatches of Bhangra.

In *The Robber Bride*, Margaret Atwood refers to Toronto's polyphonic gathering of voices as "music from elsewhere." Walking up Spadina Avenue, a wide
street vibrant with fruit venders, fishmongers, electronics importers and Sichuan
restaurants, Atwood's protagonist studies the diversity gathered around her:

> She likes the mix on the street here, the mixed skins. Chinatown has taken over
> mostly, though there are still some Jewish delicatessens, and, further up and off to
> the side, the Portuguese and West Indian shops of the Kensington Market. Rome
> in the second century, Constantinople in the tenth, Vienna in the nineteenth. A
> crossroads. Those from other countries look as if they're trying hard to forget
> something, those from here as if they're trying hard to remember. Or maybe it's
> the other way around.

Dionne Brand seems to respond to this description in her Toronto novel, *What
We All Long For*, suggesting that "as at any crossroads there are permutations of
existence. People turn into other people imperceptibly, unconsciously." She adds,

> Lives in this city are doubled, tripled, conjugated—women and men all trying to
> handle their own chain of events, trying to keep the story straight in their own
> heads. At times they catch themselves in sensational lies, embellishing or avoid-
> ing a nasty secret here and there, juggling the lines of causality, and before you
> know it, it's impossible to tell one thread from another.

These two characterizations of identity—one historical, the other invent-
ed—exemplify tensions among competing narratives of Toronto as a cultural
crossroads. In Atwood's Toronto, culture is nostalgic, wistful, unsettled, but
largely resigned to what it has gained or given up in a city described as little
more than a palimpsest of other cities. Her protagonist is a historian, an ar-
chaeologist of memory who sees herself as an observer of culture rather than a

participant in it. In Brand's Toronto, culture is hybrid and contested, engaged actively in the construction of its own memories and meanings. Brand's protagonists take culture wherever they find it—in sweaty nightclubs, impromptu street parties, Kensington Market coffee shops, each other—and weave tradition, in-jokes and borrowed memories into a pastiche that simultaneously rejects and reclaims the concept of cultural identity. They make the story up as they go along, and as a result the city they create through narrative is continually shifting and often at odds with itself.

Despite their differences, Atwood and Brand have one vital thing in common: both writers describe culture as emerging from narrative, as erupting from acts of storytelling that alternately reconstruct and reimagine the city's past and present. They challenge the anthropological claim that culture consists primarily of fixed, measurable or neutral qualities. Indeed, if culture is rooted in the stories we tell, it must necessarily involve the possibility of contradiction, forgetting and outright fabrication. This creates urgent challenges in a city like Toronto, where almost everybody has a story to tell, and where so many narratives compete for our attention. How do we navigate among them? Is a coherent narrative of the multicultural city even possible?

THE MYTH OF THE MULTICULTURAL CITY

Among Torontonians there is a widely held but inaccurate belief that the United Nations has formally declared Toronto the most multicultural city in the world. It is a statement repeated in newspaper accounts, government reports, mayoral speeches and even the City's promotional literature. Geographer Michael Doucet investigates this claim at length in "The Anatomy of an Urban Legend: Toronto's Multicultural Reputation" and finds no substantive basis for what he calls Toronto's most prominent urban legend. Nonetheless, the myth of the multicultural city has penetrated deeply into popular consciousness, perhaps in part because—as Doucet points out—Toronto *is* by any measure one of the world's most multiculturally diverse cities.[122]

Doucet attributes the persistence of this myth to Toronto's desire to achieve "world class" standing in the eyes of the international community. While there is undoubtedly validity to this diagnosis, the story is far more complex than Doucet acknowledges: in truth, the impetus driving Toronto's multicultural

---

122 Indeed, the United Nations Development Program lists Toronto second only to Miami among cities with the largest proportion of foreign-born residents in its 2004 Human Development Report (Chapter 5, page 99. Available electronically here: http://hdr.undp.org/en/media/hdro4_chapter_5. pdf). By 2006 Toronto was reported to have surpassed Miami to become the city with the greatest proportion of foreign-born residents (Francine Kopun and Nicholas Keung, "A City of Unmatched Diversity," *Toronto Star*, 5 December 2007).

myth comes not from external forces but internal ones. Germaine Warkentin and Gwendolyn MacEwen have both described Toronto as a culturally amnesic city desperately seeking its own memory, but perhaps it is more accurate to say that Toronto is a city in search of its own creation myth.

Almost all cultures have creation myths, narratives recounting the story of their coming into being. Richly metaphorical, creation myths reflect a culture's efforts to make sense of its origins, express its principles, resolve internal tensions and establish shared identity.[123] In A Dictionary of Creation Myths literary scholar David Leeming argues that creation myths serve an important etiological purpose, and adds that "[a] creation myth conveys a society's sense of its particular identity; it reveals the way the society sees itself in relation to the cosmos. It becomes, in effect, a symbolic model for the society's way of life, its world view—a model that is reflected in such other areas of experience as ritual, culture heroes, ethics, and even art and architecture."

Creation myths are associated most commonly with traditional cultures, but even a city might have its own creation myth. In Toronto, a city whose inhabitants lack access to the common history and shared traditions that give rise to identity in so many other places—a city perched, perhaps perennially, on the verge of becoming—the myth of the multicultural city seems to have special resonance. Like other creation myths, the myth of the multicultural city is rife with tensions that arise from our efforts to speak the city into being. But it is only through principled engagement with these tensions—over cultural identity, difference and the limits of tolerance—that we learn how to live together, or determine whether we can do so at all.

In The Global Soul, a popular book tracing the ascent of transnational multiculturalism, essayist Pico Iyer calls Toronto "the city as anthology." The Toronto Iyer encounters is dizzying in its diversity. Describing himself as "spinning through cultures" while visiting the city to read at the International Festival of Authors, Iyer samples "Indian Pakistani-style Chinese food," wanders into a feminist service at a Korean protestant church and visits a Scarborough high school where the students speak seventy-six different languages. Iyer connects the success of what he calls Toronto's "multicultural experiment" to the city's literary diversity. Regardless of the focus of their work—Rohinton Mistry's remembered Bombay,[124]

---

123 Popular sources on creation myths include McLeish, 1984; Sproul, 1991; Leeming, 1994; scholarly literature tends to focus on cosmogenic myths of individual cultures, but see Horsley, 2007; Aveni, 2008; McLean, 2009.

124 Despite having lived in the city and its environs for three decades, Mistry does not write about Toronto. Indeed, Iyer describes Mistry as having "lived, to all intents and purposes, in the Bombay of twenty-five years ago, even though he spent his nights in a suburb of Toronto" . Iyer adds, however, that the unique conditions of living in Canada are precisely what enable Mistry to write so profoundly and movingly about the city of his birth.

the "double foreignness" of Nino Ricci's Italian immigrants,[125] the cultural topography layered in Anne Michaels' ravines—something unique about Toronto has brought so many writers together, and Iyer struggles to discover what it is.

Iyer is not the only writer who struggles to characterize Toronto's cultural diversity. In *Playing House*, novelist Patricia Pearson describes Toronto as "a city filled with accidental citizens":

> They come from everywhere, from Argentina, Nigeria, Russia, Pakistan, but rarely because they have an explicit vision of the place; they aren't drawn by mythic images of riches and glamour like the immigrants arriving at the airports and harbours of New York. They are exiles, for the most part, who have thrown darts at a map of the world. Arriving, astonished by the cold, bewildered by hockey and our Nordic reserve, they nonetheless build their cities within our city: Chinatown, Little India, Portugal Town. Our city becomes a new city surprised by itself, doubletaking at the profusion of culture: Brazilian dance clubs, Indian cricket matches, Polish delis, Chinese newspapers, Ecuadorian snack stands, somber Italian Easter parades.

Less concerned with points of origin and more with the multiplying effects of diversity in Toronto, in *What We All Long For* Dionne Brand produces an even longer list of Toronto's cultural communities, arrayed in permutations unfolding seemingly endlessly across the page:

> In this city there are Bulgarian mechanics, there are Eritrean accountants, Colombian cafe owners, Latvian book publishers, Welsh roofers, Afghani dancers, Iranian mathematicians, Tamil cooks in Thai restaurants, Calabrese boys with Jamaican accents, Fushen deejays, Filipina-Saudi beauticians; Russian doctors changing tires, there are Romanian bill collectors, Cape Croker fishmongers, Japanese grocery clerks, French gas meter readers, German bakers, Haitian and Bengali taxi drivers with Irish dispatchers.

In contrast to Brand's ebullient inventory of cultural hybridity, novelist Stephen Marche suggests in *Raymond and Hannah* that identity in Toronto is a fleeting thing, rising and vanishing like ships adrift on an obliterating sea:

> In Toronto, nothing stays for long. There is space enough here to fit us all in. No one remembers. A city for the fish who slipped through the parts of the net that

125 Nino Ricci's Toronto novels include *Lives of the Saints* (1990), *In a Glass House* (1993) and *Where She Has Gone* (1997). The first novel is set mainly in Italy; the second and third are set principally in Toronto and powerfully evoke aspects of the Italian immigrant experience. Ricci won the Governor General's Award for *Lives of the Saints*.

are broken. The most anyone says in Toronto is, "Look, here were Native, then English, then Jewish, Italian, Portuguese, Vietnamese, and other nations will take their place in a few generations." The most anyone says is, "Look at the Muslims praying in the rush of Kennedy subway station." "Look, we will lose even the idea of mother tongue or nation."

In Marche's Toronto, multiculturalism erases difference; he concludes, "There is a dream of interpenetration, and a dream of a city that war never visits," adding, "We are pigeons, multicoloured, rustling against each other in all the public places, and the twenty-first century belongs to the colour smudge."

Like Atwood and Iyer, Pearson, Brand and Marche list Toronto's accumulated cultures as if the act of doing so will help clarify what their collected presence means. The problem with such inventories is that culture cannot be made meaningful by cataloguing its component parts: even an anthology requires thematic coherence, just as a crossroads needs signposts to guide travellers on their way. Like promotional literature depicting Toronto as "the world within a city"[126] and tourist brochures inviting visitors to "expect the world,"[127] such characterizations of diversity seem inviting but are ultimately empty because they reduce the city to a collage of the glossy but ephemeral detritus of culture, like the scattering of sequins after a parade has passed.

Even with a calendar crammed with cultural festivals,[128] the celebrated intersection of so many diverse communities in Toronto does not mean that each group enjoys equal opportunities in the multicultural city. In *Your Secrets Sleep with Me*, Darren O'Donnell writes about the economic underpinnings of racial divisions in multicultural Toronto:

Some say that the only thing race is good for is to divide the population into work categories. Those who wash the dishes will be Sri Lankan, those who drive the cabs will be African, those who run the banks will be European, those who watch the kids will be Filipino, those who mind the store will be Korean and those upon whose bodies the good life is modelled will be, more and more, a hybridization of all of the above—on TV, on billboards, in magazines.

---

126 The "world within a city" slogan has been used widely by Toronto Tourism in efforts to promote the city to visitors. *The World Within a City* is also the title of a recent scholarly study exploring the meanings of Toronto's multicultural diversity (Anisef and Lanphier, eds., 2003).
127 "Expect the World" was the slogan for the City of Toronto's unsuccessful bid to host the 2008 Summer Olympics.
128 Toronto is particularly well known for annual cultural festivals that draw tourists internationally, including Pride, Caribana, Mendhi! Masti! Masala!, BIG on Bloor, Dragon Boat races, Taste of the Danforth and—of course—Harbourfront's International Festival of Authors.

For O'Donnell, the problem is that market-oriented multiculturalism serves up culture for consumption while concealing the racial divisions that persist among those who do the producing. He adds, "it would be a mistake to believe that these beautifully mixed people represent a race-free future—that people will stop their fixation on difference and settle down to enjoying similarities. It's just a smokescreen. Part of a dazzling performance."

Austin Clarke extends O'Donnell's analysis in his novel *More*, indicting the very notion of multiculturalism for its emptiness in a city where demographic diversity often describes little more than a population partitioned rigidly into ethnic enclaves separated by socio-economic class as much as by culture:

> "Multiculturalism? Is multiculturalism you say? What is so multiculturalistic about Toronto? Toronto is a collection of ghettos. Ethnic ghettos. Cultural ghettos. In other words, racial ghettos, and—"
>
> "Oh Christ, I never looked at it this way! That's right!"
>
> "You got Rosedale: Anglo-Saxon people. Jane-Finch: black people and visible minorities. High Park: the Poles. Sin-Clair, all up there by Dufferin and Eglinton: the Eye-Talians ..."
>
> "Don't leave-out the place up north, where the cheapest house cost a million. The rich Eye-talians..."

For Clarke's protagonists, racial segregation remains a reality in the multi-cultural city: its consequences play out not only in differential employment opportunities and unequal access to residential choice but extend even to how people use public transit. In *More*, for example, Clarke's narrator spends her mornings riding the crowded subway alone, shunned by fellow passengers who will not sit beside her:

> She first wondered if all these people were uncomfortable to be so close to a black woman. And then, in time, she was sure that they were. Their silence, with heads bowed in paperback books, was their way of asking her where she came from and why didn't she go back there.

All too often this is what multiculturalism comes down to in practice: a jostling for position in close quarters based upon claims to prior arrival.

At the same time, the "go back where you came from" sentiment Clarke documents is not limited to Canadian-born Torontonians forgetful of their own immigrant past but is also expressed by foreign-born minorities hoping to fit in by distinguishing themselves from more recent arrivals. In Rabindranath Maharaj's *Homer in Flight*, a Trinidadian-Torontonian advises a newly arrived acquaintance to look for a job in Toronto, but warns, "[T]here's immigrunts allva the place," and adds, in the flat cadences of the Southern Ontario dialect he has so meticulously affected,

> Any step you take sanother immigrunt. This new preemer fella in Onterryo is trying his best bud there's too many athem. Chinese. Jamakuns. Sri Lankans. Somelees. Snabbing up all the jobs. Piddy.

In the controversial classic *Niggers This Is Canada*, Odimumba Kwamdela makes a similar observation. Two of his protagonists, immigrants from Barbados, tell a recently arrived compatriot they worry about Canada letting in "too many coloured people," adding, "Too many coloured people always spell trouble." Life in Canada has altered their pronunciation as well, a phenomenon Kwamdela suggests is a post-colonial accommodation that only emphasizes their subalternity:

> Normally they would say Ottawa or Toronto, but on this special occasion it had to be "Oddawa" and "Torona" because their white masters pronounced it that way. And if they could imitate their white masters well enough, it would undoubtedly create [a] greater impression on Jason. Sure, they were making a good try at it, considering that neither had been in Canada much over two years.

The behaviour of Maharaj's and Kwamdela's protagonists exemplifies cultural thinker Frantz Fanon's influential argument that subjugated cultures often adopt the perspectives and even the language of their colonizers, absorbing, in effect, the xenophobic attitudes projected upon them.[129] The resulting divisions within and between cultures, however, are ultimately advantageous only to the dominant group.[130]

Visible minorities are not, of course, the only Torontonians subject to interrogation about their origins. In Robertson Davies' novel *The Rebel Angels*, a graduate student named Maria Theotoky is questioned about her ethnic background by a theologian who finds her name exotic:

> "Not Canadian, I assume?"
> "Yes, Canadian."
> "Of course. I keep forgetting that any name may be Canadian. But quite recently, in your case, I should say."

129 See especially Fanon's *The Wretched of the Earth* (trans. Richard Philcox; revised edition, 2005).
130 See Gayatri Spivak's influential essay "Can the Subaltern Speak?" (1998); see also Said (1993; 2003).

"I was born here."

"But your parents were not, I should guess. Now where did they come from?"

"From England."

"And before England?"

Upon determining, at length, that Maria's parents had been born in Hungary, her inquisitor—who inventories his own Irish and Huguenot ancestry—remarks, "I think we are quite foolish on this continent to imagine that after five hundred generations somewhere else we become wholly Canadian—hard-headed, no-nonsense North Americans—in the twinkling of a single life."

Still, apart from the perils encountering wayward theologians intrigued by the etymology of exotic names, Maria is able to move freely among academic circles where her command of several languages and knowledge of Roma rituals mark her as a scholar rather than a cultural outsider. Others are not nearly as lucky: in a city where visible minorities are routinely mistaken as foreigners, even being Canadian-born is insufficient protection for Torontonians singled out because of the colour of their skin.[131] In Andrew Moodie's electrifying play *Toronto the Good*, an Ottawa-born black prosecutor who has been stopped repeatedly by police while walking or cycling along public streets shouts at a white officer, "I want to be able to walk down the street and feel like a citizen of this country!" Like Clarke's narrator in *More*, who clutches her Canadian passport like a talisman and asserts, "[T]his makes me a Canadian. I am not any damn visible minority; or immigrant!", Moodie exposes the emptiness of celebrations of multiculturalism that still leave whole segments of the population struggling to argue that they, too, belong here, that they, too, share the very same rights to the city.

Cultural theorist Stanley Fish warns us to beware of what he calls "boutique multiculturalism," a perspective he characterizes as "the multiculturalism of ethnic restaurants, weekend festivals, and high profile flirtations with the other," a multiculturalism characterized by a "superficial and cosmetic" commitment to diversity.[132] In Fish's view, celebrations of diversity that reduce culture to cooking, costume and traditional customs are in fact evasions of difference, amounting to a multiculturalism that suppresses areas of rupture in order to maintain the hollow claim that we are essentially all the same underneath. Ultimately, he writes, when confronted with real differences like racism, conflicting religious beliefs or the local consequences of global con-

---

131 Batia Boe Stolar interrogates the consequences of conflating these categories in "Building and Living the Immigrant City: Michael Ondaatje and Austin Clarke's Toronto" (2005).

132 See "Boutique Multiculturalism, or Why Liberals are Incapable of Thinking about Hate Speech," published in *Critical Inquiry* (1997).

flicts, the dominant culture cannot hope to bridge or even acknowledge them because it treats social problems as if they can be resolved by dancing together in the streets. But what happens after the bedraggled costumes are put away in the evening after the Caribana parade or Pride weekend? How do we speak to our neighbours the next day and the day after that?

In Toronto, criticism of the tendency to fixate on superficial expressions of multiculturalism while suppressing or shying away from cultural difference finds voice in the city's literature. Often it appears in the guise of satire, a subversive literary device Northrop Frye refers to as "militant irony" because of its capacity to challenge oppressive but unspoken social conventions.[133] In *Any Known Blood*, Lawrence Hill's sweeping novel exploring inheritance and identity, the mixed-race son of a black father and a white mother allows himself to be mistaken variously as French, Moroccan, Peruvian, American, Jamaican, as well as part Sikh, Jewish, Cree and Zulu, by Torontonians eager to criticize or capitalize upon the city's ethnic diversity. Ultimately, when applying for a government job as a speechwriter, he passes himself off as Algerian "to test my theory that nobody would challenge my claim to any racial identity." Nobody does, even when he is exposed as the son of a prominent black doctor and human rights activist and fired, not for misrepresenting his background but for the more defensible offence of doctoring a speech delivered by a hapless politician duped into objecting to his own government's plan to eliminate human rights legislation in Ontario.

Perhaps more pointed in its satire is Mobashar Qureshi's novel *R.A.C.E.*, in which the Toronto police set up a special drug task force to confront what it calls the Radical Association of Criminal Ethnicities, an elusive interracial gang seeking to manufacture and distribute a street drug so powerful it produces both instant anaesthesia and immediate addiction. Operation Anti-R.A.C.E. grounds its investigation in experience with ethnic gang affiliations in Toronto, explaining at a briefing:

> We are used to dealing with the Colombian Cartels, the Chinese Triads, the Italian Mafia, or the Jamaican Posse—with individuals who associate themselves with a group, most of the time race being the main factor. You were only allowed to join if you were of a certain class, certain colour, certain religion, or from a certain country.

The worrisome twist in the current investigation, the task force leader warns, is that "this group does not discriminate"—it welcomes felons of diverse

---

133 Frye, 1957.

origins into its ranks. Indeed, the problem of interracial cooperation among criminals concerns the task force as much as the drug investigation does. Ultimately, the police fear that this sort of gangland multiculturalism will spread beyond Toronto: "It will move to other major cities in Canada. Montreal, Ottawa, Vancouver, all over. It could even expand to the United States. Our mandate is to shut down this group. The pressure is on us. If this group expands there's no telling where it'll go."

But satire can go only so far. Sharper words convey more clearly the persistence of the kind of bigotry that propelled poet Earle Birney to write of 1940s Toronto in "Anglosaxon Street" that

Here is a ghetto	gotten for goyim
O with care denuded	of nigger and kike
No coonsmell rankles	reeks only cellarrot
Attar of carexhaust	catcorpse and cookinggrease

Although published nearly half a century later, remarkably similar cadences characterize Krisantha Sri Bhaggiyadatta's Toronto poem, "Let's Have Some Race Talk":

Let's have some race talk
Some pakiniggerchink talk
Let's have some race talk
Some white talk some joke talk
Let's have some lynchdeportbash talk.

Birney's and Bhaggiyadatta's emphatic words invoke conversations that the discourse of multiculturalism tends to gloss over. Racist epithets passed off as humour camouflage the violent consequences of failing to fit into the prescribed cultural categories, a sad contrast to the city's official motto: "Diversity Our Strength."[134]

In M. G. Vassanji's novel *No New Land*, a South Asian immigrant waiting on the subway platform at College Station in 1970s Toronto watches in stunned silence as a gang descends on a friend its members have targeted for racist assault:

Nanji began an instinctive step towards his compatriot, but then realized he would draw attention and stopped. At that moment a shiver ran down his spine. The three louts had come up behind Esmail and began their abuse. "Paki!" one of

---

134 "Diversity Our Strength" was adopted as the City of Toronto's official motto in 1998. It was meant to reflect not only the city's cultural diversity but also the amalgamation of six Toronto-area municipalities into the "megacity" of Toronto in 1997.

them shouted joyfully. Esmail turned toward them, looking frightened. "What do you have there, Paki? Hey, hey? Paki-paki-paki. ..."

Surrounded by silent, shuffling commuters, they punch Esmail and push him onto the tracks before running, unchallenged, out of the station. Nanji emerges from the incident unscathed but stunned, not so much by the assault itself but by his silent complicity in it:

> The whole brutal incident was shocking, the more so for being wanton and racial, directed at someone who could have been himself. In that very real sense, he too had been attacked. What ached now, and horribly, was the recollection of his own behaviour during the attack. He had not moved an inch, not uttered a syllable, to defend the man.

Even though none of the other commuters speaks out against the attackers, Nanji blames only himself. Beneath their surface veneer of social civility, he already knows that their capacity for empathy is constrained by their unmovable perception of Esmail, and therefore also of Nanji himself, as impenetrably alien. Indeed, public indignation over the incident remains strangely muted, reflecting resignation rather than outright objection:

> [T]he outrage expressed officially, although perhaps too piously, by police, newspapers, and ordinary citizens decided once and for all that the line had been overstepped, that this was beyond tolerable limits. Toronto the Good would not have it. It brought home, to everybody, the fact that the immigrants were here to stay, they could not, would not, simply go away.

The subtext of this passage—that racism remains tolerable in Toronto provided it does not step beyond seemly limits—reflects a far more common response to cultural difference, a reaction Pico Iyer refers to as "racism with a smile on its face."[135]

This latter form of racism, nearly invisible although no less deeply entrenched, finds expression in Rabindranath Maharaj's *Homer in Flight*. A Trinidadian émigré seeking an affordable Etobicoke apartment is given a guided tour by his compatriot, Vali, who assesses the surrounding buildings and advises, "I should warn you that the Paki building is dirty and always smelling of curry, the Newfie building is loaded with drunkards and the Jamaican building

---

135 Iyer, 2000. See also Odimumba Kwamdela's polemic novel, *Niggers This is Canada* (1971; revised 1986), whose entire narrative is geared toward exposing the damaging consequences of such polite or "subtle" racism.

have more drugs than a hospital." When Homer objects to these judgements, Vali laughs bitterly and responds,

> When you live here for three months, then you will really understand what racism is. I call the shots the way I see it. That is not racism. Over here racism is a sort of polite thing, not like in Trinidad. Nobody calling you nigger or coolie or names like that, but it's always inside them. Deep down. You see it in the bus when they refuse to sit by you. In the park when they suddenly change direction if they see somebody black. In the bank, when the teller's smile suddenly disappear when she look up and see a brown face before her. Over the telephone, when they recognise the foreign accent and tell you that the position is no longer available or the apartment was just rented. *That* is how racism operate over here.

Beneath benevolent expressions of cultural openness in Toronto, literary descriptions, whether of violent attacks or more subtle expressions of exclusion, reveal a city sharply divided along racial lines and seething with tensions that have only deepened in the post-9/11 era. In Deborah Ellis and Eric Walters' young adult novel *Bifocal*, a suburban high school is placed under lockdown when one of its students—a Muslim—is arrested and charged with participating in a terrorist plot. Another student, a young man of Afghan heritage whose family has lived in Canada for three generations, is targeted by fellow students, teachers and police who consider him guilty by association. Responding to a media request that members of the public report "anything suspicious" to the police, his sister retorts, "Live your life but watch your neighbours [...] What's suspicious? Muslims. We're suspicious."

At the same time, it is an error to assume that ambivalence and distrust flow only in one direction. If responses to cultural difference in Toronto range from enthusiastic if overbearing overtures to xenophobic brutality, newcomers' expectations are tempered with apprehension and, occasionally, antipathy. In Maharaj's *Homer in Flight*, for example, the protagonist's plan to emigrate from his comfortable South Asian community in Trinidad to an uncertain future in Toronto meets with opposition from family members who warn him of the perils awaiting him in Canada. As his determination mounts and the date of his emigration grows nearer, their warnings grow increasingly dire, and Homer spends his final months in Trinidad enduring his mother

> recounting horror stories about Trinidadians who left good jobs in the island only to end up on welfare, imprisoned in boxy little apartments, eating cat food and shivering with ague, consumption, pneumonia and catarrh. The severity of these diseases increased proportionately with Homer's intractability. AIDS, rabies,

flesh-eating bacteria, mad cow disease and a host of other afflictions were summoned to decorate her predictions."

Two years after landing in Toronto, Homer comes to see his emigration as the product of a peculiar insanity shared with other Trinidadians whose motives he assesses in a moment of depressing clarity:

> They did not leave their little island because of wars or famine or ethnic cleansing but because of the constant desire for romance and adventure. A ritual of escape, normally dramatized into threats and promises to leave the island, but sometimes, during moments of recklessness, actually planned and executed, so that months later, when the madness passes, the poor shivering Trinidadian finds himself trapped in a dark, cockroach-infested apartment, and then the adventure fumbles to a self-recriminatory conclusion.

Homer's flight—motivated by his eagerness to escape the crushing weight of family obligation and the anarchy he senses lurking at the edge of everyday life in Trinidad—runs aground in Toronto, where he finds himself perpetually in transit, seeking something—a sense of solidity, a source of identity, security, belonging—that he can hardly articulate and can never quite achieve. He despairs that he will end like his friend Grants, "forever trapped between two worlds, afraid to call either home, dancing in the dark."

Homer's sense of marginalization is echoed in Vassanji's *No New Land,* a novel documenting not only racially motivated hostility like the subway attack against Nanji but also the more prosaic difficulties of existing between cultures. Vassanji's protagonist, the patriarch of a family of Shamsi Muslims who fled Tanzania following political upheaval in the 1970s, worries that life in Toronto has eroded the foundations of his family and his faith. In the years since arriving, the Lalani family has established itself in Toronto—Nurdin's wife joining the extended network of Dar ex-patriots populating their Don Mills apartment building, his teenaged children adopting the dress and idiom of their peers—but Nurdin finds himself feeling isolated and unmoored.

"When does a man begin to rot?" Nurdin asks himself. Of all his transgressions—drinking beer, watching erotic films, unaccompanied visits with an unmarried female acquaintance—the one that disturbs Nurdin most greatly is having eaten a sausage pressed upon him by a co-worker, a lapsed vegetarian from Guyana who comments,

> Forget pork, man. I was not supposed to eat *meat.* Even egg. I'm supposed to think you are dirty. You think *they* are dirty. Who is right? Superstitions, all.

For Nurdin, however, eating the sausage not only violates his Muslim faith and the edict against consuming pork: it also reflects the subsuming of his identity within what he sees as the yawning morass of Canadian culture:

> The pig, they said, was the most beastly of beasts. It ate garbage and faeces, even its babies, it copulated freely, was incestuous. Wallowed in muck. Eat pig and become a beast. Slowly the bestial traits—cruelty and promiscuity, in one word, godlessness—overcame you. And you became, morally, like *them*. The Canadians.

Nurdin traces his subsequent difficulties—culminating in his arrest for an alleged sexual assault against a patient at the hospital where he works as an orderly—to this initial transgression, an act he senses has changed him irrevocably, however invisibly. Even though the charges are quickly withdrawn, the incident a misunderstanding, the experience reinforces Nurdin's sense of dissolution and drift. His inability to reconcile the old values with the new context raises the unhappy possibility that the differences are simply irreconcilable, the cultural gulf too great to be bridged.

Irreconcilable differences manifest more explosively in V. V. Ganeshananthan's *Love Marriage*, a novel tracing the consequences of Sri Lanka's long-running civil war upon a family living in contemporary Toronto. The daughter of a notorious member of the Liberation Tigers scheduled to be married to the son of a prominent Tamil businessman finds that violence has followed her across land and sea. While her extended family gathers for dinner at their Scarborough home the night before the ceremony, assailants—Tamils themselves, staking out territory in the new country—douse the wedding venue with gasoline and set it on fire. Ganeshananthan's narrator describes how strikingly the cordial rituals of the meal parallel the meticulous execution of the firebombing:

> As my mother is serving out the rice, a Tamil man whose interests in Toronto rival Suthan's is walking up to the locked doors of the Tamil community center with bolt cutters. [...] As my father asks for another helping of coconut *sambol*, the man is playing a flashlight across the walls of the main room, its decorations, its map of Sri Lanka, its Hindu gods. He has donned leather gloves, his expression unreadable. He could be doing this in another country entirely. He pours gasoline all over the rugs, and all over the wooden frame of the *m navarai*, the wedding altar Suthan has built for Janani, and which tomorrow would have been adorned with flowers.

As the final sip of tea is swallowed and the family prepares for bed, their peace is shattered by the very conflict they have crossed continents to escape:

Miles away, in a place empty of people, the stranger hands two flaming bottles to the men behind him. They roll their windows down, and the man in the driver's seat counts to three. Like twinned shooting stars, the bottles spiral through the air. Two, and then another two, the first pair shattering the hall's front windows. [...] a spark paints a stripe down a trail of gasoline, to another, to another, until a web of light tightens like a fist around the structure in which Janani was to be Married.

We are in a different country, a different time.

But the building explodes.

It explodes.

It explodes.

In a city of immigrants whose arrivals, trace entire genealogies of conflict, perhaps the very diversity upon which Toronto bases its identity becomes an intractable difficulty, although as Ganeshananthan's narrator observes tightly, "This is not a noble fight. It has nothing to do with the people dying in another country. It has to do with territory here, territory now, in this Western city."

Where do these disparate renderings of the multicultural city leave us? How do we navigate between naive optimism, expressed in municipal slogans and street festivals celebrating Toronto's cultural diversity, and violent expressions of enmity motivated by local or global conflict? Do we shrug and simply label them as end points along an inevitable continuum of positive or unpleasant encounters with difference in an otherwise successfully multicultural city? Or must we conclude that multiculturalism has failed both as policy and as social practice; that it is, as Corrado Paina writes in "Embrace the Walls,"

[...] a voice that lures us slowly to neutrality
and tolerance [...]
It's a refrain that reels off many warnings
and resembles the Pied Piper whose sounds
push us like mice into the invisible Lake Ontario
and we drown dragged down by concrete neologisms
Multiaccessmultiaddictmultiadvocatemultiarbitratormultiathlete
multiballotmultibarriomultibathroommultibombmulticavitymultiCanadian-
multichallengedmultichannelmulticitizenmulticleaningmulticlinicmulticof-
feemulticondominiummulticulturalmulticuntmultidisciplinarymultidrugmulti-
educationmultiemailmultiemissionmultiethnicmultiexclusionmultiexhibition-
multiexitmultiexterminatormultifacemultifairmultifaithmultifinemultifuck-
multinsurancenumbermultigallerymultigarbagemultigendermultigentrifica-
tionmultiglobalmultiguidelinemultihomelessmultijailmultilandlordmultinclu-
sionmultintegrationmultilingualmultilovermultinativemultimortgagemultin-

eighbourhoodmultipersonalitymultiplanningmultipoetrymultipridemultipro-
ductmultiracemultischlepmultisexmultisheltermultisoldiermultitonguemulti-
tolerantmultivictimultivoicemail

Stanley Fish offers one alternative to these quandaries. Rejecting pro-
grammatic approaches to multiculturalism that produce conceptual paralysis
or civic hypocrisy, he suggests instead that we engage in "inspired adhoccery"
in the interests of achieving a successful—or at least more honest—multiculturalism rooted in improvisation across the uneven landscape of cultural
diversity. Averring that "multiculturalism will not be one thing, but many
things," Fish writes,

> We may never be able to reconcile the claims of difference and community in a
> satisfactory formula, but we may be able to figure out a way for these differences
> to occupy the civic and political space of this community without coming to blows.

In short, Fish suggests abandoning the "ism" in multiculturalism, calling instead for open dialogue about what it means to communicate across culture
and asking us to consider whether such a thing is even possible.

In this respect Fish has much in common with prominent post-colonial
theorist Paul Gilroy, who argues in *Postcolonial Melancholia* that an organic,
emergent "multiculture" manages to sustain itself wholly independently of
state policies designed to encourage or contain expressions of cultural difference. Both Fish and Gilroy reject naive visions as well as legalistic prescrip-
tions about what the multicultural city should look like and how it should
work. While they do not make explicit where space for difference might be
made, if courts and committees and council chambers must be ruled out by
their own inability to seize the slippery nuances of culture, then perhaps we
may turn to spaces of discourse where meaning is by its very nature partial,
improvisational and subject to revision. These are the spaces of the imagination—film, art and especially literature—where the great myths of each era
are constantly dismantled and reinvented. In Toronto in particular, it is in
our literature where the myth of the multicultural city receives its critical and
creative attention.

In an era when terrorists crash hijacked airplanes into high-rise towers,
when suicide bombers march calmly onto crowded public buses and blow
themselves up, and when ethnic minorities are attacked for wearing culturally distinct clothing, Toronto stands out as a city where it is possible, indeed
necessary, to deal with our differences without coming to blows. In this city we
are enthusiastic about shawarma. We remember to say *Shalom* (Hebrew for

"peace") to one neighbour and *As-Sal mu 'Alaykum* (Arabic for "peace be with you") to the other. We attend one another's cultural festivals and acknowledge each other's holidays. At the same time, we live in a city where highly educated landed immigrants work as janitors, where poverty and discrimination drive young men into urban gangs, and where the local consequences of global conflicts leave scars that persist for generations. And yet the presence of these problems does not signal that what Pico Iyer calls Toronto's "multicultural experiment" has failed. Rather, they remind us that multiculturalism is a process requiring a deep and long-standing commitment to confronting and dealing with its challenges as well as its ideals. In this sense we owe a great debt to the city's writers for unflinchingly revealing the weaknesses—and strengths—of the multicultural city, because even if in the process we learn not only positive but also unpleasant things about ourselves, at least we will have been open to learning.

THE PLACE OF OUR MEETING WITH THE OTHER

In "Semiology and the Urban" cultural theorist Roland Barthes refers to the city as "the place of our meeting with the other," further describing it as "the privileged place where the other is and where we ourselves are other, as the place where we play the other." He uses the word *play* purposefully, invoking not only the pleasurable aspects of play but also its subversive, revelatory, even transformative qualities. For Barthes, play is never empty, never inconsequential: it is the most vital of city-building activities. By our very presence in the city—by inhabiting, building, navigating and narrating it—we appropriate and transform it, and are in turn appropriated and transformed ourselves. And what emerges is not only the city (or the self) that we wish to project, but all the other cities and all the other selves—the disordered and displaced as well as the beautiful and beloved—that exist alongside it. A living city, an open city—a successfully multicultural city—requires this discourse of play, which, at its most meaningful, offers something the language of conflict cannot provide: the promise of communication, a shared wish for reconciliation, a reaching out, a bridge—and, sometimes, a needed slap in the face.

When we "play the other" in the city, we begin to appreciate the overlapping nuances of cultural identity rather than reducing one another to catalogues of the familiar or foreign. This does not mean we take difference any less seriously. Rather, if we treat the city—and the city's literature—as prominent sites for the uneven negotiations across culture that define our era, we commit to principled engagement with difference. This means giving up certain of our conceits, including the claim that cultural openness may be expressed meaningfully by ordering takeout Thai food to celebrate the Chinese

New Year or swaying self-consciously to *mas* bands during the Caribana parade. It requires, too, the abandonment of identity politics rooted in a view of ourselves primarily as victims of history,[136] a perspective one of Rabindranath Maharaj's protagonists in "Escape to Etobicoke" characterizes as favoured by "those who continually nourish their wounds, tear away the scabs and offer their bruises for inspection. Such an elaborate preparation for sympathy, yet offended when it was given." It requires us to admit, finally, that we are uneasy with one another, and that there are things we do not, will not or perhaps cannot understand about each other. Admitting our unease seems so difficult, so at odds with the ideals of the multicultural city, and yet it is necessary if we are to have any hope of fulfilling them.

This book began with the suggestion that Toronto represents a new kind of city, one where identity emerges not from shared tradition or a long history but rather is forged out of a commitment to the virtues of diversity, tolerance and cultural understanding. It is time now to ask what tolerance can possibly mean in the multicultural city. In his challenging, controversial book, *Selling Illusions: The Cult of Multiculturalism in Canada*, Neil Bissoondath argues that tolerance amounts to little more than "putting up" with difference, intimating that "the pose of tolerance [...] can very quickly metamorphose into virulent defensiveness, rejecting the different, alienating the new." Successful multiculturalism, Bissoondath continues, requires a much stronger commitment to understanding: he observes that "Canada has long prided itself on being a tolerant society, but tolerance is clearly insufficient in the building of a cohesive society. A far greater goal to strive for would be an *accepting* society."

If Bissoondath rejects tolerance for being too narrow, Stanley Fish attacks tolerance for being too broad, observing that

> the trouble with stipulating tolerance as your first principle is that you cannot possibly be faithful to it because sooner or later the culture whose core values you are tolerating will reveal itself to be intolerant at that same core; that is, the distinctiveness that marks it as unique and self-defining will resist the appeal of moderation or incorporation into a larger whole. Confronted with a demand that it surrender its viewpoint or enlarge it to include the practices of its natural enemies—other religions, other races, other genders, other classes—a beleaguered culture will fight back with everything from discriminatory legislation to violence.

136 In *Selling Illusions: The Cult of Multiculturalism in Canada*, Neil Bissoondath objects to political positions based primarily upon a victim narrative, writing that "[t]o see oneself as a victim of history rather than as one of its victimizers, is to confer on oneself a delicious sweet-and-sour confirmation of one's own existence: deliciously sweet because you cannot be denied; deliciously sour because you have been brutalized. This life you lead is not your fault." (1994)

In a commentary interrogating cultural controversies ranging from Afro-centric education to the Islamic fatwa against novelist Salman Rushdie, Fish argues that "in the end neither the boutique multiculturalist nor the strong multiculturalist is able to come to terms with difference."

Bissoondath and Fish aptly characterize the classic dilemma of tolerance: that "mere tolerance" begrudges difference while unconditional tolerance courts absurdity by seeking to abide outright intolerance. Other critics, among them feminist,[137] post-colonial[138] and Marxist[139] scholars, challenge conceptions of tolerance on the grounds that they privilege those who do the tolerating (narrated as white, male, Western Selves) over those who are only ever provisionally tolerated (described as minority, women, immigrant Others). In reality, however, divisions between the privileged and the oppressed cannot be so conveniently categorized. Indeed, given the extent of our interrelatedness, the principle of tolerance seems to offer the only real hope that we can engage meaningfully with difference and communicate across cultures without coming to blows. Tolerance does not always lead to acceptance, but at least it is honest about its strengths and shortcomings. Moreover, because it forces us to recognize one another's shared right to the city, tolerance may represent precisely the kind of "inspired adhoccery" that Fish suggests is needed to make the multicultural city work.

How does a commitment to tolerance enable us to engage meaningfully with difference? First and most importantly, tolerance acknowledges the tensions that exist among cultural communities, particularly in a city like Toronto whose population reflects the dynamics of three centuries of global conflict and where contemporary immigration has made unlikely neighbours of Croatians, Serbs, Tamils, Sinhalese, Tutsis, Hutus, Sikhs, Hindus, Turks, Armenians, Muslims, Jews and the manifold other diasporas whose presence makes tolerance such an urgent virtue. Tolerance acknowledges, further, that social and economic power is distributed unevenly, and that individuals and minority cultures need to be protected from intolerance.

Engaging meaningfully with difference forces us to realize, finally, that even tolerance has limits. Some of the limits of tolerance are easy to agree on: that civil liberties do not extend to hate speech or hateful acts, and that racially motivated violence is more than mere assault. But other areas are more chal-

---

137 See especially Iris Young's *Inclusion and Democracy* (2002). Wendy Brown's *Regulating Aversion: Tolerance in the Age of Identity and Empire* (2006) and Anne Phillips' *Multiculturalism without Culture* (2007) also take up questions of gender alongside race and class in understandings of multiculturalism, difference and tolerance.

138 Gilroy (2005), Meeks (ed., 2007).

139 See, for example, Slavoj Zizek's essay "Tolerance as an Ideological Category" (2008) whose argument owes much to Herbert Marcuse's commentary in *Repressive Tolerance* (1969).

lenging, such as proposed introductions of Sharia law or Aboriginal sentencing circles already established in some jurisdictions alongside the established courts. A commitment to tolerance signals our willingness to engage with these difficult questions as if culture—and cultural difference—actually matter to us in the multicultural city.

Tolerance, in short, is committed precisely to the kinds of negotiation across culture that rescue multiculturalism from empty utopianism and enable us to engage meaningfully with one another. While some of these negotiations are conducted in civil courts, human rights tribunals and legislative assemblies, the great bulk of our understandings arise in the unspoken conversations between people thrust together in the streets, subways, sidewalks, elevators, offices, parks and playgrounds of this city. Urgent, embodied and living, these conversations about culture filter into the city's literature and are transmitted into the soul of the city itself. And if we are willing to listen, it is possible to discern at least four kinds of conversations about culture.

In the first of these conversations, writers respond actively to intolerance. Already in this chapter we have encountered authors, among them Austin Clarke, Andrew Moodie, Lawrence Hill, Mobashar Qureshi, Earle Birney, Krisantha Sri Bhaggiyadatta, M. G. Vassanji and Rabindranath Maharaj, who bear witness to the divisive effects of intolerance and whose protagonists resist racism by exposing it to the withering language of satire, by challenging cultural stereotypes and flatly rejecting victimhood. If further evidence is required to drive this last point home, a striking example is found in Vassanji's *No New Land*, in which one of the protagonists, when asked casually by a white lover, "Why do you Pakis come to this country?" elects not to sublimate his rage, ignore the slur or explain, yet again, that not all South Asians are from Pakistan. Instead, he responds by turning his stream of urine upon her naked body and asserting, "This is what we Pakis are going to do to you."

The second conversation is restorative, oriented toward reclaiming identity from the obliterating effects of racial prejudice, economic exclusion, political erasure and ethnic spectacles that reduce culture to cliché. In a city where cultural minorities strive for visibility, Toronto's Aboriginal inhabitants have been so thoroughly Othered they have nearly vanished from the cultural landscape. In her novel *What We All Long for*, Dionne Brand inventories the city's array of Italian, Vietnamese, Chinese, Ukrainian, Pakistani, Korean and African neighbourhoods before making the startling observation that "[a]ll of them sit on Ojibway land, but hardly any of them know it or care because that genealogy is wilfully untraceable except in the name of the city itself." In truth, contemporary Toronto sits not only on Ojibway land but on the land of the Neutrals, Huron (Wendat), Petun, Seneca, Iroquoian and Mississauga peoples, and on the land of all their ancestors who fished, farmed and fought over the region for more than ten thousand years before the first European intruders arrived in the seventeenth century. Despite the obliterating effects of three centuries of subsequent urban development, evidence ranging from spear fragments to entire villages dug periodically out of backyards and construction sites offers silent testimony to the long-standing presence of Toronto's original inhabitants. The only artifacts missing from the popular narrative are Aboriginals themselves—and their stories.

Toronto's Aboriginal writers confront a double erasure. Popular portrayals of drunk, homeless Indians panhandling outside the liquor store compete with the equally prevalent perception that "authentic" Natives do not belong in Toronto at all. Commenting on this peculiar contradiction, one Aboriginal activist has observed,

> The drunken Indian is ten feet tall, but a sober one is invisible. No one notices all the ones that they pass that are on their way to work, on their way home, on their way to committees, whatever. No one notices these ones, but everybody notices the one that is drunk on the street.[140]

Many Aboriginals are invisible in cities because of a widely held assumption that being Native is inherently incompatible with being urban. In the film *Tkaronto*, an Elder asks rhetorically, "What are we supposed to do? Leave our aboriginalness on the outskirts of town and pick it up on the way out again? Like it only exists out there?" "Out there" refers, of course, to the reservations now widely understood to be Native people's "natural" habitat. This perception persists despite the reality that more Aboriginals live in cities, including Toronto, than at any time in the past.[141]

Toronto's Aboriginal writers respond to erasure in a variety of ways. In *Big Buck City*, poet/playwright Daniel David Moses reclaims Native stereotypes through satire, converting slurs about "bush Indians" and "reservations" into jokes about prostitution and dinner plans.[142] In the novel *Through Black Spruce*, Joseph Boyden populates Toronto with a network of Natives who all seem to know each other, congregating informally at the Native Canadian Centre on Spadina, at the Meeting Place near Bathurst and Queen, or gathering to roast goose under the Gardiner Expressway. In Cherie Dimaline's *Red Rooms*, a chambermaid weaves encounters with hotel guests and their left-behind

---

140 Quoted in Proulx, 2006.
141 Proulx, 2006.
142 Daniel David Moses Moses is also the author of several other plays exploring urban aboriginal identity, among them *Coyote City* (2000), *City of Shadows* (2000) and *Kyotopolis* (2008).

items into vivid portraits of a downtown hotel's Aboriginal guests. In each of these works, the city's Native population is projected into the foreground: their lives, stories and communities dominate narratives of a city that has more than merely metaphorically "gone native."

At the same time, the Aboriginal protagonists of these works remain deeply ambivalent about a city they inhabit but are reluctant to call home. Like Boyden's Natives, congregating around a tarpaulin teepee they have erected under the Gardiner Expressway, or like Dimaline's Aboriginal hotel guests, they seem to seek out the city's marginal spaces by preference as much as necessity, their chosen transience a symbolic response to three centuries of cultural displacement. As one of Boyden's characters responds to another who objects to his panhandling: "Think of it as cheap rent for good land."

Ultimately, however, the city becomes a site for unmistakable acts of reclamation. In Dimaline's story "Room 106," a famous Cree photographer who has travelled the world documenting Aboriginal life returns to Toronto and, finally realizing what has been missing from his work, takes a photograph of himself surrounded by images of his people pinned to the wall of this anonymous urban hotel room. This arresting self-portrait, titled "Finding Home," achieves international fame as a testament to identity lost and regained. Similarly, in Moses' play *City of Shadows*, the spirits of dead Aboriginals inhabit a city filled with the broken bones of ancestors, a city inverted as its ghosts, reduced to whisperings heard on the night wind, are revealed to be the white intruders who occupy the waking city but cannot lay claim to its soul. As Moses writes in the play's epigraph (quoting legendary Suquamish chief Seattle), "All night when the streets of your cities and villages are silent and you think them deserted, they will throng with the returning hosts that once filled them and still love this beautiful land."

In the third conversation, writers inscribe their cultural narratives into the city's literary landscape for the first time. One of the earliest of these voices is Henry Kreisel, whose 1948 novel, *The Rich Man*, describes the efforts of its narrator, a Jewish garment factory worker born in Austria, to reconcile the obligations of the Old World with the opportunities of the New. Subsequent generations of writers, among them Austin Clarke, Josef Skvorecky, M. G. Vassanji, Neil Bissoondath, Nino Ricci, Antanas Sileika, Afua Cooper, Kerri Sakamoto, Shyam Selvadurai, David Bezmozgis, Lien Chao, Nitin Deckha and Anthony De Sa, extend Toronto's cultural narrative to reflect the global diaspora. More recently, organizations like Diaspora Dialogues have begun to showcase work by established and emerging writers drawn from the city's diverse communities.[143]

---

143 Diaspora Dialogues has published a series of annual anthologies called *TOK: Writing the New Toronto*, featuring new and emerging writers; see Walsh, ed., 2006; Walsh, ed., 2007; and Walsh,

Perhaps most deeply evocative of the need for culturally resonant literature is Farzana Doctor's novel *Stealing Nasreen*, in which a lesbian psycholo-
gist's flirtation with her married Gujarati teacher leads both to question their
cultural commitments. Born in Canada to Indian parents, Nasreen becomes
an object of fascination to Mumbai-born Salma and her husband, Shaffiq,
a janitor at the hospital where Nasreen works. Discovering that they have
formed an uncomfortable triangle, the three begin to renegotiate lives they
have chosen but find increasingly confining. Nasreen reconciles with her recently widowed father, agrees to a joint visit to Mumbai and even contemplates
buying a house with him, hoping these efforts will heal what she has come to
recognize as their shared emotional homelessness. Shaffiq resolves to speak
across the silence that has crept into his marriage, acknowledging what emigration has cost them and promising to help fulfill their shared aspirations.
For her part, Salma finds herself gradually, perhaps grudgingly, coming to
terms with her new life in Canada:

> The new job, this job that Shaffiq finally found after two long years in Toronto,
> holds the promise of permanent life in Canada. Now they can stay, will stay, have
> everything they need to stay. A part of her has always hoped that Shaffiq's ter-
> rible night shift job and her boring dry cleaner work would lead them to the only
> possible, rational conclusion about their big adventure in Canada; it would be a
> failure and they would have to return home. She held on tightly to this belief, even
> while she kept busy decorating their apartment, settling her children into school,
> acquiring the necessary ID, and finding work. But now things are working out for
> them and they will stay. Now they will be successful immigrants.

Despite her misgivings about coming to Canada, despite the struggles of their
first two years in Toronto, Salma finds that the city has worn down her resistance. Buoyed by Shaffiq's new job and the renewed candour of their marriage, Salma begins to map out her own future in Canada, setting aside money
for university tuition, anticipating teaching again and looking forward to the
day when she, too, can feel like she belongs in Toronto.

The fourth conversation, finally, seeks to communicate across difference,
to identify common ground and explore what might be shared—however
beautiful or terrible—in the multicultural city. In Dionne Brand's *What We
All Long For*, a young artist resolves to build a *lubaio*, a Chinese signpost, out
of discarded railway ties and found lumber she has hauled to her Kensington
Market apartment and to which she plans to affix items that represent the

---

ed., 2008. In 2009 Diaspora Dialogues branched out and began publishing stories representing
urban experiences across Canada; see Walsh, ed., 2009.

city's desires. After crafting the massive frame of the *lubaio*, Tuyen ventures forth into the city, asking people to tell her what they long for. Their longings are as varied as the city itself: "Reading, a whole year to read"; "To feel safer; safe, like when I was a child." A Somali taxi driver tells her he longs for "enough money to go home and marry four wives." A Bengali woman asks Tuyen, "Why long for anything? Longing is suffering." In addition to these stories, which she records and retains, Tuyen collects material scraps of the city—lost photographs, bank receipts, shopping lists, pages of letters—and pins them all to the *lubaio*, where they sway suspended like prayer flags. As the installation takes shape, Tuyen is stunned to discover that recent photographs she has taken in Toronto contain images of her brother, lost as a child when her parents fled Vietnam, and whose absence has been the source of the family's deepest sorrow and greatest longing.

Out of all these disparate fragments, out of all the shouted, whispered, unspoken, lost and forgotten stories she has collected, Tuyen constructs a monument to the multicultural city. As Brand writes,

> Yes, that was the beauty of this city, it's polyphonic, murmuring. This is what always filled Tuyen with hope, this is what she thought her art was about—the representation of that gathering of voices and longings that summed themselves up into a kind of language, yet indescribable.

The *lubaio* is an edifice to culture and a tangible representation of difference, but beyond all this it gives voice to the city's greatest longing: a desire to speak, even of difficult things, and the parallel need to be heard.

− 5 −

DESIRE LINES

CARTOGRAPHIES OF DESIRE

As we navigate the urban labyrinth, whenever we follow the invisible paths laid down by our longings, we trace desire lines across the city. Like the rutted footpaths worn across well-used playgrounds or the spontaneous shortcuts that materialize at street corners, desire lines mark the movements we make by choice rather than at the command of curbstones and social conventions. Radiating outward from the soul of every city dweller, they are public expressions of internal desire, a compass charting our most intimate longings.

Despite their lyrical nomenclature, we owe our awareness of these cartographies of desire not to poets but to transportation engineers, who once designed highway networks by charting destination preferences they called "desire lines."[144] Subsequently, urban planners and landscape architects used the phrase to refer to the informal footpaths worn by pedestrians deviating from paved pathways in pursuit of an efficient shortcut or playful detour.[145] More recently, desire lines have been traced across digital terrain, mapping virtual networks and documenting patterns of electronic wanderlust.[146] A thread connecting these seemingly divergent topographies of desire is an acknowledgement that between the urban imperatives of production and consumption lies a vast, corporeal landscape made by our movements in the pursuit of leisure, pleasure and play.

In Stephen Marche's novel *Raymond and Hannah,* a young man and woman meet at a party: their attraction is mutual and immediate. Raymond is a graduate student, bound to his books, while Hannah is days away from flying to Israel for a nine-month *Aliyah* program in Jerusalem. They spend six days together, and then she leaves. This could be the uncluttered conclusion to a quick fling, except they have fallen hopelessly in love and left the imprint of their union all over the city.

Throughout the novel, Marche describes their liaison in spatial language: Hannah's empty attic is a symbol of anticipation as well as absence, Raymond's basement a metaphor for the long hibernation he will endure while she is gone, every restaurant meal a plateful of proximity, the lake a ledge at the edge of infinity. Like a breath held until it must be released, the city sings a silent aubade for the lovers, begging the streets to be still:

---

144 See Goodman (ed.), 1968; Blunden, 1971. The term has reportedly been in use in its engineering context for nearly a century: reference to "desire lines" appears in land-use planning documents dating to the 1940s and desire-line calculations featured prominently in the 1955 Chicago Area Transportation Study (Fagin, 1960; Throgmorton & Eckstein, 2000).
145 Rogers, 1987; Shanks & Pearson, 2001; Myhill, 2004; Tiessen, 2007.
146 Chaplin, 1995; Paulini & Schnabel, 2008.

Transport trucks, go slowly. Pull yourself over on the side of the road. Bring the night with you into your bunks. Let Raymond and Hannah anticipate endlessly on stairs up to attics. Nights in August in Toronto are too short besides. And go slowly, street-washing men. Just let the dirt be dirty for now. Let the streets seize with filth. Let your engines stall, and stop the morning from coming.

But space and time cannot be stretched out indefinitely, and six days later the lovers learn that "[a]irports are built for Raymond waiting at doors that slide open and shut, and Hannah running through check-in, through security, through the tunnel to the airplane to sit and consider what was."

During the long months of their separation, Hannah becomes immersed in her heritage, Raymond in his studies. She grows settled, considers staying. Raymond grows melancholic and, perhaps inevitably, betrays her sexually. The thread between them, thin already, is stretched almost to the breaking point. But something inexplicable pulls them together, and when Hannah returns to Toronto it is as if all the intervening oceans have parted just for them. The city fits their contours perfectly:

> Their bodies are as beautiful as a city not cared for much. His belly and hers were two bridges facing each other across a ravine. Their hair waved like the flags over the embassies. Their mouths were two open doors leading into a single building and, lying beside each other, they spread out like one smog cloud over two smoke-stacks. They ran like water, like the subway, from one end of the city to the other. [...] Every part requires every part in a city, in a body. His hand on her thigh means her hand on his neck just so. [...] Again in Toronto, their bodies make the sound of rivers. They taste salt, emerging out of their own rivers. They have become the lake at the end of the city, perfect and serene and calm, and they start up like two pigeons among a flock of sleeping doves in the public grounds of the city. Their bodies are perfect.

Like almost everything else in Toronto, Raymond and Hannah are drawn together despite their differences. When the lovers return, the city's rough edges soften and reform around them: buildings open, bridges arch and landscapes unfold until, in the end, what remains is what was present in the beginning: the shape of a body in a city yearning only for the warmth of another.

A similar spatial lexicon structures Gordon Stewart Anderson's *The Toronto You Are Leaving*, a funny, poignant novel describing a young gay man coming out in a city just beginning to chart its sexual terrain. Set mainly in mid-1970s Toronto, in the years before Church and Wellesley became the epicentre of the city's gay ghetto, the work maps the movements of a loose network of gay men among the social spaces—gay bars, the bathhouses, the Y and Hanlan's Beach—that are already coming to define their community. Anderson's protagonist is a graduate student from Victoria who has chosen Toronto not only for its scholarly prospects but also for its sexual promise. New to the city, David meets a navigator, Tim, who becomes his first lover in an on-again-off-again relationship that quickly comes to embody the contradictions of the city itself.

Tim, a "scion of Anglo-Saxon Toronto" whose exuberant sexuality remains at unspoken odds with his upbringing, is an artist who lives in an airy high-rise at the fringes of Forest Hill, while David, a diffident academic and anxious lover, burrows into an aging Annex house near the university. Tim remains restless, leaving Toronto—and David—periodically to visit other cities—and other bodies—looking for something he never finds, while David embeds himself in Toronto, finding in it—and in Tim—a multifaceted refraction of their relationship; indeed of gay culture itself:

He had arrived in love, in a new city. From out of Tim's presence and his paths through Toronto, David had begun seeing another city, began writing it in his head. In reality, gay Toronto was a small town: its meeting places were few, faces repeated, it was banal and provincial, with the pallor of oppression. The red-brick buildings obscured the reality that hatred as well as neighbourliness and discrimination as well as friendliness could co-exist in the expanse of Metro that stretched beyond the restricted confines of the gay ghetto. For David, it seemed to hold a whole lost civilization in its ways of moving and feeling. It was an eternal city, greeting him with a kind of tacky Latinity.

David begins writing a novel called *Toronto*, its chapters laid out in the shape of his lover's body, but finds he cannot complete it because the city, like his relationship with Tim, keeps shifting and slipping away. As David muses, "He kept telling himself to hurry, to get down the words that held it. Tim, its founder and foundation, was real and solid enough, but the city wasn't. It wasn't a feeling of any sort. It was intuitive, from off to the side of the mind. It came around you only at lucky moments, like a city in the wind."

Desire encodes itself in every cell of the city. Like a mitochondrial sequence, it permeates the urban core, connecting the cerebral city—the public city of laws, culture and the mind—with the private, corporeal city of lust, anger, passion and the body. Desire is an organic algorithm, a visceral code tracing the trajectory of our myriad yearnings: for money, material success, remission from terror or the memory of it, power, possession, redemption, revenge, solidarity, solitude, love, a lucky lottery ticket, a winning hockey team or the warm press of a stranger's flesh on a crowded subway. Everything in a city leaves an imprint, with consequences novelist Katrina Onstad considers in *How Happy to Be*, musing, "What if every hand that laid itself on our bodies left a print? We could read each other better. The loneliest people would be flesh-coloured, and the most abused covered in black."

Still, sometimes in a city desire is the only thing that holds us to the people and places we love. Perhaps this is why in *Metropolis*, a volume of poems about the embodied city, Rishma Dunlop writes, "there is no consolation except in desire." Sometimes this is all we have left: an evanescent sadness passing across the soul like a row of streetlights across a wet windshield at night. As Maggie Helwig writes in her story "Canadian Movies," "I have also found flowers in the street sometimes, roses just lying across the pavement, all velvet and brittle and the colour of a heart muscle."

A GAY OLD TOWN

Urban literature is tightly wedded to narratives of heterosexual desire, but cities have always drawn the curious, the questing and the queer, whose stories are embedded just as deeply—if historically more covertly—in the city's corporeal landscape. Parallel, intersecting, yet ultimately distinguishable from heteronormative narratives of the same era, these works provide critical background to contemporary readings of queer literature because they offer historical context in addition to foregrounding many of the themes—corporeal sensuality, sexual politics and the sense of social otherness—that have characterized literature produced by later generations of gay, lesbian, bisexual and genderqueer writers.[147]

In the introduction to *Seminal: The Anthology of Canada's Gay Male Poets*, editor John Barton notes that Canada's earliest known gay poets wrote about their sexuality indirectly or delayed publication of their more revealing works, particularly during the long decades before homosexuality was decriminalized in 1969.[148] One leading example is Edward Lacey, whose groundbreaking 1965 book, *The Forms of Loss*, included homoerotic works but omitted what

147 Interested readers are directed to Peter Dickinson's thematic study of queer Canadian literature, *Here Is Queer: Nationalisms, Sexualities and the Literatures of Canada* (University of Toronto Press, 1999) as well as James C. Johnstone and Karen X. Tulchinsky's anthologies, *Queer View Mirror: Lesbian and Gay Short Fiction* and *Queer View Mirror 2* (1995, 1997), Elizabeth Ruth's Bent On Writing: Contemporary Queer Tales (2002) and Catherine Lake and Nairne Holtz's No Margins: Writing Canadian Fiction in Lesbian (2006).
148 Until 1969 in Canada, homosexual acts were punishable by imprisonment for up to fourteen years. The controversy surrounding this and other legislative easements, introduced to the House of Parliament in 1967, gave rise to then–Justice Minister Pierre Trudeau's now-famous statement that "there's no place for the state in the bedrooms of the nation."

Barton describes as Lacey's first openly gay poem.[149] This early poem, "Quintillas," crafted in the late 1950s while Lacey was an undergrad at the University
of Toronto, describes a spontaneous sexual liaison between its narrator and
another young man he encounters in an alleyway:

> [...] there in the dim
> light he signalled; I followed him
> into some intricate recess
> of patterned buildings, where with him
> I entered into congress grim
> and lovely, felt his manhood's slim
> mastery, his boyhood's loneliness.

Pressed together between the interstices of the city, the men couple in the
darkness in unspoken anonymity, parting only when dawn threatens to expose
evidence of their transgression. Afterward,

> tortured and lost; we made our way
> by separate paths out of that place,
> a sort of courtyard, foul by day,
> where neighbouring skyscrapers embrace
> and mingle, leaving lust a place
> to seek out from the winter cold,
> in cities where love is bought and sold.

Architectural erections reflecting the erotic at a brutal, mute, megalithic scale,
the surrounding high-rises shelter even as they exclude the erotic interlude
transacted in their shadows.

Another writer who evokes a similar sense of sexual tension is John Grube, whose early work (such as the poems in *Sunday Afternoon at the Toronto
Art Gallery*) is only indirectly homoerotic but whose later poetry and fiction
offer a frank retrospective of gay male sexuality in mid-century Toronto. In
"Geoffrey," from *I'm Supposed to be Crazy and Other Stories*, a young professor finds himself being seduced in the rooftop bar at the Park Plaza Hotel by
a distinguished-looking older man who takes him back to his Prince Arthur
Street apartment, slaps around and nearly strangles him, soaks him in the
shower, then proceeds to sodomize him. Afterward, Geoffrey introduces Mac

---

149 According to Barton, Edward Lacey's *The Forms of Loss* (published privately in 1965 with the
financial assistance of Margaret Atwood and Dennis Lee) was the first volume of openly gay poetry
published in Canada.

to an elite subset of the city's gay community where social and sexual affairs are conducted behind closed doors and almost wholly in code, and whose gathering places—including an axclusive club across the street from the King Edward Hotel—are open only to those accompanied by someone in the know. Inside the Nile Room, a narrow basement bar filled with well-dressed men, Mac watches the scene until another distinguished-looking older man sends him a drink. Shortly thereafter the man comes over and invites Geoffrey and Mac to join him at a private party at a Rosedale home. Mac is unsure how to respond, but Geoffrey steps in and gracefully accepts:

> "We'd love to," Geoffrey answered for both of them. "Thank you." Peter bowed almost imperceptibly to Mac and walked back to his own table. Then, Geoffrey turned to Mac. "Do you realize what an honour that was? Well...Peter is the Queen of Toronto. If he likes you, you're in, get it? He actually got up and came over for a royal visit which I've never seen him do before. [...] Everyone knows him. He's the most important person in the Toronto gay world. If he likes you, you can meet anyone." Mac knew what was left unspoken: *this is your world now.*

At a party whose attendees include politicians and a well-known stage actor, Mac gapes with star-struck absorption until Geoffrey cautions him, "[I]f you see someone you know in the outside world, for God's sake keep it to yourself, OK? I mean if you happen to see a judge, or a professor or something, don't *ever* let on, don't use the guy's real name. Do you understand?"

One reason these gatherings—and the names of the men who attend them—are so tightly scripted is because in the decades before homosexuality was decriminalized, gay men and women were subject to prosecution and harassment, and even after 1967 homophobia remained deeply ingrained in the city's culture. Although in "The Gay World" (an essay published in William Mann's 1970 book, *The Underside of Toronto*), William Johnson cheerfully avers that Toronto is "on its way to becoming the homosexual capital of North America," many Torontonians continued to consider homosexuality a form of sexual deviance, a view that made its way into the city's literature. Hugh Garner's *Death in Don Mills*, a 1975 police procedural, finds its narrative resolution in the discovery that a woman has been poisoned not by *her* jealous lover but by the jealous lover of a teenaged boy the woman's murderer fears is bisexually attracted to her. When the police storm the apartment to execute a search warrant, they find a lurid scene that, even with Garner's nod to Trudeau's famous quip about the bedrooms of the nation, reads like something torn straight from the pages of a pulp magazine:

Lying naked in each other's arms were Langenzent and Dwayne, both breathing hard from the exertions of coition. The soft bed had been pulled out and they were uncovered.

Langenzent sat up and shouted, "What the hell is this! What are you people doing here! [...] You're supposed to be cops, but you don't know the law. Don't you know that what happens in the nation's bedrooms is nobody's business any more?"

"Listen, you smart-ass, the law reads that whatever happens in the nation's bedrooms *between consenting adults* is no longer looked at as a crime."

Charging Langenzent with the woman's murder, the police use the youth's minor age as an excuse to commit him to a mental hospital. First Inspector McDumont berates the boy's father, shouting, "Seen enough now, Hardley, to know what your son is? Or didn't the fact that he was caught once before with the schoolteacher convince you that between that wife of yours and you you'd managed to bring up a homosexual?"

Well over a decade after decriminalization, gay men continued to be subject to arrest. John Grube's story "Raid," an account of a notorious 1981 police raid against Toronto bathhouses in which more than 300 people were charged for being present in what legislation continues to refer to as a "bawdy-house," not only describes the shock experienced by those arrested but also reveals schisms in the gay community. Grube describes the raid itself in language reminiscent of Kristallnacht:

"This is a bust, you goddamn cocksuckers!" the beefier of the two thugs yelled at Bob, as he now held him in a hammerlock on the floor of the cubicle. "Get your goddamn clothes on and line up in the showers with the others." [...] A few minutes later they were lined up with the other victims in the shower area, and a uniformed cop at a table was processing them slowly, one by one, filling in some kind of paper. The last thing Bob could remember before he fainted was a cop saying he sure wished those heating pipes had gas in them, the Germans really knew how to deal with queers.

Curiously enough, the raid receives its greatest support within the Attorney General's office from a closeted civil servant who believes his involvement in the raid will help further his career:

Although he was gay, it was legitimate for him to support a bust of the gay bathhouses he told himself. Being gay meant being discreet, as he and his friends were. Not rocking the boat. Good gays had long-term monogamous relationships.

They didn't have sex with twenty different guys in a weekend, in parks or in bath-houses.

Ultimately, however, neither closeted queers in the AG's office nor overzeal-ous police are able to stem the turning tide of public support. As one of the activists who organizes what becomes the city's first Pride parade muses, "Public opinion was slowly swinging around to supporting gay rights. [...] the seeds planted in the last ten years were beginning to blossom. The police were trying to block the gay community from achieving legitimacy, but it was not only surviving, it was stronger than it had ever been."

Despite police harassment, gay-bashing and persistent homophobia, from the 1970s onward queer writers and playwrights have written increas-ingly freely about their sexuality. One work that may be seen as symbolically inaugurating this era in Toronto is Scott Symons' novel *Civic Square*, pub-lished in 1969 as a limited-edition manuscript packed into a robin's-egg-blue box, reportedly because his publisher, McClelland & Stewart, was concerned about being branded a pornographer. Symons' first novel, *Place d'Armes*, re-casts Montreal as a relentlessly (homo)sexual city, but *Civic Square* is a vastly more outrageous satire of Toronto as a city at the cusp of sexual self-aware-ness. Opening with the epigraph "Cocks are beautiful," Symons goes on to describe "the Gay Queens slavering, laughing at their socially-enforced oddity: sheer guts—only *they* have the right to laugh, to cry, to see, to touch, in this city." Nearly nine hundred pages later, the novel climaxes, as it were, with an explosive sexual interlude followed by a visit to the observation deck on the roof of City Hall, where the entire city, sated and sprawled out below, appears to burst into foliage as if nurtured by spilled seed.

Still, not all writers (or their protagonists) appreciated the "out" and in-creasingly politicized culture of gay life in Toronto. One of the protagonists of Robertson Davies' *The Rebel Angels* is a disgraced ex-academic and sometime monk who attempts to shock an acquaintance by telling lurid tales of his de-bauched past. When she describes him as "one of the Gays," he responds, tartly,

Ah, but I'm not, you see; I'm one of the Sads, and one of the Uglies. The Gays make me laugh; they're so middle class and political about the whole thing. They'll destroy it all with their clamour about Gay Lib. and alternative life-styles, and all love is holy, and 'both partners must be squeaky clean.' That's putting the old game on a level with No-Cal pop or decaffeinated coffee—appearance without reality. [...] No, I want no truck with 'homo-eroticism' and the awful, treacherous, gold-digging little queens you get stuck with in that caper: I want no truck with

Gay Liberation or hokum about alternative life-styles: I want neither the love that dare not speak its name nor the love that blats its name to every grievance committee. *Gnosce te-ipsum* says the Oracle at Delphi; know thyself, and I do. I'm just a gross old bugger and I like it rough—I like the mess and I like the stink. But don't ask me to like the people. They aren't my kind.

Similarly, when Scott Symons died in 2009, *Globe & Mail* columnist Sandra Martin wrote that he "always claimed that he was homosexual, not gay, by which he probably meant that he didn't embrace the gay liberation movement as a defining political and social cause. He wasn't seeking equality, he was railing against the real foe—the Blandmen—the establishment types that he felt had betrayed Canada's British and French heritage."[150] A point that may be taken from these observations is that, despite the arguably community-building activism of the fight for gay, lesbian, bisexual, transgendered and genderqueer rights, queer identity in Toronto is hardly monolithic. Indeed, it is almost certainly far more diverse than heterosexual identity.

In his thoughtful introduction to *Making, Out: Plays by Gay Men*, dramatist Robert Wallace takes issue with efforts to distinguish "gay" (commonly denoting social and political behaviour) from "homosexual," (a biological category) arguing instead that all queer identities are socially constructed, relational and highly variable. Contemporary queer writers engaging with Toronto—among them Buddies in Bad Times Theatre co-founder Sky Gilbert, Jim Bartley (whose excellent play *Stephen & Mr. Wilde* speculates upon Oscar Wilde's relationship with Stephen Davenport, the African-American valet who accompanied Wilde during his 1882 visit to Toronto), poets R.M. Vaughan, Sandra Alland and Leah Lakshmi Piepzna-Samarasinha, novelists Peter McGehee, Todd Klinck and Greg Kramer[151] and particularly Gordon Stewart Anderson in *The Toronto You Are Leaving*—exemplify Wallace's point by tackling the overlapping subjects of homophobia, AIDS, social and sexual difference, gendered performance, desire and the intersection of queer and left politics.

Sexual politics remain a subtext in most queer literature, but increasingly often queer characters in Toronto literature seem to take their sexuality for

---

150 See Sandra Martin's essay, "His Life Was His art. Alas, It Was Not a Masterpiece." *Globe & Mail*, 27 February 2009.

151 See, for example, Gilbert's memoir, *Ejaculations from the Charm Factory*, R.M. Vaughan's *Troubled: A Memoir in Poems and Fragments*, Sandra Alland's *Proof of a Tongue*, Leah Lakshmi Piepzna-Samarasinha's *Consensual Genocide*, Peter McGehee's *Boys Like Us* and *Sweetheart*, Todd Klinck's *Tacones* and Greg Kramer's *Hogtown Bonbons*. Anthologies featuring queer literature engaging with Toronto include Lynn Crosbie and Michael Holmes' *Plush: Selected Poems of Sky Gilbert, Courtnay McFarlane, Jeffery Conway, RM Vaughan & David Trinidad* and Elizabeth Ruth's *Bent on Writing: Contemporary Queer Tales*.

granted. These include the gay twenty-something aspiring screenwriter who is the protagonist of Warren Dunford's *Soon to Be a Major Motion Picture*, the psychotherapist who falls in love with her Gujarati teacher in Farzana Doctor's *Stealing Nasreen* and the lesbian artist at the heart of Dionne Brand's *What We All Long For*. This shift is exemplified best, perhaps, by Zoe Whittall's *Holding Still for as Long as Possible*, a novel revolving around a transsexual paramedic whose bisexual girlfriend leaves him for another woman. Throughout the novel, sexuality receives about as much attention as discussions about terrorism, gentrification and what to eat for dinner. When sexual orientation does come up in conversation, such as when Josh's new partner asks about his well-being, it is more likely to be meant as a social icebreaker than a judgement or objection:

> "You gotta relax, Josh. What's up with you today?"
> "Nothing. Just girlfriend trouble."
> "Ah, that's why I do not date girls."
> I looked at him more closely. "You're gay?"
> "Yeah."
> He looked at me, just as close, and all of a sudden I saw that he knew about me. "My family has the queer gene, I guess. My sister is, at the moment, turning into my brother."
> I looked at him, wishing the subject away.
> "I don't know, man. I think that's pretty fucking cool, you know. She's always wanted it. I mean *he*. I'm always fucking that up: *he's* always wanted to be a guy. If there's anything this job has taught me, it's that life is too short to live a lie, right?"
> "Amen," I answered, lighting a smoke.

The subtext of Whittall's novel—that sexual orientation can be taken for granted as much (or as little) as anything else in the city—reflects a remarkable shift in attitudes toward sexual identity. Published half a century after the appearance of Canada's first volume of openly gay poetry, and only a decade after the most recent bathhouse raid, Whittall's novel underscores the reality that in contemporary Toronto, a city made perilous by bomb threats, pandemic scares and near-fatal bicycle accidents, people are drawn together or pulled apart less by sexual orientation than by the painful proximity of life and death.

WORKING FOR IT

Anyone who spends time in a strip club quickly realizes how little the performance of sex has to do with desire. The predominant tension—a palpable current that wafts through the air like the smell of spilled beer and stale perfume—

is one of frustration rather than promise of fulfilment. For the men (and the customers are nearly always men, or the girlfriends of men trying to pretend they are amused), visiting a strip club is a futile gesture of power and posses-sion, a marketplace where the wares remain off limits despite the calculated appearance of availability. For the women (who refer to themselves euphemis-tically as dancers), the long shifts are dominated by boredom broken only by the challenge of distinguishing between generous tippers and ass-grabbers. What prevails in this environment is an aura of mutual contempt: the custom-ers toward girls who seem eager to dance for a dangling dollar; the dancers toward those willing to pay for something they cannot possess. At the same time, however, an undercurrent of desire draws them together: the customer's delusion that a favourite performer dances only for him, or the stripper's ro-mantic notion that among the club's patrons is someone who will love her for her mind. In the end, both parties are taken in by their own performances— but who is to say it is not worth the cost?

In F. G. Paci's novel *Sex and Character*, two young men, university stu-dents eager to shed the vestiges of their virginal adolescence, stroll along Spadina to the Victory Burlesque, a theatre known for the erotic daring of its performances from the end of the war until it closed in 1975. Aroused with wondrous anticipation, they enter the faintly faded glory of the theatre, pant-ing at the promise of its posters and semi-nude statuary:

> Under the wedding cake marquee of the theatre we saw photographs of large-breasted women, with nothing but pasties and G-strings. I had to look closer to see if they were live women. Their pink-and-white bodies had the matte look of delicious bread. Further down were movie posters of scantily-clad females in soft-porn romantic adventures. [...] The inside lobby was dark and cavernous. It was an old movie palace long past its prime. A huge candy bar counter jutted out into the lobby, where the walls were festooned with more pictures of nude women. Off to the side, in a little alcove, stood the most amazing thing I had ever set eyes on. A golden plaster statue about seven feet high of a burlesque queen down to her G-string and pasties offered us the full wonders of the female body.

Despite their auspicious entrance, the first striptease performer—a nervous first-timer who fumbles her entire act—leaves the young men feeling some-what deflated:

> In the end, in her pasties and G-string, she appeared so young and virginal that I lost all excitement—and felt rather cheated. This was a girl I could go out for a coffee with, pretty enough—but no goddess at whose feet I could lay my budding

manhood. I needed an older woman, one who was practised and experienced and who could take my hand and lead me into the dark and dangerous labyrinth of sex.

When the featured attraction comes to the stage, her massive breasts as buoyant as zeppelins, the boys find their fevered expectations more than fulfilled, although one of them notices with a trickling sense of disquiet how cold and detached her gaze is:

> Look all you want, her face seemed to say, but you can never get inside. Wish and hope and drool, you cannibals, but you haven't got a chance. My door's closed.
>
> And toward the end of the performance I could clearly see that underneath her showmanship she was laughing at us. That the more she exposed her body, the more she hid herself behind her contempt. And when her abnormal breasts were fully exposed for a few seconds before the red velvet curtain closed at the end of the performance, dipping down to her navel like two huge udders, I caught the unmistakable sneer on her face.

The most shocking part of this revelation for the young man is that while he and his friend have devoured the act as if the performer was a piece of meat, she too has been thinking of them as something less than human.

Michael Holmes vividly illustrates the reason for this contempt in *Watermelon Row*, describing a lap dance in lurid, lascivious detail. A performer leads a drunk businessman to a booth in the back of "The Rail" on Yonge, where he collapses into a booth, practically gibbering with lust, and promptly vomits on her stiletto-clad foot. Still, believing himself potent and alert, he demands his dance. The stripper sets her price:

> "It's twenty, okay?"
>
> His tongue draws left to right over the edge of his teeth and just under his rubbery lip.
>
> "Okay?"
>
> He blinks the only choice he has left, pulls at his casual collar, loosens the knot of his pale tie.
>
> Jesus, he's so old.
>
> She smiles and growls and tilts his head back by chucking his stubbled-chin. He thinks of a million brilliant things to say, trolls his love-lines—they're all good. But he can't pull his eyes away from how pneumatic she is, can't stop thinking: Monsterbagos, huge fucking melons. So he says: "You're so fucking beautiful...." And then he adds: "I like this song." [...]
>
> One hundred dollars later and she's hovered over every inch of him. This

fallen angel's hands have spread out and pushed off his shoulders, the back of her wrist has caressed his cheeks, all of her lips have spilled intoxicating perfumes into his mouth, always stopping just before they kiss. Her naughty finger has grazed his lips before disappearing, deep, to the quick, between hers. Both of her thumbnails have raked up from his knees, up high on his inseam. They never got past the crease in his pants that folds over the place where his balls are cupped. Her head has dipped into his lap a half dozen times, long bleached locks have brushed the length of his cock.

He wants to explode.

He thinks he needs another drink.

He might explode.

He definitely needs another drink.

Convinced utterly that the woman's performance has been motivated by his singular charm, Holmes' drunk businessman staggers through the bar, simultaneously engorged and utterly spent. As she strides away, the stripper shudders and smirks, having succeeded in the illusion. As Holmes writes, "This is all her doing, of course. And she's good, very good, at what she does."

But in a crowded, sweaty bar filled with desperately lonely men and nervous strippers, maintaining that illusion can be a challenge. In his short story "Blazing Figures," Robert Markle describes what happens when the raunch goes off the rails:

Upstairs, second storey strip parlor built all wrong, the audience is in the dancer's lap. That close, the dancer becomes just another girl, a woman with no clothes, sweat and stretch-marks, tiny webs of veins, everyday life bruises. Perfect distance is needed to measure a vision. I hesitate to place beauty: its hopelessness is the only reality. She risked that distance, making male masturbation motions, huge hard pumping, hissing through a red slashed mouth. As the lights died and she stooped to pick up her things the man in the front row reached through the unfair distance, touched her ankle, and leapt back, stumbling, escaping. The man left, furious, humiliated, ice-cold in the finger-tips.

Having breached the invisible barrier between performer and audience, the man shatters the illusion. Beyond her failure to respond warmly to his touch, what bothers the man most is discovering that she is a real person, not the passive repository of his fantasy—whatever it might have been.

A similar humiliation unfolds in Rabindranath Maharaj's *Homer in Flight*, only in this case the aggressor is an overly enthusiastic performer fixating on a man visiting a strip club for the first time:

Some sort of Latin American music throbbed throughout the room and a woman vaulted onto the stage. The spotlight lingered on her breasts. The fresh, pliant model. She made a great fuss of caressing herself, spinning this way and that and teasingly fingering her skimpy panty. Then she took it off. Homer was disappointed. After all the provocation, the final act of undressing seemed awkwardly contrived. She offered a few tentative thrusts of her hips and left. Other women followed her on to the stage and each had her own routine. Homer's disappointment increased; after all they promised, they simply faded into women impatient to get off the stage.

Shortly thereafter, another stripper approaches Homer and sways seductively before him, inviting him to participate in a more intimate performance:

Before he knew what was happening, she was on his lap. His fingers sought the sides of the chair and gripped it. Her haunches digging into his groin felt like adamantine spikes. Something stirred; an entrapped pubic hair clung possessively, painfully. Oh god, Homer whispered silently. [...] He tried to think of the woman, his conqueror, as a nasty old pervert. He summoned a host of disgusting images. Missing teeth, blotchy skin, welts and lacerations which in the darkness he could not see. He thought of the half-price chicken leg quarters he had bought at Knob Hill Farm and the mucous membrane beneath the skin. He recalled the act of washing and cleaning the chicken legs. His erection refused to be quelled, the woman forced his hands downwards.

When the woman plunged his finger inside, he found a desperate strength, tossed her aside and ran out of the building. He ran madly, looking for a bus stop, not caring where he was carried. On the bus he held his violated finger away from his body. The finger felt hot, oily and infected.

Even in his terror, Homer knows his reaction is ridiculous. At the same time, he cannot reconcile the modest fantasies he projects upon idealized women with the aggressive, sweating, nearly naked woman who has thrown herself in his lap.

The problem, for many strip club customers, is that they do not always remember that for most performers stripping is simply a job, the act becoming rote, even mechanical. As Katherine Govier writes in *Going Through the Motions*,

Three songs. Ten minutes dancing, a slow strip-tease, for fifteen dollars. Do that four times a night for sixty dollars, and five days a week makes you three hundred. No deductions, no tax. Sounds good until you do it, until you have to face the faces out there. Lately she's been going into a cold trance while she danced, repeating to herself that it would only be ten minutes before she could skip out the door wearing next to nothing, dragging her marabou and bits of satin, leaving behind the leers, the smart-ass remarks, even the applause, with relief.

But as Govier's protagonist—nearing the end of her tether after ten years in the business—learns, sometimes it is not so easy to step away from her work. One night a disruptive drunk clambers onto the stage and grabs at her. She spins away, avoiding his outstretched arms until he suggests she come over and sit on his face. No longer willing to put up with the abuse, she wheels around and high-kicks him in the chin, shattering his jaw.

Critics—and some supporters—of sex workers suggest that women who work as strippers or prostitutes are either morally vacuous or have been pushed into the profession by poverty and an attraction to easy money. This, of course, could be said of any profession, perhaps particularly the practice of law. In *The Stroll*, Laird Stevens articulates some of the contradictions of what amounts to a seductress-victim narrative, writing,

> Society treats prostitution as a problem. [...] However, it expresses its concern about hookers in a confused and hypocritical way. First, it persecutes them: the government passes laws against soliciting and the police, for many of whom pros-titution is a victimless crime, are called upon to arrest hookers. Then, with an abrupt about-face, society feels sorry for them, denigrating them in the process: bleeding hearts within the government announce social programs to ameliorate the hookers' situation. But for society to take pity on the hookers, it must first identify them as victims, people not in charge of their own destinies. This attitude baffles and exasperates hookers, as well as wounding their pride.

In Hugh Garner's *Cabbagetown*, one of the protagonists, Myrla, becomes a prostitute in order to support herself in Depression-era Toronto. A former boyfriend, a young man she had grown up and gone to school with, counsels her to seek other employment, advice that makes her stiffen with annoyance:

> "You told me once that we all had to find our own solution, remember? I've found mine. Why should I find a job at a few bucks a week when I can make twice as much in an evening?
>
> He said angrily, "You owe it to your kid."
>
> "I owe it to my kid to make enough money to pay his board and buy him clothes, and later see that he gets a better break than you and I ever got."

For Myrla, as for many other women who become sex workers, the choice of profession is a pragmatic one in which morality—and desire—are less important than the pressing need simply to make a living in a city where too many women have little choice but to take menial jobs that keep them on their hands and knees—or on their backs.

DESIRE'S DARK SIDE

We cannot meaningfully discuss desire without acknowledging its dark side. For all the images it invokes of passionate embrace and voluptuous pleasure, desire is also about obsession, possession and violence. This is a point Dionne Brand makes powerfully in *What We All Long For* when, while gathering the city's longings for her lubaio, Brand's protagonist, an artist, realizes she cannot collect only the hopeful, happy ones. Noticing the hidden desires of abusers, murderers and rapists, Tuyen begins to expose a hidden side of the city, paying special attention to

> [t]he hideous ones. Those were the longings about bodies hurt or torn apart or bludgeoned. No one had actually confided details to Tuyen. She had intuited these, perceived them from a stride, a dangling broken bracelet—a rapist's treasure, each time he rubbed the jagged piece he remembered his ferocity [...] Some Tuyen got from newspaper articles—one about twin brothers dying at a karaoke bar: Phu Hoa Le and Lo Dai Le. The four men in bandanas came into the bar and started shooting. What were their longings—the ones dying and the ones shooting? Or, on the same page, the owners of a puppy farm with a hundred puppies mistreated in a filthy barn. Their longings would certainly surprise—she knew how people lived two lives, one most times the antithesis of the other.

But these desires are not only revelatory of the inner lives of particular individuals: they are a defining attribute of the city itself. This is not to say that cities are more likely than rural villages to harbour spectres in their shadows, but only in a city can anyone pass so close to monstrosity without necessarily knowing or recognizing it. This notion lies at the very heart of horror.

The reality that many Torontonians lead multiple lives, our outward propriety masking an internal darkness, is exemplified in Barbara Gowdy's novel *Helpless*, in which Ron, a small-appliance repairman whose public persona masks his pedophilia, abducts a nine-year-old Cabbagetown girl named Rachel and imprisons her in a basement room he has prepared to resemble a fantasy girl's bedroom, with pristine white walls, a lacy canopied bed—and bars on the window and a lock that opens only from the outside. Throughout the novel, Ron, whose tightly scripted routines enable him not only to maintain a facade of normalcy but to plot and execute Rachel's abduction, struggles with his desires, deluding himself and his seemingly addled accomplice Nancy with the fantasy that he is actually protecting Rachel from other men he describes as predators and upon whom he projects his own motives. In this way, Ron manages to rationalize a disturbing series of transgressive acts that begin with following Rachel home from school and lurking outside her home just off Parliament Street and progress inexorably toward her abduction, an event planned meticulously, even down to the duct tape he uses to bind her limbs and cover her mouth.

The bulk of Gowdy's novel is taken up with Ron's efforts to deal with Rachel's unbearable proximity. Gowdy describes Ron struggling to keep himself from opening the locked door behind which Rachel cowers and whimpers. She writes, "And yet even as he surrenders to the sensation of consciously abdicating responsibility he knows which side of him will prevail." Gowdy describes him, later, as walking "like an automaton, feeling the great resisting force of his body's machinery." As he moves closer to fulfilling the novel's great unspoken tension, Ron projects his desire upon Rachel, imagining her response to his hand on her knee, his mouth on hers. Deciding that Rachel cannot possibly be "innocent" despite being nine years old, he decides, self-righteously, that he will need to "do the resisting for both of them." Thus Ron rewrites his predation as protection, imagining that the tension emanates not from himself but from the little girl he desires.

Ron is not alone in projecting his own desires upon his helpless victim. One of the novel's other great unspoken tensions is the complicity of the media, the general public and perhaps even Gowdy's readers in Rachel's objectification and abduction. As Gowdy writes,

A child vanishing during a blackout would be a big story no matter what; make the child gorgeous, and it's huge. On Saturday the picture Mika took of her in her white-lace dress filled the front pages of all three daily papers, and yesterday the *Star* had an entire "Rachel" section. [...] Throughout these articles, Rachel's looks are underscored. "The Face of an Angel" was the *Sun*'s headline this morning, over another full-page photo. What do the editors mean to suggest? That the disappearance of a more normal-looking child would be less newsworthy or terrible? Maybe Mika is being too cynical. Rachel *does* have the face of an angel and, as he tells Celia, if ever there was a time when the media's fixation on beauty could prove useful, it's now. Let the media be enraptured is his primary feeling. Let them enrapture the public, let the public fall in love with Rachel, let the public become so personally invested in seeing her found safe that not even their own brothers and sons will be above suspicion.

Despite the constant presence of her picture, however, Rachel's own voice is disturbingly—and perhaps deliberately—nearly absent in *Helpless*. While readers are encouraged to understand and perhaps even empathize with Ron's desire, Rachel is reduced to an object, like the vintage vacuum cleaners Ron collects, preserves and admires in their restored condition. Inevitably, though, Ron cannot keep himself away from Rachel, just as he cannot keep from using one of his most precious vacuums even though he knows doing so will tarnish it and destroy much of its value in the eyes of future collectors. This tension is a clear metaphor for the behaviour of molesters who crave children for their purity and then respond with rage once they have destroyed it.

Gowdy's novel is unusual because it probes the predator's mind, but missing and murdered children figure prominently in the city's literature, just as they do in media reports, with an alarming and depressing regularity. The names of children who have been taken—among them Emanuel Jaques, Sharin' Morningstar Keenan, Nicole Morin, Alison Parrott, Andrea Atkinson, Kayla Klaudusz, Sharmini Anandavel, Cecilia Zhang, Holly Jones—are hauntingly memorable. When referenced in Toronto literature, even when some of the details are changed, they remain instantly recognizable.

In "Shoeshine Boy," one of the stories in *Barnacle Love*, Anthony De Sa describes the impact Emanuel Jaques' disappearance and murder has on the Portuguese families living in the Dundas West and Palmerston area in 1977. Jaques, a twelve-year-old who earned spending money shining shoes on Yonge Street, was abducted, raped and strangled by a group of men who were later convicted of the crime. De Sa's narrator, a young boy approximately Jaques' age, describes a neighbourhood where "every picket and dented door, the pitch of every mother's call when the streetlights came on" is familiar—until the summer of Jaques' murder. In the long days between his disappearance and the discovery of his body, rumours swirl through the community. Convalescing one afternoon on a couch in a corner of the kitchen, Antonio listens to the speculations of older family members:

> "It's been a few days now. Still not a word, not even close to finding him." I could hear my Aunt Louisa's frustration tugging at her voice.
>
> "They took his name away, you know. They gave him a new name—*Shoeshine Boy*," my Aunt Zelia replied. "This is not a Portuguese name."
>
> "What that poor boy's mother must be feeling. She must be crying like a *Magdalena*, cursing the day she came here." There was only a moment of silent contemplation. "She knows, she must know, a mother knows."
>
> "The news say he try saving money to buy a ticket for his mother, to go visit back home." Aunt Zelia added.

"I no hear that," Aunt Louisa interjected. "I hear other stories about that boy and what boys like him shining shoes do for extra money."

Later, going outside to play, Antonio learns the horrible outcome and realizes that the ground has shifted under the familiar streets he has grown up in. All at once it is as if none of the children are safe:

> I looked to Manny's veranda. All I could see was his curly black hair above the porch railing. He ran to meet me at the gate.
> "Let's go!" I said.
> "We can't."
> I saw his mother at the front door calling him inside. She sounded anxious and mad.
> "They found him on a rooftop...Yonge Street...a massage parlour...under some boards, drowned...like garbage." Manny punched the words into the still summer air. He shrugged his shoulders then, wide-eyed, whispered, "He's dead."
> I didn't need to ask *who* was dead.
> "Mannelinho!" his mother wailed.
> Manny jumped up all five steps of his porch and the screen door slammed behind him as he disappeared into the house.

Ignoring the proscription to stay inside, Antonio travels to Yonge Street on his bike, taking in the police tape and the crowd that has gathered near the crime scene, before turning around and biking home to a street that is strangely empty. Suddenly his mother materializes on the sidewalk and, tight-lipped, ushers him into the house:

> She drew her sweater tightly across her breasts, tucked her hands under her arm-pits and then shivered. It wasn't cold. Once inside I turned to see her look through the screen door before sliding the handle to LOCK. Then she closed the front door and did the same. It was the first time I heard the click of the deadbolt.

More than the television reports, more even than the police tape wrapped around the crime scene, it is this gesture that drives home to Antonio the awareness that he is "alone in a big city I didn't recognize underneath a blood-orange sun."

A similar revelation jars the protagonists of Linwood Barclay's novel *Bad Move*. Alarmed at the increasing evidence of petty crime in their established neighbourhood—syringes showing up in the alleyways, break-and-enters, a john getting a blow job in the back of a Jetta—a family finds its idle conversations about moving out of the city crystallized by one final, shocking incident. A neighbourhood girl, clearly modelled on Sharin' Morningstar Keenan, abducted and murdered steps away from her Annex-area home in 1983, disappears and is found dead:

> Four days later they found her body in a refrigerator in a second-floor apartment rented by a man, supposedly from out west, who had been going by the name Devlin Smythe. [...] His landlady called the police to say she hadn't seen him, not since that little girl disappeared, and that he was overdue with the rent. A string of minor break-ins in the neighbourhood came to an end about the same time. The police figured she hadn't lived much more than an hour after her disappearance from the playground. She'd been suffocated.

Barclay is not the only writer to invoke Sharin' Morningstar Keenan in his work. Carolyn Smart's poem "Stoning the Moon" describes the impact of the girl's murder on a woman living nearby, who hears the police loudspeakers announcing the girl's disappearance to the neighbourhood and, nine days later, learns her body has been found in the freezer of a suddenly vacated apartment on Brunswick Avenue:

> The skin of a cheek
> presses against silence
> membrane of inner ear
> knows violence
> and somewhere says *no*
> because a neighbour is afraid
> in a room downstairs
> wood and wall dividing him
> from a small girl's death
> knowing this listening and listening
> afraid

What strikes Smart's narrator is the futility of gesture in the face of such horror, the passivity of waiting, the hollowness of prayer:

> I waited for news of your death
> thinking *let it be easy*
> yet knowing he could do anything to you
> he could do it again and again
> [...]

If I believed in prayer
I would have filled a Sunday
like every other day
seeing it happen over and over
to your small self without fear
or thought for any of this
what good now to say it
but I prayed it was fast

Toronto literature is rife with accounts of other disappearances, some patterned on actual events, others presumably the product of rich and terrifying imaginations: Phyllis Brett Young's novel *Psyche*, in which a two-year-old girl is kidnapped for ransom from her wealthy parents' Toronto home and not restored to them; Richard Wright's *Final Things*, in which a grieving father seeks violent revenge on the men who have stolen his son; a generation later Andrew Pyper's *The Killing Circle* ends nearly the same way; David Gilmour's novel, *A Perfect Night to Go to China*, in which a man's young son vanishes, seemingly without a trace, leaving a father desperate to retrace his final steps while the rest of his life dissolves around him.

Like literary exorcisms, these stories recur in the city's literature, almost as if writing them is a kind of collective therapy, a warding-off, an effort to expunge all this pain from the city's psyche. In some works, as in Anthony De Sa's "Shoeshine Boy," the intent is memorial. In others, such as in Carolyn Smart's "Stoning the Moon," it is clearly a call to action. Underlying all these narratives of murdered and missing children, however, is the impossible burden borne by every sentient person in Toronto: to protect the city's innocent progeny, the most precious part of ourselves.

THE WORD MADE FLESH

In *The Poetics of Space*, French philosopher Gaston Bachelard wrote famously of the newborn child that "[b]efore he is 'cast out into the world' [...] man is laid in the cradle of the house. [...] Life begins well, it begins enclosed, protected, all warm in the bosom of the house." But long before an infant reaches the safe confines of the cradle, it makes a long and perilous journey that brings it from the farthest reaches of the cosmos: life begins like a supernova, in a burst of matter and energy transformed into pure light. A zygote flashes across the galaxy and crash-lands on the surface of the womb, where it digs itself in and transforms everything around it. Only a Darwinian can love an embryo as it is, monstrous for long weeks until it begins to assume its familiar fetal shape.

And anyone who loves a newborn baby for its soft contours and benevolent disposition would do well to remember this: that long before an infant reaches the warm confines of the cradle, life begins at the raw edge of the expanding cosmos.

As the fetus develops, it gradually takes on a mammalian form, growing hands and feet and finally a recognizable face. At some point, having been the object of one-sided conversations about its probable sex, its likely resemblance to relatives living or dead, its well-being or perhaps whether it should be brought into the world, it begins to speak back. In Timothy Findley's *Headhunter*, a woman who finds herself unexpectedly three months' pregnant and having delayed doing anything about it, wonders whether she can bear to tell her husband or her mother. Uncertain whether to have an abortion or carry through with the pregnancy, Olivia engages in silent dialogues with the fetus, who tells her things like, "*Every time you smoke one of those, you're killing me, you know,*" and, later, having heard about her mother's stillborn child, donated to the medical school and preserved in formaldehyde, asks, "*Are you going to buy me a jar, Olivia?*" Despite these dialogues, Olivia remains unsure about what to do until the afternoon she feels the symptoms of an impending miscarriage:

Something was definitely wrong. A cramp began to grow inside her. Its shape was the shape of a sling. Something wet began to flow down her inner thigh on the left side.

No. Don't.

She stepped forward. The wetness spread.

She looked at the bricks below her.

Walk.

She made her way to the edge of the street—paused and crossed over—leaned on the car and fumbled the keys. She opened the door and slid inside. [...]

She looked down.

Nothing. Still, she had to be sure. Rising slightly, she lifted her skirts until her hips were free of them. Her pantyhose were wet to just above the knee.

Not blood.

Not blood. [...]

You, she said. Are you still there?

Yes.

Olivia smiled.

Are you? said the voice.

Olivia laughed out loud. "Damn right I am!" she said.

A similar ambivalence manifests itself in Katrina Onstad's Toronto novel, *How Happy to Be*. When a thirty-something journalist, accidentally pregnant, is asked by her doctor if she has thought about what she will do if the test is positive, she responds, "I don't think there's a woman alive who hasn't run through every single what-if scenario, moved the pieces around and back again a hundred times, playing mommy like you did as a kid." But there is a huge difference between Maxime's childhood fantasies and the adult reality of her singlehood, her uneven career trajectory and the difficulty of not being entirely certain who the father is. Enumerating the complication of contemporary pregnancy, Maxime muses,

> I've thought of a Downsy baby born somewhere in my forties, when I'm alone and unemployed, and how the two of us will move into a shelter and I will carry our belongings in a plastic shopping bag down to the food bank for white bread and Kraft peanut butter handouts. I've thought about abortion, fetal sacks sucked out of my stomach with bicycle pumps. I've thought about adoption and whether I'd hire a detective to find a baby I might have handed over years ago, a wrapped package in pink that grew human limbs like mine. I've thought about it, flipping through pregnancy books for no reason, thought about how I wouldn't know how to change diapers, or what to do with the unceasing cry, and who I would ask about this stuff when it's just me and my turkey-baster baby living in the same apartment I'm in now, Marvin the donor dropping by every other Sunday, stale with last night's club sweat.

This unexpected pregnancy jars Maxime out of place, leading her to observe that "when I try, here in the doctor's office, to conjure up an image of myself with a child, my own arms holding my own child in my own apartment in my own city, I come up with white space and static." She soon flees Toronto and returns to the West Coast island of her childhood, seeking familiarity and a sense of home. There she finds her dreams shifting: "I'm dreaming of places I'm already in. I'm dreaming of the roar of the ocean." She realizes that the ocean she dreams of, however, is not the Pacific Ocean but rather an internal sea, the one in which floats her unborn child.

In *Playing House*, Patricia Pearson's unexpectedly pregnant protagonist flees in the opposite direction, catching a quick flight home to Toronto and finding herself confined in Canada by obscure immigration rules preventing her return to New York. Feeling simultaneously displaced and trapped, Freddie tries to create a nest for her unborn child in a borrowed house while whispering to herself, "I just didn't know for certain where home was." Her ambivalent partner finds the shifting landscape of pregnancy equally unrecognizable: gazing upon fetal anatomy exposed via ultrasound, he compares it to a map of Bosnia, a place neither has ever been and both can hardly imagine.

After giving birth, Freddie emerges for air in the bleary winter light and finds the city's landscape changed utterly as space, time and the narrative of her own life have all been ruptured and must now be rewritten: "We come to see that life divides at this threshold, that when we walk along the beach ever after, where the waves sprawl upward in spidery undulations to wash the shore, we will reach down with the driftwood we've idly gathered and write, not our own name, but our child's."

Margaret Atwood engages vividly with the effects of pregnancy on place in her story "Giving Birth." Exhausted but preternaturally alert after long hours of labour that have turned her body translucent and glassine, Atwood's protagonist gazes out over the city through her hospital window and notices for the first time how vulnerable Toronto's architecture seems, so much like her own body:

> the building is so thin, so fragile, that it quivers in the slight dawn wind. Jeannie sees that if the building is this way (a touch could destroy it, a ripple of the earth, why has no one noticed, guarded it against accident?) then the rest of the world must be like this too, the entire earth, the rocks, people, trees, everything needs to be protected, cared for, tended.

As these narratives suggest, few things are more powerful—or vulnerable—than the pregnant body and the life it carries, except perhaps a city in the throes of its own creation. Like a city, the pregnant body is an affront to autonomy and selfhood and a challenge to mortality. Both rend the landscape and leave it almost unrecognizable: buildings heave themselves out of the soil as dishevelled and loud as newborns. As Gwendolyn MacEwen suggests in "The Garden of Square Roots," pregnancy simultaneously accelerates and inverts the order of creation we are familiar with, reminding us that the city we live in is a corporeal place, inhabited by bodies, its structures stand-ins for gristle and sinew:

> this city I live in I built with bones
> and mortared with marrow;
> I planned it in my spare time
> and its hydro is charged from a blood niagara
> and I built this city backwards and
> the people evolved out of the buildings
> and the subway uterus ejected them —
>
> for i was the I interior

the thing with a gold belt and delicate ears
with no knees or elbows
was working from the inside out.

Like the act of city-building, the process of birth has become increasingly
mechanized, clinking with steel instruments and pulsing with electronic devices. Both, however, have their roots in the soil: silicon fused into glass in
the same way that carbon presses itself into the diamond of an eye; red clay
moulded into brick like the firm flesh of the newborn.

In many traditional cultures the placenta—a transient organ, created in
the space between mother and child, that nurtures the unborn fetus until being expelled shortly after birth—is saved and preserved until it can be buried
in the ground. This is believed variously to nurture the newborn child, predict
future fertility and protect against evil. Burying the placenta in the soil also
reminds us of the organic source of fecundity, the proximity of life and death,
and, perhaps above all, the forces that bind us to place. In Toronto midwives
routinely return placentas to women who have just given birth. Often they remain in freezers, occupying an ambivalent status between meat and medical
waste, until a place is secured to bury them, sometimes beneath a rose bush or
a newly planted tree. Still others wait for a plane ticket to a distant homeland,
where the placenta might be buried as an act of return, the diaspora brought
full circle.

Why does this need persist? Because even now, even in the age of mechanical reproduction, we require rituals to remind us that the body is genera-
tive as well as destructive and that even our largest cities rise from the soil of
the land and must eventually return to it. The placenta reminds us that pregnancy and birth are not only bodily but also intensely spatial experiences. The
terrain of fine striations across the expanding belly is a bodily cartography, a
permanent map of the progress of pregnancy. Beyond the body, however, birth
pushes us into unfamiliar territory, a displacement perhaps most acute in this
city where more people arrive than are born here. Our transience grows painful; the flesh aches for familiar soil. The trick is to remember these organic
origins and to find our way back to them. We still need stories of origin, of
ancestry, of home, and of a time when the word was made flesh and began to
dwell among us.

– 6 –

CLASS FICTIONS

THIS AIN'T NO HEALING TOWN

In *The Underside of Toronto*, a groundbreaking work of urban analysis published in 1970, sociologist John Seeley[152] challenges characterizations of the city as "Toronto the Good," adding that "[e]very city has a self-image, and every city's self-image is almost precisely a representation of what it is *not*, what it is *least*." "Toronto the Good," an expression widely used to connote propriety and civility in both Victorian and contemporary Toronto,[153] has for most of its history also been invoked ironically to refer to the city's dark side. *Of Toronto the Good*, for example, a "social study" of the city published by prohibitionist C.S. Clark in 1898, examined gambling houses, pawnbrokers, pickpockets and streetwalkers alongside the city's clergy, city government, police service and the press, deliberately interleaving virtue and vice as if one depended upon the other for sustenance. In her Depression-era poem "Queen City," Dorothy Livesay attacks Toronto the Good with savage irony:

> Take off the lid, scatter the refuse far,
> Tear down the "WELCOME" from the city-hall.
> For you're not welcome, vagabond, nor you
> Old man, nor you, farmlabourer, with sun
> Still burning in your face. Burn now with shame
> Take to yourself the bread ticket, the bed
> On John Street—fifteen cents, GOOD CLEAN
> And pluck out all the hunger from your brain.

A 1960s-era song by comedy-folk act the Brothers-in-Law called "Toronto the Good" satirized the city's image as a place of peace and order, suggesting that the repressive presence of the police was required to keep it that way. More recently, Andrew Moodie's Dora Award nominated play, *Toronto the Good*, has challenged the city's smug self-image by interrogating social inequality and the racialization of crime in Toronto's court system.

Toronto's real underside, however, is not found in bathhouses, brothels or strip clubs, in crack houses or unlicensed after hours clubs, nor even among

---

152 Sociologist John Seeley is perhaps best known for his analysis of Toronto's Forest Hill neighbourhood, thinly disguised in *Crestwood Heights: A Study of the Culture of Suburban Life* (1956).

153 The origin of "Toronto the Good" is unknown, but clearly dates to the Victorian era. In *The Heiress and the Establishment*, legal historians Constance and Nancy Backhouse report that the expression, "Toronto the Good" emerged in the 1880s and was "first coined in tribute to the moral purity campaign waged by Sir William Howland's son during the latter's term as Toronto's mayor." (2005). The phrase appears in *Debates of the Senate of the Dominion of Canada* as early as 1888 and was in wide use before the turn of the century.

inside traders, criminal fraternities or car theft rings. It exists, instead, among the city's sizable population of the poor and dispossessed, an urban under-class of people who live and work at the margins of Toronto the Good. Largely ignored by the popular media, except when they are the perpetuators (or, as is far more likely, the victims) of crime,[154] the periodic subject of research stud-ies reducing their lives to grim statistics,[155] Torontonians who live beneath the poverty line comprise a population whose experiences are neither well docu-mented nor widely understood.

In the introduction to *This Ain't No Healing Town*, an anthology of Toron-to stories whose mostly marginalized protagonists include shopkeepers, sex workers, a hangman and a homeless couple, editor Barry Callaghan observes that it is the role of the writer to deal with "what goes on in the shadows." By examining what goes on in the shadows of Toronto the Good, the city's writers humanize statistical measures of poverty and bear witness to the causes and consequences of social and economic disparity. In doing so, they reveal stories that are not part of Toronto's official narrative but that are as much a part of the city as feral cats and cracked concrete.

POSSIBILITIES OF DWELLING

In Richard Scrimger's novel *Crosstown*, a homeless drunk drifts from one end of Toronto to the other, trying to find a shelter that has been relocated, coinci-dentally, to the very west end residential street where he once owned a home. After being evicted at gunpoint from a warehouse where he has spent the night, he encounters a woman lying slack-jawed and open-eyed in an unfamil-iar doorway and decides to ask her for directions and maybe a drink. Perplexed by her silence, he does not realize the woman is dead until her corpse topples over, spilled possessions suddenly available for the taking:

> People are walking past the doorway, not looking, full of breakfast and their own troubles. I step towards the body, take the bag easily. Rigor has passed, she must be a day gone at least, I think. Three, four doorways down I see a pair of shoes sticking out. I think about stopping. He's asleep and they're better shoes than mine. But I'm more interested in what's in the bag.

154 See Rosalee Clawson and Rakuya Trice, 2000. "Poverty as We Know It: Media Portrayals of the Poor." *Public Opinion Quarterly*, vol. 64.
155 See, for example, the detailed but startlingly impersonal study, *Poverty by Postal Code: The Geog-raphy of Neighbourhood Poverty, 1981-2001*, produced in 2004 by the United Way of Greater Toronto and the Canadian Council on Social Development. Personal narratives of the subject populations are all but absent from the report's text.

Carrying off a bottle of Courage and a half-dead kitten dug out of the dead woman's bag, he sets off on a journey across town during which he is beaten by thugs, tricked into taking experimental drugs in exchange for food and cough syrup, taken in by a predator who sexually assaults him and, while trying to rescue an animated doll he mistakes for a crying baby, thrown over a bridge into the Humber River. His story proceeds with depressing inevitability—until Scrimger reveals that his protagonist was once a prominent surgeon who ended up on the streets after a deadly house fire and allegations of malpractice ended his career.

Scrimger's derelict ex-doctor has a fictional counterpart in Rosemary Aubert's novel, *Free Reign*, in which a disgraced former judge retreats to a remote tributary of the Don Valley, where he builds a hut and lives in the wilderness like a latter-day Thoreau. "I am a vagrant," he asserts, "a voyager, a wanderer, a citizen of the kingdom of free reign." The ravine offers shelter, sustenance and, equally importantly, seclusion from the family members, social workers and former law society colleagues who would like to call him to account. Despite the hardships of life in the ravine he revels in his liberty, until returning home one evening he finds his dwelling torn apart, its pieces scattered amid the underbrush:

> As I approached the hidden path, I began to feel a sense of foreboding. Maybe there's a scent left when someone trespasses. Maybe the whole forest knows when part of it is violated because of air currents or a change in light—who knows? All I know is that evening, I felt more afraid the closer I got to home.
>
> As I rounded the last bend in the path, I saw that my compound was in a shambles.
>
> Of course, I noticed the garden first.
>
> It was completely torn apart. Every plant had been pulled from its place, and the tender leaves ripped from their slender stalks. Whole rows had been scraped away, and even in the now-failing light, I could see that the seeds I'd planted had begun to sprout, small white tendrils reaching out of their casings.
>
> My hut was smashed—just a few planks propped against a tree remained—and my belongings were scattered in front of it, my blankets resting in the dust.
>
> They had even found my books, which were lying on the ground, the soft rising breeze of coming night riffling their pages.

Assessing the deliberate, methodical progress of the destruction, Aubert's judge resolves simultaneously to rebuild his shelter in a more secure location and investigate why he has been targeted, his quarters ransacked and his effects searched. It turns out not to be so easy—perhaps especially for a former judge—to leave his sheltered, domestic life behind.

Aubert's disgraced former judge is joined in the ravine, figuratively, by Derek, one of the protagonists in Maggie Helwig's novel, *Girls Fall Down*. Derek is a brilliant, schizophrenic former chemistry student who lives in a tent under a railway bridge near the Bayview extension. Like Judge Portal, Derek has retreated to the ravine for seclusion, but unlike Aubert's protagonist he does not find peace or stillness there. Helwig writes,

> Derek Rae's life in the ravine is, after its manner, a life well organized. His time is measured by the regular catastrophe of the trains passing over his head, thunderous and dirty, an assault of noise. The days and weeks are shaped by weather, the poison sun and debilitating humidity of late summer shading slowly into the long cold nights and the sheltering snow. [...] Though Derek is radically isolated, he is not in fact quite without human contact. He is known to the street nurses, for instance, who bring him the bottles of water and tins of Ensure that now constitute his entire diet.

With a mind nearly as impenetrable as the swales and thickets visitors must traverse to reach him, Derek is accessible, even in text, only in the third person.

In his impenetrability Helwig's brilliant schizophrenic has something in common with Nora, the much loved daughter of middle class parents who, in Carol Shields' novel, *Unless*, has abandoned her university studies to sit in silent vigil at the corner of Bathurst and Bloor holding a cardboard sign reading "GOODNESS." Only a few blocks away is an apparently homeless musician Dionne Brand introduces in *What We All Long For*, a classically trained pianist who composes and performs silent symphonies for an unhearing city:

> Some afternoons the musician sat in the coffee shop muttering, a short pencil in hand, scribbling musical notes onto a tattered fragment of a brown paper bag. He kept a worn leather folder of music under one arm, sometimes shifting it to the inside of his grungy coat, sometimes to the table, then back to his armpit. .[...] Oku came out of the St. George subway one day, and as he walked toward the university, he saw the musician sitting on a concrete embankment, his leather folder in his lap, his large hands making a gesture of piano playing. Oku slowed his pace, trying to avoid another unpleasant encounter. But he saw that the musician was heedlessly playing his symphony. His face was a beautiful mask of pleasure, his long fingers lustful on some arpeggio.

Having poured "all the sanity he ever had" into the silent symphony he performs before uncomfortable urban audiences, Brand's musician personifies the city's perception of those it has pushed to the margins: morally challenging, disturbingly close, but ultimately unreachable.

Despite their different experiences of homelessness, Scrimger's derelict ex-doctor, Aubert's disgraced former judge, Helwig's brilliant schizophrenic, Shields' beloved daughter and Brand's talented pianist have one remarkable thing in common: all of them are represented as gifted, if troubled, individuals whose moral qualities seem sharpened rather than dulled by the time each has spent on the streets. If they could be read as a representative sample, it would be tempting to conclude that Toronto's homeless population is comprised primarily of wayward professionals reduced to homelessness by some tragic flaw, empaths propelled by sorrow, or talented intellects driven onto the streets by an excess of creative genius. This curious narrative—a striking departure from the socio-economic reality of life on the street[156]—bears examination.

In *How the Other Half Lives: Representations of Homelessness in American Literature*, literary scholar John Allen identifies a deeply rooted dualism present in depictions of homelessness, in which narratives of homelessness are divided between romantic representations of liberty and rebellion and paternalistic portrayals of the homeless as degraded victims. In *Down to This*, a memoir of Toronto's Tent City,[157] Shaughnessy Bishop-Stall exemplifies the former image. Describing his fellow Tent City residents as "vagrant celebrities, the nobility of the bums," he adds,

> While others slip into the shelters, we're building our own houses with our hands. While they crowd around the TV in a community centre, we're stoking the fire barrel, watching sparks rise like new stars in the cold night. They're under a blanket of rules, and we're making up our own then tossing them off with a laugh. Some of them keep it tough—they live alone beneath viaducts and bridges. But we live together on the banks of the river and the lake. We've fought each other, and we'll fight each other again. But not just now.

Despite Bishop-Stall's representation of his experience, in a city like Toronto where homelessness is more likely to reflect social marginalization and economic abjection than the supposedly libertine existence of the wandering

---

156 Although some homeless individuals have fallen upon difficult times despite having had successful careers and supportive families, people who live on the streets in Toronto are disproportionately likely to have grown up in poverty, experienced domestic violence, self-identify as Aboriginal, suffer poor and deteriorating physical and mental health, battle addiction, and have spent time in prison. Moreover, while in Toronto most homeless people are assumed to be white or Aboriginal men, increasing numbers of women, children and racialized Torontonians also number among the city's homeless population. See Daly (1996), Capponi (1997, 1999), Layton (2000), the City of Toronto's *Street Needs Assessment* (2006) and Crowe (2007).

157 Tent City, located near Toronto's downtown waterfront, was a self-governing informal community of several dozen homeless who built shelters and shanties out of scavenged materials. Tent City was bulldozed in September 2002.

vagabond, the image of the degraded victim has come to dominate the imagination, alongside a closely parallel narrative in which social welfare programs
are justified only insofar as their efforts are targeted toward the "deserving
poor."[158] The "undeserving poor"—long-term alcoholics, ex-cons, hustlers,
shills and con-artists—are, except where they appear in novels like Scrimger's
Crosstown or in counter-cultural poetry such as Ted Plantos' *The Universe Ends
at Sherbourne & Queen*, simply written out of the narrative.

In research evaluating the procedures used by social agencies serving
street people, sociologist Amir Marvasti has argued that contemporary narratives of homelessness are "scripted" in order to maximize what he calls "service
worthiness." Couched in the language of efficient delivery of services such as
shelter and access to food, these narratives are nonetheless informed by what
Marvasti calls a "discourse of morality," suggesting that the narrative of the "deserving poor" has surprising persistence even among social justice advocates.
Marvasti suggests that homeless people participate actively in this process of
narrative construction, although in practice their own stories seem only rarely
to become part of the written record.[159]

Given these closely intersecting narratives, it is hardly surprising that literary representations of homelessness in Toronto reflect what appears to be a
subliminal desire to rehabilitate their homeless protagonists by writing their
lives in ways that make them sympathetic, even heroic figures deserving of ad-
vocacy and assistance. In this context, Scrimger's derelict ex-doctor, Helwig's
brilliant schizophrenic, Shields' beloved daughter and Brand's talented pianist
may be seen as vivid representations of degraded victims, laid low by circumstances (addiction, sorrow, mental illness, racism) ultimately out of their control. Even Aubert's disgraced former judge, while on the surface seemingly an
exemplar of the freethinking vagabond, is recast ultimately as a casualty requiring rescue from his homeless condition, after his hut is vandalized and he
subsequently becomes ill from something he has encountered in the ravine.

As for their heroism—a rehabilitative strategy that seems chosen to reinforce what Marvasti might call their "service worthiness"—Scrimger's protagonist rescues both a kitten and what he believes is a real baby, and Aubert's

---

158 In "The City of Dreadful Night" (*Cities of Tomorrow*, 1990) noted urban scholar Peter Hall connects the rise of social welfare programs and the development of public housing infrastructure to
a moral aversion to the squalid conditions in the slums of Victorian-era cities in Europe and North
America.

159 See Marvasti's article, "Constructing the Service-Worthy Homeless Through Narrative Editing"
(2001). Similarly, reports on homelessness in Toronto rarely incorporate more than token commen-
taries contributed by homeless people themselves. Two exceptions are Ruth Morris and Colleen
Heffren's *Street People Speak* (1988) and Cathy Crowe's *Dying for a Home: Homeless Activists Speak
Out* (2007).

judge helps save dozens of people from the Don Valley Parkway during a sudden flood. Shield's protagonist suffers serious burns while attempting to rescue a woman who has set herself on fire. Brand's homeless musician is perhaps not conventionally heroic, but his performances are a kind of benediction bestowed upon the city that has cost him his sanity. As for Derek Rae, the schizophrenic chemist living below the Bayview extension, Helwig finds valour in his willingness simply to persist in the face of mental illness, social misunderstanding and exposure to the elements:

> None of this represents the truth of Derek's existence, his passions and his miseries, the battles he wages all alone against pains and fears and the forces of universal gravitation. The raw courage that is required of him every day. His hard-won choice to continue living, when so many possibilities to stop are offered at every hand, the cars on the highway, the trains on the tracks, an end to the daily loss. None of this represents Derek's soul, scraped bloody, howling, fighting always to hang on, a solitary superhuman ordeal, unacknowledged by the world, unrewarded.

By describing Derek's heroism as a direct function of his courage simply to continue living, Helwig makes explicit something to which Scrimger, Aubert, Shields and Brand only allude. While all five novels humanize their homeless protagonists, in part by focusing on daily routines and motivations readers might reasonably relate to their own lives, Helwig goes a step further, suggesting that there is something noble, perhaps even saintly, about Derek: as if by presiding, trembling and shouting, in a tent high above the ravine floor he has come to possess some garbled but vital truth about suffering and redemption.

The suggestion that the city's most marginalized citizens—the homeless, the insane—have access to special knowledge is an idea that resonates throughout Helwig's novel. This view is borne out further by one of Helwig's minor characters, a panhandler who believes he is being held hostage by terrorists and who appears throughout the novel like an oracle, offering prescient commentary about the city and its troubles to those who are prepared to listen and read between the lines. Indeed, an encounter with this street sage makes Helwig's protagonist speculate that "maybe people died on the street not from cold or heat or hunger but only because no one got enough attention," and to wonder to himself, "How much of this [...] can a street contain? How much, before it all breaks down?"

Evidence of things breaking down is found most visibly in the intricate relationship between homelessness and mental illness. Although popular portrayals of homelessness exaggerate the extent of mental disturbance among street people, about one third of the city's homeless population is estimated to be in need of psychiatric help.[160] At the same time, the causal connection between mental illness and homelessness is difficult to establish given that extreme poverty, social isolation, continuous hunger and prolonged exposure to the elements—typical conditions of life on the streets—can themselves contribute to both addiction and poor mental health. An additional complicating factor is that the practice of deinstitutionalizing psychiatric patients without providing adequate community support has significantly increased the ranks of the visibly mentally ill homeless in cities like Toronto.[161] Indeed, the narrator of Pat Capponi's novel, *Last Stop Sunnyside,* describes her Parkdale neighbourhood—best known, perhaps, for its proximity to the Queen Street Mental Health Centre[162]—as "a dumping ground for alcoholics, drug addicts, ex-cons and de-institutionalized mental patients." Even so, another of Capponi's protagonists, an elderly woman renting a bed in a run-down King Street rooming house, challenges the caricature of the incoherent street person, telling a neighbour, "I'm not crazy, you know. I spent a few years on the streets, and maybe I was yelling, but I was never crazy. I was just confused, wondering where everyone had gone, my family, my friends." With this explanation in mind, anyone prepared to pay attention to stories told about life on the street may learn something important, not only about what it is like to be homeless, but also about the duty of care we owe to one another in this city and, perhaps ultimately, about the significance of home and what it means to dwell.

In "Discrete Environments: Those Which Do Not Dwell," an essay examining homelessness as a philosophical problem, phenomenologist Raymond Koukal borrows the concept of dwelling introduced by influential German philosopher Martin Heidegger[163] to examine the nature of our collective responsibility toward the homeless. Defining "dwelling" not only in terms of the necessity of being housed, but also as requiring concern, or care, for the dwelling of others, Koukal describes what it is like to move through the urban environment, encountering others whose dwelling we recognize because it is similar to our own. At the same time, the city is filled with those who exist in space but are not able to dwell in it:

---

160 See Gerry Daly's book *Homeless: Policies, Strategies, and Lives on the Street* (1996). Daly points out, however, that it is difficult to gauge the extent of mental illness among the homeless and adds that even well-meaning researchers and activists bring considerable political and moral baggage to the task.

161 See Capponi, 1992 and 2003; Daly, 1996; Crowe, 2007.

162 In the century-and-a-half since it was first built, the Queen Street Mental Health Centre has operated under a variety of official and unofficial names, including the Provincial Lunatic Asylum and 999 Queen Street West. Currently it is a residential site of the Centre for Addition and Mental Health (CAMH).

163 In "Building Dwelling Thinking," (*Basic Writings*, trans. David Farrell Krell, 1997; 1993), Heidegger writes that to dwell is to build, as well as "to cherish and protect, to preserve and care for."

Within this closeness that is dwelling in the *polis* I encounter, more and more frequently, those which do not dwell. I find that the homeless "jut" into my environment, without belonging to it. [...] On the same pavement where I walk they scuttle out of where they do not belong to another location where they do not belong, and every gesture of their mortal bodies reveals their resignation to not belonging.

Pat Capponi makes a similar observation in *The Corpse Will Keep*, writing that "[l]ike some lost infantry battalion on a long, endless march, the homeless have to keep moving; their legs must carry them from agency to agency, from street corner to temporary shelter."

But is it not only the homeless whose dwelling has been ruptured. As Koukal adds,

Those of us which dwell swirl in eddies about the homeless, not indifferent, not concerned, not solicitous, but disturbed. We respond either with something like negation or something like charity, but in either case these confrontations disrupt our environment because we have encountered something out of place, something-we-do-not-know-what-to-do-with.

Again, Koukal's analysis seems echoed in Pat Capponi's writing. Capponi's narrator, herself a psychiatric survivor struggling to find her feet in a Parkdale rooming house, describes the difficulty of encountering the city's truly homeless:

I learned not to stare at the haunted men and women who would rummage through public garbage receptacles that had already been picked through half a dozen times before, in search of food or some discarded treasure. And I wouldn't stand open-mouthed, staring at those who, like pigeons swooping down on crumbs of bread, grabbed up cigarette butts from gutters and sidewalks, straightening up long ones and immediately lighting them, the shorter ones going into torn pockets for later.

Distressed by these encounters, unable to reconcile her own precarious dwelling with their absolute homelessness, Capponi's narrator acknowledges, "There were days when I simply went back to my room and cried, overwhelmed by the misery I had witnessed. [...] I would hide out for a day or two, shaken and miserable, determined never to venture out of these walls again."

Ultimately, Koukal argues, the presence of the homeless in the *polis* corrodes any possibility of our own dwelling, rooted as it is in our collective failure to cultivate the dwelling of others. This is an urgent matter for all of us, because in a city like Toronto there are so many ways to be homeless. The City of Toronto, for example, defines homelessness as "a condition of people who live outside, stay in emergency shelters, spend most of their income on rent, or live in overcrowded, substandard conditions and are therefore at serious risk of becoming homeless."[164] By the City's own reckoning, over half a million people—one quarter of the City's population—live in poverty and are therefore considered precariously housed. In 2002 over thirty thousand different individuals stayed in shelters, including nearly five thousand children. A 2006 homeless "census" conducted by the City counted over 800 people living directly on the streets, a number it admits does not begin to measure the number of "hidden homeless" staying out of sight in ravines or alleyways or "couch surfing" in efforts to stay off the streets.[165]

In the story "1001 Names and Their Meanings," Andrew Pyper describes Toronto as "a long street with doorways that cost too much to enter." Given what Heidegger calls "the state of dwelling in our precarious age," it is no wonder that Koukal concludes, "[i]t remains to be seen whether or not the discrete dissonance of the homeless among us will bring us to an authentically poetic reckoning, or to a time so destitute that even the efforts of the poets will be rendered futile."

CLASS FICTIONS

Toronto is a city wrapped in the rhythms of work. All night vehicle surge and recede along the urban expressways, as fluid as arteries, their lights pulsating as if propelled by the city's beating heart. At dawn packed buses flounder in the curb lane, wallowing like migrating manatees. An hour later the subway is stuffed with commuters who sway in silent communion as the train scythes around a curve in the tunnel, while above them, at kitchen counters and crowded street corners, coffee cups are raised and lowered and raised again in sleepy salute to the day.

In this precise, punctual, tightly scripted city—"New York run by the Swiss," as playwright Peter Ustinov is claimed to have once remarked—we rely on these rhythms. Torontonians shove past sidewalk laggards and chafe at waiting in line. We view the weather report—snow squalls in Barrie, flurries along the 401, light rain near the lakeshore—less as a meteorological phenomenon than as a kind of calculus for plotting our commute into work. In this city, where time is indistinguishable from money, we shout into cell phones whenever there is a lane closure, a lag on the subway line or a stalled streetcar

164 City of Toronto, 2003. *Report Card on Housing and Homelessness.*
165 City of Toronto, 2006. *Street Needs Assessment: results and Key Findings.*

in our path. We are always in a hurry to get to work, as if failing to do so on time would jeopardize not only our gainful employment but the very essence of our being.

In *The Work and the Gift*, literary scholar Scott Cutler Shershow describes the "double necessity of work" as a paradox that arises from the imperative to perform the obligatory labour that sustains our material existence despite deriving the bulk of our identity from the parallel impulse to build, craft or otherwise create works with intrinsic value, such as a hand-knit scarf, a literary masterpiece or a well laid wall. This tension, arguably inherent in human endeavour, turns destructive whenever works are subsumed beneath the demands of work. In distinguishing works from work, Shershow belongs to an intellectual tradition stretching from Hegel, who emphasized the transcendent qualities of work performed in the creation of works, to Hannah Arendt, who distinguished work, as an end in itself, from labour, or work as a means to an end. For his part, Marx maintained that all work is devalued under the alienating conditions of industrial capitalism, which he argued reduces workers to automatons, separates working people from the products of their labour, pits workers against one another as a class and estranges them even from the core of their own essence.[166] Marx's view is echoed by urban theorist Henri Lefebvre, who wrote succinctly in *The Production of Space* that "products have vanquished works.".

In Emily Schultz's Toronto novel, *Heaven is Small*, the imperative to work and the impulse to create works are pitted quite literally against one another. Gordon Small, a failed writer who has died without noticing the event of his own passing, travels to suburban Don Mills to apply for a job as a proofreader at Heaven, the world's largest publisher of romance fiction. Reminded daily of his status as drone, Gordon grows increasingly uneasy about the recursive qualities of his work environment, where little seems to change except the titles of the texts he proofreads. There is also something decidedly strange about his coworkers. Day after day, they wear the same clothes, have the same conversations and enact the same workplace rituals. None of them leaves the building. Gordon notices that he does not sweat, defecate or feel sexual arousal. Gradually but inexorably he reaches the disturbing conclusion that he and his colleagues are dead, and that their employment at Heaven represents some kind of afterlife limbo.

Schultz's characterization of Heaven's lifeless labour force aptly evokes the alienating conditions of contemporary workplace environments that reduce employees to walking automatons and exert influence over their personal lives.[167] And indeed, the significance of Heaven's working conditions is not

---

166 See James Reinhart's distillation of Marx's four dimensions of alienation in *The Tyranny of Work* (1987).
167 See, for example, Fleming & Spicer, 2004, "You can checkout anytime, but you can never

lost entirely on Gordon's colleagues, one of whom inventories Heaven's reliance on nineteenth century Taylorist labour management practices, observing that their work lacks intellectual content, tasks are mechanized, routinized, simplified and fragmented, and even their wages are calculated to keep them compliant.[168] "Coercion outweighs consent," Gordon's co-worker declares, adding, "a bona fide industrial plant stands above you, my friend ... the wheels of romance turn with Fordism."

Schultz's bleak satire of contemporary white-collar work exaggerates but otherwise confirms experiences described in other Toronto fictions. The female protagonist of Margaret Atwood's *The Edible Woman*, a recent university graduate who designs and delivers surveys for a downtown market research company, chafes against the knowledge that her job offers no opportunity for advancement mainly because, as a young woman, even in late 1960s Toronto, she will be expected to leave her job as soon as she marries. In the meantime, she remains suspended, like a pressed flower or an insect preserved in amber, between the structural layers of a company where even the interior geography of the building reinforces the organizational hierarchy:

> On the floor above are the executives and the psychologists—referred to as the men upstairs, since they are all men—who arrange things with the clients; I've caught glimpses of their offices, which have carpets and expensive furniture and silk-screen reprints of Group of Seven paintings on the walls. Below us are the machines— mimeo machines, I.B.M. Machines for counting and sorting and tabulating the information; I've been down there too, into that factory-like clatter where the operatives seem frayed and overworked and have ink on their fingers. Our department is the link between the two: we are supposed to take care of the human element.

In the gendered landscape of Seymour Surveys, Marian works in an open office laid out like a classroom, where only the head of the department enjoys a modicum of privacy:

---

leave": Spatial Boundaries in a High Commitment Organization. *Human Relations*, 57(1).
168 Frederick Winslow Taylor is credited with having institutionalized Scientific Management as a system for maximizing management control in the workplace. Taylorist work practices, which became common in the early years of the twentieth century but persist even in contemporary workplaces, centred on the routinization, simplification and fragmentation of tasks. In *White Collar*, a groundbreaking midcentury study of American middle class working life, noted American sociologist C. Wright Mills argued that an inevitable side effect of "scientific management" is a disenfranchised, alienated workforce prone to indolence and sometimes outright sabotage. In efforts to forestall such behaviour, companies typically respond with a combination of increased surveillance, behavioural profiling and morale-boosting schemes designed to produce what Mills calls "cheerful robots."

We are spread out in a large institutional-green room with an opaque glassed cubicle at the end for Mrs. Bogue, the head of the department, and a number of wooden tables at the other end for the motherly-looking women who sit deciphering the interviewers' handwriting and making crosses and checkmarks on the completed questionnaires with coloured crayons, looking with their scissors and glue and stacks of paper like a superannuated kindergarten class. The rest of us in the department sit at miscellaneous desks in the space between.

Subject to continual scrutiny in a building where even an occasional retreat to the ladies' washroom does not guarantee a moment of respite, Marian comes to understand her prospects in spatial terms, musing, "[w]hat, then, could I expect to turn into at Seymour Surveys? I couldn't become one of the men upstairs; I couldn't become a machine person or one of the questionnaire-marking ladies, as that would be a step down. I might conceivably turn into Mrs. Bogue or her assistant, but as far as I could see that would take a long time and I wasn't sure I would like it anyway." Still, conditioned to doing what is expected of her, Marian toils away at her work until, shortly after disclosing that she is engaged to be married, she learns that her position has been terminated by a boss who "preferred her girls to be either unmarried or seasoned veterans with their liability of unpredictable pregnancies well in the past."

A similar ennui pervades the downtown law office where Mitchell, an aspiring screenwriter in Warren Dunford's *Soon to Be a Major Motion Picture*, works as a temp typing legal correspondence "for a tense, middle-aged lawyer who was preparing thirty precisely detailed letters regarding the estate of another tense, middle-aged lawyer who had recently succumbed to a heart attack." Noticing that his superior resembles the actor Gregory Peck, Mitchell passes the tedious hours composing scandalous sexual fantasies about him:

> After lunch—teriyaki chicken amid the jostling crowds in the food court downstairs—I worked on another porn story, this one starring me and Gregory Peck. We were setting up for a presentation in the oak-panelled boardroom. I was kneeling down, plugging in the slide projector. He put his hand on my shoulder ... When he suddenly called me into his office, I had to hold the note pad in front of my crotch.

Despite its arousing effects, the *frisson* of this fantasy cannot survive the bland atmosphere of the office environment—"[t]he flatness of his monotone immediately deflated my interest,"—and Mitchell returns regretfully to his work.

Nearly as passive but far less obedient, the protagonist of Katrina Onstad's novel, *How Happy to Be* is a newspaper columnist who deals with workplace ennui by showing up shortly before noon, filing fraudulent expense claims ("six forty-dollar cab rides in two days. A receipt I found on the street for gumboots. A $200 restaurant tab."), sleeping under the desk in her newsroom cubicle and getting falling-down drunk at company party functions, all in hopes of getting fired. When rumours start swirling that *The Daily*, a conservative newspaper headquartered in suburban Don Mills and modelled on the iconic but belea-guered *National Post*, is about to be sold, she resolves to be the first person laid off by the future owners, mentally calculating the size of her hoped-for severance package. In the end, however, she isn't sure she will be able to last that long. Flown to Los Angeles on a film studio press junket, she walks out of an especially vapid media scrum and takes an unscheduled leave of absence:

> I write the Big Cheese an e-mail. I tell him I've left the junket early, that I can't do junkets any more, that no paper should do junkets any more, and I actually type the word *integrity* with the same fingers that are used to typing the words *glam* and *hot* and then I tell him I'm taking a break, that I'm tired and I'm taking a break and he can fire me if he wants to, but I need sleep.

A few weeks later, uncertain about returning to *The Daily*, on a place returning from Vancouver Maxime notices a news broadcast announcing that the news-paper has at last been sold. She laughs both ruefully and with relief upon learn-ing that the entire *Daily* staff has been fired, meaning that she will receive her hoped-for severance package after all: "The scene is a suburban office building with a stream of distraught professionals being escorted from its doors. One of them—and this is weird—is Marvin in his gigantic rave pants, and there's the Editor, almost serene, and Heather the Up-Talker, and Hard-Working Deb-bie wiping away her tears. *The Daily* has been sold to BFD Television. Mohsen is idling in the driveway waiting to take everyone back to the city."

Although as Schultz, Atwood, Dunford and Onstad's protagonists dem-onstrate, most "take-this-job-and-shove-it" fantasies play out in pure passive-aggression, occasionally a beleaguered employee will feel pushed far enough to take aggressive action. In David Eddie's novel, *Chump Change*, a young man who works at the Toronto headquarters of the "Cosmodemonic Broadcasting Corporation" writing continuity scripts for television news segments encoun-ters the viperfish environment that prevails in the city's media and entertain-ment industries. Describing his colleagues as "the most venal, petty, nasty crew it's ever been my displeasure to work with," he adds,

> I realize every office has its share of assholes, but in the newsroom the propor-tions seemed all out of whack. Most offices, I've found, break down something

like this: 5 percent of the people are cool or "allies," 10 percent are assholes; and the other 85 percent are indifferent, neutral. But in the Cosmodemonic crackhouse, it was more like 5 percent cool people; 85 percent assholes; and 10 percent real fucking assholes.

In an environment populated by ambitious media professionals vying for plum positions as producers and anchors, competition is the principal social currency. Personally comfortable with being "just a cog, a tooth on a cog, in the vast Cosmodemonic machinery," Eddie's protagonist learns quickly that his easygoing disposition offers little protection from being singled out for abuse. In the end, he decides to exact revenge by leaping in front of the camera during a live news broadcast and planting a lipsticked kiss on one of the anchors, a notorious bully, before ripping open his own shirt to reveal a message reading "I QUIT!"

If the comedic quality evident in these narratives seems to downplay the burned-out bitterness that has come to dominate contemporary workplace environments,[169] it must be pointed out that Gordon, Marian, Mitchell, Maxime and David are all well-educated white collar workers who can afford their ennui. Each of these protagonists, even ghostly Gordon, has a firm sense that something more meaningful lies beyond the confines of their cubicles, even if none of them are entirely sure what it is. In the meantime, they have the luxury to appreciate the absurdity of their circumstances, and perhaps this is why Marian's roommate, a woman who works in an electric toothbrush factory, often intones airily, "What else do you do with a B.A. these days?"

In Toronto we have grown accustomed to think of the big battles over work as having been fought elsewhere and a long time ago, in Germany and England or perhaps in Winnipeg.[170] In an era of employment standards acts, employment insurance, human rights commissions and public health care, most of us have come to take work—if not always our own jobs—for granted. As unionization levels continue to decline,[171] we consider strikes an intrusion

---

169 See, for example, "Growing workplace disloyalty 'no big surprise': Workplace expert," *National Post*, 14 July 2009. For critical commentary on contemporary alienation, see Franco Berardi's *The Soul at Work* (Semiotext(e), 2009) as well as James Rinehart's classic *The Tyranny of Work* (1987).
170 The 1919 Winnipeg General Strike is considered a turning point in Canadian worker activism and labour relations. See David Bercuson's book, *Confrontation at Winnipeg: Labour, Industrial Relations, and the General Strike* (McGill-Queen's University Press, 1990).
171 In 2009, 26.4% of all workers in Ontario were members of unions. While public sector workers have a high rate of unionization at about 70%, fewer than 20% of private sector workers were represented by unions. These numbers have declined steadily since the 1970s. Part-time and service-sector workers—the only "growth" industries in Canadian labour markets—are least likely to be represented by a union. Source: Statistics Canada, August 2009. *Perspectives on Labour & Income*, 10(8). For an examination of contemporary labour trends in Canada, see John Godard's *Industrial*

into the orderly progress of urban life, particularly when the striking workers are public servants who process paperwork, pick up our garbage or drive the buses many of us take to work. We have grown even to dislike the word "worker," with its connotations of lunch buckets and blue collars, preferring to think of ourselves as professionals, specialists, agents and consultants. We watch television programs like *The Office* with rueful recognition, but fail to see in them any meaningful assessment of our own working lives. If we are unhappy, overworked, undervalued or toil in unsafe conditions, we blame our insufficient education, lack of Canadian experience, bullying boss or infighting coworkers. If we sense that some structural imbalance underpins the relations of production, we joke about it or keep our mouths shut. Everyone has to make a living, don't they?

But making a living in Toronto is not something many working people have ever been able to take for granted. Labour historians confirm that Dickensian working conditions persisted in many Toronto factories until well into the twentieth century.[172] Even in contemporary Toronto there are garment sweatshops that pay piece-work rates lower than the minimum wage [173] and reports of undocumented workers abused and robbed by unscrupulous employers.[174] If it seems an exaggeration to draw parallels with early twentieth century factory conditions, one has only to turn to media accounts of fatal industrial accidents such as the 2009 incident in which four construction workers fell to their deaths on Christmas Eve from scaffolding hanging against the thirteenth floor of an Etobicoke apartment building. An investigation indicated that they were all non-unionized migrant workers; published reports suggested their safety harnesses were not attached to safety cables and that the workers had not been made aware of their legal right to refuse unsafe work.[175] In this light, representations of working conditions from the nineteenth century to the present day can tell us much about what has—or has not—changed about work in Toronto.

Set in turn-of-the-century Toronto, Barbara Greenwood's exhaustively researched children's story, *Factory Girl*, describes the working conditions endured by a twelve year old girl forced to leave school in order to support her widowed mother and younger siblings. Turned away by every business she approaches, finally she is directed down a dark and squalid lane to the Acme

Relations, the Economy, and Society, 3rd ed. Toronto: Captus Press, 2005.
172 See Piva (1979), Kealey (1980), Frager (1992), Baskerville and Sager (1998), Godard (2005).
173 Ng et al, 1999.
174 Bustos, Alejandro, 15 August 2005. "Workers cheated, sexually exploited; Employers threaten deportation," *Toronto Star*, B.02.
175 "4 migrant workers die in plunge from highrise," *Toronto Star*, 25 December 2009; "Worker 'didn't feel safe' before scaffold collapsed," *Toronto Star*, 23 January 2010.

Garment Company, a factory known to hire underaged girls. For twelve hours a day Emily stands at a long table with other young girls, mainly Eastern European immigrants, snipping loose threads from shirtwaists while sewing machines thunder all around them in a room made murky by lubricating oil and airborne dust. Tedious and exhausting, the long hours are interrupted only by a single break and the lurking presence of the foreman, who responds harshly to the slightest suggestion of inattention:

> The clock was on the wall behind her. She daren't turn and look again. The boss had shouted at her the first and last time she'd looked. That seemed an eternity ago, and even then her feet were numb. Now sharp pains ran across her shoulders and down her back. If she twisted her head to relieve the pain in her neck, she jostled the girl beside her, who glared silently but ferociously.

Angry with her bullying boss but even more fearful of being fired, Emily finds herself fibrillating between fury and terror, directed not only at the foreman but at her own sense of silenced helplessness about working conditions she is powerless to change:

> Filthy floors. Dust in the air so thick it made Katya cough until she spat up blood. And just yesterday there was Anna, fired when a sewing machine needle ran through her finger and blood stained the sleeve she was sewing.

When a City inspector pays an unexpected visit, the foreman orders the youngest-looking girls to hide in a wooden crate to escape detection. Subsequently, social reformers and a newspaper reporter approach the girls, hoping to expose abuses in the garment industry but encountering only silence. Emily tries to convince her coworkers to speak to the reporter, arguing, "he wants to help. Clean up that filthy place. Get us fair pay. The newspaper could change things ... make them better." But as her coworker Magda retorts, "You lose us job! [...] He write in paper, how I buy bread? Little sisters starve in street!" Soon afterward, a spark from the foreman's cigar sets fabric scraps ablaze and the factory floor erupts into a chaos of overturned chairs, burning shirtwaists and women desperate to escape. Trapped by the raging fire, Emily and Magda struggle to move burning bolts of fabric blocking the only fire escape. Emily manages to escape with one of the other factory girls, but Magda dies in the inferno, another anonymous casualty of turn-of-the-century labour conditions until Emily resolves to tell her story to the reporter, musing, "[i]f people knew about the factories and the way working girls have to live, maybe they *would* change things."

Judi Coburn's novel *The Shacklands* traces the beginnings of such change. Like Emily in *Factory Girl*, Greenwood's protagonist is a young girl forced to seek work in the garment industry after a family tragedy. Like Greenwood's story, Coburn's novel is also based on historical fact. Hired by the T. E. Braime Clothing Company, located in the heart of Toronto's garment district on King Street near Bathurst, Jessie is dismayed to learn that her meagre salary of six dollars will be reduced each week by a one dollar deduction for thread. When the company announces an increase in the thread deduction in February of 1910, Jessie joins sixty of her coworkers in a strike that quickly captures the attention of the city's media.[176] Although the "overall girls," as the media dubs them, do not win the strike, their efforts have resonated with the city's working people, and they are buoyed by a sense of change in the air. As one of the strike organizers tells Jessie, "We didn't really lose, you know. There are at least fifty women who won't let an employer treat them like that again. Most of them now have better jobs than before."

Despite these small gains, by the time the great Depression descended upon Toronto in 1929, work was in short supply and vulnerable workers, particularly the predominantly foreign-born labourers in the garment industry, were forced to accept lower wages and longer hours in exchange for the ephemeral privilege of keeping jobs upon which their entire lives depended. In *Stitch*, a contemporary opera about the history of the city's garment industry, librettist Anna Chatterton interweaves speech cadences with the ceaseless thrum of sewing machines to emphasize the inescapable interplay between garment workers' lives and their work:

She one stitch
She two hundred stitch
She three hundred thousand stitch
She four hundred ten thousand stitched herself into an old woman
She stitched herself into a crone
She stitched her breath
She stitched a gasp

---

176 Coburn's novel is based on historical fact: T. E. Braime was a real company, and in 1910 sixty of its female employees voted to strike against the thread deduction. A labour perspective on the strike—and on labour conditions experienced by women in Toronto more generally—is provided in Ruth Frager's book, *Sweatshop Strife: Class, Ethnicity, and Gender in the Jewish Labour Movement of Toronto, 1900-1939* (University of Toronto Press, 1992). Christina Burr provides further background on the gendered nature of work and labour activism in the garment industry in *Spreading the Light: Work and Labour reform in Late-Nineteenth-Century Toronto* (University of Toronto Press, 1999; see especially chapter 7, 'Bring the Girls into the Fold': Work, Family and the Politics of Labour reform in the Toronto Garment Trades).

She stitched a stifle
She stitched a last...
She stitched her coffin
She stitched her life
She stitched herself out of life[177]

Chatterton's lyrics resonate powerfully with the work of Lithuania-born Yiddish poet Yudica (Yehudit Zik), who describes a similar blend of pessimism and determination motivating a previous generation of garment workers, uncertain whether their sacrifices will lead to any advantage in the new land:

Thinly fragile is dawn's early air. Spadina, street of stores and factories. Lies under a web of gray And dreams the dream of workers' fortunes.

Individual steps on echoing sidewalks Merge with hundreds of steps together. A sound that comes from laneways and streets. A sound of toilers, of hands occupied. Spadina, the street of the Labour Lyceum. With stairs and chambers for labouring men. With their own judges, with laws that are just—Only unity is missing among the worker masses.

How many dreams are buried in the walls Of the massive bricked in shops—Of the young, who gave up their schooling Fortune and future to find in work?

Spadina, the street of worker struggles—I give you in example my personal fate: My child, which I leave in gray mornings. Hungry, abandoned, in rooms among strangers. My sorrow, wandering without direction through ruined worlds. Through horrible sufferings of peoples bleeding To the clanging of wheels, machines and irons. You soak in my tears and my youth.

Spadina, the street of stores and factories. Of people who wait and pine for work— The day that'll unite us all Will be the golden key to freedom.[178]

The cadences of Yudica's lines, evident even in translation—the steady tramping of feet, the heavy pulse of the machines—are meant as an unmistakable call to action. In a city then held in the thrall of labour activist Emma Goldman,[179] it was an appeal that could not possibly go unheard.

---

177 *Stitch* (lyrics by Anna Chatterton, music by Juliet Palmer) was first produced in 2008 through World Stage. Lyrics quoted with permission.
178 These lines were published in Yudica's book, *Shpliters* (1943); translated and quoted in Fuerstenberg, 1996.
179 Anarchist and activist Emma Goldman, who died in Toronto in 1940, where she had lived on an off during the 1930s, was both revered and reviled for her outspoken political beliefs. Goldman motivates protagonists to action in a number of Toronto novels, including John Miller's *A Sharp Intake of Breath* (2006) and Steven Hayward's *The Secret Mitzvah of Lucio Burke* (2005). Interestingly, Goldman was born in Kovno, the same district in Lithuania where activist poet Yudica grew up.

In Steven Hayward's novel, *The Secret Mitzvah of Lucio Burke*, a young woman, whose parents had met and married on the picket line during an eighteen week strike against the Timothy Eaton Company in 1911, responds a similar call. Ruthie Nodelman works as a bookkeeper and occasional coat model at Gutman Fur, located at the very heart of the garment district in the Darling Building on Spadina Avenue. Although Ruthie's own working conditions are undeniably pleasant—her most onerous responsibility is parading across the showroom wrapped in luxurious fur—the ceaseless reverberation of sweatshop sewing machines on the floor above strengthens Ruthie's conviction that little has changed since her parents' days on the picket lines:

> [T]he girls in the sweatshop on the floor above were working at full speed, and she could hear nothing but the mechanized rattle of Singers and the garment trucks being rolled through rows of sewing machines [...] the sound of those poor women working late into the night—without any rights, or a minimum wage, or any protection whatsoever from anything that might be done to them.

A recent convert to communism, one afternoon Ruthie sets aside the volume of Marx she keeps in the showroom and walks up one flight of stairs to McMullen Fabrics, where she sits herself down at one of the machines and begins speaking, in low but urgent tones, about workers' rights to the girls labouring on the factory floor. Just as she seems to be winning their support she is discovered by the foreman, who lifts her bodily and throws her out of the factory. Shortly afterward, Ruthie begins planning the direct action she hopes will provoke a workers' revolution in the City of Toronto:

> [W]hat she has in mind is a kind of general strike, a mass demonstration. If she cannot get into McMullen Fabrics herself, if she cannot speak directly to the girls whose sewing machines punctuate and sometimes drown out her reading of *Das Kapital*, she will communicate with them in other ways. She will go into every dress shop on Spadina, and spread the word that on a particular day there will be a walkout. The walkout will be Ruthie's message to those girls on the floor above her, a sign to them—but not just to them, to them all, to all the girls in all the non-unionized shops who think they've no choice about working sixteen hours a day—a sign of what is possible, a sign that there is nothing to be afraid of. On exactly the same day, Ruthie tells Lucio, at exactly nine in the morning, all the girls, all the finishers and sleeve drapers, all the alteration hands and stenographers, all the pressers and stock girls and dressmakers and buttonhole-machine operators and cloakmakers and embroiderers and trimmers and body makers and drapers, and all the girls who work in the flower and feather factories on King Street, and all the

paper-box makers in the Empire Building near Dundas—she has been drawing up a list—all of them will walk out, all at once.

On the appointed day, the walkout does in fact happen. Hundreds of girls and women and boys and men pour onto Spadina Avenue, clutching the leaflets Ruthie has prepared. The entire city seems to stop, and even the sewing machines in the sweatshop upstairs pause for a few minutes as if in expectant, revolutionary silence. Then they start up again and the crowds on the street below begin to disperse. What Ruthie has not realized in her diligent reading of Marx and in her studious attendance at the lectures of Emma Goldman is that even a workers' revolution requires leadership: the downtrodden will not rise up and demand change entirely on their own.

But engaging in civil disobedience in Depression-era Toronto is a high-stakes game, and one in which demonstrating workers—and even those who write about them—are all too likely to be caught between a police baton and a work camp. The creators of *Eight Men Speak*, a 1933 play challenging the arrest and incarceration of labour activists, were threatened with arrest when the controversial production opened in a Spadina Avenue theatre. In Howard Akler's *The City Man*, a newspaper reporter covering a labour demonstration is nearly arrested in the melee:

He covers a labour protest at College and Spadina. Almost at the intersection before folks are suddenly shoulder to shoulder. Feet on the march and placards held high. A gathering of the local needle trades, shmatte workers filing from the west and the south toward the grass-and-stone nexus of Queen's Park. [...]

Voices Yiddish and Ukrainian squish together in the sparse wiggle room of protest, a polyglot glut of tongues that needs nearly a whole minute to ease into harmony.

FAIR WAGE!

FAIR WAGE!

FAIR WAGE!

FAIR WHHH-eeeeeeeeeeeeeeeeeeeeeeeeeeee!

First come the police whistles and then the quartet of cops who jump down the front steps of the station. Others follow. Push and shove, push and shove. Eli gets grabbed by the collar and spun around.

Star man, says Eli. *Star* man!

What're you doing here?

Trying to get a story.

The officer draws his truncheon, knuckles going white at the ridge. Well, he says, get it and go.

Other protests erupt in similar violence. In Earle Birney's, novel, *Down the Long Table*, a graduate student attends a workers' demonstration held at Queen's Park late in the fall of 1932. At first the protest seems peaceful; a mass of dark coats clustered around a single speaker:

> Framed by the dim interior of the stand a man leaned hatless, straw hair cox-combed by the wind, shouting, "...work...name of the single unemployed of this Province...fullscale program...union wages..." The wind, and the honk and squeal of traffic, shredded his sentences, which in any case came jerkily, slowly, from the swaying figure. "Twenty cents a day...starvation...Bennett government...slave camps...winter..." In a ragged topcoat buttoned to the neck he rocked, beat on the railings with bare fists. "Organize...bosses...mass action..." Above him a canvas banner bellied: WORKLESS UNITE—JOIN PROTEST MARCH TO CITY HALL MONDAY.

When a second speaker takes the podium, seemingly without warning, a pha-lanx of police motorcycles descends upon the crowd, surrounding it with ba-tons drawn and orders it to disperse. As the demonstrators file through the police cordon, the speaker and event chairman are isolated and arrested:

> The back of the long line was suddenly convulsed with struggling figures; the police had converged, batons flashing. [...] A thin little man charged back toward them, brandishing a spindly placard, but the nearest policeman brought a baton down with a long swing; the thin man clutched his head, staggered, sagged to the grass.

But if the force used to subdue the demonstration seems extreme, it quickly becomes clear that many of the attendees have played calculated roles in this theatre of protest.

Invited along for lunch, Birney's graduate student is told that the event has been staged in hopes that reports of police brutality would elicit sympa-thetic newspaper headlines. The protestor knocked unconscious by a police baton is described as "expendable" and then dismissed as a "Trotskyite bas-tard" guilty of "trying to grab the limelight for his uh counter-revolutionary faction by uh—by ultra-leftist putschism."[180] Gordon learns that even the baby carriage he saw knocked over by a police motorcycle had in fact been filled with pamphlets. Only long months later, after he has been drawn into one of the warring factions of the Canadian workers' movement, does Gordon realize that the continuous campaigning and endless agit-prop have little to do with

---

180 In the Stalinist era, followers of Trotsky were considered counter-insurgents and class enemies; Trotskyism has since become fashionable on the ideological left.

workers' rights and everything to do with the ideological ambitions of the organizers. This is a bitter revelation to Gordon, who has given up everything for a cause he realizes has accomplished nothing while the unemployment lines get longer and the Depression drags on.

A similar cynicism propels Ken Tilling, the protagonist of Hugh Garner's *Cabbagetown*, to reject the entreaties of a fellow-traveler hoping to covert him to the Cause. Having traveled from one coast to the other in search of work before returning to Toronto, and having been starved and beaten and imprisoned and robbed along the way, Ken declares,

I've seen the working stiff being kicked around all over the North American continent. [...] You don't even have to go anywhere outside this town to see that the system is rotten and has broken down. Right here in good old Tory British Toronto you have the same problems they have anywhere else. Just because I don't use Commie words like 'labour power', *petit-bourgeois*, or 'surplus value' doesn't mean I can't see what's wrong. I'm just not interested in your new civilization or your new religion or your new politics, or whatever the hell it is. I'm just interested in pork chops for the poor, jobs for those who want to work, bugless beds and free hospitalization.

More than a century after trade unions and other labour organizations first took up the cause of workers' rights in Toronto, and in the long decades since legislation was gradually and grudgingly enacted to even out the balance between employers and working people, it is easy to forget the appalling factory conditions that led to violent demonstrations and labour stoppages in the first half of the twentieth century. It is easy, too, to forget the rigid social schisms that divided people by class. Yet, many of these same divisions persist today and have even deepened in an era of global outsourcing, lean production and contingent labour. The difference is that the new working class—including the cashiers, cleaners and food service workers who keep the global economy running—has become largely invisible. This new working class consists disproportionately of recent immigrants, some lacking English language skills or Canadian qualifications but many simply encountering the subtle workplace racism that persists even in multicultural Toronto. Less likely to be represented by unions than all other classes of employees,[181] disproportionately likely to be injured on the job[182] and typically excluded from health care packages and pension plans because of their part-time or contingent status, these "grey collar" workers occupy a parallel universe in many of the same spaces frequented

181 Statistics Canada, August 2009. *Perspectives on Labour & Income.*
182 Fournier et al, 2005; Singh, 2004.

by the visible workforce, hard at work opening up coffee shops and food courts before the executives and office managers arrive in the morning, and emptying garbage cans and cleaning toilets long after the secretaries and even the IT people have gone home at night.

In M. G. Vassanji's *No New Land*, a South Asian immigrant discovers that his long overseas career as a salesman cannot even get him a retail job selling shoes in Canada:

> Braving the punishing cold, you beat the footpaths, searching for vacancies. You do Yonge Street, then Bloor, Dundas, and Queen, the East End, then the West. Taking refuge in donut shops, using precious change to make phone calls doomed by the first word, the accent. I am a salesman, I was a salesman. Just give me a chance. Why don't they understand we can do the job? "Canadian experience" is the trump they always call against which you have no answer.

The rejections are unvarying, apart from one interview when, after detailing his extensive overseas experience, Nurdin is told he is "overqualified" for the position.

Similarly, in Rabindranath Maharaj's *Homer in Flight*, a man who once worked for the government in Trinidad hands out hundreds of resumes without receiving a request for a single interview. The "help wanted" section of the newspaper lists only jobs he cannot apply for: "Canadian degree...previous Canadian experience required...Canadian accent required...Canadian experience preferable...Ontario letter of standing required." Finally, Homer secures work at a suburban factory where the supervisor likens the production line to a high-speed highway, warning, "the efficient workers reach their destinations quickly and easily while the malfunctioning workers end up maimed, mangled or dead." Mindlessly mixing chemicals alongside a crew comprised mainly of migrant workers, Homer feels his dreams of successful citizenship slipping slowly away.

Other unemployed outsiders do not fare even this well. In Austin Clarke's story, "Canadian Experience," a Barbadian-born man travels to First Canadian Place—a building he once worked in as a cleaner—to apply for an executive position with a bank, knowing already that he will be rejected for the colour of his skin or the cut of his suit. When the elevator stops at the fourteenth floor he stands frozen while the doors open and close on an elegantly appointed reception area filled with stylish, staring women. Collecting his courage as the elevator rises to the fiftieth floor and makes its descent, he finds himself immobilized again:

No one enters, even though it stops two times in quick succession. And then it stops once more, and the door opens, and he is facing the same office with BANK written on the glass, cheerless and frightening, and seeing the same chrome, the rugs and the black and pearls of the women. Just as he moves to step out, the closing door, cut into half, and like two large hands, comes at him. He gets out of the way just as the blue eyes of one of the women approaching the elevator door to see what he wanted are fixed on him.

As soon as the elevator reaches the ground floor he retreats from the building rather than risk further humiliation. Hours later, standing on a subway platform, he weighs his failed prospects against his mounting debts, which are all he has to show for the eight years he has spent in Canada. In the end, realizing his options are exhausted, he laughs bitterly and steps off the edge of the platform as the train pulls into the station.

In the introduction to *Nine Men Who Laughed*, the collection of short stories in which "Canadian Experience" appears, Austin Clarke analyses the precarious position the immigrant—a term he rejects because it reduces the foreign-born person to a single facet of his existence—is placed in by a culture that relies on his labour but will not grant him any real freedom of movement in the city. Clarke writes,

> Some say that life imitates art. For the "immigrant" in these stories there is no life and there is no art. There is no "life" because they do not live freely nor with any semblance of mutual, creative relationships. The "immigrant" is merely *living*.
> "How are things, man?"
> "Living, man. I just here, living."

This criticism is taken up by literary scholar Batia Boe Stolar in her essay "Building and Living the Immigrant City." Contrasting Clarke's West Indian workers with the immigrant city-builders celebrated in novels like Michael Ondaatje's *In the Skin of a Lion*, Stolar points out that Clarke's protagonists are relegated to menial service sector jobs that contribute to the urban economy but do not permit them to stake any claim to the city's cultural identity or belong to its built environment. Instead, they inhabit rented rooms and employers' attics, existing in the city's interstices and expending all their productive energy on tasks that sustain their material survival without ever leaving room for anything more.

It is this final point that brings us back to Scott Cutler Shershow's analysis of work in *The Work and the Gift*. The most grievous wrong of contemporary capitalism, Shershow argues, is not only that it consigns entire classes of people to "endless labour" so that the rest of us may consume more cheaply and conveniently, or even that the exchange is so appallingly unequal, but that it sabotages our capacity for generosity. The end of work, Shershow argues, will not be found in a proletarian utopia populated by liberated workers, as most Marxist theorists would have it. Nor will it emerge amid an elitist celebration of Works. If there is to be any alternative to the excesses and inequalities of industrial capitalism, it will unfold, rather, in what Shershow calls a "community of unworking." By this Shershow does not mean precisely that people will not work or produce Works, but rather than both work and Works might be unharnessed, at least partly, from the empty desperation of the compulsion to produce and consume.

"Living well," Shershow adds, needs to be decoupled from what he calls "the fatal conjunction of work and the gift"—a garbled notion of work in which effort is equated with moral righteousness, paired with an equally distorted concept of charity in which the unemployed or needy are blamed for conditions of material scarcity over which they have limited control. And if this seems a tall order, and one likely to be undone by the pressing practical problems of deciding how the necessary tasks will continue to be done, Shershow suggests that it would be worthwhile to start by questioning the necessity of those tasks in the first place.

In one sense this is a perennially ongoing project: as Shershow points out, "we already live these questions" through labour activism and employment standards legislation. At the same time, however, there is a need to pay heed to what Shershow calls "aesthetic or theoretical or religious questions" about work. And this is where literature comes in. Just as literary representations of race and identity expose willing readers to the challenges of dealing with difference in multicultural Toronto, and just as imaginative renderings of gender and sexuality offer insight into the manifold qualities of desire, so too do class fictions give us a chance to look beyond the blinkers of our own misery or privilege, to understand and perhaps even empathize with the working lives of others.

− 7 −

CITY LIMITS

SUBURBAN GOTHIC

In *Blind Crescent*, Michelle Berry's unsettling 2005 novel set in an unnamed Ontario suburb, six houses on a cul-de-sac harbour residents separated by a common but unspoken crisis. A single mother struggles to cope with young toddlers while suppressing unrequited fantasies about the divorced father who lives next door, a young man buckles under the burden of caring for his ailing parents, a 500-pound synaesthete is compelled to eat by the colours he tastes in everything around him, a brittle family crumbles around the edges of its outwardly perfect life and a squatter holes up in an abandoned house whose previous owner hanged himself from a basement rafter. A gunman stalks the nearby metropolitan highways, and as the novel unfolds with deliberate DeLilloesque detail, it seems possible that the shooter could be any one of the people living on Blind Crescent. Even the unlikely suspects are marked by silent complicity, noticing disturbing patterns of neighbourhood behaviour but remaining too caught up in the minutiae of private misery even to protect themselves.

The suggestion that violence seethes beneath the tranquil surface of suburban Southern Ontario is not unique to *Blind Crescent*. In *Bad Move*, Linwood Barclay's darkly comedic 2004 novel set in a thinly fictionalized version of Oakville, a downtown homeowner tires of the nightly accumulation of condoms and crack pipes in his Toronto neighbourhood and moves his family to a suburb where he quickly concludes boredom must be the leading cause of death. Soon, troubling discoveries begin to tarnish his tranquility, among them the revelation that the neighbourhood accountant moonlights as a dominatrix and the landscaper across the street uses his garage as a grow-op. Even more alarming is his growing suspicion that the subdivision's land development corporation is controlled by the mob. Zack's diminishing peace is shattered permanently when he stumbles across the bludgeoned corpse of an environmental activist floating face down in a local creek. Caught in an escalating cycle of extortion and murder, Zack realizes far too late that suburbia cannot provide an escape from the violent proclivities people carry with them.

Novels depicting cruelty and criminality in suburban settings may be traced to the origins of contemporary Canadian suburbia. One of the earliest, Hugh Garner's *Death in Don Mills*,[183] set in what urban analyst John Sewell calls "Canada's first corporate suburb," contrasts the bland, orderly reputation

---

183 Garner wrote three Inspector McDumont mystery novels, all engaging with different Toronto neighbourhoods, including *The Sin Sniper* (1970), *Death in Don Mills* (1975) and *Murder has Your Number* (1978). A fourth McDumont mystery, *Don't Deal Five Deuces* (1992), was completed by Paul Stuewe after Garner's death. Stuewe is also the author of the only biography of Garner published to date: *The Storms Below: The Turbulent Life and Times of Hugh Garner* (1988).

of 1970s-era Don Mills with the sordid reality of activities transacted behind the community's closed doors. A married businessman, dropping off a neatly wrapped packet of waste before embarking on his precisely timed morning commute, discovers the naked body of his neighbour, stabbed and stuffed into the garbage chute of their otherwise immaculate Don Mills apartment building. A police investigation exposes the dead woman's private predilection for booze, boys and promiscuous sex, and, more tellingly, uncovers a tangled network of drug dealers, sexual "deviants," sociopaths and killers living at 1049 Don Mills Road and permeating the community at large.

Given popular portrayals of suburbia as bland and monolithic, it seems curious that Toronto's suburbs should have attracted such dark imaginings. Perhaps it is the undifferentiated suburban landscape—rows of seemingly identical houses, the stark, treeless terrain, silent playgrounds and curvilinear streetscape confounding efforts at coherence—that provides the perfect backdrop to these narratives, as if behind the closed California shutters and the impassive facades of locked garage doors are secrets more disturbing than the storyline of any gothic novel.

THE GEOGRAPHY OF NOWHERE

In "Rewriting White Flight," literary scholar Paul Milton examines the cultural disconnect between the suburban dream that has propelled generations of city dwellers to seek peace and privacy at the urban periphery, and a parallel discourse that casts suburbia (and, by extension, suburbanites) as homogenous, exclusionary and seething with unresolved frustration with its failure to live up to its inhabitants' materialistic aspirations. Tensions between unfulfilled suburban ambitions and the depressing emptiness of suburban experience produce a peculiar sort of ennui. On one hand, Milton observes, "Nothing [...] of any consequence ever really happens on a crescent. These are the sites of complacent banality, of the here and now, of everydayness. Art is about the there and then. Excitement takes place elsewhere." At the same time, Milton points out that suburban writing is also rife with "narratives of frustration, broken dreams, broken marriages, and failed families," adding that "many writers represent the suburbs as soulless and their families as dysfunctional. More often than not, the suburbs are represented as sites of everyday monotony leading to dissatisfaction or as the quiet backdrop against which gothic horror or absurdity takes place." The result of these tensions is nostalgia tinged with self-loathing and regret, sentiments portrayed vividly not only in novels where death and violence drive the narrative, but also in literary representations of everyday suburban life.

One source of suburban regret is the destruction of natural landscapes and rural farmland bulldozed under blocks of tract housing. A character in *Death in Don Mills* appears to be modelled loosely on Charles Sauriol,[184] the Canadian naturalist who devoted the bulk of his life to preserving natural areas in the Greater Toronto Area, particularly the Don Valley. Having long since traded his cabin for a tidy apartment in Don Mills, Garner's protagonist observes with regret how irrevocably suburbia has altered the Toronto landscape, recalling, "The country around here was half-wild in those days, especially down in the river valley. During the Depression we had squatters who moved into log cabins and tarpaper shacks down there. And there were always a lot of hoboes." In Garner's novel the cabins and hoboes have been replaced by disaffected young men of no fixed address who loiter outside the Don Mills Centre looking to score or sell drugs.

In *Bad Move*, regret is expressed as a kind of guilty nostalgia for a landscape Barclay's narrator cannot remember and can barely imagine:

When you stood next to Willow Creek, held your breath, and listened to the sounds of the shallow waters flowing by, you could almost imagine you weren't a few hundred yards from a soulless subdivision. [...] What had this entire area looked like before the developers took over? What had the land where our house now stood been before the surveyors marked out where the streets would go, and the bulldozers came in and levelled everything? Had it been woodlands? Had it been farmland? Did corn used to come out of the ground where we now parked the cars? How many birds and groundhogs and squirrels had to relocate once the builders broke ground on Valley Forest Estates?

Standing on the banks of Willow Creek, "surrounded by some of the only trees within a five-mile radius," Barclay's protagonist acknowledges feeling "like a hypocrite" for living the suburban dream upon this denuded landscape. At the same time, however, he attempts to rationalize his presence, adding, "at least our house didn't back up onto a marshland. It's not like we were tossing our trash into the creek." Still, Zack remains ill at ease in suburbia, fibrillating uncomfortably between rationalization and regret over what has been lost or

<hr />

184 A lifelong advocate of wilderness preservation, Charles Sauriol co-founded the Don Valley Conservation Association and subsequently led the Metropolitan Toronto and Region Conservation Authority in establishing conservation areas throughout the greater Toronto area. An expert on the history and ecology of the Don Valley, he wrote four books about the Don (*Remembering the Don, Tales of the Don, Trails of the Don* and *Pioneers of the Don*), a treatise on apiary (*A Beeman's Journey*) and a memoir (*Green Footsteps: Recollections of a Grassroots Conservationist*). Sauriol received many public accolades and awards for his work, and was named to the Order of Canada in 1989. He died in 1995.

destroyed, dimly aware that it is his own culpability that keeps him from feeling a sense of belonging there.

Memories of misbegotten youth and a sense of frustrated nostalgia propel other narratives of suburbia. The protagonist of Russell Smith's 1998 novel *Noise*, returns via Greyhound bus to a thinly fictionalized version of Kitchener to attend his brother's graduation from law school, passing through a stultifying, recursive semi-urban wasteland of strip malls and industrial parks along the entire route:

> The factories and warehouses passed, long, flat, windowless buildings, all in the same corrugated white material. Miles of parking lots, the same signs in every strip mall: McDonald's, Petsworld, Adults Only Video. Occasionally there would be a Lighting Unlimited or an Arby's, but on the horizon, approaching, would always be a McDonald's, a Petsworld or an Adult's Only. [...] Closer to Munich he opened his eyes. The signs were more idiosyncratic along this highway. They passed a lot stacked with lengths of huge pipe, steel and concrete, and the sign, JUST PIPE. A brightly lit restaurant called Megabite. Rows of new brick houses with garages, mud all around them: Freehold Towne Houses. Software Depot. About Bedrooms.

James' mother picks him up at the Munich bus station and together they drive through seemingly unpopulated subdivisions with names like Woodcrest Village and Sherwood Park, while James experiences the disturbing sensation of being dragged backward through time, his adulthood vaporizing like exhaust fumes under the highway lights. Turning into the driveway of the familiar split-level, James encounters his father engaged in a uniquely suburban ritual:

> They pulled into the driveway of the house James had grown up in and James saw his father in a circle of light on the front lawn. He was kneeling, his head close to the grass and his bum in the air. He wore shorts, and his legs were white. His bald patch glowed; the spotlight was over the garage door. James called to him as he opened the car door, but his father only grunted. He seemed to be scrabbling at something in the grass.

Rather than greeting his long-absent son, James' father brandishes a plastic ruler in his general direction and instructs from his position on the lawn, "Watch that, that's just seeded. And careful of the edging," before accounting for his peculiar behaviour:

> "Just measuring. I tell Georg to keep it exactly two point five centimetres, but there are patches where it varies. I'll have to speak to him." He waved at the far edge of

the lawn. "Burnt patches over there, too, I think it's some kind of fungus, from having leaves on it too long. I told him."

The visit goes downhill from there. James endures a celebratory family dinner at the local Howard Johnson's by drifting regularly into the hotel bar to drink a series of compensatory cocktails. Civil exchanges with his brother are marred by the inevitable resurrection of sibling rivalry. Depressingly, James discovers that his former classmates—most of whom have married, moved to other suburbs and engaged in professions he derides for their banality—are nonetheless doing far better than he is. The contrast disquiets James, whose stalled literary ambitions have reduced him to writing snarky arts reviews for one of the city's alternative weekly newspapers. Then, amazingly, James runs into a high school friend with whom he has an intense discussion about classical music, the kind of conversation he knows he can never have in the city, where his passion for Scriabin, Prokofiev and Poulenc would mark him as unbearably quaint. The contradiction leaves him aching and feeling utterly unmoored, unable to belong either in Toronto, where he cannot keep up with his own hipster image, or the suburban hometown he has rejected for its cultural smallness.

Ray Robertson's protagonist revisits a similar suburban landscape in 2000's *Gently Down the Stream*, noticing upon returning to his parents' home in suburban southwestern Ontario how utterly their tastes, interests and desires have diverged from his own:

He and mum made out alright. A split-level ranch-style prefab in a freshly bulldozed subdivision with a winterized garage equipped with a colour TV and beer fridge for him, wall-to-wall everything inside the house for her (pink hand towels you don't dare dirty proudly on display on the bathroom counter, a rock garden out back just like the one she saw on *Home and Garden Television*), they got the stuff they wanted.

The problem for Hank is that, unlike his parents, not only does he not have what he wants, he is not even sure what it is. Restless, dissatisfied, he sabotages his marriage and, on the very weekend they are scheduled to move into the semi-detached fixer-upper they have bought just off Roncesvalles Avenue in Toronto's west end, flees by bus to his parents' Chatham-area home and holes up in their suburban basement, shocked into awareness only because he is unable to find comfort there either.

It is a telling characteristic of Toronto literature that, in recollections of youth, so many hometowns, however remote,[185] are recast as suburbs of

185 Russell Smith's "New Munich" is an hour and a half outside the city by bus, while the version of Chatham Ray Robertson describes in *Gently Down the Stream* is nearly 300 kilometres away.

Toronto. Represented in ways that emphasize contrasts between past and present, parochial and urbane, they underscore the compulsion to escape suburbia that drives so many young protagonists eager to crack open the cast of their upbringing. Despite admitting having had no tangible reason to reprove the suburbs, Paul Milton writes, "still I learned to hate my life there" and adds, "having grown up among the balloon frames and fields of mud, my dreams lay elsewhere, and all that I had learned and read fanned my discontent. The suburbs, I learned, was a place from which you must escape, a not-so-old sow that eats its farrow."

In one sense this is, of course, a familiar literary trope: that of the young scion breaking away from family to seek fame or fortune and make a mark on the world. At the same time, however, those who choose this exodus must struggle against the currents that pushed their parents out of the inner city. Returning is, in some ways, like Lot's wife gazing back at Sodom and being turned into a pillar of salt, and perhaps this is what accounts for the paralysis experienced by both Smith's and Robertson's protagonists. Only once they have reconciled their urban ambitions with their suburban upbringing are James and Hank able to achieve traction in their lives, at last escaping what Emily Schultz describes in *Joyland* as the kind of place where "nothing changed except the television commercials" and where "parents were without history, without future."

Suburban women's experiences have been pathologized for half a century in popular sociological analyses such as *The Split Level Trap* and Betty Friedan's *The Feminine Mystique*, which attribute the misery of suburban women's lives to an excess of material wealth and a poverty of meaning. Underpinning their ennui is a patriarchal division of life and labour that leaves suburban women trapped in what Phyllis Brett Young describes in *The Torontonians* as a "gilt-edged suburban labyrinth."[186] Young's protagonist is a bored housewife who faces the banality of a suburban existence revolving around Cuisinarts and backyard cookouts. Her despair is rooted in the realization that, despite the success of her twenty-year marriage, the accomplishments of her grown children and the demands of a social life that keeps her busy with charity drives and bridge tournaments, she ekes out an utterly empty, lonely existence in Rowanwood, a fictional Toronto suburb standing in approximately for Leaside:

---

186 Notable for its frank depictions of middle-class suburban women's angst, *The Torontonians*—an international bestseller when first published in 1960—is an important forerunner of more pointedly feminist works such as Betty Friedan's *The Feminine Mystique*, which first appeared in 1963, and Margaret Atwood's first novel, *The Edible Woman*, first published in 1969 and also set in Toronto.

If you had been a stranger from another planet, you might have wondered if Rowanwood was inhabited at all. You would not have understood the phenomenon of mid-morning doldrums. You had to live in Rowanwood to know that the men had all left the boxes in which they lived for other boxes in the business section downtown; to know that the women were either hidden inside cleaning the former, or had gone off in smaller mechanized boxes to the shopping plaza. These things explained to you, you, the stranger from another planet, would still fail to understand why the women should spend so much time shut up in their boxes. You would, if you had come equipped with any knowledge of the civilization you had invaded, wonder how on Earth women had allowed themselves to be hoodwinked into believing what the manufacturers wanted them to believe—that they had never had it so good.

Belatedly aware that her single-minded pursuit of the Good Life has brought little more than a beautiful carpet and a buckwheat lawn, Karen contemplates suicide as the only avenue of escape from a suburban life in which she is slowly but inexorably suffocating.

Suburban novels of the ensuing decades reinforce this depressing account of suburban women's experiences, from the social-climbing housewives of *Death in Don Mills* who lie about their husbands' occupations and sneer upon hearing that their neighbour—a "loose woman," in their eyes—has been murdered, to the image-obsessed wife, mother and marketing executive in Michelle Berry's *Blind Crescent* who judges the single mother next door not so much for failing to live up to the standards of *House Beautiful* as for giving away how hard it is to keep up the act. The spectre of suicide raised in *The Torontonians* recurs, too, in Barbara Gowdy's novel *Falling Angels*, when the family matriarch makes good on the promise of self-destruction, heaving herself off the roof of her suburban split-level and leaving only secrets and lies behind. Despite the promises of suburbia, morbid despair figures in these novels far more than the fulfilment of any dream. As Karen observes in *The Torontonians*, "[Y]ou were, whether you recognized it or not, caught in a maze similar to that in which scientists put white mice to see if they had sufficient intelligence to find their way out. If the mice were not intelligent enough to solve the puzzle, they ran round and round and round until they went out of their minds."

In *The Geography of Nowhere: The Rise and Decline of America's Man-Made Landscape*, Howard Kunstler sums up this last sentiment, denouncing the contemporary North American suburban landscape as

depressing, brutal, ugly, unhealthy, and spiritually degrading—the jive-plastic commuter tract home wastelands, the Potemkin village shopping plazas with their vast parking lagoons, the Lego-block hotel complexes, the "gourmet mansardic" junk-food joints, the Orwellian office "parks" featuring buildings sheathed in the same reflective glass as the sunglasses worn by chain-gang guards, the particle-board garden apartments rising up in every meadow and cornfield, the freeway loops around every big and little city with their clusters of discount merchandise marts, the whole destructive, wasteful, toxic, agoraphobia-inducing spectacle that politicians proudly call "growth."

Kunstler's views echo those of influential urban theorist Henri Lefebvre, who in *The Production of Space* wrote succinctly of contemporary cities that "everything here resembles everything else," adding that "repetition has everywhere defeated uniqueness, [and] the artificial and contrived have driven all spontaneity and naturalness from the field."

Given the strength of these indictments, and given that the aforementioned novels represent their suburban settings in a uniformly negative manner, it is tempting to conclude (as does the protagonist in *The Torontonians*) that suburbia represents "an evolutionary *cul de sac.*" This seems a depressing summation of a now-massive metropolitan region that, in little more than half a century, has expanded to house and employ more than half the population of the Greater Toronto Area. But given the continuous exodus of city-dwellers to the urban periphery, alongside the influx of recent immigrants and second-generation suburbanites who bypass downtown dwelling entirely,[187] it is clear that something more meaningful pulls people to the suburbs than the prospect of a multi-vehicle garage and a verdant lawn. Indeed, an emerging body of Toronto literature indicates that the city's suburbs are continually being inhabited and imagined in new ways, suggesting that if there is redemption to be found in suburbia, it will rise out of a rapidly changing cultural landscape.

THE MYTH OF THE MONOCULTURAL SUBURB

In *White Diaspora*, literary scholar Catherine Jurca suggests that the eschatological quality present in so many suburban novels reflects their authors' collective sense of cultural loss. Since the late nineteenth century, middle- and upper-class North Americans have migrated to suburbs to escape conditions they feared or found distasteful about cities: overcrowding, pollution, poverty

187 For further analyses of the social, cultural, economic and environmental consequences of suburban growth in the greater Toronto area, see John Sewell's *The Shape of the Suburbs* (2009), Julie-Ann Boudreau, Roger Keil and Douglas Young's *Changing Toronto: Governing Urban Neoliberalism* (2009) and Mohammad Qadeer and Sandeep Kumar Agrawal's Evolution of Ethnic Enclaves in the Toronto Metropolitan Area 2001-06 (*Canadian Geographer*, forthcoming).

and (as the well-documented phenomenon of "white flight" indicates) immigration and ethnic diversity. Ultimately, Jurca argues, these fears have shown up in novels portraying their middle-class suburban protagonists as members of a diaspora driven from cities, seeking an Anglo-Saxon homeland but finding themselves perennially displaced at the urban fringe. Ironically invoking the language of dispossession, Jurca explains that "the term *white diaspora* is designed to emphasize and lay bare the role of the novel in promoting a fantasy of victimization that reinvents white flight as the persecution of those who flee, turns material advantage into artifacts of spiritual and cultural oppression, and sympathetically treats affluent house owners as the emotionally dispossessed."

An examination of Toronto's suburban literature would, at first glance, seem to confirm this analysis. Seemingly without exception, the protagonists of *Blind Crescent, Bad Move, Death in Don Mills, Noise, Gently Down the Stream, Joyland, The Torontonians* and *Falling Angels* are white, middle-class suburbanites (or the children of white, middle-class suburbanites) grappling with a sense of dispossession and spiritual homelessness. Even novels featuring protagonists of colour often seem to bear out, if ironically, the narrative of white, middle-class oppression. One such novel, David Chariandy's *Soucouyant*, from 2007, is set in Old Port Junction, a suburban neighbourhood resembling the Scarborough Bluffs community of Port Union where Chariandy grew up. A post-war suburb with pretensions of authenticity,[188] Port Junction describes itself strenuously as "The *Traditional* Community by the Lake," mainly because, as Chariandy writes, "[i]t was considered one of the last remaining 'good' parts of Scarborough, meaning distant from the growing ethnic neighbourhoods to the west." Port Junction hosts an annual Heritage Day parade whose promotional literature invites "*everyone*" to participate, "since the Heritage Day parade was being revamped these days to recognize 'people of multicultural backgrounds,' and 'not just Canadians.'" One year, Trinidad-born Adele, suffering from senile dementia and living in an old house lodged between the railway tracks and the edge of the Scarborough bluffs, makes a surprise appearance in the parade clad only in a bra and several pairs of underwear, her dark skin luminous in the spring light. While a couple of costumed citizens extricate themselves from the parade to steer Adele home to her mortified son, an alarmed and indignant crowd gathers around them, muttering, "[W]hat kind of people are we allowing to live here, anyway?"

Post-colonial scholars, chief among them Homi Bhabha and Gayatri Spivak, argue that racialized minorities are vulnerable to the barrage of negative

---

188 Robert Bonis's *A History of Scarborough* (1969) conveys some of this sense of historical immanence.

images they encounter in the dominant discourse.[189] Dionne Brand articulates this vulnerability eloquently in *What We All Long For*, describing a Vietnamese family who, despite having accumulated material wealth in the years since arriving as refugees, find their accomplishments remain inadequate and the suburban dream elusive:

> Tuyen's family is rich, newly rich. They have a giant house in Richmond Hill, where rich immigrants live in giant houses. Richmond Hill is a sprawling sub-urb where immigrants go to get away from other immigrants, but of course they end up living with all the other immigrants running away from themselves—or at least running away from the self they think is helpless, weak, unsuitable, and always in some kind of trouble.

Worn down by the trauma of their flight from Vietnam and the trials of two decades spent reassembling the pieces of their life in Canada, Tuyen's parents buy a house in Richmond Hill, as if this visible symbol of the suburban dream will enable them to transcend their perceived foreignness. Brand adds,

> They hate that self that keeps drawing attention, the one that can't fit in because of colour or language, or both, and they think that moving to a suburb will somehow eradicate that person once and for all. And after all the humiliations of being that self—after they've worked hard enough at two or three jobs and saved enough by overcrowding their families in small dour rooms and cobbled together enough credit—immigrants flee to rangy lookalike desolate suburbs like Richmond Hill where the houses give them a sense of space and distance from that troubled im-age of themselves.

Toronto-born Tuyen considers her parents' house artificial, and observes that

> [t]he whole development seemed highly contrived, as if it were made all of card-board and set down quickly and precariously. Someone's idea of luxury, which was really antiseptic, and for all its cars and spaciousness, it was nevertheless rootless and desolate.

But to her parents, the big suburban house is meant to represent arrival, as if at long last it will enable them to escape their memories of flight and foreign-ness, and the fear that in some important way they will always remain refu-gees, adrift forever on a crowded boat on the South China Sea.

189 See Homi Bhabha's *The Location of Culture* (1994) and Gayatri Spivak's "Can the Subaltern Speak?" (1988).

Dreams of suburban homeownership and attendant images of security and arrival also feature prominently in Rabindranath Maharaj's *Homer in Flight*. But where Maharaj's protagonist has hoped to find stability and order, he experiences social isolation and crushing loneliness instead. At first the city's order impresses Homer, its immaculate streets a striking contrast to the corruption and humid decay that had compelled him to leave Trinidad. During the hour-long car trip from Toronto's international airport to his cousin's suburban home on the eastern outskirts of the city, Homer marvels at the tidy landscape of subdivisions and factories they pass on Highway 401, remarking to himself how

> everything is well-preserved: the houses, the landscape, the people. He focused on the neatness: each house was embellished with a colourful garden, a well-maintained lawn and a tree. They all looked similar. He felt that if he closed his eyes and opened them after one minute, he would not notice any difference. Just like a *Flintstones* cartoon, with the same building appearing over and over, he thought.

Surprised to hear the name of the suburban community his cousin Grants lives in, Homer asks, somewhat rhetorically, "Ajax? Like the bleach cleaner?"

In Ajax—named after a battleship, Homer is informed—he settles into his cousin's basement and dreams of homeownership and big American cars. A conversation with Grants explains the significance of his cousin's suburban address:

> I ... we bought the house during the boom years. Cost a fortune then. There was plenty money around and immigrants were buying houses left, right and centre. They still do, you know. Other Canadians are different from us. They see nothing wrong about living their entire lives renting an apartment or condo, but in the back of every immigrant's mind there is always one fixed thought: when can I afford a house? It gives us security. Security.

But the security Grants enjoys eludes Homer. Moving to Etobicoke in search of work, he rents an ill-furnished high-rise apartment and joins a ragged army of immigrant men who toil at low-paying factory jobs in the city's industrial suburbs. Early one morning, travelling home exhausted and dirty after a long night shift, he realizes how far away his dreams have become:

> The bus arrived and Homer slipped his two loonies into the slot and headed for a seat at the back. Young women on their way to offices, immaculately attired, sat at the front, while closer to Homer were ragged-looking middle aged men with

dirty knapsacks between their legs and overused safety boots. [...] Perhaps it was because they looked tired and sleepy, but Homer could not help thinking that they appeared ill at ease. Maybe they were all foreigners, migrants functioning solely on the success stories they had been told of earlier migrants, enduring the thin comforts of this life with a fatalistic exhaustion, dreaming of their own success stories five years from now. Maybe they have already given up on themselves, Homer thought, their lives sucked dry, HHthinking instead of their children.

Even after Homer meets and marries a fellow Trinidadian, his dreams of security and self-possession seem as elusive as they had in Trinidad. To save money, Homer and his new wife move into the basement of her sister's Burlington home, where his strenuously Canadianized in-laws reduce their melodious names to monosyllables and derive all of their social significance from television talk shows. After his marriage breaks down, Homer moves into a decrepit Hamilton apartment house and, despite finally securing a satisfactory position as a school librarian, falls into a depression deepened by isolation and loneliness. The orderly suburbs he once admired from afar have managed simultaneously to trap and exclude him, and the social protocols remain impenetrable. Every interaction brands him as an outsider, but returning to Trinidad is unthinkable. Homer has no idea how to move forward, but it is far too late to go back.

Homer's sense of liminality is echoed in M. G. Vassanji's *No New Land*. But where Homer experiences crushing loneliness and social exclusion in suburbs he finds cold and uninviting, Vassanji's protagonists are buffered by a tightly knit cultural community that bolsters their efforts to make a place for themselves in the new country. In *No New Land*, the Lalani family joins an established community of Tanzanian ex-patriots living in a Don Mills high rise. Their address, 69 Rosecliffe Park Drive, has achieved legendary status among South Asians in East Africa mainly because its inhabitants have recreated their home city of Dar Es Salaam in the building's corridors and common spaces:

Sixty-nine Rosecliffe Park. The name still sounds romantic, exotic, out of a storybook or a film. Sometimes it's hard to believe you are here, at this address, sitting inside, thinking these thoughts. [...] But then you step out in the common corridor with its all too real down-to-earth sights, sounds, and smells, and you wonder: *This*, Sixty-nine Rosecliffe? And you realize that you've not left Dar far behind. "Twenty floors." Nurdin once did a small calculation for his wife. "Twelve homes in each—you have two hundred and forty families—that's three good-sized blocks of any street in Dar." Except that the variety found here at Sixty-nine would not be found in any street in Dar. Here a dozen races mingle, conversant in at least as many tongues.

Although the lobby doors at 69 Rosecliffe revolve continuously with departures to and arrivals from school or work, other residents are able to conduct vital commerce without ever leaving the building. Each floor has its speciality: on the sixth level, Gulshan Bai prepares tiffin for a steady stream of customers who carry her meals to work in plastic containers; on the fourteenth floor, Sheru Mama and her husband, Ramju, make chappatis in the traditional manner; there is even a halal butcher. It is possible to buy toiletries at all hours from an apartment on the ground floor, and a continuous open house operates on the eighteenth floor where residents play cards, drink tea and share gossip about Dar and the fates of their fellow emigrants. Encounters in the corridors confirm the presence of practitioners eager to dispense legal, medical or spiritual advice. Awash in familiar faces and routines, 69 Rosecliffe is a slice of sovereign soil transplanted halfway around the world, a vertical version of Dar that has just happened to take root in suburban Don Mills.

It is when the residents of 69 Rosecliffe step outside that they run into trouble. For their children it is easy to weave multiple identities into a tapestry of Canadian vernacular, hijab silk, university applications, Quran classes and games of street hockey. But their parents, making the immigrant sacrifice, despair that their own prospects are limited because they lack an acceptable accent and the ephemeral qualification called "Canadian experience." Still, the building at 69 Rosecliffe Park, and the weekly mosque held nearby at a school gymnasium on Eglinton Avenue, represent a start, a defensible beachhead in this improbable corner of Don Mills where Dar's exiles have made their new home.

As these four novels suggest, visible minorities seeking shelter in Toronto-area suburbs routinely encounter bigotry, poverty and cultural isolation. At the same time, however, even while underscoring the sort of deep-seated racism Jurca argues is endemic in suburban literature, the novels of Chariandy, Brand, Maharaj and Vassanji emphasize another reality: that Toronto-area suburbs are culturally far more diverse than broad-brush analyses of North American suburbia have typically accounted for. This is not to say that racial tensions do not exist, but rather that they are less a cause or consequence of "white flight" than a product of cultural conflicts analogous to those found within the inner city itself. The prototypical suburb—a white, middle-class bedroom community segregated from the inner city by race and income—is increasingly the exception in the Greater Toronto Area. There many suburban municipalities, including Vaughan, Markham and Mississauga, are culturally more diverse than the downtown core and "inner suburbs" like Scarborough[190] and Rexdale[191] attract large numbers of recent immigrants seeking affordable housing

190   See Pico Iyer's discussion of multicultural Scarborough in *The Global Soul* (2000).
191   In "Thirty Days in Jamestown" (*Toronto Life*, December 2006), Shaughnessy Bishop-Stall de-

and who work in mid-city industrial enclaves.[192] Even Don Mills, a community novelist Lawrence Hill describes in his memoir, *Black Berry, Sweet Juice*, as being so monoculturally white in the 1960s that he became conditioned to think of his black features as ugly,[193] has undergone a profound cultural shift as residents of Chinese, South Asian and Middle East origin have trickled into its perimeter while transforming the adjacent high-density inner suburban communities of Flemingdon and Thorncliffe Park.[194] As geographers Larry Bourne and Damaris Rose observe laconically in "The Changing Face of Canada," "diversity has suburbanized."

The extent to which Toronto's inner and outer suburbs have diversified is far more than a merely demographic measure, however. Diversity is also a quality of the imagination, marking the invisible moment when the urban narrative becomes truly representative of the lives lived within its orbit. Seeming to write in anticipation of this moment, in "Canada Geese and Apply Chatney" Sasenarine Persaud describes a Guyanese immigrant who wanders the sprawling parkland of Eglinton Flats in Weston, watching Canada geese gather before their long migration south for the winter. Inspired by hunger and recollections of home, Writerji enlists two friends who wring the necks of enough geese to fill the freezer of their Emmett Avenue apartment. A week later the trio visit friends whose Scarborough apartment overlooks Morningside Park. During their visit, Writerji disappears into the woodland surrounding Highland Creek and returns with a bounty of crabapples:

Next thing he coming back with he hand full a them small sour apple. He can't believe all them apple falling on the grass and wasting. People wasteful in Canada he muttering over and over. Writerji want help to pick some nice green apple on them tree. Why? He thinking just like how yuh use green mango, or bilimbi, or barahar to make achaar and chatney why not green apple. And right then mango scarce in Toronto, cost a fortune. Them days was not like nowadays when you gat West Indian store every corner. Them days you only get fruits from the West

scribes the racial and religious conflict and community that exists among the European, Caribbean and African residents of a public housing project in inner-suburban Rexdale.
192 Bourne and Rose, 2001; Murdie & Teixeira, 2003; Siemiatycki et al., 2003; Boudreau et al., 2009.
193 Among other works, Lawrence Hill is also the author of *Any Known Blood* (1997), a novel interrogating identity and racial politics in Toronto, Oakville and Philadelphia.
194 Although Don Mills "proper" (the distinctive four-quadrant 1950s development radiating outward from Lawrence Avenue and Don Mills Road) remains predominantly white, in 2006 nearly 40 percent of its residents self-identified as visible minorities. By contrast, 77 percent of Flemingdon Park's population consists of visible minorities, while almost 75 percent of Thorncliffe Park residents describe themselves as visible minorities (source: City of Toronto, Neighbourhood Profiles for Banbury-Don Mills, Flemingdon Park and Thorncliffe Park).

Indies when anybody coming. But that apple-chatney taste good with them geese we bring for Prem and Kishore.

For Writerji, cooked goose and apple chatney represent more than a meal: they are a confirmation that creativity and cunning will help carry him through the months of privation while "waiting for he name and number" in an immigration queue. They are also a cultural affirmation, a taste of the familiar in this foreign land. And what else is chutney, after all, but an idiosyncratic blend of ingredients meant to unify the disparate ingredients of a meal?

THE NEW TORONTONIANS

In *The Urban Experience*, geographer David Harvey reminds us that a city—and its suburbs—should be understood as a process rather than a thing. In this light, it is important to remember that Toronto's suburbs did not appear out of nowhere at mid-century, emerging all at once from the landscape like earthbound Leviathans. In his 1898 book, *Toronto the Good*, C. S. Clark wrote of the city's diurnal migration of suburbanites who "come down every morning to [do] business in crowds between the hours of seven and nine, and literally pour out of it between the hours of four and seven in the evening." The suburban commuters Clark refers to are mainly the wealthy inhabitants of Rosedale, Moore Park and the Annex, at the time still distinguished from the rest of the city by a combination of social class and legal jurisdiction.[195]

At the same time, however, working-class suburbs had also begun to make their muddy appearance in undeveloped areas west of the city. In *Unplanned Suburbs*, geographer Richard Harris traces the development of these communities, established through the subdivision of large landholdings into building lots purchased primarily by immigrants attracted to industrial jobs located along the Grand Trunk and Canadian Pacific rail lines. Some residents bought developer-built homes in rapidly growing industrial suburbs like the Town of West Toronto Junction[196] but many others settled in an area known as "the Shackland," a district of self-built homes and squatters' shanties centred on St. Clair in the Earlscourt area around Dufferin Street and extending west into the Junction.[197]

---

195 The City annexed Moore Park in 1910, and while the eponymous Annex had been absorbed by the City in a phased annexation beginning in 1883, its residents continued to think of themselves as distinct from the rest of the city, a conceit that arguably continues to the present day.
196 Fragmented histories of the Junction are told in *West Toronto Junction Revisited* (ed. Joan Miles and Diana Fancher; 4th edition, 1999) and *The Leader and Recorder History of the Junction* (ed. Diana Fancher, 2004).
197 See Harris, 1996; also Byers & Myrvold, 1999; and Solomon, 2007.

Set in 1909 just as the Junction, Carlton Village and Earlscourt areas were being incorporated into the City of Toronto, Judi Coburn's young adult novel *The Shacklands*, depicts the circumstances of a working-class family living in a tarpaper shack on Silverthorn Lane, subsequently developed into a real street located just east of St. Clair and Old Weston Road. Coburn evokes a community perched well beyond the edges of the city's established limits:

> Up on the heights the small black roofs crowded together at the crossroads. Along the edge of the wide empty ribbon of St. Clair Avenue, trees creaked and bent. The Avenue's straight east-west swath linked the isolated clusters of rooftops: those of the meat-packing plant and surrounding dwellings at the Keele crossroad to the west, those of the village of Carlton at Old Weston Road, the rooftops spreading in increasing numbers farther east across fields, to another cluster at the next crossroads—the Shacklands. No human illumination marked this country road, only the gleam of the rain beating down on its slick surface. But down over the edge of the escarpment, where the flats sloped gently to the lake, the densely roofed town of Toronto was outlined in a regular grid pattern by the yellow halos of streetlamps.

Far from the pastoral tranquility of turn-of-the-century suburban Rosedale or the smug insularity of the Annex during the same era, life in the Shacklands has less in common with contemporary images of suburbia than the wilderness conditions experienced by Susannah Moodie's protagonists in her 1852 classic, *Roughing It in the Bush*. Coburn writes:

> [A]lthough the Robertsons' new home was for now just a tiny shack, the family had been warmly welcomed by the Dixons, who owned a small store on Silverthorn Lane just up the road from the Robertsons' home. The Dixon store prospered, and in the summer its verandah and yard bustled with activity from early morning until late in the evening. [...] Neighbours often came to buy provisions and stopped to chat. Behind the house big washtubs with washing boards stood outside on a trestle table; a squat potbellied stove with a stovepipe rising up into the air heated water nearby, and a couple of clotheslines stretched out to the edge of the clearing. The Dixons' pump supplied the water for several houses, and the women would congregate to do their washing. [...] The Robertsons' shack was farther north on the lane just before the land rose steeply to a heavily wooded ridge of land known as "The Bush."

If this sketch of the Shacklands seems incongruous with popular representations of suburbia, her description of the interior of the Robertsons' shack, viewed from its doorway as the bereaved family returns home from their mother's burial in Prospect Cemetery, undoes the image entirely:

The plank walls of their one-room dwelling seemed to have moved closer together in their absence. The table stood in the middle of the room covered with a checked tablecloth and upon it, the oil lamp. Behind, against the back wall, sat the large stove, which served as both heater and cooker. The children tried hard not to look at the curtained-off bed in the back corner where their mother had died. In the other back corner, below the small window, was a washing-up counter, where a few dishes had been left to dry beside the metal wash basin. [...] Against the side wall was a day bed that pulled out for Ned and Thomas to sleep in at night. They had to nail newspapers to the wall behind when cold October winds sent icy drafts through the cracks.

Like many Shacklands families, the Robertsons endure a frigid winter in their shanty before building a solid two-story frame house on their lot the following spring. Although few Shacklands residents are trained carpenters, they work together with neighbours, gradually transforming the rough and rutted landscape into a recognizable residential suburb.

Working-class suburbs were not only a phenomenon of the early part of the century. An acute housing shortage and a surge in European immigration following World War II spurred new growth on the city's outskirts well before incorporated subdivisions like Don Mills, marketed to the middle class, came to dominate the suburban landscape.[198] In *The Suburban Society*, a study of urban change in mid-century Toronto, sociologist Samuel Clark described the bulk of suburban residents as "people in impoverished circumstances prepared to accept whatever the country had to offer them." In many cases what these residents—many of whom were war veterans or refugees—were prepared to accept were unserviced, undeveloped building lots available for a few hundred dollars. In *Pioneering in North York*, historian Patricia Hart refers to these suburbanites as "the New Pioneers," writing that

many bought land and started to build their own houses. They dug basements, covered them over, then paused to regroup their finances, and as the idea became known, others followed suit. They were somewhat derisively called "cave dwellers." Slowly, these houses have been finished, sometimes after a nudge from the municipal authorities, but for a number of years "cave dwellers" walked daily to a pump near the centre of the community for water.

In his 1997 collection of linked stories, *Buying on Time*, Antanas Sileika describes a family from Lithuania, displaced by the ravages of World War II, who buy a building lot in an undeveloped corner of Weston:

198 See Harris, 1996; Solomon, 2007.

Our street had half a dozen other houses on it, but none of them were finished. People dug the foundations and laid the basement blocks. Then they waited and saved. When a little money came in, they bought beams and joists and studs. Then they waited some more. The Taylors stood out because a contractor had built their house from start to finish. We stood out too. We moved in before the above-ground walls went up.

"You want us to live underground?" my mother had asked. "Like moles? Like worms?"

"No," my father said, "like foxes."

For the children, it is easier to accept living underground as "normal," given that the skeletal house offers the first prospect of stability they have known in their lives. As Sileika's young narrator observes,

It was true that others lived in houses that were already built, while we lived in the basement as the house was being raised above us. But normal houses belonged to that other race of people, Canadians, who wore suits to work. Before the basement, we had lived in a rented wooden shack on the edge of a farm. Before that there had been the DP camp in Germany, which I couldn't remember much, except for all the bomb craters filled with water where the children fished hopelessly all day.

Months later, when the shell of the house is complete, the family moves above ground and settles into its newly painted rooms. They begin to feel smug about their suburban surroundings:

Not for us the dark houses of the city on tree-lined streets, where there were no driveways and the wretchedly small windows left the interiors in perpetual gloom. We had large picture windows in the living rooms, and on the smaller windows of our bedrooms were curtains with pictures of cowboys on bucking horses.

Their sense of arrival grows nearly complete when a Canadian family moves into a tarpaper shack down the street, cramming nine children into a tattered dwelling with an outhouse and rutted yard. "Now that our outhouse was gone," Sileika's narrator reflects, "we had someone *we* could look down on."

By the 1950s, the period in which Sileika's stories are set, Toronto's suburban landscape was shifting toward the middle-class mould that has dominated the popular imagination ever since its first appearance along the curvilinear streets of Don Mills. No other novel has captured this transitional moment better than Phyllis Brett Young's *The Torontonians*, which brings to full circle the tensions between the city and the layered landscapes of its suburbs. *The Torontonians* is not only one of Canada's first suburban novels[199] but is also an early example of the sort of suburban satire subsequently popularized in American novels like Don DeLillo's *White Noise* and television shows like *Desperate Housewives*. Reportedly the first novel to feature Viljo Revell's City Hall on its cover,[200] *The Torontonians* exposes the conceits and preoccupations of a city believing itself to be perched at the very edge of modernity. The novel depicts four populations dwelling (then as now) in uneasy coexistence: the staid Toryish urban establishment of the Annex and Forest Hill; the ambitiously modern movers and shakers of the downtown core; the voracious materialists of its sprawling suburbs; and, making room among themselves in the interstices of the city, the "New Canadians" beginning their own transformations of Toronto.

A study in contrasts, *The Torontonians* suggests that in 1960 Toronto was a far more complex and contested city than contemporary representations imply. Regularly recalled as a flat and featureless Anglo-Saxon landscape where you couldn't watch a film or get a drink on Sunday,[201] at the same time Toronto seethed with race, class and gender divisions roiling just beneath the surface of a city whose cultural terrain was shifting as inexorably as the price of a cocktail at the Park Plaza Hotel. The novel's principal tension, however, is the cultural divide between the city core and its rapidly growing suburbs; its subtext is the question of whether they reflect two different, perhaps opposed, ways of life.

Although the city portrayed in *The Torontonians* is predominantly Anglo-Saxon, by 1960 a third of Toronto's population consisted of foreign-born immigrants. In the novel these "New Canadians" are the perennial beneficiaries

199 When *The Torontonians* was first published in 1960, an unhappy local reviewer wrote, "Don Quixote tilted at windmills, Phyllis Brett Young tilts at the sacred cows of suburbia, poking fun at the ranch-type bungalow, the bigger and better electrical appliances, the strange tribal customs of the natives such as the barbecue and the "inverted snobbery [which] dictated that servants did not belong to the Good Life." The reviewer went on to insist that Young's suburban satire "fails dismally" because of its "stock characters" and "slick dialogue" and its apparent "nostalgia...for the Toronto of Rosedale" (Joan Walker, 1960. "She Ridicules Suburbanites," *Globe & Mail*, 22 October 1960). Despite the reviewer's objections, and despite critic Robert Fulford's dismissal of the novel as "strictly from *Ladies' Home Journal*" ("Lament for a Dead Toronto," *Toronto Star*, 25 October 1960), *The Torontonians* was an international bestseller, released subsequently in the U.K. as *The Commuters* and in the U.S. as *Gift of Time*. *The Torontonians* was reissued in 2007 by McGill-Queen's University Press.
200 Although Toronto landmarks figure regularly in the cover artwork of literary works engaging with Toronto, Viljo Revell's City Hall appears on the cover of only a few works, among them Phyllis Brett Young's *The Torontonians*, published before construction had begun on the already-famous design. City Hall also appears on the cover of Rosemary Aubert's Harlequin Romance novel *Firebrand*, whose plot revolves around a municipal librarian's love affair with the mayor.
201 See, for example, Margaret Atwood's 1982 profile of Toronto, "The City Rediscovered," published in the *New York Times*, in which she describes mid-century Toronto as a place "where you lived when you weren't having fun."

of charitable bridge tournaments held in the manicured salons of suburban Rowanwood,[202] whose population consists mainly of wealthy businessmen and their wives who have migrated north in search of the "Good Life" where everybody, as one housewife puts it in the novel, "should live in ranch-style bungalows and be just like themselves."

If *The Torontonians* satirizes mid-century Rowanwood for its homogeneity, it is worth noting that cultural commentators worry that many of Toronto's contemporary suburbs—such as Markham with its large Chinese population, Brampton with its concentration of South Asians and the preponderance of Italian neighbourhoods in Woodbridge—are at risk of developing into ethnic enclaves as insular and homogenous as Rowanwood. But just as these contemporary suburbs are far more open than the census records might suggest, even Rowanwood is more diverse than it appears. A neighbourhood housewife takes as a lover a Polish count (or so he tells her) fallen upon hard times. The neighbourhood's most powerful businessman conceals the secret of his slum upbringing. A single mother is quietly subsidized by a neighbour. It turns out that much of Rowanwood is busy concealing facets of difference in order to compete for the dubious rewards of middle-class consumption.

Perhaps this is why the novel's protagonist finds herself drawn to the city spread out below Rowanwood, musing that "It was only below the Hill that you came into direct contact with the core of vitality that was the true essence of the city," and adding, "Here you were acutely and excitingly aware of the steady heart-beat of a really great metropolis, fresh blood continuously pumped into it from the four corners of the globe." Chafing at the banality of a materialist existence that has reduced her to a consumer of Cuisinarts, carpets and backyard cookouts, and desperate and bored while her husband commutes downtown to work in the city's corporate canyons, Karen seeks to diagnose precisely what is wrong with suburbia, describing it as "an impossible compromise" between city and countryside. She concludes that suburbia is an "evolutionary cul-de-sac," and adds:

> A city with a future, like an individual with a future, could never remain static for long, could not afford to expand indefinitely along the lines of least resistance. The suburbs, as they now existed, were the city's lines of least resistance. The towering buildings to the south were the real yardstick of its stature.

But rejecting suburbia requires confronting the harsh social and economic realities of life in the city below the Hill. Karen realizes that the "towering

---

202   Rowanwood is a fictionalized version of the approximate area where Moore Park and Leaside intersect. Jane Pitfield's *Leaside* (2nd edition, 2000) is a useful complement to Young's novel.

buildings" of the downtown core loom above the long-standing slums of the Ward and the city's first Chinatown, even then being cleared for the construction of the new City Hall and an adjacent collection of commercial towers. She discovers that her best friend's husband, now one of the city's most powerful executives and a Rowanwood neighbour, had grown up in one of those same slums. Stumbling out into the downtown sunlight after this stunning revelation, Karen sees Toronto's polyglot mix of cultures reflected in the city's "uneven stratification of brick and granite record[ing] more than a hundred and fifty years of architectural trial and error." Walking north along Yonge Street, she revels as if for the first time in the "vivid turbulence" of the city's diversity unfolding all around her.

Reading *The Torontonians* half a century after it was first published, one is of course struck by the city it omits: the CN Tower not yet even a figment in the city's imagination, the genuine cultural diversity that in 1960 has yet to appear, the astonishing sprawl that has turned Leaside from a suburb into midtown.

But one is struck even more by the similarities. Toronto remains divided between north and south, although current demographic data confirm that the immigrants who comprise nearly half the city's population are more likely to occupy the inner and outer suburbs, while the chattering classes have pushed their way back into the city beneath the Hill, retaking old territory in the Annex and Parkdale. In the downtown core, land developers and ambitious politicians seek to remake the city in their own image. In short, read not simply as a novel but as social commentary on the city and its suburbs, *The Torontonians* offers a fresh perspective on the conceits and preoccupations of a city that still believes itself to be perched at the very edge of modernity.

– 8 –

IMAGINING TORONTO

IMAGINING TORONTO

> So give me time   i want
> i want to know
> all your squares & cloverleafs
> [...]
> i can hear your beat-
> ing centre   will i
> will i make it
> are there maps of you
> i keep circlingimagining
> parks fountains   your stores
> back in my single bed i wander
> your stranger dreaming
> i am your citizen

Earle Birney, "I Think You Are a Real City"

This book began as an invitation to develop a new undergraduate course for the Department of Geography at York University, where I teach and conduct research on urban identity and the cultural significance of place. While putting together the syllabus for what became, in 2006, the Imagining Toronto course, I thought it might be possible to identify a dozen Toronto novels and at least as many poems; just enough literary material, in other words, to sustain twelve weeks of study. It did not occur to me that there would be much more—that there was more to the city's literature, in fact, than anyone had ever estimated.

Like many readers, I was already familiar with the "Toronto canon," a short list of literary works—among them Hugh Garner's *Cabbagetown*, Margaret Atwood's half-dozen Toronto novels, Dennis Lee's *Civil Elegies*, Michael Ondaatje's *In the Skin of a Lion* and Anne Michaels' *Fugitive Pieces*—that have won enough awards, sold enough copies or been adopted in enough undergraduate university courses to remain profitably in print. Browsing my library shelves, however, I began to notice many other equally prominent Canadian novels set partly or entirely in Toronto, including Morley Callaghan's *Strange Fugitive*, Mordecai Richler's *The Incomparable Atuk*, Robertson Davies' *The Rebel Angels*, Neil Bissoondath's *A Casual Brutality* and Timothy Findley's *Headhunter*. I discovered, moreover, that I had copies of four anthologies of Toronto stories: William Kilbourn's *The Toronto Book*, Morris Wolfe and Douglas Daymond's *Toronto Short Stories*, Cary Fagan's *Streets of Attitude* and Barry

Callaghan's *This Ain't No Healing Town.* By this time I had begun to pick up small press novels and poetry chapbooks at used bookshops and garage sales, and the vivid representations of Toronto in three such works—Basil Papadimos's *The Hook of It Is,* Maggie Helwig's *Talking Prophet Blues* and Richard Scrimger's *Crosstown*—supported my growing sense that far more Toronto literature existed than was widely acknowledged.

I began to amass my own library of Toronto literature. I haunted used bookstores, moiling methodically in their shelves for books that looked as if they might be set in Toronto. I typed "Toronto" into the electronic databases of online booksellers and was delighted to discover scores of novels, short-fiction anthologies and poetry collections engaging in some way with the city. I trolled the city's libraries on the prowl for out-of-print volumes, my fingers tracing patterns shaped like skylines on the dusty shelves. I scoured publishers' backlists, scanned the archives of literary journals and searched through decades of book reviews published in Canadian newspapers and magazines. Poring over the thirty-five-year history of the Toronto Book Awards[203] produced a reading list that kept me busy for months. Friends, colleagues and complete strangers contacted me to recommend books they had read or written. My study, a converted sunroom at the back of our home, began to sag visibly under the weight of the hundreds and then thousands of Toronto books I stuffed into its jury-rigged shelves. I created an online inventory of Toronto literature[204] and have received so many suggested additions it is difficult to keep up to date. And still, even after the extensive research that has resulted in this book, every time I pick up an unfamiliar Toronto novel at a book sale or receive another invitation to a poetry launch, I am struck with the simultaneously exhilarating and terrifying sense that I am merely scratching at the surface of the city's literature.

At this point it must surely be apparent that claims Toronto lacks its own literature are patently untrue. The hundreds of books discussed in the preceding chapters—representing only a sampling of the enormous volume of literature engaging with the city—provide ample evidence that Toronto is richly imagined. The range, diversity and quality of the works discussed in this book should also go a long way toward defeating critics who insist that Toronto literature cannot possibly measure up to writing produced elsewhere. Given that literary works set in Toronto regularly win prestigious national and inter-

---

203   Established in 1974, the Toronto Book Awards honour "authors of books of literary or artistic merit that are evocative of Toronto." The awards are given annually, and a complete list of finalists and winners is available online at http://www.toronto.ca/book_awards/.

204   The Imagining Toronto Library, an electronic inventory of literary works engaging with Toronto, is available online at http://www.imaginingtoronto.com.

national literary awards[205] and are popular globally in English and translated editions, denying their significance seems absurd. The preceding chapters have attempted to show how literature gives Toronto a sense of its shape and identity. They have argued, variously, that the ravines are the repository of the city's memory, that we derive much of our identity from belonging to neighbourhoods, that our faith in multiculturalism is a kind of creation myth, that rifts across culture, class and gender rupture and reform the city's moral terrain, that "desire lines" link us despite our social and sexual differences, and that the suburbs tell us more about the city's origins and ambitions than we might have guessed. If Toronto is truly to know itself, to appreciate its origins, to understand its challenges and aspirations and to gain a solid sense of identity, then it must learn to value its own stories. As John Bentley Mays writes in *Emerald City*,

> Living fully and mindfully anyplace, I believe, involves giving thought to all the rhythms we move within—the personal ones, from birth to death, but also the historical ones, preserved and recalled by the artifacts of architecture and urban planning, art and writing and music.

Robert Fulford makes a similar point in *Accidental City: The Transformation of Toronto*:

> A successful city fulfills itself not by master plans, but through an attentiveness to the processes that have created it and an awareness of its possibilities. It achieves a heightened identity by giving form to memory and providing space for new life.

Mays' and Fulford's comments bring us back to the place this book began, with Michael Ondaatje's suggestion that before the real city could be seen it

---

205 Conspiracy theories (duly noted in the first chapter) aside, Toronto books regularly win prestigious national and international literary awards. Michael Redhill's Toronto novel, *Consolation*, was longlisted for the 2007 Man Booker Prize; Margaret Atwood won the Man Booker prize in 2000 for *The Blind Assassin*, and has been shortlisted for the Booker three times. Toronto books that have won Governor General's Awards include John Hayes' *Rebels Ride at Night* (1953), Hugh Garner's *Best Stories* (1963), Raymond Souster's *The Colour of the Times* (1964), Margaret Atwood's *The Circle Game* (1966), Dennis Lee's *Civil Elegies* (1972), Josef Skvorecky's *The Engineer of Human Souls* (1984), Gwendolyn MacEwen's *Afterworlds* (1987), Nino Ricci's *Lives of the Saints* (1990), Rosemary Sullivan's *Shadow Maker* (1995), Dionne Brand's *Land to Light On* (1997), Richard Wright's *Clara Callan* (2001), David Gilmour's *A Perfect Night to Go to China* (2005), Karolyn Smardz Frost's *I've Got a Home in Glory Land* (2007) and Jacob Scheier's *More to Keep Us Warm* (2008). Scotiabank Giller Prize winners include Vincent Lam, for *Bloodletting & Miraculous Cures* (2006), and Joseph Boyden, for *Through Black Spruce* (2008). Literary works engaging with Toronto have also won or been shortlisted for the Trillium Book Award, the Griffin Poetry Prize and the Commonwealth Writers' Prize.

had to be imagined, and Jonathan Raban's observation that the imagined city is as real as the city we can find on any map.

For nearly half a century literary critics have remained preoccupied with Northrop Frye's claim that the principal riddle of cultural identity in Canada is not "Who am I?" but rather "Where is here?" But in what even Frye predicted would be a post-national age, it seems more urgent than ever to ask "Who are we?" and "What—if anything—do we believe in?" That these are no longer national questions but instead local ones is borne out by Dennis Lee, who in *Civil Elegies* laments Torontonians' ignorance of our history—including the unfulfilled promise of the 1837 Rebellion—writing that "in the city I long for men complete / their origins" before deploring

> that not
> one countryman has learned, that
> men and women live that
> they may make that
> life worth dying.

George Jonas responds directly to Lee in "City Elegy," writing,

> yes: it is not
> skyscrapers subways green belts
> theatres neighbourhoods children
> but war that forges a city and no city
> lives that has not lived through war

My husband, who was born behind the Iron Curtain and grew up in the Middle East before coming to Toronto in his teens, likes to tell people that being Canadian means having nothing to declare. His concern is that living in a soft-spoken and materially wealthy city dulls Torontonians to the need to have opinions about anything other than the state of the housing market or the playoff prospects of the Toronto Maple Leafs. But if having nothing to declare is one of Toronto's shortcomings, in some ways it is also a virtue, particularly for those who have come here because they are tired of living in places where people have far too much to declare. In this sense, Toronto *is* a city that has lived through war, and if we have been slow to assert our identity and cautious about claiming ideological authority it is we are first committed to the task of figuring out the scope—and the limits—of tolerance. This task is an urgent one, particularly in a city like Toronto where we are thrown together by collisions of history that have left us lacking shared traditions or a common cultural language. If we are to learn to live together—or discover, in an era of escalating international conflict, whether we can do so at all—we must be able to listen to one another speak. We need to pay attention to the city's stories because we, too, are part of the narrative. We engage actively in imagining Toronto whenever we move through its streets and experience how boring, bigoted, violent, ugly, peaceful, powerful, glittering and beautiful it is.

Toronto's reputation as a dull city—a city where, as Bert Archer once claimed, no one lives in the imagination—is deceptive. In a 1954 essay called "How Can a Writer Live in Toronto?" Morley Callaghan described Toronto's reputed parochialism as a "necessary illusion" that stimulates the literary imagination:

> I come now to my acceptance of the reality of my life in Toronto. I walk around the streets, I go from house to house, nursing my necessary illusion that the orderly life of the place and the simple friendliness of the people is a discipline for me. I deceive myself into thinking that I live a monastic life, but that like a monk in his cell in the long night, my imagination may be stretched and strained and fired and make for me the stuff of exalted dreams.

It is the desire for drama, Callaghan continues, that awakens the writer's muse; the unfulfilled longing for experiences larger than life. He concludes, finally, that

> [i]f you stay in Toronto, the longing remains deep in the soul, and since it can't be satisfied you can't be wearied, and your mind and your imagination, should become like a caged tiger. O Toronto! O my tiger city!

Callaghan's prescription applies even more powerfully today in a city populated increasingly by exiles, marooned here by war or economic circumstances, who write potently of displacement and the longing for home. It suggests, further, that coming to terms with Toronto, however we may experience or perceive it, is not only one of the city's greatest challenges but may well be one of its most meaningful opportunities. As we negotiate our identity through literature, we learn to appreciate the densely interwoven panoply of stories we tell about ourselves and one another, and in doing so we begin to recognize and fill gaps in the city's narrative, because as the city changes, its stories must change too.

In an article tracing the shifting demographics among Toronto's cultural producers, Philip Marchand wrote once about the emerging generation of authors he hoped would produce "startling novels about Jamaican gang warfare in Toronto or the conflict between the God of Islam and the hedonism of techno clubs on Queen St." While analogous literary terrain has already been surveyed,[206] Toronto remains a city practically pulsating with stories not yet told. Toronto has produced no novels, for example, engaging with Rexdale's expanding Somali community and only one set among Malvern's Tamils.[207] Apart from Richard Scrimger's Scarborough coming-of-age novel, *Into the Ravine*, there are few *bildungsromans* set in the city's contemporary suburbs, although *Scarborough Stories*, playwright Catherine Hernandez's work-in-progress, seems poised to change this dynamic.[208] While preoccupations with race, class and gender are recurring themes in Toronto literature, many emerging stories—of economic migrants living underground to avoid deportation,[209] of entire families sharing single motel rooms because historically high rents have pushed them out of their homes,[210] of sex workers taking the struggle for statutory protection from the street to the Supreme Court of Canada[211]—have not yet made the leap from newspaper headlines to novel ideas. Wild creatures, including falcons, feral cats, raccoons, deer, coyotes, opossums and the occasional black bear, have reinhabited Toronto in numbers in recent years but remain nearly invisible in the city's literature. Finally, Toronto's new social and civic spaces—among them the Pacific Mall, Yonge-Dundas Square, Gerrard India Bazaar, the Don Valley Brickworks and the rehabilitated lower Don—have become integral to the city's character but have only begun to make their appearance in print. Still, it is clear that over time these new stories cannot help but infuse themselves into the city's story. We need only be prepared to listen.

In "Toronto: A City in Our Image," a 2005 essay anticipating his return to Toronto after several years spent making films and producing a radio show in Paris, writer Erik Rutherford mused, "I feel that life will be better in Toronto, not because I have better friends or a better job there, but because the city itself will allow things to happen." Describing Paris as an impenetrable, polished jewel, a place that has been reduced to a pastiche of itself because everything is already a metaphor for something else—a city that is, in short, history—Rutherford goes on to argue that Toronto, nascent, incomplete, forgetful of its beginnings—a city wide open, not only to the future, but to inter-

---

206 See, for example, Deborah Ellis and Eric Walters' *Bifocal*, Mobashar Quereshi's *R.A.C.E.*, Austin Clarke's *More*, Andrew Moodie's play *Toronto the Good* and M. G. Vassanji's *No New Land*.
207 See V. V. Ganeshananthan's *Love Marriage* (2008).
208 See Sarah B. Hood's review of *Scarborough Stories*, "She needn't Bluff about her locale," *National Post*, 31 May 2008.
209 "Illegal immigrants tell tales of their lives in the shadows," *Toronto Star*, 2 September 2003.
210 "We have absolutely nothing," *Toronto Star*, 7 September 2009.
211 "Sex workers set to launch landmark challenge," *Toronto Star*, 5 October 2009.

pretation—is "conducive to self-realization, brimming with opportunities to mould its malleable stuff in our own image." Rutherford's comments echo the words of poet Corrado Paina, who writes of Toronto in "Embrace the Walls" that "We are unfinished humans / in an unfinished city."

Four years before being named the city's third poet laureate, Dionne Brand observed of Toronto that "the literature is still catching up with the city, with its new stories." Brand's own work has explored some of these new stories: her Toronto Book Award–winning novel, *What We All Long For*, features as protagonists a group of young men and women representing the contemporary face of Toronto and breaks new ground, too, by culminating in the sprawling suburb of Richmond Hill. Her Griffin Poetry Prize–shortlisted *Thirsty* describes Toronto—"the city that's never happened before"—as a concatenation of "impossible citizens" heaved into one another, as if the entire city was a single overcrowded bus hurtling along Dufferin Street on a weekday morning shortly after dawn. On the occasion of her appointment as poet laureate in 2009, Brand spoke of the hard love she has for Toronto, quoting from *Thirsty* to characterize Toronto as a place

> where nothing is simple,
> nothing, in the city there is no simple love
> or simple fidelity

In Toronto our fidelity is complicated by forgetfulness, by simultaneously destructive and aggrandizing urges, by cultural insularity, civic envy and a collective fear of failing to measure up to some external measure of what a city is supposed to represent. But it is a fidelity all the same, and in it we discover our capacity for tolerance, accommodation and the hard love that foregrounds our narratives of life in this city.

During the five years I have spent researching Toronto literature and the three years it has taken to write this book, my own fidelity has grown increasingly complicated. For much of this period I viewed the city's stories historically or through the lens of their representations of the contemporary city. But after my daughter was born, I began to think much more concertedly about the city that has yet to unfold.

My daughter is a city child, born into a landscape of gleaming high rises, graffiti-stained alleys and verdant ravines. Her reference points are urban ones: streetcars and subway trains, stray cats, conniving raccoons, recycling trucks, jackhammers, concrete wading pools and the cadence of strangers in constant motion around her. Like most Toronto children, she is already coming to terms with the consequences of her hybrid heritage—a mix of my Aboriginal and Anglo-Saxon ancestry and my husband's Romanian and Middle Eastern background—as part of the long process of deciding who she will become. In important ways her life has already been shaped by this city, and so naturally she has been introduced to its stories, beginning with Dennis Lee's classic *Alligator Pie* and Allan Moak's *A Big City ABC*. Her bedroom bookshelves are well stocked with books to grow on, and together we read a new one almost every night.

In truth, though, these stories are for us more than they are for her: like all children she was born knowing exactly where the real and the imagined city meet. We are the ones who must remember how to make our way back to the city within the city, the city at the centre of the map.

ACKNOWLEDGEMENTS

I am exceedingly grateful to the following individuals and organizations for encouraging and supporting the Imagining Toronto project from its inception to the appearance of this book:

The staff, students and faculty of the Geography Department at York University deserve many thanks for sustaining the creative and collegial environment that has helped nurture the Imagining Toronto project. I am particularly grateful to Karen Cunningham for inviting the course proposal that turned into this book.

Thank you to *Spacing Magazine*, *Open Book Toronto*, Reading Toronto, the *Toronto Star*, *Eye Weekly*, Coach House Books' *uTOpia* series, CBC Radio One, the Goethe-Institut Toronto, the Festival of Architecture & Design, Walk21, the Osgoode Constitutional Roundtable, Jane's Walk and Doors Open Toronto, where many of the ideas appearing here were published or presented in an earlier form.

I am deeply grateful to Denis De Klerck for inviting me to write for Mansfield Press, and to Stuart Ross for his many gifts as a poet, editor, literary resource and friend.

I acknowledge with considerable appreciation the support of the Toronto Arts Council and the Ontario Arts Council in the form of literary grants supporting the completion of this work.

Above all, I am grateful to my husband, Peter Fruchter, for solidarity and perspective, and to our daughter, Katherine Aurora—the living embodiment of her name, which means "pure light."

SOURCES

Adam, Graeme Mercer and Ethelwyn Wetherald, 1887. *An Algonquin Maiden: A Romance of the Early Days of Upper Canada.* Montreal: John Lovell & Son; Toronto: Williamson & Company.

Adams, Mary Louise, 1994. Almost Anything can Happen: A Search for Sexual Discourse in the Urban Spaces of 1940s Toronto. *Canadian Journal of Sociology,* 19(2): 217-232.

Akler, Howard, 2005. *The City Man.* Toronto: Coach House.

Allen, John, 2001. *How the Other Half Lives: representations of Homelessness in American Literature.* Unpublished PhD dissertation. Milwaukee, WI: Department of English, University of Wisconsin-Milwaukee.

Anderson, Gordon Stewart, 2006. *The Toronto You Are Leaving.* Toronto: Untroubled Heart.

Anisef, Paul and Michael Lanphier, eds., 2003. *The World in a City.* Toronto: University of Toronto Press.

Ali, Ansara, 1992. *The Sacred Adventures of a Taxi Driver.* London, Ontario: Third Eye.

Alland, Sandra, 2004. *Proof of a Tongue.* Toronto: McGilligan Books.

Archer, Bert, 2005. 'Making a Toronto of the Imagination." In *uTOpia: towards a New Toronto,* eds. McBride, Jason and Alana Wilcox. Toronto: Coach House: 220-228.

Armstrong, Kelley, 2006. *Broken.* Toronto: Random House Canada.

Armstrong, Kelley, 2001. *Bitten.* Toronto: Random House of Canada.

Arnason, David and Mhari Mackintosh, 2005. *The Imagined City: A Literary History of Winnipeg.* Winnipeg: Turnstone Press.

Arthur, Eric [revised by Stephen A. Otto], 2003. *Toronto: No Mean City.* 3rd ed, revised. Toronto: University of Toronto Press.

Atwood, Margaret, 1969. *The Edible Woman.* Toronto: McClelland & Stewart.

Atwood, Margaret, 1972. *Survival.* Toronto: Anansi.

Atwood, Margaret, 1976. *Lady Oracle.* Toronto: McClelland & Stewart.

Atwood, Margaret, 1977. *"Giving Birth."* In Dancing Girls & Other Stories. Toronto: McClelland & Stewart.

Atwood, Margaret, 1979. *Life Before Man.* Toronto: McClelland & Stewart.

Atwood, Margaret, 8 August 1982. "The City Rediscovered." *New York Times.*

Atwood, Margaret, 1988. *Cat's Eye.* Toronto: McClelland & Stewart.

Atwood, Margaret, [1993] 1994. *The Robber Bride.* Toronto: Seal.

Atwood, Margaret, 2000. *The Blind Assassin.* Toronto: McClelland & Stewart.

Aubert, Rosemary, 1985. *Firebrand.* Toronto: Harlequin.

Aubert, Rosemary, 1997. *Free Reign.* New York: Bridge Works Publishing.

Aveni, Anthony, 2008. Bringing the Sky Down to Earth. *History Today,* 58(6): 14-21.

Bachelard, Gaston, trans. Maria Jolas [1964] 1994. *The Poetics of Space.* Boston: Beacon Press.

Backhouse, Constance and Nancy L. Backhouse, 2005. *The Heiress vs. the Establishment: Mrs. Campbell's Campaign for Legal Justice.* Vancouver: University of British Columbia Press.

Bain, Alison L., 2003. Constructing Contemporary Artistic Identities in Toronto Neighbourhoods. *The Canadian Geographer*, 47(3): 303-317.

Baraness, Marc and Larry Richards, 1992. *Toronto Places: A Context for Urban Design*. Toronto: University of Toronto Press.

Barclay, Linwood, 2004. *Bad Move*. New York: Bantam.

Bartley, Jim, 1993. *Stephen & Mr. Wilde*. Winnipeg: Blizzard Publishing.

Baskerville, Peter and Eric W. Sager, 1998. *Unwilling Idlers: The Urban Unemployed and their Families in Late Victorian Canada*. Toronto: University of Toronto Press.

Batten, Jack, 2004. *The Annex: The Story of a Toronto Neighbourhood*. Erin, ON: Boston Mills Press.

Baraness, Marc and Larry Richards, eds., 1992. *Toronto Places: A Context for Urban Design*. Toronto: University of Toronto Press for the City of Toronto.

Barr, Robert, November 1899. "Literature in Canada, Part One." *The Canadian Magazine*, XIV, 1: 3-7.

Barr, Robert, November 1899. "Literature in Canada, Part Two." *The Canadian Magazine*, XIV, 2: 130-136.

Barr, Robert, [1907] 1973. *The Measure of the Rule*. Toronto: University of Toronto Press.

Barthes, Roland, 1986. "Semiology and the Urban." In *The City and the Sign: An Introduction to Urban Semiotics*, ed. Mark Gottdiener and Alexandros Lagopoulos. New York: Colombia University Press, 87-98.

Barton, John and Billeh Nickerson, eds., 2007. *Seminal: The Anthology of Canada's Gay Male Poets*. Vancouver: Arsenal Pulp Press.

Baute, Nicole, 26 December 2008. "Our Lost Greenwich Village," *Toronto Star*, p. A19

Bell, Margaret, July 1913. "Toronto's Melting Pot." *The Canadian Magazine of Politics, Science, Art and Literature*, vol. XLI: 234-242.

Benjamin, Walter [ed. Rolf Tiedemann; trans. Howard Eiland and Kevin McLaughlin], 2002. *The Arcades Project*. Cambridge, MA: Harvard University Press / Belknap.

Berardi, Franco [trans Francesca Cadel & Mecchia Guiseppina], 2009. *The Soul at Work: From Alienation to Autonomy*. Los Angeles: Semiotext(e).

Berchem, F.R., 1977. *The Yonge Street Story: 1793-1860*. Toronto: McGraw-Hill Ryerson.

Bercuson, David Jay, 1990. *Confrontation at Winnipeg: Labour, Industrial Relations, and the General Strike*. Montreal; Kingston: McGill-Queen's University Press.

Berry, Michelle, 2005. *Blind Crescent*. Toronto: Penguin.

Berton, Pierre, 1961. *The New City: A Prejudiced View of Toronto*. Toronto: MacMillan.

Betts, Gregory, ed., 2007. *Lawren Harris in the Ward: His Urban Poetry and Paintings*. Toronto: Exile Editions.

Bezmozgis, David, 2004. *Natasha and Other Stories*. Toronto: Harper Collins Canada.

Bhabha, Homi, [1994] 2004. *The Location of Culture*. London; New York: Routledge Classics.

Bhaggiyadatta, Krisantha Sri, 1981. *Domestic Bliss*. Toronto: Is Five Press.

Big Rude Jake, 1996. *"Cold Steel Hammer."* From Blue Pariah. Toronto: Big Rude Records.

Birney, Earle, 1955. *Down the Long Table*. Toronto: McClelland & Stewart.

Birney, Earle, 1971. *Rag & Bone Shop*. Toronto: McClelland & Stewart.

Birney, Earle, 1977. *Ghost in the Wheels: The Selected Poems of Earle Birney*. Toronto: McClelland & Stewart.

Bishop, Dorothy, 1970. "The Story of John Mitchell." In *The Yellow Briar*, Patrick Slater. Toronto: Macmillan of Canada, 1-44.

Bishop-Stall, Shaughnessy, 2004. *Down to This: Squalor and Splendour in a Big-City Shantytown*. Toronto: Random House Canada.

Bishop-Stall, Shaughnessy, December 2006. Thirty Days in Jamestown. *Toronto Life*, 40(12): 70-80.

Bissell, Claude, 1981. *The Young Vincent Massey*. Toronto: University of Toronto Press.

Bissell, Claude, 1986. *The Imperial Canadian: Vincent Massey in Office*. Toronto: University of Toronto Press.

Bissoondath, Neil, [1988] 1989. *A Casual Brutality*. Toronto: Penguin.

Bissoondath, Neil, 1994: *Selling Illusions: The Cult of Multiculturalism in Canada*. Toronto: Penguin.

Bloom, Ronna, 1996. *Fear of the Ride*. Ottawa: Carleton University Press.

Blunden, W.R., 1971. *The Land-use Transport System*. Oxford: Pergamon Press.

Bobet, Leah, 2004. "Midnights on the Bloor Viaduct." *On Spec*, 16(2).

Bonis, Robert R., 1968. *A History of Scarborough*. Scarborough, ON: Scarborough Public Library.

Boudreau, Julie-Anne, Roger Keil and Douglas Young, 2009. *Changing Toronto: Governing Urban Neoliberalism*. Toronto: University of Toronto Press.

Bouraoui, Hédi, [trans. Elizabeth Sabiston] 2008. *Thus Speaks the CN Tower*. Toronto: CMC Editions.

Bourne, Larry S. And Damaris Rose, 2001. The Changing Face of Canada: The Uneven Geographies of Population and Social Change. *Canadian Geographer*, 45(1): 105-119.

Bowering, George, ed., 1971. *The Story So Far*. Toronto: Coach House.

Boyden, Joseph, [2001] 2008. *Born With a Tooth*. Toronto: Cormorant.

Boyden, Joseph, 2008. *Through Black Spruce*. Toronto: Viking Canada.

Brady, Liz, 2004. *See Jane Run*. Toronto: Second Story Press.

Brand, Dionne, 1989. "At the Lisbon Plate." In *Sans Souci and Other Stories*. Toronto: Women's Press.

Brand, Dionne, 2002. *Thirsty*. Toronto: McClelland & Stewart.

Brand, Dionne, 2005. *What We All Long For*. Toronto: Knopf.

Bremer, Sidney, 1992. *Urban Intersections: Meetings of Life and Literature in United States Cities*. Urbana; Chicago: University of Illinois Press.

Bridle, Augustus, 1924. *Hansen: A Novel of Canadianization*. Toronto: Macmillan.

Brook, Calvin, 2008. "The Gardiner Expressway." In *Concrete Toronto: A Guidebook to Concrete Architecture from the Fifties to the Seventies*, ed. Michael McClelland and Graeme Stewart. Toronto: Coach House, 182-185.

Brown, Ron, 1997. *Toronto's Lost Villages*. Toronto: Polar Bear Press.

Brown, Wendy, 2006. *Regulating Aversion: Tolerance in the Age of Identity and Empire*. Princeton, NJ: Princeton University Press.

Bruce, Harry, 1968. *The Short Happy Walks of Max MacPherson*. Toronto: Macmillan of Canada.

Bryden, Diana Fitzgerald, 2004. *Clinic Day*. London, ON: Brick Books.

Burdick, Alice, 2002. *"Spadina Way."* In Simple Master. Toronto: Pedlar Press.

Burnham, Clint, 1991. *Allegories of Publishing: The Toronto Small Press Scene*. Toronto: Streetcar Editions, Streetcar Number Eleven.

Burnham, Clint, ed., Winter 1994. Toronto Since Then (Part 1). *Open Letter*, 8(8).

Burnham, Clint, ed., Summer 1994. Toronto Since Them (Part 2). *Open Letter*, 8(9).

Burr, Christina, 1999. *Spreading the Light: Work and Labour Reform in Late-Nineteenth-Century Toronto*. Toronto: University of Toronto Press.

Bush, Catherine, 1993. *Minus Time*. New York: Hyperion.

Bustos, Alejandro, 15 August 2005. "Workers cheated, sexually exploited; Employers threaten deportation," *Toronto Star*, B.02.

Butler, Juan, 1970. *Cabbagetown Diary*. Toronto: Peter Martin.

Byers, Nancy and Barbara Myrvold, 1999. *St. Clair West in Pictures: A History of the Communities of Carlton, Davenport, Earlscourt, and Oakwood*. 2nd edition. Toronto: Toronto Public Library.

Cain, Stephen, 2001. *Torontology*. Toronto: ECW Press.

Cain, Stephen, 2002. *Imprinting Identities: An Examination of the Emergence and Developing Identities of Coach House Press and House of Anansi Press (1967-1982)*. Unpublished PhD thesis. Toronto: Department of English, York University.

Cain, Stephen, 2005. Mapping Raymond Souster's Toronto. In *The Canadian Modernists Meet*, ed. Dean Irvine. Ottawa: University of Ottawa Press, 59-75.

Cain, Stephen, 2006. Annexing a Space for Poetry in the New Toronto. In *The State of the Arts: Living with Culture in Toronto*, ed. Alana Wilcox, Christina Palassio and Jonny Dovercourt. Toronto: Coach House, 90-99.

Callaghan, Barry, ed., 1995. *This Ain't No Healing Town: Toronto Stories*. Toronto: Exile Editions.

Callaghan, Morley, 1928. *Strange Fugitive*. New York: Charles Scribner's Sons.

Callaghan, Morley, 1970. "How Can a Writer Live in Toronto?" In *Canada: A Guide to the Peaceable Kingdom*, ed. William Kilbourn. Toronto: Macmillan: 312-314.

Calvino, Italo, [trans. William Weaver] 1974. *Invisible Cities*. Orlando, FL: Harcourt / Harvest.

Cameron, Bill, 2003. *Cat's Crossing*. Toronto: Random House Canada.

Capponi, Pat, 1992. *Upstairs in the Crazy House: The Life of a Psychiatric Survivor*. Toronto: Viking Canada.

Capponi, Pat, 1997. *Dispatches from the Poverty Line*. Toronto: Penguin.

Capponi, Pat, 1999. *The War at Home: An Intimate Portrait of Canada's Poor*. Toronto: Penguin.

Capponi, Pat, 2003. *Beyond the Crazy House*. Toronto: Penguin.

Capponi, Pat, 2006. *Last Stop Sunnyside*. Toronto: HarperCollins.

Capponi, Pat, 2008. *The Corpse Will Keep*. Toronto: HarperCollins.

Casey, Edward S., 1993. *Getting Back into Place: Toward a Renewed Understanding of the Place-World*. Bloomington, IN: Indiana University Press.

Cat City (film), 2009. Written and directed by Justine Pimlott. Toronto: Red Queen Productions.

Caulfield, Jon, 1994. *City Form and Everyday Life: Toronto's Gentrification and Critical Social Practice*. Toronto: University of Toronto Press.

Chambers, Chris, 1999. *Lake Where No One Swims*. Toronto: Pedlar Press.

Chaplin, Sarah, 1995. Desire Lines and Mercurial Tendencies: Resisting and Embracing the Possibilities for Digital Architecture. *Leonardo*, 28(5): 409-414.

Chariandy, David, 2007. *Soucouyant*. Vancouver: Arsenal Pulp Press.

Chatterton, Anna (librettist) and Juliet Palmer (music), 2008. *Stitch*.

Chiocca, Olindo Romeo, 2005. *College Street*. Toronto: Guernica.

Christian, Christian, n.d. "I am Frightened by the Gladstone." Orgasmmagazine.

City of Toronto Planning Board, 1968. *Plan for Yorkville*. Toronto: City of Toronto.

City of Toronto, 2003. *Ravine and Natural Feature Protection By-Law*. Brochure. Toronto: City of Toronto, Urban Forestry, Parks, Forestry & Recreation.

City of Toronto, 2003. *Report Card on Housing and Homelessness*. Available online at: http://www.toronto.ca/homelessness/pdf/reportcard2003.pdf

City of Toronto, 2006. *Street Needs Assessment*. Toronto: Shelter, Support and Housing Administration. Available online at: http://www.toronto.ca/legdocs/2006/agendas/committees/cms/cms060705/ito23.pdf

Clark, C. S., 1898. *Of Toronto the Good: A Social Study: The Queen City of Canada As It Is*. Montreal: The Toronto Publishing Company. [Reprinted in 1970 by Coles the Book People.]

Clark, Trevor, 1989. *Born to Lose*. Toronto: ECW Press.

Clarke, Austin, 1967. *The Meeting Point*. Toronto: Macmillan of Canada.

Clarke, Austin, 1971. *When He was Free and Young and He Used to Wear Silks*. Toronto: Anansi.

Clarke, Austin, 1973. *Storm of Fortune*. Boston; Toronto: Little, Brown.

Clarke, Austin, 1975. *The Bigger Light*. Boston; Toronto: Little, Brown.

Clarke, Austin, 1986. *Nine Men Who Laughed*. Toronto: Penguin.

Clarke, Austin, 2008. *More*. Toronto: Thomas Allen.

Clawson, Rosalee A & Rakuya Trice, 2000. Poverty as we know it: Media portrayals of the poor. *Public Opinion Quarterly*, 64(1): 53-64.

Coburn, Judi, 1998. *The Shacklands.* Toronto: Second Story Press.

Cochrane, Jean, 2000. *Kensington.* Toronto: Boston Mills Press.

Cohen, Matt, 1972. "Spadina Time." In *Columbus and the Fat Lady and Other Stories.* Toronto: Anansi.

Cohen, Matt, 1988 [writing under the pseudonym "Teddy Jam"; illustrated Eric Beddows, 2000]. *Night Cars.* Toronto: Groundwood Books / Anansi.

Cohen, Matt, 2000. *Typing: A Life in 26 Keys.* Toronto: Random House of Canada.

Colombo, John Robert, 1984. *Canadian Literary Landmarks.* Toronto: Houndslow Press.

Cook, Ramsay, 1985. *The Regenerators: Social Criticism in late Victorian English Canada.* University of Toronto Press.

Cooke, Nathalie, 1998. *Margaret Atwood: A Biography.* Toronto: ECW Press.

Coopersmith, Penina, 1998. *Cabbagetown: The Story of a Victorian Neighbourhood.* Toronto: James Lorimer.

Crosbie, Lynn and Michael Holmes, eds., 1995. *Plush: Selected Poems of Sky Gilbert, Courtnay McFarlane, Jeffery Conway, R.M. Vaughan & David Trinidad.* Toronto: Coach House.

Crosbie, Lynn, 1996. *Pearl.* Toronto: Anansi.

Crosbie, Lynn, 1998. *Queen Rat: New and Selected Poems.* Toronto: Anansi.

Crowe, Cathy, 2007. *Dying for a Home: Homeless Activists Speak Out.* Toronto: Between the Lines.

Cullen, Don, 2007. *The Bohemian Embassy: Memories and Poems.* Hamilton, ON: Wolsak & Wynn.

Daly, Gerald, 1996. *Homeless: Policies, Strategies, and Lives on the Street.* London; New York: Routledge.

Dault, Gary Michael, Tony Urquhart, 1989. *Cells of Ourselves.* Erin, ON: Porcupine's Quill.

Dault, Gary Michael, 1996. *Flying Fish And Other Poems.* Toronto: Exile Editions.

Daurio, Beverley, 1992. *Internal Document: A Response to Clint Burnham's 'Allegories of Publishing: The Toronto Small Press Scene.'* Toronto: Streetcar Editions, Streetcar Number 12.

Davie, Michael B., 2004. *Why Everybody Hates Toronto.* Toronto: Manor House.

Davies, Robertson, 1970. *Fifth Business.* Toronto: Macmillan of Canada.

Davies, Robertson, 1972. *The Manticore.* Toronto: Macmillan of Canada.

Davies, Robertson, 1975. *World of Wonders.* Toronto: Macmillan of Canada.

Davies, Robertson, 1981. *The Rebel Angels.* Toronto: Macmillan of Canada.

Davis, Lauren B., 2002. *The Stubborn Season.* Toronto: HarperCollins Canada.

Dearing, Sarah, 2001. *Courage My Love.* Toronto: Stoddart.

Debord, Guy-Ernest, [trans. Ken Knabb] 1958. "Theory of the Derive." *Internationale Situationniste #2.*

De Certeau, Michel [trans. Steven Rendall], 1984. *The Practice of Everyday Life.* Berkeley: University of California Press.

Decoursey, Elaine, Donn Kerr, Dan Ring and Matthew Teitelbaum, 1989. *Saskatoon Imagined*. Saskatoon, SK: Mendel Art Gallery.

De Klerck, Denis and Corrado Paina, eds., 2006. *College Street, Little Italy: Toronto's Renaissance Strip*. Toronto: Mansfield Press.

Demchinsky, Bryan and Elaine Kalman Naves, 2000. *Storied Streets: Montreal in the Literary Imagination*. Toronto: Macfarlane, Walter & Ross.

Dendy, William, 1993. *Lost Toronto*. 2nd edition. Toronto: McClelland & Stewart.

den Hartog, Kristen, [2002] 2005. *The Perpetual Ending*. San Francisco: MacAdam/ Cage.

Dennis, Richard, 1995. Private landlords and redevelopment: "The Ward" in Toronto, 1890-1920. *Urban History Review*, 24(1), 21-35.

Dennis, R.J., 2000. Morley Callaghan and the moral geography of Toronto. *British Journal of Canadian Studies*, 14(1): 35-51.

Denoon, Anne, 2002. *Back Flip*. Erin, ON: Porcupine's Quill.

Dent, John Charles, 1888. *The Gerrard Street Mystery and Other Weird Tales*. Toronto: Rose Publishing Company.

De Sa, Anthony, 2008. *Barnacle Love*. Toronto: Doubleday Canada.

Dewdney, 2000. *Signal Fires*. Toronto: McClelland & Stewart.

Dewdney, Christopher, 2008. *Soul of the World*. Toronto: Toronto: Harper Collins.

Dey, Claudia, 2008. *Stunt*. Toronto: Coach House.

Di Cicco, Pier Giorgio, 1977. *The Sad Facts*. Vancouver: Fiddlehead Poetry Books

Dickinson, Peter, 1999. *Here is Queer: Nationalisms, Sexualities and the Literatures of Canada*. Toronto: University of Toronto Press.

Dieterman, Frank and Ron Williamson, 2001. *Government on Fire: The History and Archaeology of Upper Canada's First Parliament Buildings*. Toronto: Eastendbooks.

Dimaline, Cherie, 2007. *Red Rooms*. Penticton, B.C.: Theytus Books.

Di Nardo, Desi, 2008. *The Plural of Some Things*. Toronto: Guernica.

Doctor, Farzana, 2007. *Stealing Nasreen*. Toronto: Inanna.

Donegan, Rosemary, 1985. *Spadina Avenue*. Vancouver; Toronto: Douglas & McIntyre.

Donnell, David, 1980. *Dangerous Crossings*. Windsor, ON: Black Moss Press.

Doucet, Michael J., 2001. "The Anatomy of an Urban Legend: Toronto's Multicultural Reputation." Toronto: CERIS Working Paper No. 16. Joint Centre of Excellence for Research on Immigration and Settlement.

Drache, Sharon Abron, 1993. *The Golden Ghetto*. Victoria, BC: Beach Holme.

Dubro, James, 2004. "Introduction" to reissue of Morley Callaghan's *Strange Fugitive*. Toronto: Exile Editions.

Duffy, Dennis, 2001. Furnishing the pictures: Arthur S. Goss, Michael Ondaatje and the Imag(in)ing of Toronto. *Journal of Canadian Studies*, 36(2): 106-129.

Dunford, Warren, 1998. *Soon to Be a Major Motion Picture*. Toronto: The Riverbank Press.

Dunford, Warren, 2001. *Making a Killing*. Toronto: Penguin.

Dunlop, Rishma, 2005. *Metropolis*. Toronto: Mansfield Press.

Duval, Paul, 2000. *Berryman Street Boy: Growing up in Yorkville*. Whitby, ON: Somerville Publishing / Vol Lotz Publishing.

Edmondson, Jill, 2009. *Blood and Groom*. Toronto: Dundurn.

Edwards, Justin D., 1998. Strange Fugitive, Strange City: Reading Urban Space in Morley Callaghan's Toronto. *Studies in Canadian Literature*, 23(1): 213-227.

Edwards, Justin D. And Douglas Ivison, eds., 2005. *Downtown Canada: Writing Canadian Cities*. Toronto: University of Toronto Press.

Ellis, Deborah and Eric Walters, 2007. *Bifocal*. Markham, ON: Fitzhenry & Whiteside.

Evernden, Neil, 1992. *The Social Creation of Nature*. Baltimore; London: Johns Hopkins University Press.

Eyles, Nick, 2004. *Toronto Rocks: The Geological Legacy of the Toronto Region*. Toronto: Fitzhenry & Whiteside.

Faessler, Shirley, 1988. *A Basket of Apples and Other Stories*. Toronto: McClelland & Stewart.

Fagan, Cary and Robert MacDonald, eds., 1990. *Streets of Attitude: Toronto Stories*. Toronto: Yonge & Bloor Publishing.

Fagan, Cary, 1990. *City Hall and Mrs. God: A Passionate Journey Through a Changing Toronto*. Stratford, ON: Mercury Press / Aya Press.

Fagin, Henry, 1960. Improving Mobility Within the Metropolis. *Proceedings of the Academy of Political Science*, 27(1): 57-65.

Fancher, Diana, ed., 2004. *The Leader and Recorder's History of the Junction*. Toronto: West Toronto Junction Historical Society.

Fanon, Frantz, [trans. Richard Philcox] 2005. *The Wretched of the Earth*. New York: Grove.

Farewell Oak Street, 1953. Ottawa: National Film Board of Canada.

Fawcett, Brian, 2003. *Local Matters*. Vancouver: New Star Books.

Findley, Timothy, 1988. "Stones." In *Stones*. Toronto: Viking.

Findley, Timothy, 1993. *Headhunter*. Toronto: HarperCollins.

Firth, Edith, 1983. *Toronto in Art: 150 Years Through Artists' Eyes*. Toronto: Fitzhenry & Whitside.

Fish, Stanley, 1997. Boutique Multiculturalism, or Why Liberals are Incapable of Thinking about Hate Speech. *Critical Inquiry*, 23(2): 378-395.

Fleming, Peter and Andre Spicer, 2004. "You can checkout anytime, but you can never leave": Spatial Boundaries in a High Commitment Organization. *Human Relations*, 57(1): 75-94.

Fournier, Michel et al, Spring 2005. Barriers in Access to Compensation of Immigrant Workers who have Suffered Work Injuries. *Canadian Issues*, 94-98.

Frager, Ruth, 1992. *Sweatshop Strife: Class, Ethnicity, and Gender in the Jewish Labour Movement of Toronto, 1900-1939*. Toronto: University of Toronto Press.

French, William, 1964. *A Most Unlikely Village: An Informal History of the Village of Forest Hill*. Toronto: Village of Forest Hill

Frye, Northrop, 1957. *The Anatomy of Criticism: Four Essays*. Princeton, N.J.: Princetown University Press.

Frye, Northrop, [1965] 1971. Conclusion to a *Literary History of Canada*. Reprinted in *The Bush Garden: Essays on the Canadian Imagination*. Toronto: Anansi, 213-251.

Fuerstenberg, Adam, 1996. Yudica: poet of Spadina's sweatshops. *Canadian Woman Studies*, 16(4): 107-111.

Fulford, Robert, 25 October 1960. "Lament for a Dead Toronto." *Toronto Star*, page 18.

Fulford, Robert, 1996. *Accidental City: The Transformation of Toronto*. Boston: Houghton-Mifflin.

Fulford, Robert, 2001. *2001 Real Estate Guide*. Toronto Life, 35(2).

Funston, Mike, 23 February 2009. "Dog owners defend coyote after dog killed." *Toronto Star*.

Galt, John, [1831] 1971. *Bogle Corbet*. Toronto: McClelland & Stewart.

Ganeshananthan, V.V., 2008. *Love Marriage*. New York: Random House.

Gardiner, Scott, 2007. *King John of Canada*. Toronto: McClelland & Stewart.

Garner, Hugh, 1950. *Cabbagetown*. [abridged edition]. Toronto: White Circle.

Garner, Hugh, 1962. *The Silence on the Shore*. Toronto: McClelland & Stewart.

Garner, Hugh, 1964. *Author, Author*. Toronto: Ryerson.

Garner, Hugh, [1953] 1964. "Bohemia on the Bay." In *Author, Author*, 116-119. Toronto: Ryerson.

Garner, Hugh, 1968. *Cabbagetown*. [restored edition]. Toronto: Ryerson.

Garner, Hugh, 1970. *The Sin Sniper*. Toronto: Simon & Schuster / Pocket Books.

Garner, Hugh, 1975. *Death in Don Mills*. Toronto: McGraw-Hill Ryerson.

Garner, Hugh, 1978. *Murder Has Your Number*. Toronto: McGraw-Hill Ryerson.

Garner, Hugh [completed by Paul Steuwe], 1992. *Don't Deal Five Deuces*. Toronto: Stoddart.

Gatenby, Greg, 1999. *Toronto: A Literary Guide*. Toronto: McArthur.

Gibson, Graeme, 1993. *Gentleman Death*. Toronto: McClelland & Stewart.

Gibson, Sally, 1984: *More Than an Island: A History of the Toronto Island*. Toronto: Irwin.

Gibson, Sally, 2006. *Inside Toronto: Urban Interiors, 1880-1920*. Toronto: Cormorant.

Giese, Rachel, August 2010. Priority One: Suicides on the Subway Tracks—How Many, How Often and How to Stop Them. In Toronto Life

Gifford, Jim, 2004. *Hurricane Hazel: Canada's Storm of the Century*. Toronto: Dundurn.

Gilbert, Sky, 2000. *Ejaculations from the Charm Factory*. Toronto: ECW Press.

Gilmour, David, 2005. *A Perfect Night to Go to China*. Toronto: Thomas Allen.

Gilroy, Paul, 2005. *Post-colonial Melancholia*. New York: Columbia University Press.

Godard, John, 2005. *Industrial Relations, the Economy, and Society*. 3rd edition. Toronto: Captus Press.

Gold Jr., Cad (aka Cad Lowlife) and Rob Siciliano, circa 1998. "Parkdale, Scummy Parkdale." Unpublished performance poem. Used with permission.

Goodman, William I., ed., 1968. *Principles and Practice of Urban Planning.* 4th edition. Washington, DC: International City Managers' Association.

Gould, Allan, 1991. *Fodor's Toronto.* New York: Random House.

Govier, Katherine, 1982. *Going Through the Motions.* Toronto: McClelland & Stewart.

Govier, Katherine, [1985] 2005. *Fables of Brunswick Avenue.* Toronto: Harper Perennial.

Govier, Katherine, 1992. "Union Station." In *Toronto Places: A Context for Urban Design*, eds. Marc Baraness and Larry Richards, 40. Toronto: University of Toronto Press.

Gowdy, Barbara, 1989. *Falling Angels.* Toronto: Random House of Canada.

Gowdy, Barbara, 2003. *The Romantic.* Toronto: HarperCollins.

Gowdy, Barbara, 2007. *Helpless.* Toronto: HarperCollins.

Grady, Wayne, 1995. *Toronto the Wild.* Toronto: Macfarlane, Walter & Ross.

Greenwood, Barbara, 2007. *Factory Girl.* Toronto: Kids Can Press.

Griffiths, Huw, Ingrid Poulter and David Sibley, 2000. "Feral Cats in the City." In *Animal Spaces, Beastly Places: New Geographies of Human-Animal Relations*, ed. Chris Philo and Chris Wilbert, 56-70. London; New York: Routledge.

Grube, John, 1966. *Sunday Afternoon at the Toronto Art Gallery.* Fredericton, NB: Fiddlehead Poetry Books.

Grube, John, 1997. *I'm Supposed to be Crazy and Other Stories.* Toronto: Dartington Press.

Grube, John, 2002. *God, Sex & Poetry.* Toronto: Dartington Press.

Hall, Peter, 1990. *Cities of Tomorrow.* Oxford, UK: Basil Blackwell.

Harris, Richard, 1996. *Unplanned Suburbs: Toronto's American Tragedy, 1900 to 1950.* Baltimore; London: Johns Hopkins University Press.

Harrison, Robert Pogue, 2003. *The Dominion of the Dead.* Chicago; London: University of Chicago Press.

Hart, Patricia W., 1968. *Pioneering in North York.* Toronto: General Publishing.

Harvey, David, 1989. *The Urban Experience.* Baltimore: Johns Hopkins University Press.

Hayes, Derek, 2008. *Historical Atlas of Toronto.* Vancouver: Douglas & McIntyre.

Hayward, Steven, 2005. *The Secret Mitzvah of Lucio Burke.* Toronto: Knopf.

Heidegger, Martin [ed. David Farrell Krell], 1993. *Basic Writings.* New York: HarperCollins.

Heffron, Dorris, 1971. *A Nice Fire and Some Moonpennies.* Toronto: Macmillan of Canada.

Heighton, Steven, 2000. *The Shadow Boxer.* Toronto: Knopf.

Helwig, David, 1969. *The Streets of Summer.* Ottawa: Oberon.

Helwig, Maggie, 1989. *Talking Prophet Blues.* Kingston: Quarry Press.

Helwig, Maggie, 1997. "Canadian Movies." In *Gravity Lets You Down.* Ottawa: Oberon.

Helwig, Maggie, 2008. *Girls Fall Down.* Toronto: Coach House Books.

Henderson, Stuart Robert, 2007. *Making the Scene: Yorkville and Hip Toronto, 1960-1970.* Unpublished PhD dissertation. Kingston, ON: Queen's University, Department of History.

Henighan, Stephen, 2002. "Vulgarity on Bloor: Literary Institutions From CanLit to TorLit." In *When Words Deny the World.* Erin, ON: Porcupine's Quill, 157-178.

Henighan, Steven, 2006. "Kingmakers." *Geist*, volume 63: 61.

Henry, Frances, Patricia Hastings & Brian Freer, 1996. Perceptions of Race and Crime in Ontario: Empirical Evidence from Toronto and the Durham Region. *Canadian Journal of Criminology*, 38(4): 469-476.

Hill, Lawrence, 1997. *Any Known Blood*. Toronto: HarperCollins.

Hill, Lawrence, 2001. *Black Berry, Sweet Juice: On Being Black and White in Canada*. Toronto: HarperCollins Canada.

Holden, Alfred, December 1997. *The Forgotten Stream*. Taddle Creek, Vol. 1, No. 1.

Holmes, Michael, 1992. *got no flag at all*. Toronto: ECW Press.

Holmes, Michael, 1993. *Satellite Dishes from the Future Bakery*. Toronto: Coach House.

Holmes, Michael, 1994. *james i wanted to ask you*. Toronto: ECW Press.

Holmes, Michael, 1998. *21 Hotels*. Maxville, ON: above/ground press.

Holmes, Michael, 2000. *Watermelon Row*. Vancouver: Arsenal Pulp Press.

Hood, Hugh, 1973. *The Governor's Bridge is Closed*. Ottawa: Oberon.

Hood, Hugh, 1975. *The Swing in the Garden*. Ottawa: Oberon.

Hood, Hugh, 1979. *Reservoir Ravine*. Ottawa: Oberon.

Hood, Hugh, 1982. *Black and White Keys*. Toronto: ECW Press.

Hood, Sarah B., 31 May 2008. "She needn't Bluff about her locale." *National Post*.

Hopkins, J. Castell, 1913. Canadian Literature. *Annals of the American Academy of Political and Social Science*, 45(1): 189-215.

Hopkinson, Nalo, 1998. *Brown Girl in the Ring*. New York: Warner / Aspect.

Horning, Lewis Emerson and Lawrence J. Burpee, 1904. *Bibliography of Canadian Fiction*. Victoria University Library Publication No. 2. Toronto: William Briggs.

Horsley, Katrice, 2007. Storytelling, Conflict and Diversity. *Community Development Journal*, 42(2): 265-269.

Howison, John, [1821] Facsimile edition 1970. *Sketches of Upper Canada*. Toronto: Coles.

Huff, Tanya, 1991. *Blood Price*. New York: Daw.

Hughes, Isabelle, 1947. *Serpent's Tooth*. Toronto: Collins.

Hughes, Isabelle, 1949. *Time in Ambush*. Toronto: Collins.

Hughes, Isabelle, 1952. *Lorena Telforth*. London: Peter Davies.

Hughes, Isabelle, 1954. *The Wise Brother*. Toronto: Ryerson.

Humphreys, Helen, 1997. *Leaving Earth*. Toronto: HarperCollins.

Hutcheson, Stephanie, 1978. *Yorkville in Pictures, 1853-1883*. Toronto: Toronto Public Library Board, Local History Handbooks. Number 2.

Hyde, Anthony, 1 August 1987. "Turning Toronto the Terrible into Myth." *Ottawa Citizen*, C3.

Iyer, Pico, 2000. *The Global Soul: Jet Lag, Shopping Malls, and the Search for Home*. New York: Knopf.

James, Cathy, 2001. Reforming reform: Toronto's Settlement House movement, 1900-20. *The Canadian Historical Review*, 82(1): 55-90.

Jameson, Anna Brownell, 1839, *Winter Studies and Summer Rambles in Canada*. Volume 1. New York: Wiley and Putnam.

Jarvis, Thomas Stinson, 1890. *Geoffrey Hampstead*. New York: D. Appleton and Company.

Jennings, Maureen, 2003. *Let Loose the Dogs*. New York: Thomas Dunne Books / St. Martin's Minotaur.

Jiles, Paulette, [1986] 2003. *Sitting in the Club Car Drinking Rum and Karma Kola*. Vancouver: Poestar / Raincoast.

Johansen, Emily, 2008. "Streets are the dwelling place of the collective": Public Space and Cosmopolitan Citizenship in Dionne Brand's *What We All Long For*. *Canadian Literature*, volume 196: 48-62.

Johnson, William, 1970. *The Gay World. In The Underside of Toronto*, ed. W.E. Mann, 322-333. Toronto: McClelland & Stewart. Jones, Daniel, 1994. *The People One Knows: Toronto Stories*. Toronto: Mercury Press.

Johnston, Wayne, 1994. *Human Amusements*. Toronto: McClelland & Stewart.

Jones [Daniel Jones], 1985. *the brave never write poetry*. Toronto: Coach House.

Jurca, Carolyn, 2001. *White Diaspora: The Suburb and the Twentieth-Century American Novel*. Princeton, NJ: Princeton University Press.

Kilodney, Crad, 1990. *Girl on the Subway And Other Stories*. Windsor, ON: Black Moss Press.

Kaminer, Michael, 5 July 2009. "Skid Row to Hip in Toronto," *New York Times*.

Kealey, Gregory S., [1980] reprinted 1991. *Toronto Workers Respond to Industrial Capitalism, 1867-1892*. Toronto: University of Toronto Press.

Keith, William John, 1992. *Literary Images of Ontario*. A project of the Ontario Historical Studies Series for the Government of Ontario. Toronto: University of Toronto Press.

Kenneally, Michael, 2005. Inscribing Irish Identities in Upper Canada: Patrick Slater's The Yellow Briar. *The Canadian Journal of Irish Studies*, 31(1): 60-66.

Kidd, Kenneth, 8 March 2009. "The Star unveils unique map of neighbourhoods. *Toronto Star*, page A8-9.

Kilbourn, William, ed., 1970. *Canada: A Guide to the Peaceable Kingdom*. Toronto: Macmillan of Canada.

Kilbourn, William, 1976. *The Toronto Book: An Anthology of Writings Past and Present*. Toronto: Macmillan.

Kilbourn, William, 1984. *Toronto Remembered*. Toronto: Stoddart.

Kingwell, Mark, 2008. "All Show." In *Toronto: A City Becoming*, ed. David Macfarlane. Toronto: Key Porter, 169-187.

Klinck, Todd, 2007. *Tacones*. Vancouver: Anvil Press.

Kluckner, Michael, 1988. *Toronto The Way It Was*. Toronto: Whitecap Books.

Kopun, Francine and Nicholas Keung, 5 December 2007. "A City of Unmatched Diversity," *Toronto Star*.

Koukal, D. Raymond, 1996. Discrete Environments: Those Which Do Not Dwell. *International Studies in Philosophy*, 28(2): 63-73.

Kramer, Greg, 1999. *Hogtown Bonbons*. Toronto: The Riverbank Press.

Kreisel, Henry, 1948. *The Rich Man*. Toronto: McClelland & Stewart.

Kunstler, James Howard, 1994. *The Geography of Nowhere: The Rise and Decline of America's Man-Made Landscape*. New York: Touchstone.

Kwamdela, Odimumba, [1971] 1986. *Niggers This Is Canada*. Revised Edition. Brooklyn, NY: Kibo Books.

Lacey, Edward A., [n.d. but presumed late 1950s]. "Quintillas." In *Seminal: The Anthology of Canada's Gay Male Poets*, ed. John Barton & Billeh Nickerson, 121. Vancouver: Arsenal Pulp Press.

Lake, Catherine and Nairne Holtz, eds., 2006. *No Margins: Writing Canadian Fiction In Lesbian*. Toronto: Insomniac Press.

Lakey, Jack, 19 June 2009. "Fur Flies over Bluffers Park cat colony." *Toronto Star*.

Lam, Vincent, 2006. *Bloodletting and Miraculous Cures*. Toronto: Doubleday Canada.

Latour, Bruno, [trans. Catherine Porter] 1993. *We Have Never Been Modern*. Cambridge, MA: Harvard University Press.

Layton, Irving, 1973. *Lovers and Lesser Men*. Toronto: McClelland & Stewart.

Layton, Jack, 2000. *Homelessness: The Making and Unmaking of a Crisis*. Toronto: Penguin.

Lee, Dennis, ed., 1968. *T.O. Now: The Young Toronto Poets*. Toronto: Anansi.

Lee, Dennis, 1974; illustrations Frank Newfeld. *Alligator Pie*. Toronto: Macmillan of Canada.

Lee, Dennis, [1974] 1994. *Civil Elegies*. Toronto: Anansi.

Lee, Dennis, 1984. "When I Went Up To Rosedale." Quoted in Kilbourn, William. *Toronto Remembered: A Celebration of the City*. Toronto: Stoddart.

Lee, Dennis, [illustrations by Gillian Johnson], 2001. *The Cat and the Wizard*. Toronto: Key Porter.

Leeming, David Adams [with Margaret Adams Leeming], 1994. *A Dictionary of Creation Myths*. Oxford; New York: Oxford University Press.

Lefebvre, Henri [trans. Donald Nicholson-Smith], 1991. *The Production of Space*. Oxford, UK: Blackwell.

Levy, Sophie, 2001. *Torontology*. Unpublished Master's Thesis. Toronto: Department of English, University of Toronto.

Lewis, Wyndham, [1954] 1983. *Self Condemned*. Santa-Barbara, CA: Black Sparrow Press.

Ley, David, 2003. Artists, Aestheticisation and the Field of Gentrification. *Urban Studies*, 40(12): 2527-2544.

Livesay, Dorothy, 1972. "Queen City." In *Collected Poems: The Two Two Seasons*. Toronto: McGraw-Hill Ryerson.

Lizars, Robina and Kathleen MacFarlane, 1897. *Humours of '37: Rebellion Times in the Canadas*. Toronto: William Briggs, 1897.

Lonergan, Peter, 1993. *Leslieville*. Toronto: Lugus Publishing.

Lorimer, James and Myfanwy Phillips, 1971. *Working People: Life in a Downtown City Neighbourhood*. Toronto: James Lewis & Samuel Ltd.

Lyons, Don, 1984. *Yorkville Diaries*. Toronto: Elephant Press.

MacDonnell, Susan, et al, 2004. *Poverty by Postal Code: The Geography of Neighbourhood Poverty, City of Toronto, 1981-2001*. Toronto: United Way of Greater Toronto and the Canadian Council on Social Development.

MacEwen, Gwendolyn, 1966. *A Breakfast for Barbarians*. Toronto: Ryerson Press.

MacEwen, Gwendolyn, 1972. *Noman*. Ottawa: Oberon.

MacEwen, Gwendolyn, 1982. *Earthlight*. Toronto: General.

MacEwen, Gwendolyn, 1985. *Noman's Land*. Toronto: Coach House.

MacEwen, Gwendolyn, 1987. *Afterworlds*. Toronto: McClelland & Stewart.

Macfarlane, David, ed., 2008. *Toronto: A City Becoming*. Toronto: Key Porter.

MacKinnon, Steve, Karen Teeple and Michele Dale, 2009. *Toronto's Visual Legacy: Official City Photography from 1856 to the Present*. Toronto: Lorimer.

MacLean, Kath, 1998. *For a Cappuccino on Bloor & Other Poems*. Fredericton, NB: Broken Jaw Press.

Maharaj, Rabindranath, 2010. *The Amazing Absorbing Boy*. Toronto: Knopf Canada.

Markle, Robert, 1995. "Blazing Figures." In *This Ain't No Healing Town: Toronto Stories*, ed. Barry Callaghan, 149-156. Toronto: Exile Editions.

McNamee, Graham, 2003. *Acceleration*. New York: Dell Laurel-Leaf.

Maharaj, Rabindranath, 1997. *Homer in Flight*. Fredericton, NB: Goose Lane Editions.

Maharaj, Rabindranath, 2002. "Escape to Etobicoke" in *The Book of Ifs and Buts*. Toronto: Vintage, 159-168..

Mann, W.E., ed., 1970. *The Underside of Toronto*. Toronto: McClelland & Stewart.

Marchand, Philip, 1994. *Deadly Spirits*. Toronto: Stoddart.

Marchand, Philip, 23 November 2002. "Literati leave Big Smoke out in the cold: Book prize judges, and our authors, snub Toronto." *Toronto Star*, J04.

Marchand, Philip, 5 November 2006. "What's Toronto's story." *Toronto Star*.

Marche, Stephen, 2005. *Raymond and Hannah*. Toronto: Doubleday Canada.

Marche, Stephen, 31 December 2005. "Drab and dull, yes, but we write a mean novel." *Toronto Star*, M2.

Marche, Stephen, 20 October 2007. "Raging against the tyranny of CanLit." *Toronto Star*.

Marcuse, Herbert, 1969. Repressive Tolerance. In *A Critique of Pure Tolerance*, eds. Robert Paul Wolff, Barrington Moore Jr. And Herbert Marcuse. Boston: Beacon Press, 95-137.

Marny, Suzanne, 1909. *Tales of Old Toronto*. Toronto: William Briggs.

Marshall, Joyce, 1957. *Lovers and Strangers*. Philadelphia; New York: J.B. Lippincott Company.

Marvasti, Amir B., 2002. Constructing the Service-Worthy Homeless Through Narrative Editing. *Journal of Contemporary Ethnography*, 31(5): 615-651.

Martin, Sandra, 27 February 2009. "His life was his art. Alas, it was not a masterpiece." [retrospective essay on Scott Symons] *Globe & Mail*.

Matheson, George, 1996. *Hogs and Cabbagers*. Lumby, BC: Kettle Valley Publishing.

Mathews, Vanessa, 2004. *The Art of Ideology: Theorizing Artists and Gentrification in the Space of Yorkville, Toronto*. Unpublished Master's thesis. Toronto: Department of Geography, York University.

Mathews, Vanessa, 2008. *Artcetera: Narrativising Gentrification in Yorkville, Toronto*. Urban Studies, 45(13): 2849-2876.

Mays, John Bentley, 1994. *Emerald City*. Toronto: Viking.

Mays, John Bentley, May 2006. Walking off the Map: Hymns to the Unknown City Beneath our Feet. *The Walrus*.

McAree, J.V., 1953. *Cabbagetown Store*. Toronto: The Ryerson Press.

McClelland, Michael and Graeme Stewart, eds., 2007. *Concrete Toronto: A Guide to Concrete Architecture from the Fifties to the Seventies*. Toronto: Coach House.

McBride, Jason and Wilcox, Alana, eds., 2005. *Utopia: Towards a New Toronto*. Toronto: Coach House Books.

McCaffery, Steve, 1988. "In Tens/tion: Dialoguing with bp." In *Tracing the Paths: Reading ≠ Writing "The Martyrology*, ed. Roy Miki, 72-94. Vancouver: Talonbooks.

McFetridge, John, 2006. *Dirty Sweet*. Toronto: ECW Press.

McGehee, Peter, 1991. *Boys Like Us*. Toronto: Harper Collins.

McGehee, Peter, 1992. *Sweetheart*. Toronto: Harper Collins.

McLaren, Jack, 1956. *Let's All Hate Toronto*. Toronto: Kingswood House.

McLean, Stuart, 2009. Stories and Cosmogonies: Imagining Creativity Beyond "Nature" and "Culture." *Cultural Anthropology*, 24(2): 213-245.

McLeish, Kenneth, 1984. *In the Beginning: Creation Myths from Around the World*. Harlow, UK: Longman.

McNamee, Graham, 2003. *Acceleration*. New York: Dell Laurel-Leaf.

Meeks, Brian, ed., 2007. *Culture, Politics, Race and Diaspora: The Thought of Stuart Hall*. London: Lawrence & Wishart.

Meredith, Alden G., 1928. *Mary's Rosedale and Gossip of Little York*. Ottawa: Graphic.

Micallef, Shawn, 2010. *Stroll: Psychogeographic Walking Tours of Toronto*. Toronto: Coach House / Eye Weekly.

Michaels, Anne, 1996. *Fugitive Pieces*. Toronto: McClelland & Stewart.

Michaels, Anne, 1999. *Skin Divers*. Toronto: McClelland & Stewart.

Miles, Joan and Diana Fancher, eds., 1999. *West Toronto Junction Revisited*. 4th edition. Toronto: Toronto: West Toronto Junction Historical Society.

Miller, Jeffrey, 2005. *Murder's Out of Tune*. Toronto: ECW Press.

Miller, John, 2006. *A Sharp Intake of Breath*. Toronto: Simon & Pierre / Dundurn.

Mills, C. Wright, [1951] 2002. *White Collar: The American Middle Classes*. Oxford; New York: Oxford University Press.

Millner, George F., 1914. *The Sergeant of Fort Toronto*. Boston: Gorham.

Milton, Paul, 2005. "Rewriting White Flight: Suburbia in Gerald Lynch's Troutstream and Joan Barfoot's Dancing in the Dark. In *Downtown Canada: Writing Canadian*

Cities, eds. Justin D. Edwards and Douglas Ivison, 166-182. Toronto: University of Toronto Press.

Moak, Allan, 1984, 2002. *A Big City ABC*. Montreal; Toronto: Tundra Books.

Moir, John S., 1965. *Rhymes of Rebellion*. Toronto: Ryerson Press.

Moodie, Andrew, 2009. *Toronto the Good*. Produced at the Factory Theatre, Toronto.

Morey, Mike, 2003. *Uncle Dirty*. Denver, CO: Escape Media.

Moritsugu, Kim, 2003. *The Glenwood Treasure*. Toronto: Simon & Pierre / Dundurn.

Morris, Ruth and Colleen Heffren, 1988. *Street People Speak*. Oakville: Mosaic Press.

Moses, Daniel David, 1998. *Big Buck City. A Play in Two Acts*. Toronto: Exile Editions.

Moses, Daniel David, 2000. *Coyote City and City of Shadows: Necropolitei*. Toronto: Imago Press.

Moses, Daniel David, 2008. *Kyotopolis. A Play in Two Acts*. Toronto: Exile Editions.

Moss, John, 2008. *Still Waters*. Toronto: Dundurn.

Moure, Eirin, 2001. *Sheep's Vigil by a Fervent Person*. Toronto: Anansi.

Mugerauer, Robert, 1994. *Interpretations on Behalf of Place*. Albany, NY: State University of New York.

Mulvaney, C. Pelham, 1884. *Toronto: Past and Present*. Toronto: W.E. Caiger. [facsimile edition reprinted in 1970 by Ontario reprint Press.]

Murdie, Robert A. And Carlos Teixeira, 2003. Towards a Comfortable Neighbourhood and Appropriate Housing: Immigrant Experiences in Toronto. In *The World in a City*, eds. Paul Anisef and Michael Lanphier, 132-191. Toronto: University of Toronto Press.

Murphy, Phil, 1984. *Summer Island*. Ottawa: Oberon.

Myhill, Carl, 2004. Commercial Success by Looking for Desire Lines. In *Proceedings of the 6th Asia Pacific Computer-Human Interaction Conference*, ed. M. Masoodian, S. Jones & B. Rogers. Rotorua, NZ.

Nelson, Frederick, 1908. *Toronto in 1928 A.D.* Toronto: National Business Methods & Pub. Co.

Ng, Roxana, Renita Yuk-Lin Wong and Angela Choi, 1999. Homeworking: Dream Realized or Freedom Constrained? The Globalized Reality of Immigrant Garment Workers. *Canadian Woman Studies*, 19(3): 110-114.

Nichol, Barbara, 1997. *Dippers*. Toronto: Tundra.

Nichol, bp, 1982. *The Martyrology Book V*. Toronto: Coach House.

Nichol, James W., 2002. *Midnight Cab*. Toronto: Knopf.

Oberman, Sheldon [illustrator Les Tait], 1995. *The White Stone in the Castle Wall*. Toronto: Tundra.

O'Donnell, Darren, 2004. *Your Secrets Sleep with Me*. Toronto: Coach House.

Ondaatje, Michael, [1987] 1996. *In the Skin of a Lion*. Toronto: Vintage.

Onstad, Katrina, 2006. *How Happy to Be*. Toronto: McClelland & Stewart.

Osbaldeston, Mark, 2008. Unbuilt *Toronto: A History of the City that Might have Been*. Toronto: Dundurn.

Paci, F.G., 1993. *Sex and Character*. Ottawa: Oberon.

Paci, F.G., 1996. *The Rooming House*. Ottawa: Oberon.

Paina, Corrado, 2000. *Hoarse Legend*. Toronto: Mansfield Press.

Paina, Corrado, 2008. *Souls in Plain Clothes*. Toronto: Mansfield Press.

Papadimos, Basil, 1989. *The Hook of it Is*. Enismore, Ont.: Emergency Press.

Paris, Erna, 1976. "Ghetto of the Mind: Forest Hill in the Fifties." In *The Toronto Book*, ed. William Kilbourn. Toronto: Macmillan of Canada, 98-105.

Patriarca, Gianna, 1994; 1996. *Italian Women and Other Tragedies*. Toronto: Guernica.

Paulini, Mercedes and Marc Aurel Schnabel, 2008. Surfing the City: Towards Context-Aware Mobile Exploration. *Proceedings of the 13th Annual Conference of the Association of Computer Aided Architectural Design in Asia, Chiang-Mai, Thailand, 9-12 April*.

Pearson, Mike and Michael Shanks, 2001. *Theatre/Archaeology*. London; New York: Routledge.

Pearson, Patricia, 2003. *Playing House*. Toronto: Random House Canada.

Persaud, Sasenarine, 1998. "Canada Geese and Apple Chatney." In *Canada Geese and Apple Chatney*. Toronto: TSAR Books.

Philip, Neil, 2001. *The Great Mystery: Myths of Native America*. New York: Clarion.

Phillips, Anne, 2007. *Multiculturalism Without Culture*. Princetown, NJ: Princeton University Press.

Piepzna-Samarasinha, 2006. *Consensual Genocide*. Toronto: TSAR.

Pitfield, Jane, ed., 2000. *Leaside*. 2nd edition. Toronto: Natural Heritage / Natural History.

Pitt, Steve; illustrations Heather Collins, 2004. *Rain Tonight: A Story of Hurricane Hazel*. Toronto: Tundra.

Piva, Michael J., 1979. *The Condition of the Working Class in Toronto, 1900-1921*. Ottawa: University of Ottawa Press.

Plantos, Ted, 1977. *The Universe Ends at Sherbourne & Queen*. Toronto: Steel Rail Publishing.

Pollock, Francis, 1937. *Jupiter Eight*. Toronto: Thomas Nelson & Sons.

Pollock, Jack, 1989. *Dear M: Letters from a Gentleman of Excess*. Toronto: McClelland & Stewart.

Pool, Sandy, 2009. *Exploding into Night*. Toronto: Guernica.

Powe, B.W., 1995. *Outage*. Toronto: Random House of Canada.

Preville, Philip, February 2008. "Toronto's Traffic Time Bomb." *Toronto Life* magazine.

Proulx, Craig, 2006. Aboriginal Identification in North American Cities. *The Canadian Journal of Native Studies*, XXVI, 2.

Pupo, Mark, August 2006. Facts and Fiction: A roundtable discussion on Toronto literature with Sheila Heti, Andrew Pyper and Shyam Selvadurai. *Toronto Life* (online feature), www.torontolife.com/features/facts-fiction/

Pyper, Andrew, 1996. *Kiss Me*. Erin, ON: Porcupine's Quill.

Pyper, Andrew, 2008. *The Killing Circle*. Toronto: Random House.

Purdy, Al, 1968. *Wild Grape Wine*. Toronto: McClelland & Stewart.

Purdy, Sean, 1997. Industrial efficiency, social order and moral purity: housing reform thought in English Canada, 1900-1950. *Urban History Review*, 25(2): 30.

Qadeer, Mohammad and Sandeep Kumar Agrawal, forthcoming. Evolution of Ethnic Enclaves in the Toronto Metropolitan Area 2001-06. *Canadian Geographer*. A presentation summarizing the study findings is available at http://ceris.metropolis.net/ events/seminars/2009/20090206QadeerAgrawalSemPres.pdf.

Quarrington, Paul, [1989] 1997. *Whale Music*. Toronto: Vintage.

Quarrington, Paul, 2008. *The Ravine*. Toronto: Random House Canada.

Quinn, Philip, 2008. *The Subway*. Toronto: BookThug.

Qureshi, Mobashar, 2006. *R.A.C.E.* Toronto: Mercury Press.

Raban, Jonathan, 1974. *Soft City*. London: Collins Harvill.

Rakoff, Alvin, 2007. *Baldwin Street*. New York; Charlottetown: Bunim & Bannigan.

Rayburn, Alan, 1994. "The real story of how Toronto got its name." *Canadian Geographic*, September / October: 68-70.

Redhill, Michael, ed., 1996. *Blues & True Concussions: Six New Toronto Poets*. Toronto: Anansi.

Redhill, Michael, 2006. *Consolation*. Toronto: Doubleday Canada.

Reeves, Wayne, 2007. "From the Ground Up: Fragments Towards an Environmental History of Tkaronto." In *GreenTOpia: Towards a Sustainable Toronto*, ed. Alana Wilcox, Christina Palassio and Jonny Dovercourt. Toronto: Coach House, 2007. Pp. 64-75.

Reid, John, 1974. *The Faithless Mirror*. Toronto: Darkwood Press.

Ricci, Nino, 1990. *Lives of the Saints*. Dunvegan, ON: Cormorant.

Ricci, Nino, 1993. *In a Glass House*. Toronto: McClelland & Stewart.

Ricci, Nino, 1997. *Where She Has Gone*. Toronto: McClelland & Stewart.

Richardson, Karen and Steven Green, eds., 2004. *T Dot Griots: An Anthology of Toronto's Black Storytellers*. Trafford.

Richler, Mordecai, 1963. *The Incomparable Atuk*. London: Andre Deusch.

Richler, Noah, 2006. *This Is My Country, What's Yours?: A Literary Atlas of Canada*. Toronto: McClelland & Stewart.

Rinehart, James W., 1987. *The Tyranny of Work: Alienation and the Labour Process*. 2nd edition. Toronto: Harcourt Brace Jovanovich Canada.

Roberts, Charles G.D., 1891. *The Canadian Guide-Book*. New York: D. Appleton and Company.

Robertson, J. Ross, [1911] facsimile edition 1973. *The Diary of Mrs. John Graves Simcoe, Wife of the First Lieutenant-Governor of the Province of Upper Canada, 1792-6*. Toronto: Coles.

Robertson, Ray, 2002. *Moody Food*. Toronto: Random House of Canada.

Robertson, Ray, 2005. *Gently Down the Stream*. Toronto: Cormorant.

Robinson, Percy J., [1933] reprinted 1965. *Toronto During the French Regime, 1615-1793*. Toronto: University of Toronto Press.

Rogers, Elizabeth Barlow, 1987. *Rebuilding Central Park: A Management and Restoration Plan.* Cambridge, MA: MIT Press.

Rose, Albert, 1958. *Regent Park: A Study in Slum Clearance.* Toronto: University of Toronto Press.

Rosengarten, Herbert, Summer 1976. Admirable Purpose. Review of The Faithless Mirror. *Canadian Literature,* vol. 65: 115-117.

Rosenthal, Joe [illustrator] and Adele Wiseman [text], 1964. *Old Markets, New World.* Toronto: Macmillan of Canada.

Ross, Stuart, 2005. *Confessions of a Small Press Racketeer.* Vancouver: Anvil Press.

Ross, Stuart, 2006. "In the small press village: New trends in adequate stapling." In *The State of the Arts: Living with Culture in Toronto,* eds. Alana Wilcox, Christina Palassio and Jonny Dovercourt. Toronto: Coach House, 254-261.

Ruddy, Jon, 1980. *The Rosedale Horror.* Toronto: Markham, ON: PaperJacks.

Ruppert, Evelyn S., 2006. *The Moral Economy of Cities: Shaping Good Citizens.* Toronto: University of Toronto Press.

Russell, Victor L., ed., 1984. *Forging a Consensus: Historical Essays on Toronto.* Toronto: University of Toronto Press.

Rust-D'Eye, George, [1984] 1993. *Cabbagetown Remembered.* Toronto: Stoddart.

Ruth, Elizabeth, ed., 2002. *Bent On Writing: Contemporary Queer Tales.* Toronto: Women's Press.

Rutherford, Erik, 2005. "Toronto: A City in our Image." In *uTOpia: Towards a New Toronto,* eds. Jason McBride and Alana Wilcox. Toronto: Coach House, 16-21.

Rynor, Becky, 14 July 2009. "Growing workplace disloyalty 'No big surprise': Workplace expert. National Post.

Said, Edward, 1979. *Orientalism.* New York: Vintage.

Said, Edward, 1994. *Culture and Imperialism.* New York: Vintage.

Sale, Medora, 1990. *Murder in a Good Cause.* New York: Charles Scribner's Sons.

Salutin, Rick, 1976. *1837: William Lyon Mackenzie and the Canadian Revolution.* Toronto: Lorimer.

Sauriol, Charles, 1981. *Remembering the Don.* Scarborough, ON: Amethyst Communications.

Sauriol, Charles, 1984. *Tales of the Don.* Toronto: Natural Heritage / Natural History.

Sauriol, Charles, 1984. *A Beeman's Journey.* Toronto: Natural Heritage / Natural History.

Sauriol, Charles, 1991. *Green Footsteps: Recollections of a Grassroots Conservationist.* Toronto: Hemlock Press.

Sauriol, Charles, 1992. *Trails of the Don.* Toronto: Hemlock Press.

Sauriol, Charles, 1995. *Pioneers of the Don.* Self-published.

Savigny, Annie G., 1888. *A Romance of Toronto.* Toronto: William Briggs.

Scadding, Henry, [1873; 1878] edited and abridged by Frederick H. Armstrong, 1987. *Toronto of Old.* Toronto: Dundurn.

Scadding, Henry, 1891. Etymology of Toronto: Why I Prefer "Place of Meeting" to "Trees in the Water" as the Probably Meaning of the Word "Toronto." A paper read before the Pioneer and Historical Society of the County of York, Ont., October 6th, 1891. Toronto: Press of "The Week."

Schick, Irvin C., 1999. *The Erotic Margin: Sexuality and Spatiality in Alterist Discourse*. London: Verso.

Schultz, Emily, 2006. *Joyland*. Toronto: ECW Press.

Schultz, Emily, 2009. *Heaven is Small*. Toronto: Anansi.

Scott, F.R. and A.J.M. Smith, eds., 1967. *The Blasted Pine: An Anthology of Satire, Invective and Disrespectful Verse Chiefly by Canadian Writers*. Toronto: Macmillan.

Scrimger, Richard, 1996. *Crosstown*. Toronto: The Riverbank Press.

Scrimger, Richard, 2007. *Into the Ravine*. Toronto: Tundra.

Scrivener, Leslie, 23 November 2008. "The Enigma of Lake Ontario's 11,000-year-old footprints," *Toronto Star*.

Seeley, John, 1956. *Crestwood Heights: A Study of the Culture of Suburban Life*. New York: Basic Books / Toronto: University of Toronto Press.

Seton, Ernest Thompson, 1898. *Wild Animals I Have Known*. New York: Charles Scribner's Sons.

Seton, Ernest Thompson, 1903. *Two Little Savages*. Toronto: William Briggs.

Sewell, John, 1993. *The Shape of the City: Toronto Struggles with Modern Planning*. Toronto: University of Toronto Press.

Sewell, John, 2009. *The Shape of the Suburbs: Understanding Toronto's Sprawl*. Toronto: University of Toronto Press.

Seymour, Murray, 2000. *Toronto's Ravines: Walking the Hidden Country*. Richmond Hill, ON: Boston Mills Press.

Shanks, Michael and Mike Pearson, 2001. *Theatre/Archaeology: Disciplinary Dialogues*. Florence, KY: Routledge.

Sheppard, Edmund Ernest, 1889. *A Bad Man's Sweetheart*. Toronto: Sheppard Publishing Company.

Shershow, Scott Cutler, 2005. *The Work & the Gift*. Chicago: University of Chicago Press.

Shields, Carol, 2002. *Unless*. Toronto: Random House Canada.

Siemiatycki, Myer, Tim Rees, Roxanna Ng and Khan Rahi, 2003. Integrating Community Diversity in Toronto: On Whose Terms. In *The World in a City*, ed., Paul Anisef and Michael Lanphier, 373-456. Toronto: University of Toronto Press.

Sileika, Antanas, 1997. *Buying on Time*. Erin, ON: Porcupine's Quill.

Sinclair, Lister, 1948. 'We All Hate Toronto." In *A Play on Words & Other Radio Plays*, ed. Lister Sinclair. Toronto: J.M. Dent.

Singh, Susan Singh, 2004. Why deaths, injuries still mar workplaces. *Canadian HR Reporter*, 17(13).

Sinnett, Mark, 2009. *The Carnivore*. Toronto: ECW Press.

Slater, Patrick, [1933] 1941. *The Yellow Briar*. Toronto: Macmillan.

Smart, Carolyn, 1986. *Stoning the Moon*. Ottawa: Oberon.

Smith, Russell, 1994. *How Insensitive*. Erin, ON: Porcupine's Quill.

Smith, Russell, 1998. *Noise*. Erin, ON: Porcupine's Quill.

Smith, Russell, 11 December 2002. "Dear [non-] reader, it might not be your fault." *Globe & Mail*, R1-R2.

Solnit, Rebecca, 2000. *Wanderlust: A History of Walking*. New York: Penguin.

Solomon, Lawrence, 2007. *Toronto Sprawls: A History*. Toronto: University of Toronto Press.

Souster, Raymond, 1953. *Shake Hands with the Hangman: Poems, 1944-52*. Toronto: Contact Press.

Souster, Raymond, 1964. *The Colour of the Times*. Toronto: Ryerson Press.

Souster, Raymond, 1972. *Selected Poems*. Ottawa: Oberon.

Souster, Raymond, 1973. *The Colour of the Times / Ten Elephants on Yonge Street*. Toronto: McGraw-Hill Ryerson.

Souster, Raymond, 1975. *Double-Header: As Is and Lost & Found*. Ottawa: Oberon.

Souster, Raymond, 1980. *Collected Poems of Raymond Souster*. Volume One, 1940-55. Ottawa: Oberon.

Souster, Raymond, 1984. *Queen City*. Ottawa: Oberon.

Souster, Raymond, 1986. *It Takes All Kinds*. Ottawa: Oberon.

Speisman, Stephen, 1979. *The Jews of Toronto: A History to 1937*. Toronto: McClelland & Stewart.

Spencer, Guylaine, November/December 2005. "The Allure of Atwood's Toronto." *Americas*, 57(6): 14-21.

Spivak, Gayatri Chakravorty, 1988. "Can the Subaltern Speak?" in *Marxism and the Interpretation of Culture*, ed. Cary Nelson and Lawrence Grossberg. Urbana, IL: University of Illinois Press: 271-313.

Sproul, Barbara C., 1991. *Primal Myths: Creation Myths Around the World*. San Francisco: HarperSanFrancisco.

Statistics Canada, August 2009. *Perspectives on Labour & Income*, 10(8).

Stein, David Lewis, 1967. *Scratch One Dreamer*. Toronto: McClelland & Stewart.

Stein, David Lewis, 1971. *My Sexual and Other Revolutions*. Toronto: new press.

Stein, David Lewis, 1978. *City Boys*. Ottawa: Oberon.

Steuwe, Paul, 1988. *The Storms Below: The Turbulent Life and Times of Hugh Garner*. Toronto: James Lorimer.

Stevens, Laird [as told to be John Davidson], 1986. *The Stroll: Inner City Subcultures*. Toronto: NC Press.

Stolar, Batia Boe, 2005. Building and Living the Immigrant City: Michael Ondaatje's and Austin Clarke's Toronto. In *Downtown Canada: Writing Canadian Cities*, ed. Justin D. Edward and Douglas Ivison. Toronto: University of Toronto Press: 122-141.

Stone, Laura, 28 May 2008. "Black bear captured in Pickering." *Toronto Star.*

Sullivan, Rosemary, 1995. *Shadow Maker: The Life of Gwendolyn MacEwen.* Toronto: HarperCollins.

Sullivan, Rosemary, 1998. *The Red Shoes: Margaret Atwood Starting Out.* Toronto: Harper Flamingo Canada.

Sward, Robert, 24 July 1982. "Hunting rare books a rewarding pursuit." *Toronto Star,* page E.5.

Symons, Scott, 1967. *Place D'Armes.* Toronto: McClelland & Stewart.

Symons, Scott, 1969. *Civic Square.* Toronto: McClelland & Stewart.

Symons, Scott, 26 April 1979. "The Cherished-Loathed Rosedale Myth." *Globe & Mail,* page 7.

Sypnowich, Peter, 4 April 1970. "The moral endurance of Morley Callaghan." *Toronto Star.*

Tambar, Jaspreet, 16 March 2010. "West-end neighbourhood to be called 'Junction Triangle." *Toronto Star.*

Tepper, Anderson, 12 December 2005. "Northern Exposure: Can you hear that literary buzz? It's coming from Toronto". *Vanity Fair.*

Thompson, T. Phillips, 1873. *The Political Experiences of Jimuel Briggs.* Toronto: Flint, Morton & Co.

Throgmorton, James A. And Barbara Eckstein, 2000. Desire Lines: The Chicago Area Transportation Study and the Paradox of Self in Post-War America. Birmingham, UK: The 3Cities Project.

Thurman, Mark, 1987. *Cabbagetown Gang.* Toronto: NC Press.

Tiessen, Matthew, 2007. Accepting Invitations: Desire Lines as Earthly Offerings. *Rhizomes: Cultural Studies in Emerging Knowledge,* vol. 15. <http://www.rhizomes.net/ issue15/tiessen.html>

Tkaronto, (film) 2007. Written and directed by Shane Belcourt. Produced by The Breath films.

Trask, Rick, 1989. *Toronto Jokes: Tronna Roast #1.* Port Sydney, ON: Upalong Enterprises.

Tuan, Yi-Fu, [1974] 1990. *Topophilia: A Study of Environmental Perception, Attitudes, and Values.* Morningside Edition. New York: Columbia University Press.

Tuan, Yi-Fu, 1977. *Space and Place: The Perspective of Experience.* Minneapolis; London: University of Minnesota Press.

Tulchinsky, Gerald, 1992. *Taking Root: The Origins of the Canadian Jewish Community.* Toronto: Lester& Orpen Dennys, 1992.

Turner, Victor, 1967. Betwixt and Between: The Liminal Period in Rites de Passage. In *The Forest of Symbols: Aspects of Ndembu Ritual,* pages 93-111. Ithaca, NY: Cornell University Press.

Turner, Victor, 1974. *Dramas, Fields, and Metaphors: Symbolic Action in Human Society.* Ithaca, NY: Cornell University Press.

Turner, Victor and Edith Turner, 1978. *Image and Pilgrimage in Christian Culture: Anthropological Perspectives*. New York: Columbia University Press.

Type, David, 1984. *Just Us Indians*. Toronto: Playwrights Canada.

United Nations Development Program (UNDP), 2004. *Human Development Report 2004: Cultural Liberty in Today's Diverse World*. New York: United Nations Development Program.

Van Gennep, Arnold, [1960] 2004. *The Rites of Passage*. London; New York: Routledge.

Vassanji, M.G., [1991] 1997. *No New Land*. Toronto: Vintage.

Vaughan, R.M., 2008. *Troubled: A Memoir in Poems and Fragments*. Toronto: Coach House.

Vermeersch, Paul, 2005. *Between the Walls*. Toronto: McClelland & Stewart.

Wallace, Robert, ed., 1992. *Making, Out: Plays by Gay Men*. Toronto: Coach House.

Walker, Joan, 1960. "She Ridicules Suburbia." *Globe & Mail*, 22 October: page 16.

Walsh, Helen, ed., 2006. *TOK Book 1: Writing the New Toronto*. Toronto: Zephyr Press.

Walsh, Helen, ed., 2007. *TOK Book 2: Writing the New Toronto*. Toronto: Zephyr Press.

Walsh, Helen, ed., 2008. *TOK Book 3: Writing the New Toronto*. Toronto: Zephyr Press.

Walsh, Helen, ed., 2009. *TOK Book 4: Writing the New City*. Toronto: Zephyr Press.

Walters, Eric, 2007. *Safe as Houses*. Toronto: Doubleday Canada.

Warkentin, Germaine, December 2005. Mapping Wonderland. *Literary Review of Canada*, 13(10):14-17.

Warkentin, John, 2010. *Creating Memory: A Guide to Outdoor Sculpture in Toronto*. Toronto: City Institute at York University / Becker Associates.

Weinzweig, Helen, 1980. *Basic Black With Pearls*. Toronto: Anansi.

White, Randall, 1993. *Too Good to be True: Toronto in the 1920s*. Toronto: Dundurn.

Whittall, Zoe, 2009. *Holding Still For As Long As Possible*. Toronto: Anansi.

Whitzman, Carolyn, 2009. *Suburb, Slum, Urban Village: Transformations in Toronto's Parkdale Neighbourhood, 1875-2002*. Vancouver: UBC Press.

Wilcox, Alana, Christina Palassio and Jonny Dovercourt, eds., 2006. *The State of the Arts: Living with Culture in Toronto. uTOpia Volume Two*. Toronto: Coach House.

Wilcox, Alana, Christina Palassio and Jonny Dovercourt, eds., 2007. *GreenTOpia: Towards a Sustainable Toronto*. Toronto: Coach House.

Williamson, Ronald F., ed., 2008. *Toronto: An Illustrated History of its First 12,000 Years*. Toronto: James Lorimer & Company

Wilson, Robert Charles, 2000. *The Perseids and Other Stories*. New York: Tor.

Winspur, Steven, 1991. "On City Streets and Narrative Logic." In *City Images: Perspectives from Literature, Philosophy, and Film*, ed. Mary Ann Cawes, 60-70. Amsterdam: Gordon and Breach.

Wise, Leonard and Allan Gould, 2000. *Toronto Street Names: An Illustrated Guide to Their Origins*. Willowdale, ON: Firefly Books.

Wolfe, Morris and Douglas Daymond, eds., 1977. Toronto Short Stories. Toronto: Doubleday Canada.

Wolff, Elana, 2006. *You Speak to Me in Trees*. Toronto: Guernica.

Wolfreys, Julian, 1998. *Writing London: The Trace of the Urban Text from Blake to Dickens*. Hampshire, UK; New York: Palgrave / St. Martin's.

Woodcock, George, 1972. Callaghan's Toronto: the Persona of a City. *Journal of Canadian Studies*, 7(2): 21-24.

Wright, Richard and Robin Endres, eds., 1976. *Eight Men Speak and other plays from the Canadian Workers' Theatre*. Toronto: New Hogtown Press.

Wright, Richard B., 1980. *Final Things*. Toronto: Macmillan of Canada.

Wyatt, Rachel, 1977. *The Rosedale Hoax*. Toronto: Anansi.

Wynne-Jones, Tim, 1982. *The Knot*. Toronto: McClelland & Stewart.

Yee, Paul, 2005. *Chinatown: An illustrated History of the Chinese Communities of Victoria, Vancouver, Calgary, Winnipeg, Toronto, Ottawa, Montreal and Halifax*. Toronto: James Lorimer & Company.

York, Alissa, 2008. "Rock Dove." In *TOK Book 3: Writing the New Toronto*, ed. Helen Walsh, 13-19. Toronto: Zephyr Press.

York, Alissa, 2010. *Fauna*. Toronto: Random House Canada.

Young, Frederick, 1902. *A Pioneer of Imperial Federation in Canada*. London: George Allen.

Young, Phyllis Brett, 1959. *Psyche*. Toronto: Longmans, Green and Company.

Young, Phyllis Brett, 1960. *The Torontonians*. Toronto: Longmans. Reissued in 2007 by McGill-Queen's University Press.

Young, Iris Marion, 2002. *Inclusion and Democracy*. Oxford, UK: Oxford University Press.

Zizek, Slavoj, 2008. Tolerance as an Ideological Category. *Critical Inquiry*, 34(2): 660-682.

AUTHOR INDEX

Amy Lavender Harris teaches in the Department of Geography at York University, where her work focuses on urban identity and the cultural significance of place. She is a contributing editor with *Spacing Magazine,* where she writes a regular column on Toronto literature. Her work has also appeared in *Open Book Magazine, Canada: A Literary Tour, Reading Toronto, GreenTOpia* (Coach House, 2007), *The State of the Arts: Living with Culture in Toronto* (Coach House, 2006), *Plan Canada and the Ontario Planning Journal.* Amy lives in Toronto with her husband and daughter.

OTHER BOOKS FROM MANSFIELD PRESS

POETRY

Stephen Brockwell & Stuart Ross, eds., *Rogue Stimulus: The Stephen Harper Holiday Anthology for a Prorogued Parliament*
Diana Fitzgerald Bryden, *Learning Russian*
Alice Burdick, *Flutter*
Margaret Christakos, *wipe.under.a.love*
Pino Coluccio, *First Comes Love*
Gary Michael Dault, *The Milk of Birds*
Pier Giorgio Di Cicco, *Early Works*
Christopher Doda, *Aesthetics Lesson*
Rishma Dunlop, *Metropolis*
Jason Heroux, *Emergency Hallelujah*
Jeanette Lynes, *The Aging Cheerleader's Alphabet*
David W. McFadden, *Be Calm, Honey*
Leigh Nash, *Goodbye, Ukulele*
Lillian Necakov, *The Bone Broker*
Peter Norman, *At the Gates of the Theme Park*
Catherine Owen & Joe Rosenblatt, with Karen Moe, *Dog*
Corrado Paina, *Souls in Plain Clothes*
Jim Smith, *Back Off, Assassin! New & Selected Poems*
Robert Earl Stewart, *Something Burned Along the Southern Border*
Priscila Uppal, *Winter Sport: Poems*
Steve Venright, *Floors of Enduring Beauty*
Brian Wickers, *Stations of the Lost*
Natasha Nuhanovic, *Stray Dog Embassy*

FICTION

Marianne Apostolides, *The Lucky Child*
Kent Nussey, *A Love Supreme*
Tom Walmsley, *Dog Eat Rat*

NON-FICTION

Pier Giorgio Di Cicco, *Municipal Mind*
Amy Lavender Harris, *Imagining Toronto*